Essentials
of
Risk Financing

Essentials
of Risk Financing
Volume II

Margaret Wilkinson Tiller, CPCU, ARM, FCAS, ASA, MAAA, MCA
President
Tiller Consulting Group, Inc.

James D. Blinn
Consultant
Tillinghast a Towers Perrin Co.

John J. Kelly, CPCU, CLU, ARM, AAI, ChFC
Alexander & Alexander

Edited by
George L. Head, Ph.D., CPCU, ARM, CSP, CLU, FIRM
Vice President
Insurance Institute of America

First Edition • 1988

INSURANCE INSTITUTE OF AMERICA
720 Providence Road, Malvern, Pennsylvania 19355-0770

©1988
INSURANCE INSTITUTE OF AMERICA
*All rights reserved. This book or any part thereof
may not be reproduced without the written
permission of the publisher.*

Second Printing • December 1990
Library of Congress Catalog Number 88-80993
International Standard Book Number 0-89462-043-6

Printed in the United States of America

Table of Contents

CHAPTER 7

Retention—Implementing the Chosen Options

INTRODUCTION

The preceding chapter considered the overall wisdom and feasibility of retention as a risk financing strategy for any organization. This chapter applies the preceding analysis to more specific risk financing decisions for particular losses. This analysis rests on concepts developed in several earlier chapters: forecasting, amounts of loss, and claims payment patterns from Chapter 2, the matching of needs for funds to sources of such funds at the times and in the amounts needed from Chapter 1, and from Chapter 6, the characteristics of the losses the organization may choose to retain beyond its mandatory retentions. The underlying objective is to minimize the adverse effects that financing recovery from accidental losses has on the organization's cash flows in terms of both (1) the overall expected present value of the organization's future net cash flows and (2) the variability of its net cash flows from one accounting period to another.

The first part of this chapter focuses on the characteristics of particular loss exposures that affect the extent to which an organization may choose to retain losses from these exposures. The second part of the chapter focuses on the retention of specific exposures including property, workers compensation, other medical expense, and several types of liability exposures.

EXPOSURE CHARACTERISTICS RELEVANT TO
RETENTION DECISIONS

The three key characteristics of loss exposures that affect risk retention decisions are (1) the legality of retention in a particular jurisdiction, (2) the claims development and payout patterns of losses from a specific exposure, and (3) the frequency and severity of losses from that exposure. Answers to questions regarding legality determine whether retention is a feasible alternative; the remaining two characteristics affect the extent to which retention is attractive to an organization's senior management and owners. Even when a jurisdiction allows retention of an exposure, however, the requirements imposed on a self-insurer may dramatically affect the attractiveness of retention.

Legality

For most loss exposures, neither state nor federal laws restrict how an organization finances recovery from any resulting losses. However, for many liability exposures, state and federal laws often require that an organization has insurance so that claimants can be assured adequate compensation for harm they have suffered. When these laws allow particular organizations or groups of organizations to use retention rather than insurance, these alternatives are quite uniformly referred to as *self-insurance*, although this label is a contradiction in terms. In the context of any particular jurisdiction's statute, however, self-insurance does describe the risk retention procedure used to meet the financial responsibility requirements that most individuals and organizations meet by purchasing commercial insurance. These requirements typically pertain to funding arrangements, claims handling practices, and reporting procedures.

When risk retention is allowed as self-insurance by law, its major disadvantage is the burden of meeting the different requirements from state to state and within the state where an organization operates. While there is no federal regulation as such on self-insurance, federal insurance and other risk financing requirements are imposed on organizations governed by the following:

- *The Interstate Commerce Commission (ICC)*, which governs motor carriers.

- *The United States Longshoremen's and Harbor Workers' Act*, which requires employers to provide compensation benefits for their injured or diseased employees.

- *The Resource Conservation and Recovery Act (RCRA) and Comprehensive Environmental Response, Compensation, and Liability Act (CERCLA),* which imposes financial responsibility requirements on various parties producing, handling, or disposing of hazardous substances that could create pollution liability.

- *The Employee Retirement Income Security Act (ERISA),* which requires employers to act as fiduciaries in guaranteeing specified minimum retirement benefits to their covered employees.

State and federal regulations are not the only factors that affect an organization's decision and/or desire to retain loss exposures. Business firms and other borrowers also face insurance and/or risk retention requirements in bond covenants, leases, loan agreements, letters of credit, and other contracts. These agreements may restrict the ability of an organization to retain exposures even more narrowly than do legislative requirements. States have extended the regulation of self-insureds to each of the areas discussed below.

Other Assessments States may also assess other charges against self-insurers for such items as assigned risk plans, administrative funds, maintenance funds, second-injury and disability funds for workers compensation, and uninsured motorists' funds. These charges typically are handled in a manner similar to premium taxes.

Filing An organization wishing to retain its workers compensation, automobile liability, or other designated exposures often needs to file for approval in each state where an exposure exists and retention is permitted. Along with the application, financial and other reports, which may vary between states, are required.

Reports States generally also require that reports be filed as frequently as quarterly and that they contain information regarding loss experience, such as losses paid, reported or incurred losses, and loss reserves. These reports are used for calculating taxes and other assessments against each self-insurer. If a state requires that excess insurance is maintained by self-insurers, these reports also must document such excess coverage.

Security A qualified self-insurer typically must post some security to guarantee that it will meet its obligations with respect to retained loss exposures. State insurance codes typically establish a minimum security deposit and leave to the discretion of the insurance department the precise amount each self-insurer must maintain in the form of surety bonds, notes, cash, securities, or letters of credit. These security deposits may be required long after an organization ceases to act as a qualified self-insurer. Before a state will permit the withdrawal of any security deposits, it must be assured there are no future claims to be paid. With workers compensation, for example, this may be several years, depending on state laws regarding filing requirements for new claims or the reopening of past claims.

Payout Patterns

Recall from Chapter 2 that a payout pattern for a particular type of loss describes the timing of payments to a claimant to finance recovery from a loss that has been reported. Also recall that a loss may have occurred but not been reported for years. Chapter 2 also described how claim reporting patterns may extend the interval between the time a loss occurs and the initial reporting of that loss; payout patterns become relevant only after the initial loss is reported. This discussion assumes, for simplicity, that the organization establishes no reserves for losses incurred but not yet reported and that, therefore, claims reporting patterns are not relevant to its risk retention planning.

There are three general types of payout patterns, any one or all of which may apply to a given case or exposure:

- *Short:* A short payout pattern is when losses are paid relatively quickly after they have been reported. Property, net income, and many life and health losses are likely to produce such payout patterns. (Liability losses, in contrast, are characterized by lengthy payout patterns. Losses associated with short payout patterns are generally easy to value, and they result in relatively quick settlements with no future payments. An example of a short payout pattern is given in Exhibit 7-1.

- *Annuity:* An annuity payout pattern is when periodic payments are made for a specified number of years or for the life of a claimant or other individual. While this pattern normally is similar to a long payout pattern because the payments are made over a number of years, claims involving annuities have a defined end. Annuities are commonly used in workers compensation and other bodily injury cases. The use of *structured settlements* in liability claims also is resulting in more annuity payouts. Exhibit 7-2 is an example of a twenty-five-year annuity payout pattern.

- *Long:* A long payout pattern extends over a number of years and often includes payments to many claimants. Therefore, unlike an annuity payment pattern, a long payment pattern is

Exhibit 7-1
Short Payout Pattern*

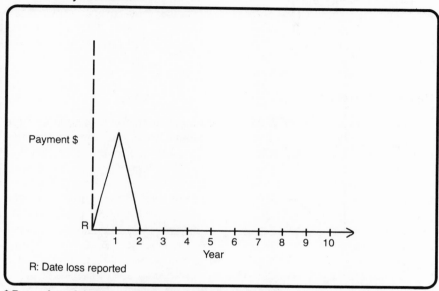

R: Date loss reported

* Data adapted from A.M. Best & Co., Oldwick, NJ

not limited by the life of any individual or clearly identifiable small group of single claimants. Thus, in Exhibit 7-3 the dashed portion of the "curve" shows payments extending indefinitely. Events that cause injury to widespread groups of claimants who, for example, are injured by a defective model of a particular product or by environmental pollution, give rise to long payment patterns. This payment structure often amalgamates compensation for bodily injury, property damage, loss of income, and perhaps less tangible harm.

In practice, a payout pattern can combine any of the elements from these basic patterns. In addition, because these patterns apply only after a loss has been reported, they may be preceded by a lengthy interval between the occurrence and the report of a loss. For example, a medical malpractice claim could be first reported ten years after the event occurred and could be resolved with a structured settlement that includes an annuity for the life of the claimant.

The payout pattern associated with a specific exposure influences the desirability of retaining that exposure. There are, however, two distinct views regarding the attractiveness of long and short payout patterns. One potential benefit of retaining exposures with long payout

Exhibit 7-2
Annuity Payout Pattern*

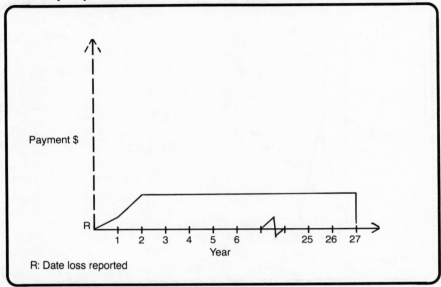

* Data adapted from A.M. Best & Co., Oldwick, NJ

patterns is the interest and other income that can be made on money that is held with the organization to make future payments on presently incurred reported and/or unreported claims. For example, if an event in 19X0 results in a liability of $1 million that is paid over a period extending to 19X9, the present value of the liability in 19X0 is significantly less than $1 million due to the time value of money.

There are also disadvantages to long payout patterns. First, the ultimate value of a liability claim will normally increase the longer it remains outstanding, or "open." As explained in Chapter 2, an event reported in 19X0 that may be worth only $1 million in that year could grow to several million dollars by 19X9 because of (1) economic and legal inflation and (2) aggravation of the harm that first gave rise to the claim. Second, loss exposures with long payout patterns are characterized by much more uncertainty in terms of the frequency and the severity than are those with short payout patterns. Organizations retaining exposures are not usually comfortable with a high degree of uncertainty regarding future payments for known and unknown losses.

As a result, exposures with short payout patterns are generally viewed as more desirable candidates for retention. However, the uncertainties involved in long payout patterns should not discourage retention. If an organization keeps good records of its losses and has a

Exhibit 7-3
Long Payout Pattern*

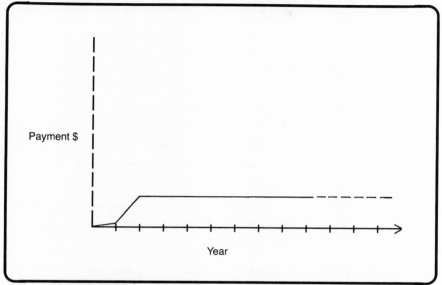

* Data adapted from A.M. Best & Co., Oldwick, NJ

sufficiently large exposure base or can obtain credible loss data elsewhere, loss frequency and severity and payout patterns can be forecast with considerable certainty.

Frequency and Severity

The frequency and severity of losses from an exposure is the third characteristic that affects the desirability of retention. Exposures with high loss frequency and low loss severity are typically deemed the most attractive for retention. A high frequency of losses (not necessarily a large number of exposure units) results in better predictability of loss experience. Low severity means that there will not be any catastrophic losses that may be beyond the organization's financial capacity. These types of exposures belong in Cell 3 of Exhibit 7-4. Because of the high frequency of claims, losses from exposures are often anticipated and funded in advance although some organizations choose to pay such losses from current revenues or assets as they occur.

Exposures generating high severity losses with a low frequency of occurrence are the least desirable to retain. Insurance is best suited for financing the often catastrophic losses from such exposures, which belong in Cell 2 of Exhibit 7-4. Organizations with losses having a high

Exhibit 7-4
Impact of Frequency and Severity on Risk Retention Decision

		Frequency of Losses	
		High	Low
Severity of Losses	High	1. Bankruptcy	2. Catastrophic Losses: Purchase Insurance
	Low	3. Retention: Funded	4. Retention: Unfunded

severity and a high frequency (Cell 1) are, from a practical standpoint, nonexistent—it could not stay in business with such losses. Low severity losses with a low frequency of occurrence (Cell 4) are not generally significant concerns. These small losses that occur infrequently are generally retained and financed with current assets.

APPLICATIONS OF THESE CHARACTERISTICS TO SPECIFIC EXPOSURES

To determine the feasibility of retaining an exposure, an organization should analyze it in terms of the three preceding characteristics. Each characteristic as it relates to a specific exposure should be studied over an extended period. Only by this type of careful analysis can a sound choice about retention be made.

The particular exposures described here—property, workers compensation, other medical expense, and several types of liability exposures—are only a sample of a great many exposures. They do illustrate the principles involved in making a decision about retention.

Property

Exposures to an organization's property are generally very well suited to retention. The only negative factor usually associated with retaining property losses is a low frequency level and, therefore, greater difficulty in predicting future losses.

The legal impediments to retaining property losses typically come from creditors of the organization who have a secured interest in the property and from lease agreements for property that is not owned. In addition, there may be situations in which an organization is required to insure property in its custody and owned by others. If the organization maintains a sound risk retention program, however, these creditors and bailors may waive their insurance requirements.

As mentioned, the payout pattern from property losses is typically very short. A major property loss may take one or two years to resolve with perhaps several insurers, but this is still a short time relative to liability loss payout patterns.

Although the frequency of property losses is usually low, thus making it difficult to predict future losses, severity is limited to the value of the property. This creates a cap on maximum potential loss and is one of the most desirable features of retaining property exposures. However, the net income losses stemming from property damage—an exposure distinct from the property damage itself—are potentially catastrophic and usually require insurance, perhaps excess insurance over a substantial retention.

Medical Expenses

The property losses just described are associated with damage to or destruction of tangible objects. The losses from all the other exposures treated in this chapter are not limited in such a definitive way. The remaining losses all entail expenditures to meet streams of loss-related expenses or reductions in revenue for an organization or individual. In theory, although fortunately not in fact, these costs are limitless.

One of the most common expense-related exposures retained by organizations is employee medical costs. These generally consist of two distinct exposures. First, organizations have a contractual responsibility for medical expenses provided as an employee benefit. Second, organizations have a statutory responsibility to provide workers compensation benefits to their employees who suffer work-related injuries or illnesses. For our purposes, medical expenses will include not only both these disability types of costs but also employees' income benefits provided by workers compensation coverage.

As further explained in Chapter 10, medical expenses provided as part of an employee benefits program are generally viewed as an attractive exposure to retain. From a legal standpoint there are usually no restrictions or requirements beyond what may be required in a labor union contract. The payout of medical expenses tends to be very short for most illnesses and injuries. Disability income loss may result in long payouts, but such payments are usually in the form of an annuity and, as a result, very predictable. An organization with a large number of employees also will probably have a high frequency of claims, which will enhance the attractiveness of retaining medical expense losses. Furthermore, the severity of medical expense losses is generally limited. Often an employee benefit program includes a cap on the benefits that will be paid to any employee or covered dependent, making the cost of this exposure relatively certain. Moreover, organizations purchase major medical insurance as catastrophic protection against those few illnesses or injuries producing substantial, extended medical costs. Organizations with many employees hire outside administrators to handle medical expense claims, thus often avoiding possible conflicts and bad feeling between employees and the organization that may occur when a company settles its employees' claims.

The second large medical expense exposure facing an organization is for workers compensation benefits. The relatively high frequency and statutorily limited severity of this exposure makes it an attractive candidate for retention if the organization has a large number of employees and a credible number of claims. Nevertheless, the ease with which workers compensation claims can be filed and reopened raises the severity of these claims as compared to medical benefits provided by most employee benefit plans.

Exhibit 7-5 shows a typical payout pattern for workers compensation claims, both medical expense and income benefits. For example, four years after the end of the year in which an employee is disabled, 73.5 percent of the ultimate value of the claims arising in that year have been paid. After nine years, 87.3 percent of all ultimate claim values have been paid. This implies that 12.7 percent of the value of claims still remains to be paid out nine years after the close of the year an accident or injury occurred. This payout pattern indicates that most claims are resolved fairly quickly, which leads many risk management professionals to conclude that workers compensation claims have a short payout pattern.

There is, however, a small percentage of claims that take a long time to pay in full. For these kinds of claims a structured settlement based on insured annuities relieves an organization of much of the uncertainty associated with an extended payout pattern.

The logic and mechanics of claim reporting and payout patterns were detailed in Chapter 2, where somewhat different percentages were entered into the patterns analyzed. The student should not be concerned about relatively small differences between the pattern described here and those in Chapter 2. In fact, these differences suggest the importance of developing and regularly updating loss data, which will generate reporting and payment patterns appropriate for each organization.

The legality of retaining the workers compensation exposure can be very complex, especially for employers with employees in many

Exhibit 7-5
Workers Compensation Payment Pattern*

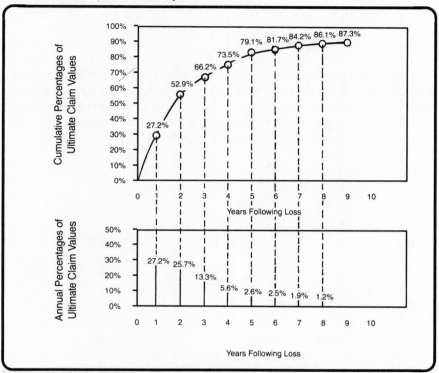

* Data adapted from A.M. Best & Co., Oldwick, NJ

states. Each state or territory has its own minimum qualifications and reporting requirements. In fact, North Dakota, Puerto Rico, Texas, the Virgin Islands, Wyoming, and all Canadian provinces prohibit self-insurance of workers compensation statutory benefits. In the forty-seven states that do permit employers to self-insure workers compensation, requirements also vary depending on whether the risk retention program is for a group of employers or for an individual employer. Illinois is a good example of the extent of state regulation. Exhibit 7-6 summarizes the states' requirements. Comparable state requirements for automobile liability, products liability, professional liability, and some other exposures apply, in varying degrees, in most states. The exhibit should be studied only for its general content; the details in the regulations in any particular state are not germane to the educational objectives of this text.

Exhibit 7-6
Illinois Workers Compensation Self-Insurance Requirements and Regulations*

SPECIAL TAXES AND FEES:

INDIVIDUALS

On July 15 and January 15 of each year, the self-insured employer pays a sum to the Rate Adjustment Fund equal to .5 percent of all compensation payments made during the preceding six months. An additional amount, equal to .125 percent of such payments, is made to the Second Injury Fund on July 15 and January 15. A pro-rata assessment covering the cost of the Self-Insurer's Security Fund also can be made. This assessment cannot exceed 1.2 percent of the benefits paid in the preceding calendar year by an employer.

REQUIRED APPLICATION AND/OR RELATED FORMS:

INDIVIDUALS

1. Application for Self-Insurance. Form I.C. 50

2. Self-Insurer's Guaranty Agreement.

3. Self-Insurer's Escrow Agreement. Form I.C. 51 (12-26)

4. Self-Insurer's Security Bond. Form I.C. 52

5. Certificate of Excess Insurance - Workmen's Compensation Act and Workmen's Occupational Diseases Act Form I.C. 46 (2-76)

6. Annual Report Questionnaire of Illinois Self-Insured Employers.

GROUPS

1. Application for Service Company.

2. Statement of Education, Prior Occupation, Business Experience and Supplementary Information.

3. Application for Individual Pool Member.

INITIAL FILING REQUIREMENTS:

An applicant for self-insurance must file the following information:

INDIVIDUALS

1. A loss history for the last three years;

continued on next page

2. Indicate who will administer the program;

3. A list of locations to be self-insured and the numbers of employees at each location; and

4. The most recent financial statement certified by a CPA. (While the application calls for a certified statement, a company can use its annual report or its 10(K) report in an application. Affiliates, subsidiaries, and divisions can be included.)

GROUPS

Groups of employers with similar characteristics or members of a bona fide professional, commercial, industrial or trade association can pool their risks through self-insurance. An application for group self-insurance requests:

1. Biographical information on the risk manager (and officers and directors, if a corporation);

2. Information that demonstrates the administrator has adequate resources to run the program;

3. The most recent financial statement of the administrator (10(K) report if a publicly-held corporation);

4. The compensation for the administrator;

5. The pooling agreement;

6. A plan of operation;

7. Individual applications for members; and

8. Written evidence of a fidelity bond for the administrator's employees and officers.

The fidelity bond is based on the assets held by the administrator. If assets are less than $500,000, the bond is $20,000 plus 6 percent of the assets. The other limits that are required are:

Assets		Bond
More Than	But Not More Than	
$ 500,000	$ 1,000,000	$50,000 plus 4.0% of assets over $ 500,000
1,000,000	3,000,000	70,000 plus 3.0% of assets over $1,000,000
3,000,000	5,000,000	130,000 plus 2.0% of assets over $3,000,000
5,000,000	10,000,000	170,000 plus 1.5% of assets over 5,000,000
10,000,000	—	245,000 plus .75% of assets over 10,000,000

The gross annual combined payroll of the members must be at least $10 million.

continued on next page

All members of a group self-insurer must agree to be jointly and severally liable, and all members of a self-insurance group must have similar risk characteristics or be members of a bona fide professional, commercial, industrial or trade association.

EXCESS INSURANCE REQUIREMENTS:

INDIVIDUALS

The Industrial Commission views the purchase of specific and aggregate excess insurance as necessary unless specifically waived.

GROUPS

Group self-insurers must buy specific excess coverage and may buy aggregate excess coverage. The specific excess retention cannot exceed 20 percent of the projected annual premiums to be received from members. Annual aggregate excess "coverage of not less than 90% excess or not more than 110% of the projected annual premiums to be received . . ." by the group may be purchased. There must be a minimum annual aggregate coverage of $2 million excess of a pool's retention.

SECURITY OR BONDING:

INDIVIDUALS

A self-insurer must post a bond or deposit securities in escrow in amount not less than $200,000. Escrow deposits must be cash, negotiable United States government bonds, or negotiable general obligation bonds of the state of Illinois.

A surety for a self-insurer cannot cancel its bond before the Industrial Commission of Illinois and the principal have received 60 days' notice of such cancellation.

GROUPS

The reserve for group self-insurers, however, can be maintained in United States obligations (or obligations of United States agencies), certificates of deposit, time deposits, or demand deposits in a bank in Illinois, savings certificates issued by savings and loans in Illinois, some business obligations, obligations of political subdivisions, and bonds or securities issued by any state.

AVERAGE TIME FOR APPLICATION APPROVAL:

Thirty days for group self-insurers.
Ninety to 100 days for individual self-insurers.

RENEWAL FILING REQUIREMENTS AND OTHER REPORTS:
Certificates are continuous until cancelled.

INDIVIDUALS

An annual questionnaire and the latest annual financial statement (certified by a CPA) must be filed by individual self-insurers.

continued on next page

GROUPS

Group self-insurers must file a financial statement for the preceding calendar year by April 1 of each year, and quarterly statements may be required. By June 1, a group self-insurer must file an audited financial statement for the preceding calendar year.

GENERAL PROVISION:

Group self-insurance service companies must apply to the Insurance Department for approval to conduct business. Every group self-insurer must maintain reserves equal to all outstanding claims discounted at a rate not to exceed 5 percent per annum. The reserve may be reduced by amounts recoverable from authorized reinsurers. New group self-insurer members must be reported to the Insurance Department within five days after they become members. To be eligible to join an existing group, an employer must:

1. Have 20 employees and $250,000 of gross annual payroll;

2. Have 10 employees and $125,000 of gross annual premium (if the employer has been engaged in business in Illinois for at least three years); or

3. Have five employees and $62,500 of gross annual payroll (if the employer has been engaged in business in Illinois for at least five years).

The minimum eligibility requirements can be waived if:

1. An applicant has been in business at least five years in Illinois;

2. An applicant agrees to make its books available for inspection to the Insurance Department during the time it is a group member; and

3. The pool administrator certifies that it has reviewed an applicant's financial records and finds an applicant is solvent and financially stable.

Illinois permits group members to be liable for 20 percent of the medical expenses per employee, up to a limit of $5,000. The balance of the medical expenses is paid by the group.

GROUNDS FOR CANCELLATION OF A SELF-INSURANCE CERTIFICATE:

A certificate is cancellable after reasonable notice and a hearing if a self-insurer is found to be in financial difficulty or is practicing a policy of delay or unfairness in settling claims.

* Reprinted with permission from Claude C. Lilly III and H. Glenn Boggs, *The Self-Insurance Manual* (Chatsworth, CA: National Insurance Law Service Publishing Company, looseleaf revised and supplemented periodically), January 1987, pp. WC IL-1—WC IL-4.

Liability

The desirability of retaining liability exposures varies with the type of liability. The four liability exposures that will be discussed here are automobile, general, pollution, and medical malpractice.

Automobile Liability Bodily injury and property damage liability resulting from automobile accidents is an exposure commonly retained by organizations with large fleets of vehicles. A few organizations fully retain all such losses. Many more organizations retain the full amount of exposures to physical damage losses to their vehicles and purchase excess insurance for catastrophic automobile liability losses.

While anyone is free to retain physical damage losses to their own vehicles, each state has its own regulations regarding qualifications for an organization to self-insure its automobile liability. These regulations are much less extensive than those for workers compensation. In general, the requirements specify that the organization must do the following:

- have a minimum number of registered vehicles, typically twenty or twenty-five, but often substantially fewer,
- submit a current list of vehicles and update loss experience,
- submit current financial statements,
- submit a surety bond or other financial guarantee.

In addition to state requirements, the Interstate Commerce Commission (ICC) imposes requirements for motor carriers seeking to qualify as self-insurers. The specific ICC requirements vary with an organization's financial strength, the proven reliability of its retention program, and its safety program. Exhibit 7-7 shows a typical payout pattern for automobile losses. Only three years after the close of the year in which a claim is reported, 80.8 percent of the ultimate value of all losses has been paid. After nine years, this figure rises to 98.7 percent. Although this is one of the shortest payout patterns of all liability exposures, a higher degree of certainty can be achieved for automobile liability than for all other liability claims.

The frequency of an organization's automobile liability claims is a function of the number of vehicles the organization owns and/or operates: the larger the number of vehicles, the higher the frequency and the greater the predictability of losses. The severity of automobile liability losses is generally not large; there are, however, very significant exceptions. To illustrate the arithmetic, automobile liability claims in most major cities in the United States were less than $4,000 in the early 1980s; however, a few such liability claims reached tens of

Exhibit 7-7
Automobile and General Liability Payout Patterns*

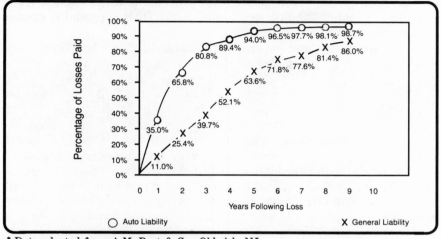

* Data adapted from A.M. Best & Co., Oldwick, NJ

millions of dollars. Risk management professionals can always imagine cases in which a vehicle is involved in a serious accident with a school bus. Therefore, most organizations retain the lower "layers" of automobile liability losses while purchasing excess liability insurance for major claims.

General Liability Organizations often choose to retain smaller losses from their general liability exposures for bodily injury or property damage suffered by persons visiting their premises or affected by their off-premise operations. The ease and desirability of retaining such losses varies with the organization's activities, loss experience, and financing capabilities. In practice, many organizations retain claims up to a specified limit and then purchase an umbrella policy to provide excess coverage for general, automobile, products, and employer's liability. There are a few state or federal regulations for retention of general liability exposures. However, many business contracts, bond covenants, and other agreements have provisions regarding insurance and risk retention such as the highly diverse hold harmless and other indemnity provisions examined more fully in Chapter 9.

The payout pattern of general liability claims, typified in Exhibit 7-7, is longer than for workers compensation and automobile liability claims. Four years after the close of the year of their occurrence, only 52.1 percent of the ultimate value of general liability claims has been paid. After nine years, 86 percent of the ultimate value of all such claims has been paid. This payout pattern makes general liability a less attractive retention alternative than workers compensation and automobile liability. However, it does not preclude an organization from retaining general liability exposures, which are capped by excess insurance.

The frequency and severity of general liability claims are very closely related to the nature of the organization's operations and its size. For example, a chain of retail stores may have a high frequency of liability claims related to events, such as slips and falls, that occur on its premises. While each claim is low in terms of severity, this type of organization can incur a substantial aggregate annual cost for administering and settling these claims. On the other hand, a basic chemical manufacturing company may have a very low frequency of general liability claims with very high severity for those claims that do occur— for example, an accident that releases toxic material into the general community. The attractiveness of risk retention for general liability exposures, therefore, will be a function of an organization's exposures and financing capabilities.

Pollution Liability   Environmental Impairment Liability (EIL), commonly referred to as pollution liability, is retained by most organizations because EIL insurance is very difficult and expensive to obtain. Some organizations, particularly those with serious exposures, have established funded reserves or captives as formalized techniques for retaining those exposures or have joined with other firms in their industries to share them. In addition, risk control has become very important for reducing these exposures.

The legality of retaining pollution risks is a function of the organization's specific exposures. ICC regulations apply to transporters that haul hazardous wastes. Superfund and RCRA regulations (described in ARM 55) have an impact on the owners and operators of hazardous waste management facilities.

The payout pattern of pollution liability claims is generally very long. Claims usually are paid much later than ten years after having been reported. Some sudden and accidental pollution-related events may have much shorter payout patterns, but these tend to be less severe.

The frequency of pollution liability claims for any one organization is typically very low; however, the severity of pollution losses can be great. As a result, pollution exposures need to be carefully evaluated, controlled, and financed.

Medical Malpractice Liability   Medical malpractice is an example of an exposure that is difficult to retain, especially for individual doctors. Other professionals face comparable exposures and risk

Exhibit 7-8
Medical Malpractice Payment Patterns*

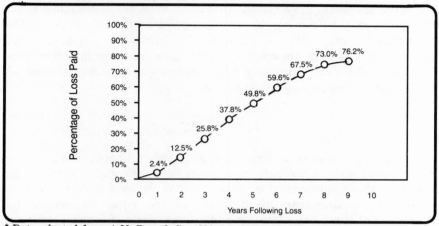

* Data adapted from A.M. Best & Co., Oldwick, NJ

management challenges within their own specialties. It is increasingly difficult for medical persons and other professionals to obtain or afford malpractice insurance, so they have been forced to retain these exposures on an individual basis or through professional associations and other groups.

There are few legal impediments to a physician, a hospital, or other professional or organization retaining malpractice exposures. However, a hospital does not require insurance to be or to remain accredited. Nevertheless, hospitals may require their physicians to maintain medical malpractice insurance to keep their hospital privileges. Because it is difficult to secure such physician coverage at affordable rates, some hospitals allow their physicians to join groups to finance claims from this exposure.

The payout pattern for medical malpractice shown in Exhibit 7-8 is the longest of those shown in this chapter. Four years after the end of the year in which claims have been reported, only 37.8 percent of the ultimate value of all claims has been paid; after nine years, this percentage rises to 76.2 percent. One quarter of all claims, therefore, will not be paid for at least ten years after they have been reported. Furthermore, many malpractice claims are not recognized or reported until a decade or more after the physician's alleged error. These long reporting and payout patterns increase the difficulty of predicting both the number and size of future claims. Generally, the longer a claim remains outstanding, the greater the potential loss becomes.

The frequency of medical malpractice claims for an individual physician is usually quite low, but it varies most significantly from one specialty to another. Frequency also may slowly be rising, especially in the more litigious jurisdictions. However, even for a hospital, claim frequency may be too low to establish good predictability. Adequate predictability may still be achieved for individual physicians and hospitals if loss data are combined with data from similar physicians and hospitals. Thus, relatively low frequency is one reason medical professionals join to pool this exposure.

SUMMARY

Applying the general principles described in Chapter 6 regarding organization-wide aggregate mandatory and optional retentions to decisions about appropriate optional retention levels for individual loss exposures requires careful attention to the legal restrictions on retentions of these exposures, the payout patterns of losses stemming from these exposures, and the frequency and severity of the losses.

Retention is legally restricted not only by statutes but also by the various contracts into which an organization may enter. Statutes may mandate at least minimum amounts of insurance. They also may establish qualifications in terms of size, financial strength, and sound risk management that an organization must meet to be considered a self-insurer exempt from mandatory insurance requirements. Organizations that do meet these qualifications must follow filing, reporting, and security requirements and must pay premium taxes and other insurance-like assessments. Leases, promissory notes, bond indentures, and indemnity agreements between noninsurers are some of the business contracts that may further limit an organization's legal power to choose to retain an exposure. The organization's creditors or indemnitees may seek to require the organization to insure an exposure as a way of guaranteeing the organization's financial strengths.

Exposures generating losses with short payout patterns are more attractive as optional retentions than are those with longer patterns. This is true because the shorter the interval between the initial reporting of the loss or claim and the final payment to restore that loss or claim, the greater the predictability of the ultimate payout and the less the uncertainty associated with the retention. Moreover, as a complement to short payout patterns, the rapid reporting of losses and claims—which reduces the significance of potential losses or claims incurred but not reported—also reduces the uncertainty inherent in a given level of retention. However, for organizations that can accept the unpredictability associated with losses that have long payout patterns, financing retained losses through installment or annuity payments may be particularly attractive. By retaining losses and making the payments, these organizations can control and use more cash for a longer time than organizations who have transferred such losses.

The frequency and the severity of losses from a given exposure also affect optional retention levels. Losses that are frequent, and therefore more predictable, are more suited to retention. (Still, excess insurance should be considered to protect the organization from unexpectedly aggregating losses if the frequency suddenly rises.) Losses with inherently limited severity are easier to fully retain than those with an unlimited or unpredictable level of severity. For the latter, insurance or other transfer above some moderate level of retention is most appropriate. Exposures involving losses that are both frequent and severe are rarely encountered because few organizations can thrive, or even survive, in such a hostile environment.

Property, medical expense (for workers compensation and employee benefit plans), and a selection of liability exposures represent the various legal requirements, payout patterns, and frequency/severity combinations that are likely to influence an organization's decision about optional retentions. Because these three characteristics vary from one organization to another, the risk management professional should study them in light of each exposure that is a potential optional retention. From any given combination of characteristics, the reasoning in Chapters 1, 6, and 7 points to a level of retention that maximizes the expected present value of an organization's future net cash flows while holding the variability of its annual net cash flows within tolerable limits.

CHAPTER 8

Captives and Pools

INTRODUCTION

In principle, the management of an organization's risk financing program is simplified and made more logical by distinguishing between risk retention and risk transfer. The logic for this distinction has at least three sources. First, where it relies on retention, an organization must be prepared to generate money internally to pay for losses; where it relies on transfer, an organization must assure itself that the outside sources to which it looks for funds will be able and willing to provide this money in appropriate amounts. Second, retained losses make direct demands on an organization's cash flows; these demands are typically less predictable than the payments the organization makes to secure funds from outside sources. Third, any risk transfer typically can be only as reliable as the contract establishing that transfer is enforceable; therefore, through successful risk retention, an organization can become more self-sufficient and confident about its source of funds.

Yet, in financial reality, this highly logical distinction between retention and transfer often becomes blurred. For example, borrowing funds to pay for losses may appear to be transfer because the money comes from the lender, a source outside the organization. However, this hides the essential fact that borrowing actually reduces the organization's credit resources, cutting its ability to borrow further for other purposes. In the end, the organization has actually retained the loss since it must draw on its own funds to repay the lender and to finance other activities. Further, the ideal line between retention and transfer begins to fade when considering various loss-sensitive insured cash flow plans, which establish the upper and lower limits of an organization's insurance costs while allowing it to secure many of the investment income and control-of-funds advantages that usually characterize traditional forms of retention. In addition, the formation of affiliated insurance subsidiaries to meet the risk financing needs of one or more parent organizations has raised complex, important questions about whether such captive insurers represent retention or transfer. Somewhat similar questions have been spawned by insurance pools, risk retention groups, and insurance purchasing groups that have been formed in response to the difficulties that some insureds have experienced in obtaining traditional insurance at reasonable cost.

Building on the discussion of traditional forms of insurance and reinsurance in Chapters 4 and 5, and on the examination of the more widely recognized retention techniques in Chapters 6 and 7, this chapter explores the somewhat uncharted risk financing territory that lies between clear transfer and retention. Pools and captives are discussed in addition to the variety of insured cash flow plans, which, from the perspective of financial management, combine elements of retention and transfer.

For educational purposes the chapter deals with some aspects of retention and transfer that are not yet fully resolved by federal and state tax and insurance officials. Without making an effort to resolve or to take a position on these legal issues, this chapter discusses risk financing techniques primarily from an internal financial management perspective, considering how various "hybrid" retention/transfer financing techniques can enhance the cost-effectiveness of an organization's risk financing program.

CAPTIVES AND POOLS—DEFINITIONS AND TYPES

A captive insurer (more accurately, an affiliated insurer) and a pool are two very closely related risk financing techniques. Both involve more structured risk financing than do the simpler forms of retention; yet both give an organization more control over its risk financing program than does the purchase of commercial insurance. A captive organized to meet the risk financing needs of only the one organization that founded and fully owns it (its *single parent*) is quite different from a pool, which is at least two organizations that join to form a single entity through which they finance recovery from specified losses of either organization. However, this distinction between a single parent captive and a pool dissolves with group or association captives, which have several parents. It thus becomes difficult to operationally define the point at which adding more parents to a captive creates a risk financing mechanism that managerially functions as a pool.

For income tax purposes, however, the distinction between a captive and a pool is crucial: both federal tax and state insurance regulators typically view a captive as a risk retention device but consider a pool as a risk transfer mechanism. If a risk financing arrangement is considered retention, then the following are true from a tax and regulatory perspective:

- Any transactions between a parent and a captive are not insurance; as a consequence to the captive, no insurance premium taxes are payable, and the indemnitor is not regulated as an insurer.
- Periodic or other payments the parent makes to the captive are not tax deductible to the parent as business expenses for insurance premiums.

If a risk financing arrangement is considered as a transfer like a pool, then the following are true:

- The enterprise formed by the pool usually is considered insurance and typically must pay premium taxes and be regulated as an insurance company.
- Payments made by each participant to the enterprise are typically tax deductible to participants as insurance premium expenses.

Given these facts, the line between a captive as a risk retention mechanism and a pool as a risk transfer mechanism is significant in determining the after-tax cost of various risk financing alternatives and in assessing the degree of regulatory freedom available to those who finance loss exposures through a given mechanism. Locating this line is made more difficult by the growing popularity of multi-parent captives, whose tax and regulatory status is uncertain in many jurisdictions.

Against this background the following discussion explores the distinctions between captives and pools with an eye to their tax and regulatory status. However, to keep this discussion in perspective, three caveats should be recognized. First, the decision to form or join a captive or pool—or any other form of risk financing—should be made primarily on the basis of internal financial management and overall operating efficiency, not on the basis of tax or regulatory statutes, which may be changed at any time. (In fact, for public and other organizations that pay no income taxes, the income tax differences between retention and transfer are not always germane.) Second, the following discussion presumes that the tax authorities will continue to treat payments for risk transfers as tax deductible expenses, while treating additions to reserves for retention as non-tax deductible. Third, this discussion does not consider the question of whether payments (regardless of whether they are or are not "premiums" of some other risk transfer) from an indemnitee to an indemnitor might possibly be tax deductible to the indemnitee as a general ordinary and necessary business expense.

Definitions

To distinguish between various types of captives and pools, it is best to examine first the generic differences between all captives and all pools. These differences also will clarify how a captive and a pool differ from a mutual insurance company.

Captive Because risk financing techniques evolve in response to market forces and tax and regulatory statutes, the definitions of these techniques also change in response to similar forces. The concept and definition of an *affiliated insurer,* colloquially but universally also called a *captive,* has evolved rapidly as organizations seeking to use captives (and the brokerage and insurance organizations striving to meet their needs) have attempted to develop mechanisms that qualify as insurance (or other transfer devices) within the meaning of the tax statutes. (Achieving tax deductibility of premium payments historically has been a more important concern for parents and participants than the burdens of complying with state laws imposing premium taxes on insurance and regulating the activities of insurers.) One of the best current definitions of captive is that it is a subsidiary owned by one or more parent organizations established primarily to insure the exposures of its owner(s). The words subsidiary and primarily the exposures of its owner(s) are crucial to this definition.

A *subsidiary* of one or more parents is an organization that may be legally separate from but is managed by its parents. Within the bounds of sound risk financing practice, the activities of a captive are guided by the best interests of the parents in terms of the types of losses financed, the ratemaking and underwriting practices, and the captive's strategies for investing its reserves and other available funds. The captive operates "primarily" to provide risk financing for its parents in the sense that (1) most of the exposures dealt with through the captive are those of the parents, (2) most of the capital for founding the captive comes from the parents, and (3) the management of the captive is controlled by persons who are also employees of the parents.

Pool A risk financing pool is one application of the general concept of pooling that is used throughout commerce. As typically defined in a dictionary, a *pool* is an association of persons or organizations formed to combine their resources for some common

advantage. By extention, pool also may refer to the member participants in or the resources of such an association. In a risk financing
context the common advantages a pool seeks for its member participants relate to cost-effective management of funds for financing
recovery from accidental losses. Thus, in this context, a risk financing
pool may be defined as an association of persons or organizations that
combine their resources for their common advantage in managing
funds to finance recovery from accidental losses.

Thus, a pool must have more than one participant or parent. Unlike
captives, there can be no single-parent pools. Pooling also suggests the
creation of an entity that is not only legally distinct from each of its
participants but also is equal to each of its creators. The implication is
that the managers of a pool, perhaps appointed to represent the pool
participants, make judgments intended to be independent of the
participating organizations and to serve the long-term mutual interests
of the group as a whole as distinct from each of its members. In
principle, a pool's continuing existence and viable operation are
independent of, not controlled by, any one owner.

As a *mutual association,* a pool usually operates on a not-for-
profit basis (in contrast to most captives, which are profit-seeking). To
further its members' shared risk financing interests, most pools unlike
most captives periodically distribute to their participants any excess
earnings from underwriting or investment operations that are not
needed to support the pool's risk financing activities. Such distributions
usually are proportional to the size of the exposures (as measured by
loss potentials or premium volumes) of the participants. If underwriting and investment activities do not generate enough funds to
sustain the pool's risk financing activities, the participants may be
further assessed, usually on the same proportional basis. Decisions on
such "dividends" earned or additional assessments typically are made
by an executive committee that takes an active, democratically oriented
role in the major policy-making decisions of the pool. However, usually
they are not involved in its routine daily operations (which are handled
by persons paid by and answerable to the pool itself).

Mutual Insurers Like a pool, a mutual insurer is a not-for-profit
organization that collects funds from many participants. These funds
are called premiums or contributions and are used together with
investment earnings on them to pay insured losses. Also like a pool, a
mutual periodically distributes any funds that are excess in the sense
that they are not needed to meet participants' risk financing needs.
Some mutuals also reserve the right to levy additional assessments
against participants if more funds are needed to meet unexpected,
especially heavy covered losses; however, for business reasons, few

mutuals choose to exercise this right. There is generally no substantive legal question that the protection such a mutual organization provides to its participants is risk transfer, that the transaction constitutes insurance, and that payments made by each participant to the mutual are tax deductible to that participant.

The differences between a pool and a mutual insurer are, therefore, matters of degree. The members of a pool are usually few and operate in the same industry or have other substantial common economic interests beyond their participation in this risk financing mechanism. In contrast, a mutual insurer may provide risk financing for many hundreds or thousands of organizations in highly different industries; the participants may have few other common interests beyond their participation in the mutual. Therefore, the insureds in a mutual do not ordinarily engage directly in its management, particularly in major strategy or policy decisions that would typically be of great concern to, and substantially controlled by, the participants in a pool or the parents of a captive. While the insureds in a mutual theoretically own the enterprise and vote on the appointment of key officers and directors, they normally cannot control this management any more effectively than can the individual stockholders of a widely held public corportion. Because these size and control differences between pools and mutuals are matters of degree, there may be little practical difference between a very large pool and a very small mutual.

Captive/Pool/Mutual Growth   Arrayed in terms of increasing numbers of participants, captives, pools, and mutual insurers form a continuum ranging from the single-parent captive to the mutual with many thousands of insureds. History bolsters logic documenting this array: some of today's largest property-liability mutual insurers began as very small pools of perhaps eight or ten organizations in a single industry (for example, lumber, hardware, and commercial nurseries) or in a particular area (such as towns in New England and counties in the Midwest). The exact point in their growth at which multi-parent captives cease to be risk retention devices for each parent and become mutual insurers (providing risk transfer for them all) is not clear and is more a matter of practice than of logic.

In principle, even a two-parent captive could be a pool or mutual insurer if this risk-financing entity is independently managed, has its own separately viable existence, and follows sound insurance practices. Conversely, a captive with even several thousand small nominal parents and a few dominant large ones might still effectively be a risk retention mechanism for the largest parents if the others have no effective voice in its management.

Therefore, the significant distinctions between multi-parent captives, pools, and mutuals primarily affect the managerial status of those who operate the risk financing venture. The captive, pool, or mutual provides risk transfer if it is managed as a viable organization that is separate from its participants and whose executives operate it for its own long-term financial strength and well-being apart from the shifting financial needs of any one parent or participant.

Types

The preceding section explained the generic differences between captives, pools, and mutuals. This background provides a basis for distinguishing between the various types of captives and pools.

Types of Captives Captives are usually classified in terms of their sponsors. They may be pure captives, association captives, group captives, risk retention groups, or rent-a-captive arrangements.

Pure Captive. A pure captive is wholly owned by the single parent for whose benefit it operates. A pure, or *single-parent,* captive—because it provides risk financing for no other entities except its one parent—is the clearest example of *captive insurance* as true risk retention, not transfer. From the perspective of financial management, a pure captive provides no economically separate entity to which the parent's loss exposures can be transferred. At most, a single-parent captive can provide a highly structured mechanism for gathering data on loss exposures, levying charges against the various departments and operations within the organization, reflecting their respective exposures, and providing claims management for the parent organization. Properly operated, a single-parent captive can provide highly controlled, effective, and efficient risk retention.

Association Captive. An association captive has more than one parent, all of which belong to a particular industry or professional association and all of which have similar loss exposures and risk financing needs. Many of the early single-industry mutual insurers that sprang up along the Atlantic Coast of the United States in the nineteenth century established precedents for modern association captives. When a sufficient number of parents achieve an adequate spread of risk that will generate credible loss statistics, and when captive management is strong enough to make implement decisions independent of its parents, an association captive can function much like a pool or mutual. If it meets these qualifications, such an association captive can provide risk financing that, from a managerial perspective, is equivalent to risk transfer.

Group Captive. A group captive is similar to an association captive except that it is not sponsored by a trade association or professional society. Its two or more parents consequently do not have such closely similar exposures or comparable risk financing needs. It follows that the participants in a group captive tend to be united solely by their common interest derived from owning the group captive.

The distinction between risk retention and risk transfer is less clear in light of group captives. In some situations, the focus on risk financing has led tax authorities to examine whether the parents of a group captive (especially those with few members) operate the captive for legitimate risk financing reasons beyond merely seeking income tax deductions for "premiums" they have paid for "insurance" from their captive. These authorities have been reluctant to grant tax deductibility for risk financing arrangements of "fictitious groups" formed primarily to gain tax advantages rather to achieve other, more "real," benefits. These authorities, backed by the courts, generally have held that fictitious groups are really risk retention mechanisms in disguise.

In other cases, especially when the parents have demonstrable risk financing or risk control needs not met by existing insurance markets, group captives have generally been recognized as true risk transfer mechanisms. This is because, first, they clearly were formed and continue to operate for reasons unrelated to taxes, and second, they are managed independent of the particular interests of any individual participant. Such group captives grew out of the tradition of the industry-centered and community-centered mutuals of nineteenth-century America.

Risk Retention/Purchasing Group. The terms *risk retention group* and *risk purchasing group* originated in the federal Risk Retention Act of 1981 (most recently amended in 1986), which was passed in response to a "products liability crisis" that arose from the rising costs and decreasing availability of products liability coverage from commercial insurers during the preceding year. This act was written to help organizations in any industry to meet their liability risk financing needs by (1) forming their own mutual risk financing organization (a risk retention group) or (2) establishing a buyers' cooperative (a purchasing group) to secure insurance in regular commercial markets for the group on a more efficient and favorable basis than could an individual member.

To encourage organizations to combine their resources to finance their products liability losses through association captives or pools, the act freed risk retention groups from much of the insurance regulation that might otherwise have hampered the effective pooling and financing of these exposures. Once licensed in any state, a risk retention group can operate anywhere in the nation, provided that it deals "primarily" in risk financing of the participants' products liability and completed

operations exposures. A risk retention group differs from an association or group captive (or a pool) principally because its operations are
covered by this federal law rather than by the state statutes under
which most association or group captives function or the insurance
codes governing pools and mutuals. Risk retention groups are special
because this federal law makes them so: they qualify as insurers while
being exempt from many otherwise burdensome provisions of state
insurance codes.

Other organizations, unable or unwilling to finance their liability
losses through risk retention groups, were encouraged by the act to
cooperate in making collective purchases of liability coverage from the
commercial insurance market. The act is based on the assumption that
a well-managed buyers' cooperative usually is more attractive to the
insurer and the members than are the members individually because
(1) the total premium generated by the cooperative merits more
underwriting, rating, and loss control attention than does any single
member of the cooperative; (2) the members of the cooperative can
obtain better loss control and other risk management services from
independent providers than can the individual members; and (3) the
cooperative possesses more bargaining leverage with insurers and
service providers than do many of its individual members.

Therefore, the Risk Retention Act authorizes firms in any industry
to form purchasing groups for liability insurance and to otherwise
cooperate in managing their liability loss exposures. The act excuses
the members of such groups from liability for many forms of collusion
under antitrust laws and fictitious group statutes, provided their
activities are limited to management of the participants' liability
exposures. These exemptions enable these groups to engage with
impunity from both federal and state laws in activities that restrain
trade in insurance markets and to enjoy income tax advantages that
would otherwise be denied to fictitious groups.

Rent-A-Captive. Some existing pure, association, or group captives are willing to "rent" their facilities—such as underwriting, rating,
claims management, and accounting and financial expertise—to other
organizations that would like to confirm the feasibility and benefits of a
captive before forming their own enterprise. For a fee that usually
reflects the degree of underwriting risk and the amount of effort
required to accommodate the "renter," an existing captive agrees to let
one or more renters participate in the captive arrangement as if they
intended to be permanent parents. Such an arrangement can generate
additional revenue and a wider exposure base for the original parents
of the captive while allowing new firms to test the wisdom of forming
their own enterprises. Some insurance brokerage organizations and

insurers have formed captives principally to make rent-a-captive services and facilities available to those clients who want to try the captive risk financing mechanism.

An Alternative Classification: Pure and Broad Captives. The description of a pure captive as one having a single parent is the most widely accepted definition of this type of organization. However, many authorities and practitioners use the term *pure captive* with a different meaning in a classification that recognizes only two types of captive, pure captives and broad captives. In this classification a pure captive is one that provides risk financing only for its parents, regardless of how few or numerous, otherwise related or unrelated, they may be. In contrast, a *broad captive* in this classification is one that also provides risk financing for organizations that are not its parents. In short, a pure captive provides risk financing only for its parent; a broad captive meets others needs as well.

A subsequent section in this chapter describes the advantages of or the reasons for employing a captive. One of these may be to use it as a device for entering the commercial insurance and reinsurance market as a seller of coverages to other organizations. Thus, one reason a parent may choose to form a broad captive is to implement a long-term, general marketing strategy for the parent and its corporate affiliates.

Two other reasons a broad captive may have special appeal relate more directly to an organization's risk financing needs. First, accepting "outside" business may provide an organization's captive with a broader base of loss exposures and a more credible set of loss statistics from which to develop more meaningful premium rates—in short, to form a better *risk pool.* Second, one of the criteria that tax authorities sometimes use to evaluate the independence of an affiliated insurer (and thus the tax deductibility to the parent of "premiums" paid to the captive) is the percentage of outside business the captive underwrites; therefore, providing substantial risk financing for a significant number of outside organizations may enhance a parent's likelihood of being allowed a tax deduction for payments to its own captive.

Types of Pools The classification of pools is not as complex as that of captives. This probably is because regulatory and tax authorities and codes recognize that pools are insurers. Therefore, the tax deductibility of premiums paid by participants to pools for insurance has been largely unchallenged. Consequently, several of the basic distinctions among types of captives generally have not been considered relevant when analyzing pools. Such distinctions may be based, for example, on the number of parents or whether they write substantial amounts of insurance on "outside" exposures of entities other than their parents (distinctions once thought useful in obtaining tax deductibility for "premiums" paid to these captives).

Pools are classified in terms of (1) the organizational characteristics shared by their participants, (2) the types of coverage they provide, and (3) whether they operate in the primary insurance or in the reinsurance market. A *municipal pool* provides risk financing for municipalities (and perhaps for other public entities), while a *public utility pool* focuses on the risk financing needs of electric, natural gas, and other utility firms. Similarly, a *products liability pool* provides only (or at least primarily) products liability protection for its participants, while a *malpractice pool* centers on professional liability exposures of its participants. A *nuclear reinsurance pool* is a mechanism through which insurers can combine through reinsurance the nuclear exposures of their policyholders. Any given pool can be classified by any two or more of these three characteristics. For example, at one time two nuclear reinsurance pools flourished, one primarily serving stock insurers and the other primarily mutual insurers.

RETENTION VERSUS TRANSFER—PRACTICE MODIFIES THEORY

By the definitions of captive and pool in the preceding section, risk financing through a captive is retention, while risk financing through a pool is transfer. This distinction between captives and pools is consistent with the sharp contrast that exists, in principle, between using internal funds to pay for accidental losses (retention) and using external funds for this purpose (transfer).

Recall from ARM 54 and Chapter 1 of this text that while every organization ultimately can expect to pay for its own losses whether their cost initially has been retained or transferred, retention includes financing techniques by which funds for losses originally come from within an organization or its financial family; transfer encompasses all techniques by which funds for losses first come from external sources. Thus, charging off losses as current expenses, using funded or unfunded reserves, borrowing, and relying upon a captive insurer are all forms of retention, while contractual transfers of risk financing and insurance (including pools) are all risk transfer.

Principles with "Soft" Edges

Despite the theoretically sharp distinction between retention and transfer, much of the discussion in this chapter deals simultaneously with both captives and pools, making statements that apply equally to both. This structure of this discussion about captives and pools implicitly raises the question as to whether the distinction between retention and transfer is as sharp as the principles would suggest. In practice, many innovative risk financing techniques are "hybrids" of retention and transfer. They include elements of both techniques, leaving somewhat unclear the point at which a particular risk financing measure ceases to be a member of one "family" and joins the other.

Biology provides a useful analogy. Biologists classify any living organism as either an animal or a plant just as risk management professionals have been taught to think of a risk financing technique as retention or transfer. For biologists, the distinction is useful in studying and classifying the behavior of living things: for example, plants manufacture their own food, animals do not; plants continue growing as long as they live, animals stop growing when they reach maturity; plants occupy a fixed location, animals move about; the individual cells of plants have rigid outer perimeters, those of animals are flexible. In risk financing, retention involves drawing upon internal funds, transfer draws on external funds; retention implies being able to control the use of an earned income from one's own funds, transfer entails surrendering that control and income; additions to internal reserves for retained losses are not tax deductible, payments to external transferees are.

These features are useful as long as the basic plant/animal or retention/transfer distinction remains clear. But the biological creativity of nature and the financial ingenuity of risk management professionals have blurred some of these distinctions. In nature, many microscopic creatures that move like animals also can generate their own food like plants; a few creatures who spend their lives anchored plant-like to one spot consist of individual cells with flexible perimeters. In risk financing, recent decades have seen the development of *insured cash flow plans* which, while containing elements of insurance protection, also allow an insured considerable control of and much of the investment income generated by funds the insurer holds as reserves. Flexible, *loss-sensitive rating plans* also permit an organization's insurance premium costs to vary with its loss experience in recent rating periods. Controlling and earning returns on funds held ready to pay losses, as well as risk financing costs that vary with loss experience, are both key characteristics of retention—yet these cash flow plans also offer insurance protection to keep loss costs within predetermined boundaries.

In short, while there are in biology still highly significant differences between plants and animals and, in risk financing, still some very useful distinctions between retention and transfer, creative developments challenge traditional thinking in both fields. Because the distinctions between captives and pools parallel the distinction between retention and transfer, creative developments in captives and pools also pose such challenges. Pools clearly have the two hallmark characteristics of insurance: (1) transfer of the financial burden of specified losses from one group (participants/transferors/indemnitees) to a separate, unaffiliated transferee/indemnitor (the pool itself); and (2) the sharing or combining of loss exposures (colloquially, the *pooling of risks*). Even when a pool has as few as two participating indemnitees, it has both these essential characteristics of insurance and can, at least in principle, therefore be classified as a transfer mechanism. Several currently prominent and highly successful mutual insurance companies serving the general public once began in just this fashion when a few businessowners banded together for mutual protection when they felt that the then existing commercial insurance markets were not meeting their needs. Their small pools grew to become outstanding general insurers.

Just as clearly as pools constitute transfer, *some* captive insurance arrangements are clearly a retention mechanism. For example, when a captive has only one parent and "insures" the loss exposures of no other entity, there is neither any shifting of the financial burden of losses to an economically independent entity nor any pooling of loss exposures. However, as such, a single-parent, single-indemnitee captive grows in one or both of two directions—by acquiring more parents who are of different corporate or economic "families" or by indemnifying entities that are not its owners. This growing and diversifying captive begins to take on the characteristics of a pool and begins to approach what state and federal statutes term "engaging in the business of insurance."

Determining exactly when such a diversifying captive ceases to be a retention device for one or a few parents and begins to engage in the business of insurance is very important but very difficult. It is important because as long as a captive is a retention device, (1) the "premiums" the parent pays to the captive typically are not tax deductible, (2) the captive does not need to comply with the highly complex and costly regulations by which every United States and most foreign jurisdictions regulate how an insurer shall operate, and (3) these jurisdictions normally do not collect insurance premium tax revenues from risk financing mechanisms deemed to be retention. However, once a captive crosses the boundary into transfer by providing "insurance" to a founder or to some other indemnitee, then all three of these conditions are reversed. It is difficult to decide if and when this reversal should be implemented because the precise boundary between retention and transfer is not always clear and because the

United States legal system delegates to each jurisdiction much independent authority to resolve for itself the retention/transfer issue. The taxation and regulation of captive insurance arrangements consequently have been the subject of much litigation and numerous administrative hearings, many of which have reached conflicting decisions.

A Historical Note on "Cash Flow" Plans

Many of the reasons for the blurring of the distinction between retention and transfer can be traced to insureds' desire to improve control of their own funds in order to make more efficient use of their financial resources. Rather than simply surrendering a predetermined number of premium dollars to an insurer at the beginning of a coverage period and waiting to perhaps collect some indemnity payments for losses that may or may not happen—and meanwhile "helping" an insurer to invest these dollars for its own benefit—financially perceptive insureds have looked for financially beneficial uses for these insurance dollars. Insurers and their intermediaries have sought to respond to these insureds' wishes by devising or agreeing to various plans for (1) deferring some premium payments, (2) establishing loss-sensitive rating systems, and (3) allowing insureds to participate in investment earnings. Because the development of pools and captives has been stimulated by this same creative environment, it is instructive to review briefly the history that has generated not only captives and pools, but also the many risk financing techniques that combine elements of retention with elements of transfer.

The early 1950s witnessed the development of guaranteed-cost, coordinated programs of property and liability insurance using standardized policies designed for typical organizations. As offered by some insurers, these policies also featured rating plans that reflected individual insureds' recent loss experience, reducing coverage costs for insureds with favorable loss records.

The 1960s brought high deductibles, verging into *self-insurance* and *self-insured retentions (SIRs)* backed by excess insurance, including umbrellas, and/or reinsurance. Also in this decade single-parent captives became a means of retaining not only loss exposures but also premium dollars within their founders' corporate families. While it was at first thought that this might allow tax deductibility of "premiums" paid to captives that were actually holders of internal self-insurance reserves, the tax status of captive-oriented plans has remained in doubt. Both the Internal Revenue Service and the Federal Tax Court have been quite consistent in resisting new attempts by parents to achieve tax deductibility payments to captives by minimizing the importance of the insurance-like features of what the federal authorities see as retention mechanisms. Cases litigated from the 1960s to the present have elaborated on federal authorities' basic premise that payments for risk financing transfers are tax deductible to the transferor/indemnitee, but additions to reserves for retention programs are not tax deductible.

During the 1970s one popular trend combined the use of captives with *fronting arrangements* through primary insurers and reinsurers. This allowed an organization to retain exposures (and funds) through its captive while attempting to meet the then-current, very restrictive tax regulations for the deductibility of "insurance" premiums paid to a captive. Most of the cash flow plans described under the next heading originated in the 1970s. Beginning then and continuing to the present, insurers have been especially receptive to and inventive of insurance rating innovations, premium-deferral schedules, and procedures for allowing insureds to participate in investment earnings.

During the 1980s, multi-parent captives have become a growing force in insurance markets, especially for professional and trade associations seeking liability coverages for their members. These and other groups also have been forming pools to combine their members' exposures in a mutual insurance arrangement or to form marketing groups whose combined premium volume empowers them to negotiate effectively with commercial insurers.

Cash Flow Plans Combining Retention with Transfer

Cash flow plan is an imprecise term applied in various contexts to many insurance-based risk financing measures, most of which have developed since the mid-1970s. In its most exact sense, cash flow plan refers only to modifications in the practice that requires insurance premiums to be paid at the beginning of coverage periods. By thus deferring the cash payment of a portion or all of a premium, an insured can use these dollars until they must finally be paid. More loosely defined cash flow plans also encompass *loss-sensitive rating plans*, which allow an insured with favorable loss experience to pay less for insurance, and *investment-credit plans*, which allow an insured some control of or some investment earnings from reserves held to pay future losses.

Thus, all cash flow plans *decrease* the expected present value of an insured's cash outflows for insurance (thereby *increasing* the expected present value of the insured's overall net cash flows if other factors remain unchanged), while placing upper limits on the insured's risk financing costs if its accidental losses happen to be frequent or severe. In cash flow plans the (1) use of funds that otherwise would initially be paid out as insurance premiums, (2) reduced risk financing costs if loss experience is favorable, and (3) investment earnings on loss reserves are all characteristics of traditional forms of retention. In contrast, the limit on risk financing costs if loss experience is adverse, (also provided by cash flow plans), is an "insurance element" and is a key characteristic of traditional forms of transfer. Thus, cash flow plans combine elements of retention and transfer, merging in practice the two principally distinct families of risk financing techniques.

The following subsections describe a variety of cash flow plans to illustrate briefly some ways of combining retention with transfer. The combinations can be as diverse as the imaginations and negotiating powers of risk management professionals representing buyers or sellers of insurance. Therefore, the following sketch may be only a preview of innovations; it is representative, but not exhaustive.

Deferred Premiums Deferred premium plans are an alternative to paying an entire annual (or any other periodic) premium at the beginning of a coverage period. They allow an insured to pay fractions of this premium each month, quarter, or at any other interval. Such a payment schedule gives the insured longer use of the yet unpaid portion of the premium, thus decreasing the present value of premium outlays. In exchange for the right to defer premium payments, the insured usually must pay the insurer interest on the unpaid portion of the premium. For premium deferral to strengthen an insured's net cash flows, the after-tax interest rate on this "loan" from the insurer should be less than the after-tax rate of return the insured can generate from using the unpaid portion of the premium in its own operations.

Lagged Premium Payments Some types of insurance on exposures with fluctuating values (such as inventories or gross receipts) require insureds to periodically report actual values and then to pay premiums based on these reported values. Premiums for such *reporting form coverages* are traditionally payable within thirty days of the end of the period for which values have been reported and coverage has been in effect. By extending the deadline for premium payments to sixty, ninety, or more days beyond the end of this coverage period, an insurer can grant an insured more time to use dollars that otherwise would have flowed to the insurer. In effect, lagged premium payments grant the insured an interest-free loan (as long as premium rates are not raised to compensate for the deferral of premium payments).

Retrospective Rating Plans Two loss-sensitive rating plans are called retrospective rating plans because the insured's premium for coverage during a particular period is based on the insured's loss experience during that policy period. Subject to a maximum and a

Exhibit 8-1
The Operation of a Retrospective Rating Plan

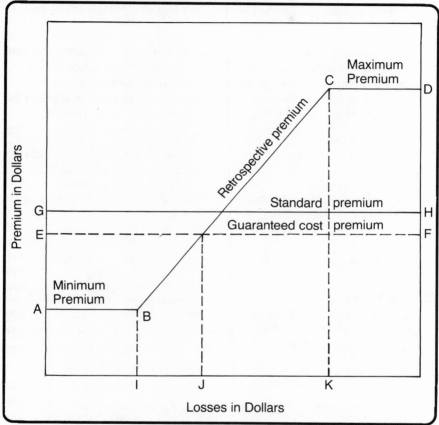

minimum premium, this final premium varies directly with the insured's current loss experience as schematically shown in Exhibit 8-1. One of these two types of retrospective rating plans is based on an insured's losses incurred during the period; the other is based on the insured's losses paid during the period.

Retrospective Rating Formula—Incurred Losses. This plan also is known as an *incurred loss retro plan.* The final premium is determined by the following *retrospective rating formula.*

$$\begin{array}{c}\text{Indicated}\\\text{retro}\\\text{premium}\end{array} = \left(\begin{array}{c}\text{Basic}\\\text{premium}\end{array} + \begin{array}{c}\text{Converted}\\\text{losses}\end{array} + \begin{array}{c}\text{Excess}\\\text{loss}\\\text{premium}\end{array}\right) \times \begin{array}{c}\text{Tax}\\\text{multiplier}\end{array}$$

The components of this formula, known as *retro factors*, are interrelated. When one of these is changed, the others also change.

Basic Premium.   The basic premium has the following characteristics:

- It provides for insurer expenses, profit, and contingencies, but does not include loss adjustment expense or tax expense.
- It includes a charge for the insurance protection above the maximum premium amount less a deduction in recognition of the minimum premium.

Retrospective rating uses *standard premium* as its starting point. A standard premium is the product of multiplying the basic (manual) premium rate by the number of exposure units and then multiplying again by an experience modifier. Standard premium is developed with guaranteed-cost rating procedures for the applicable lines of coverage but does not use a premium discount. That is:

$$\text{Standard premium} = \text{Rate} \times \text{Exposure} \times \text{Experience modifier}$$

Exhibit 8-1 shows that the standard premium normally is greater than the guaranteed-cost premium. The difference between the two (GE in Exhibit 8-1) reflects the *premium discount.* The standard premium is then multiplied by the basic premium factor to develop the *basic premium:*

$$\text{Basic premium} = \text{Standard premium} \times \text{Basic premium factor}$$

The basic premium factor used in the calculation may be taken from a rating manual or determined by actuarial analysis. It is interrelated with the other factors used in the formula:

- The basic premium factor (and hence the basic premium) will decrease if the minimum premium is decreased. The insurer receives no less than the minimum premium even if there are no losses at all. The higher the minimum premium, the better the chance that premiums will be more than high enough to reflect losses, and the insurer will earn an extra profit.
- The basic premium factor will decrease if the maximum premium is increased. The insurer receives no more than the maximum premium, regardless of the amount of covered losses. The higher the maximum premium, the lower the chance that

the insurer will have to pay insured losses that are not directly reflected in the premium it collects.

Converted Losses.   Once the terms of a retrospectively rated plan have been agreed on and accepted by the insurer and insured, losses are the only independent variable. Incurred losses (that is, paid and reserved losses) are multiplied by a *loss conversion factor* (LCF) to develop *converted losses:*

Converted losses = Incurred losses × Loss conversion factor

This is the second element in the formula used to develop the indicated retro premium.

Since *incurred losses* (e.g., paid plus reserves) are used in the formula, conventional retrospective rating plans are often referred to as *incurred loss retros* to distinguish them from *paid loss retros,* discussed later.

Excess Loss Premium.   Sometimes an insured will purchase a *loss limitation* to limit *individual* (per claim or per occurrence) losses to a specified level and reduce the effect of unusually large single losses on the retro premium. The amount of loss limitation may range from $10,000 to a maximum of 50 percent of the plan premium.

The loss limitation is a different type of insurance element than the maximum premium. The loss limitation has an effect similar to specific excess coverage, whereas the maximum premium has an effect comparable to aggregate excess coverage. The maximum premium is the most the insured will have to pay to the insurance company in the event aggregate loss experience is very poor (either a few individual large losses or an aggregation of small losses). A loss limitation, on the other hand, places a cap on the dollar amount of a large loss to be plugged into the formula. It eliminates or reduces the possibility that one or a few unusually large "freak" losses will require the insured to pay the maximum premium, even though loss frequency is low and experience is otherwise favorable.

Tax Multiplier.   Taxes are a separate factor in the retro formula and are assessed on the basic premium, converted losses, and excess loss premium through the application of a *tax multiplier.* The tax multiplier varies by line of insurance coverage and by state. It provides for state premium taxes and miscellaneous taxes such as assigned risk pool surcharges, second injury fund assessments, licenses, and fees.

Operation of Retrospective Rating Plans—Incurred Losses. Retrospective rating plans are generally subject to annual premium adjustment calculations until all losses are paid or until an agreement is reached between the insurer and the insured such that, even though some losses may still be open, it is time to close the plan based on the probable outcome. Adjustments are usually made six months after policy expiration and annually thereafter. Each adjustment involves "plugging" the insured's updated loss experience into the formula and determining if an additional or return premium is due.

As can be seen in Exhibit 8-1, the *retro additional* and *retro return premiums* are constrained by the minimum and maximum premiums agreed to at the inception of the policy. For example, as losses approach the level specified in K, the premium approaches the maximum. However, the insured will never pay more than the maximum premium even if losses greatly exceed the level represented by K. Likewise, the insured will never pay less than the minimum premium even if losses are much lower than the level represented by I.

The minimum and maximum are usually expressed as a percentage of the standard premium. For example, the minimum might be 60 percent of standard and the maximum might be 150 percent of standard. This approach automatically adjusts the minimum and maximum premium amount if there is any variation in standard premium from the amount forecast at the inception of the policy.

A retrospective rating plan rewards an insured for successful loss control. When losses are low, an insured's net cost is lower than what it would be under most prospective rating approaches. Referring again to Exhibit 8-1, the premium will be less than that of a guaranteed cost program (E) if losses are lower than the amount represented by J. Conversely, an insured with poor loss experience may pay a premium in excess of standard premium. Again referring to Exhibit 8-1, the insured's premium will be more than that of a guaranteed cost program (E) if losses are higher than the amount represented by J.

Under an incurred loss retro plan, the insurer holds loss reserves until losses are paid and retro adjustments are made. Retro adjustments typically occur over several years, and the insured forfeits cash flow until such adjustments are completed.

Retrospective Rating Plans—Paid Losses. A conventional *incurred* loss retrospective rating plan is intended to produce a final cost that reflects an insured's actual loss experience. Through the plan, the insured eventually recoups any surplus premium payments if losses are controlled, and the insurer collects additional premiums if losses are not controlled. However, the insured party does not have use of the "reserve dollars" held by the insurer for losses incurred but not yet paid. As discussed, portions of these loss reserves will not be paid out for several years or will be paid at amounts lower or higher than the established reserves.

A paid loss retrospective rating plan offers the insured cash flow features that are absent in the incurred loss retro plans. *The retrospective rating formula used with a paid loss retro is identical to that of an incurred loss retro except that it calculates earned premium on the basis of paid losses rather than incurred losses.* During the (often) extended period of time between loss events and actual payment of claims, the *insured* holds the unpaid premium and unpaid loss reserves and uses them to generate income. In other words, the insured holds funds that would have been held by the insurer under plans such as incurred loss retrospective rating plans or guaranteed-cost plans. These funds are *eventually* paid to the insurer when needed to pay the claimants, but the insured holds them until then.

Under a paid loss retro, the insurer may increase its profit factor or levy a special interest charge, offsetting—at least in part—the income it forgoes because it does not collect premiums in advance of the loss payouts.

Differences Between Retro Plans. A paid loss retro plan differs from an incurred loss plan in the timing of premium payment.

- Under an incurred loss retro the insured pays an advance premium based on the estimated standard premium. The actual earned premium is periodically calculated (approximately six months after policy expiration and annually thereafter until all claims are closed or other agreement is made) and the premium is adjusted either through an additional or return premium.
- Under a paid loss retro the amount of the standard premium is the same; however, it is not all paid to the insurance company during the policy period. Rather, the insurer agrees to accept a substantially reduced amount in advance. The amount required at policy inception consists of the nonloss portion of the standard premium plus a loss fund deposit.

The basic premium represents the largest portion of the nonloss premium. As in an incurred loss retro, the basic premium in a paid loss retro includes charges for administrative expenses, sales commissions, loss control services, insurer profit and contingencies, and a net insurance charge reflecting the selected minimum and maximum premium levels. Payment terms for the basic premium are negotiable, but it is common for the basic premium to be divided by twelve and paid in equal monthly installments.

The excess loss premium—to pay for a loss limitation if applicable—is payable at the same time the basic premium is paid. If the basic premium is paid through twelve monthly installments, the excess loss premium is divided by twelve and paid along with the basic.

In addition to the payment of the basic and excess loss premiums, a paid loss retro program requires an advance deposit to establish an *escrow loss fund*. The purpose is to provide funds from which the insurance company will pay claims, pending periodic reimbursement by the insured. The escrow loss fund, or what remains of it, is returned to the insured upon termination of the paid loss program or when all claims are settled. The initial deposit for the loss fund, which must be paid in advance, is subject to negotiation with the insurance company. However, the deposit fund is usually equal to two to two and one-half months of estimated paid claims derived from *reasonably anticipated loss payments*.

As noted, the insurer pays claims out of the escrow loss fund, and the insured periodically replenishes the fund. Reimbursement to the fund may be based on the exact amount paid by the insurer or on a projected paid loss schedule established at the beginning of the program. If reimbursement is on a projected schedule, the insurer generally will maintain the right to request additional funds in the event claims are paid out faster than expected.

Claims handling charges for services provided by the insurer may be collected in advance. The insured may be required to pay estimated claims service charges developed by multiplying expected losses by the loss conversion factor. These estimated costs are an advance charge to the insured and may be included in the initial program payment. Generally, however, the insured will not be obligated to an advance payment for claims handling expenses. Rather, the loss conversion factor will be applied to those paid losses covered by each periodic billing to the insured.

State premium taxes are estimated at the inception of the program and paid in advance by the insured. The estimated standard premium (manual premium developed using an estimated exposure base) is multiplied by the applicable tax multiplier to calculate the estimated taxes payable. Advance payment of taxes by the insured follows the basic premium payment stream. That is, if the basic premium is paid to the insurer in twelve equal monthly installments, the estimated taxes are divided by twelve and paid monthly in addition to the basic; if the basic premium is paid in full at the inception of the plan, estimated taxes are also paid in full.

In simpler terms, the cost elements payable to the insurer of a paid loss retro are the following:

- basic premium (stated percentage of the standard premium),
- excess loss premium if applicable (charge for elected loss limitations),
- estimated premium taxes (estimated standard premium × tax multiplier),
- claims handling service charges (applied as negotiated), and

● paid losses (billed as negotiated).

Since the insured's advance premium payment and interim billings represent payments for only the basic premium (insurer expenses), state premium taxes, excess loss premium, paid losses (escrow fund) and claims handling expenses, the insured is required to provide financial security to the insurer for the difference between the estimated standard premium and the total premium actually paid at inception. The financial security reduces the insurer's credit risk. It also provides the insurer with an asset that may be counted in its surplus. The most commonly used financial security is a "clean," irrevocable letter of credit from an insurer-approved domestic bank. The insurer will also require a commitment from the policyholder to increase or decrease the financial security provided in order to accurately reflect any fluctuations from the original amount due as a result of audits or retro adjustments.

Under a paid loss retro plan the insured basically provides funds for losses only when there is actual payment to claimants and does this by periodically reimbursing the escrow fund. Loss dollars usually represent 50 to 70 percent of the premium dollar for liability and workers compensation insurance; therefore, the paid loss approach effectively defers a large portion of the advance premium requirements of other types of plans such as incurred loss retros.

The premium deferment carries a value that increases as the length of time premium payments are deferred is extended. Workers compensation, general liability, and products liability insurance coverages have traditionally involved very significant periods between loss occurrence and loss payment. Although most losses are generally reported in the initial two to three years after policy inception, only a fraction of incurred losses are actually paid during that time period. As a result, the insured retains the use of substantial funds held for unpaid loss reserves and may use them to generate additional income. Dollars that would otherwise be committed to advance insurance premiums may support collateral or become available for general business use.

In summary, incurred and paid loss retrospective rating plans are different ways of defining losses that are used to calculate final premiums. The plans have different effects on the timing of an insured's premium payments, while both plans normally have cash flow advantages over guaranteed-cost insurance for an insured. In addition, a paid loss retro permits an insured to defer premium payments for longer than in an incurred loss retro. For liability and other coverages involving long-term claims payouts, the incurred losses in any given period are likely to be much greater than the paid losses. Therefore, the paid loss retro permits greater postponing of final payment adjustments so that (unless the insured is due a premium refund at the end of the retrospective rating period) the insured has more time to use money that would have been paid sooner to the insurer even under an incurred loss retrospective rating plan.

Discounted (Net Present Value) Premium Plan Regardless of whether the premium for a property and liability coverage is computed on a guaranteed-cost or any loss-sensitive basis, the premium normally anticipates that the insurer will establish reserves for unearned premiums and for losses and will benefit from investment earnings on funds in these reserves. Many insureds question whether an insurer is entitled to any or all of these investment earnings on funds that, in their view, the insurer has not yet "earned" by either paying losses or providing protection during loss-free periods.

In response to this attitude, some insurers project their expected earnings from these invested reserves and credit insureds with all or a portion of these investment earnings. Such credits reduce the policyholder's insurance costs by lowering the premium to the present value of what the premium otherwise would have been if discounted at the after-tax rate of interest the insurer anticipates on its invested reserves. The higher this discount rate (and the greater the portion of investment earnings the insurer agrees to credit to the insured), the lower the discounted premium.

Compensating Balances Plan Many commercial banks require their business borrowers to leave on deposit specified minimum balances. This effectively reduces the true amounts these borrowers are able to borrow from their banks, increasing the borrowers' costs of loans. These balances often are known as *compensating balances*, indirect payments to banks for serving their commercial customers.

Some insurers offer insureds opportunities to "liberate" at least a portion of these mandatory compensating balances by using insurance premiums to offset some of the bank's requirements. These insurers agree that all or most of the premium an insured pays the insurer will be deposited by the insurer in the insured's bank and, by agreement with the bank, will be considered to be part of the insured's compensating balance. This allows the insured initially to reduce its actual compensating balance by the amount of the deposited insurance premium. Any insured losses the policyholder later incurs are then paid out of the deposited premium, thus forcing the insured to then increase its actual compensating balance by the amount of these insured losses. As long as insured losses paid by the insurer from this deposit do not exceed the premium first deposited in the insured's bank, the insured enjoys use of some of the funds that otherwise would have been paid as insurance premiums, much as if the organization had initially retained these losses.

Captive Insurance It is important to recognize the role of captive insurance in the evolution of insurance-based cash flow plans. The plans described in the preceding sections involve external commercial insurers not affiliated with insureds but providing many of the benefits of retention while affording the insured some protection against unexpectedly severe losses. Where these commercial insurers have been unable to fully meet insureds' expectations, some insureds have taken the next logical step—forming their own insurer to provide what they feel they need and deserve.

The result was the rapid formation of many captive insurance companies in the 1970s. However, this led many insurance regulators and the federal tax authorities to scrutinize the new captive operations to ensure that they truly were operating as independent insurance enterprises. To be regulated, taxed, and otherwise recognized as insurers, these new ventures would actually have to perform the economic functions of insurance companies and not be a disguised mechanism for retention by their founders. When regulators determined that captives operated as genuine insurers, they have been treated like any other commercial insurer—in particular, premiums paid to these insurers have been tax deductible for the parents. In contrast, when captives have not been truly independent but appear to have primarily been managed to retain losses for their parents or to achieve other financial benefits, insurance and tax authorities have treated them as devices for retention. Parents have been denied income tax deductions for insurance premiums paid to these captives.

The litigated cases suggest that a captive will be treated, *for tax purposes*, as a retention device unless most of the following conditions are met:

- The senior operating executives of the captive responsible for its daily operations are not employees of any parent.
- The captive has adequate capital and charges sufficient premium rates for the exposures it underwrites.
- The captive holds adequate amounts and appropriate forms of reinsurance, and no parent directly or indirectly participates in this reinsurance or any related retrocession.
- The captive is managed as a true insurance enterprise, and its accounts are not managed for the principal purpose of benefiting any parent.
- The captive is prepared to accept applications for coverage from organizations that are not its parents. (Having a meaningful

percentage of such outside business is often persuasive evidence of a captive's independence.)

These criteria collectively define what operational independence means for a captive. When the captive operates independently of its parents' economic family, the captive is able to accept exposures to accidental loss as insurance because these exposures have actually been transferred to an entity that is financially separate from any parent.

Most captives have failed or have chosen not to undertake these tests of independence required to gain both status for themselves as insurers and income tax deductibility of premium payments for their parents. Deductibility of premium payments to captives, once a crucial goal for some, has largely been resolved; the federal tax authorities' stand against deductibility largely has prevailed. Therefore, when tax considerations were important motives for forming captives, the initial expectations of their founders have been somewhat frustrated. Truly effective captives bring other, more significant risk financing benefits to their parents.

DECIDING TO ESTABLISH A CAPTIVE OR POOL

Financing accidental losses through a captive or pool strengthens the risk management programs of an organization only if the following are true. First, the benefits to be derived from a captive or pool exceed the costs of such an arrangement and second, establishing and operating a captive or pool is feasible *in practice* for the organizations that found and use it. Thus, the decision to establish a captive or pool requires (1) weighing benefits and costs "on paper" and (2) determining the practicality of actually operating a captive or pool.

Weighing Benefits and Costs

The decision to inaugurate or to join a captive or pool essentially should be a financial one. Pride or prestige in owning or founding an insurance company or angry frustration with current but probably temporary conditions in commercial insurance markets generally are not valid reasons for establishing or joining a captive or pool. Therefore, making a good decision requires an objective analysis of financial benefits and costs.

Benefits of a Captive or Pool The benefits of forming or joining a captive or pool can be broadly classified as reduced insurance costs, improved net cash flows, more stable insurance markets, improved insurance coverage, fewer regulatory restrictions, improved loss control and claims services, coordination of insurance programs for organizations operating in many jurisdictions, and more ready access to reinsurance and retail insurance markets.

Reduced Insurance Costs. Many organizations with favorable loss experience under commercial insurance often feel that their insurance costs are higher than necessary because commercial insurers' rating systems seem inadequately responsive to a favorable loss record. A captive may improve the perceived rating equity by making each insured's premium more flexible, especially in terms of rate credits. Insurance costs also may be reduced because a captive or pool can achieve greater operating efficiency than can a commercial insurer operating in a broader market: for example, a captive or pool may have greatly reduced marketing costs, thus passing on lower costs than would a commercial insurer to the insured or parent. Moreover, if the parents of a captive or participants in a pool already practice sound loss control or claims administration, the captive or pool need not provide these services, thus enabling it to eliminate the related premium "loadings" a commercial insurer normally would charge all insureds. There may be additional reductions in premium rates because the captive or pool can generate a higher rate of investment income on its unearned premium and loss reserves than commercial insurers can achieve or will credit to insureds as premium savings.

Improved Net Cash Flows. Reduced insurance costs naturally lessen an organization's cash outflows for risk financing. Beyond this one direct cash flow effect, the insurance and reinsurance operations of captives and pools can generate positive net cash inflows for their parents or participants. Money once spent on commercial insurance can stay in the captive or pool regardless of whether it is the primary insurer or a reinsurer of coverages initially placed through fronting insurers, which reinsure with the captive or pool.

To the extent that the captive or pool generates revenue from its underwriting or investment activities that is not needed to support its operations, the revenue can be returned as dividends to the parent or participating insureds, thus providing a new source of cash inflow. (To the extent that the captive or pool cedes coverage and premiums to a reinsurer, allowing cash to "escape," this new source of net cash flow is reduced.) In short, by functioning as their own insurers and keeping funds within their own corporate families, participants in a captive or pool eliminate the net outflow of cash to pay for outside insurance coverage.

More Stable Insurance Markets. The executives of captive insurers and pools recognize their close relationships with their parents and participants: were it not for their special insurance needs, these captives and pools probably would not exist. Therefore, captives and pools usually strive to be especially reliable sources of insurance, quite resistant to the market fluctuations that prompt commercial insurers to alter the prices and availabilities of their coverages. While captives and pools cannot always meet their parents' and participants' coverage needs, a sense of a common purpose and interests usually leads the management of captives or pools and their insureds to establish mutually satisfactory coverage arrangements.

Moreover, the option of placing its coverages with a captive or pool often gives a parent or participant special leverage in commercial insurance markets. Knowing that a potential insured has a captive or pool alternative, commercial insurers may be willing to offer insurance on more competitive terms to attract or hold business. Whether a potential insured actually intends to use the captive or pool may not matter; a commercial insurer perceiving the captive or pool as a threat to its market share may become more accommodating to insureds.

Improved Insurance Coverages. Captives or pools that serve insureds who have special coverage needs are likely to be established in jurisdictions whose insurance codes grant them great freedom to offer broader coverages than typically are available in commercial insurance markets. Captives in particular are able to provide their parents with coverages not usually available in commercial insurance markets, thereby more fully meeting the unique or specific needs of their parents.

Given the special relationship between parent and captive, insurance commissioners often reason that—with respect to the scope of exposures to be transferred—captives and their parents require fewer regulations than do commercial insurers in more generalized markets. Captives (and to some extent pools) thus have been somewhat successful in overcoming regulatory underwriting restrictions to insure some perils that often have highly limited commercial insurability such as strikes, floods, medical malpractice, and products liability.

Fewer Regulatory Restrictions. The special knowledge of one another that a captive or pool and its insureds can be expected to have is one of three justifications for allowing captives, pools, and their insureds more freedom than in a traditional insurance relationship. A second source of freedom is the ability of the parents or participants to select a captive's or pool's legal domicile, the jurisdiction with primary regulatory authority. By choosing a domicile whose insurance code best suits the founders' needs with respect to coverages, rating plans, and/or investment practices, founders can free themselves from certain undesirable regulations. (The statutes in any jurisdiction can, however, be revised, thus creating a less favorable regulatory environment than the founders first anticipated; they may choose to remain in that environment or to dissolve and reestablish their captive or pool in a more favorable jurisdiction.)

A third source of coverage flexibility is an organization's access to reinsurance markets through its captive (or a group of organizations through its pool). As explained in Chapter 5, reinsurers normally deal with insurers and other reinsurers, not directly with insureds. However, by using a captive or pool as its negotiating agent, an organization or group can deal directly in the reinsurance market, entering into reinsurance, excess and umbrella insurance, and retrocession arrangements as a buyer or provider of coverage. The relatively unregulated realm of reinsurance thus permits an organization to obtain coverage from a wide range of insurers and reinsurers. Given this freedom, parents of a captive or the participants in a pool have, in principle, access to virtually any available insurance coverage.

Improved Loss Control and Claims Services. A particular organization or group may feel that it requires a greater degree or special type of loss control or claims management services than seems available at a reasonable price from commercial insurers. Establishing a captive or pool may well be a cost-effective way of obtaining tailored service, especially if the captive or pool generates economies of scale or concentrations of special expertise that the individual organizations could not achieve alone. Moreover, the status of a captive or pool as a "third party," officially organized and staffed as an entity separate from its insureds, is likely to give a captive or pool greater autonomy and authority in dealing with the insureds' personnel and claimants, thus upholding the principles of sound insurance administration with greater objectivity.

Coordination of Insurance Programs in Many Jurisdictions. International and even numerous, widespread national organizations often have difficulty obtaining uniform insurance coverages because insurance codes differ from state to state and/or country to country. Some jurisdictions require that certain insurance contract provisions follow a prescribed wording. They may also mandate that loss exposures located within their boundaries be insured to specified limits or by an insurer domiciled within these boundaries. The ability to insure, reinsure, or retrocede certain types of risks through a captive or pool—with the captive or pool dealing as necessary with various local insurers and reinsurers—can greatly simplify the design and control of a coordinated insurance program for a far-flung organization. The captive or pool also can administer loss control and claims service programs much more consistently than the organization's (or its insurers') personnel could from scattered locations. Poorly administered, a multi-national or multi-state insurance program can be chaotic; placing the risk financing challenges in the hands of the competent, central management of a captive or pool can greatly reduce administrative costs and achieve more coherent results.

Improved Access to Reinsurance and Retail Insurance Markets. Beyond allowing an organization or group to secure better coverage for itself, a captive or pool can enable its participants to sell insurance for the underwriting and investment profits this activity may bring. Once a captive or pool has successfully met the insurance needs of its founders, it may wish to expand its markets to a broader group of insureds or to a wider range of coverages. In fact, several of today's largest property and liability insurers began as highly specialized "mutual" insurers of firms in a particular industry or territory who once chose to pool their exposures because they found their insurance markets very limited. Drawing on these models fashioned a century or more ago, many founders of today's captives or pools seek to enter— and eventually to generate substantial profits from—the general insurance and reinsurance market.

Costs Establishing a captive or pool requires a commitment of substantial resources in capital and personnel. Moreover, choosing to finance recovery from accidental losses through a captive or pool logically entails abstaining from other retention or insurance alternatives. Either of these requirements may impose on an organization heavy burdens in the form of (1) unexpectedly costly or ineffective risk financing and (2) great difficulties disengaging from the captive or pool and returning to more traditional risk financing techniques.

Unexpectedly Costly and Ineffective Risk Financing. The founders of a captive or pool need to anticipate substantial initial capital expenses for establishing itself in a new jurisdiction, for hiring personnel to conduct insuring and investing operations, and for obtaining the space, equipment, and supplies for daily operations. An organization that is considering joining an existing captive or pool also needs to be prepared to bear its share of these expenses often without any guarantee (or even expectation) that these outlays will be recoverable if the captive or pool is dissolved or if the organization later elects to withdraw from it.

Beyond these initial capital requirements and ongoing expenses, the most significant and least predictable expense for any risk financing program is its outlays for accidental losses. If these losses prove to be much larger than anticipated (especially in the early years or if a captive or pool lacks adequate reinsurance), the captive or pool may face insolvency or may require infusions of new capital. In either case, a parent of a captive or a participant in a pool is likely to encounter unanticipated demands for more capital as the only alternative to failure, with the concomitant loss of all participants' initial investment. In addition to loss expenses, any of the normal ongoing insurance costs including loss control, claims handling, ratemaking, underwriting, accounting, and financial management may prove much higher than expected. This can slowly drain the resources of the pool or captive, consequently raising the premiums that must be assessed against each participant. If the premiums must increase, then participants with favorable loss experience may claim that they are entitled to pay lower assessments than others, perhaps leading to many of the pricing and availability problems that first led the participants to join the captive or pool.

The operating results of a captive or pool also may be disappointing. Starting and managing a property and liability risk financing mechanism so complex that it resembles an insurance company requires access to a wide variey of actuarial, financial, legal, loss control, underwriting, and general management skills. The cash flow, underwriting, and investment projections underlying the decision to launch or join a captive or pool may have assumed that personnel with these skills would merge into a cohesive team to produce "model" underwriting and investment results. In fact, some of this expertise may be entirely lacking, or those with a crucial skill may not function efficiently with their fellows as envisioned. For example, the rate charges of captives or pools may prove inadequate, loss control deficient, claims handling erratic, or the senior management of the captive or pool may not receive the expected degree of commitment from participants. For these or other reasons, the captive or pool simply may not produce the results at the costs that were projected when the plan began or when some later members joined the enterprise.

Difficulties Shifting to Other Alternatives. Before making a new venture, especially one whose success is directly tied to the skillful management of events so uncertain as accidental losses, it is prudent to consider if other options will be available at a reasonable cost if the enterprise fails or if one of the participants chooses to abandon it. Those who form or join a captive or pool are making long-term commitments to one another and to others who may have claims against the captive or pool. In Chapter 2, the demonstration that accident-related legal claims may take decades to indemnify implies that the commitment cannot simply be financially or ethically abandoned. Therefore, arrangements for (1) allowing any one participant to withdraw or (2) winding up the entire enterprise should be explicitly detailed in the charter or other founding documents of the enterprise.

For a single-parent captive, terminating the enterprise or withdrawing from a particular line of coverage is usually relatively simple. This single parent can absorb any outstanding losses once financed through the captive through a more elementary type of retention and search for other financing alternatives for future losses. Liability claims once financed through the captive are automatically transferred back to the parent, which must either accept or attempt to retroactively insure claims. As long as the parent itself remains solvent, the demise of the captive only forces the parent to temporarily increase its burden of retained losses until it can arrange new risk financing.

In a multi-parent captive or pool one member's withdrawal—or a unanimous decision to terminate the enterprise—is likely to cause more perplexing difficulties. In these situations care must be taken not only to protect the rights of outside claimants (to whom the withdrawing member(s) may eventually become liable) but also to preserve equities among the departing and/or remaining participants in the captive or pool. For both these purposes the articles of incorporation, by-laws, or other key documents related to the venture should detail how the assets of the captive or pool, its continuing expenses and income, and its obligations to participants are to be apportioned. The founders of a captive or pool have considerable latitude in determining these apportionments; more important than the precise terms of these apportionments is that the allocations be clear and implemented as stated at the appropriate times.

A Note on Taxes Tax considerations can be advantages or disadvantages for captives or pools depending on the tax statutes and their interpretation in a given jurisdiction at a given time. Some of these considerations include (1) the income deductibility of participants' payments to a captive or pool, (2) the obligation to pay premium taxes for having engaged in the "business of insurance," and (3) the tax status of net cash flows that a captive or pool may generate and pay as dividends to its participants.

To briefly recap the discussion in Chapter 4, current United States federal tax law appears to bestow the advantage of premium tax deductibility on pool participants but not on organizations using captives or other retention arrangements. However, these statutes or their interpretation may change, or risk management professionals may construct risk financing programs that legitimately earn tax deductibility for payments to captives. Therefore, rather than conclude that any given tax treatment is or is not a relative advantage of the particular financing technique, the risk management professional should recognize that tax advantages and disadvantages, like other strengths and weaknesses of various risk financing alternatives, should be weighted (ideally, expressed in present values of expected net cash flows) so that they can be considered as are the other costs and benefits of risk financing alternatives.

Determining Feasibility of a Captive or Pool

If an organization's risk management professional and its senior executives agree that forming or joining a captive or pool would, in principle, benefit the organization, sound risk financing next calls for a detailed feasibility study. This study should determine whether or not the captive or pool would also be practical in reality.

A proper feasibility study is not a sales presentation. Therefore, a feasibility study that merely documents a previous conclusion should be suspect. (In fact, one particularly meaningful criterion for selecting an external expert to lead a feasibility study is how often the expert has recommended *against* a captive or pool, and the reasons for such negative recommendations.) A proper feasibility study should explore, via a team of experts, whether the organization possesses, and can have continuing access to, the financial, managerial, and other resources needed to operate or participate in a captive or pool.

Because establishing a captive or pool entails the regulatory, accounting, and financial complexities of starting an insurance company, any feasibility study should be conducted by a team of specialists. The leader is often someone associated with a risk management consulting or insurance brokerage firm, many of which also are prepared to manage the ongoing operations of any captives or pools. Before retaining an expert, it is good practice to reach a preliminary agreement with this expert on the scope, purposes, schedule, and cost of the study. More specifically, a full-scale feasibility study should be preceded by general agreement between the interested organization(s) and the outside expert with respect to the following:

- Possible alternative forms of organization for the captive or pool (for example, stock, mutual, or reciprocal).
- Types and amounts of property, liability, net income, or personal loss exposures the organization(s) may wish to finance through the pool or captive.
- Jurisdictions in which the organization(s) may wish the captive or pool to be domiciled.
- Amounts of initial capital and annual expenses the founding organizations visualize allotting from their own resources to the captive or pool until it becomes self-supporting.
- Types of services (actuarial, financial, legal, managerial, and the like) the captive or pool will require and the possible sources for them.

- Cost of the feasibility study itself, the procedures for conducting it, the subjects to be included in the study, and a timetable for its completion.
- Whether the ultimate goal of the captive or pool is to grow beyond the needs of its current participants to serve wider markets and eventually to become a general insurance company.
- Benefits anticipated from the study even if it should recommend against establishing a captive or pool. (These benefits might include a thorough analysis of the organizations' risk management programs and recommendations for improvements.)

Based on such a preliminary agreement, representatives from the client organization and the consulting organization should be chosen for the study team. The study should involve two distinct parts: a *risk management analysis* and an *operational analysis*.

The basic purpose of the risk management analysis is to determine the types of losses that could best be financed through the captive or pool. To achieve this purpose, the team must analyze the organizations' loss history, current loss exposures, and the existing means of treating these exposures including the ability to retain losses less than the *attachment points* of the protection offered by the captive or pool. This information can be a basis for discussions with reinsurers, captive management companies and other specialists who might provide services to the captive or pool. Moreover, the risk management portion of a feasibility study should better enable the managements of the participating organizations to view their risk management programs as a whole, with or without a captive or pool, rather than merely considering the captive or pool as an isolated proposal.

The purpose of the operational analysis is to project the costs and benefits the participants could expect from the most reasonable use of a captive or pool and to compare these cost/benefit relationships with those of other risk financing alternatives. To achieve this purpose, price quotations must be secured from reinsurers, captive management companies, and other service organizations for all activities relevant to the operations of the captive or pool. Prices also should be obtained for each of the other risk financing alternatives. The study should structure this information to compare the costs and benefits of alternatives under a variety of scenarios involving expected levels of accidental losses, especially severe loss levels, as well as particularly favorable loss experience. It is not sufficient for a captive or pool to appear feasible under only favorable conditions—it should also appear reliable during the worst forseeable times.

The final feasibility study should structure its findings and recommendations to include a brief summary and index of the entire report, a detailed discussion of the alternative risk financing techniques and the costs and benefits projected for each, a summary of the legal and tax implications of the captive or pool for the participants, and if a captive or pool is recommended, a time sequence for the steps needed to implement this recommendation.

ESTABLISHING AND OPERATING A CAPTIVE OR POOL

In establishing a captive or pool, risk management professionals and senior executives must make a number of crucial decisions as to the nature and scope of their enterprise. Once the enterprise is established, they also must make numerous decisions about how it will operate on a daily basis.

Establishing a Captive or Pool

The decisions made at the outset about the (1) organizational form, (2) domicile, (3) initial and continuing capitalization, (4) method of providing coverage, and (5) types of coverage provided are among the most important decisions ever confronting the management of a captive or pool because they shape all its future activities.

Organizational Form For establishing formal risk financing mechanisms for retention or transfer, property and liability insurance history and traditions provide three basic models: a *stock organization,* a *mutual organization,* and a *reciprocal organization.* They are usually defined as follows in an insurance setting:

- A stock insurer is an incorporated insurer with capital contributed by stockholders to whom any earnings are distributed as dividends on their shares.
- A mutual insurer is an incorporated insurer owned by its policyholders to whom earnings are distributed as dividends in some equitable manner.
- A reciprocal (or a reciprocal exchange) is an unincorporated group of individuals or organizations called subscribers who mutually insure one another, each separately assuming individual shares of each insured loss exposure.

With the exception of a single-parent captive, which has only one owner, any other captive or any pool can be operated by its parents or participants as a stock organization, a mutual organization, or a reciprocal.

Before 1969, most captives were formed as stock organizations for any of several reasons. First, the original founders' ability to determine who shall hold the stock and to prohibit or limit transfers of the stock ensures complete ownership and control of the captive by its parents. Second, a stock organization can be more easily liquidated when it has fulfilled its objectives and is no longer needed; the owners clearly have the right to discontinue their enterprise without raising any regulatory concerns about whether persons or organizations receiving risk financing protection through the enterprise have been equitably treated. Third, for dealing within reinsurance markets, stock organizations of a given capital size typically are regarded as financially more reliable than all but the largest of mutual and reciprocal organizations.

Beginning in the 1970s, mutual and reciprocal forms of organization have become significantly more popular than they were before that time. Especially for association and group captives, the mutual or reciprocal framework has been appealing because of the ability to expand or contract its operations as participants' risk financing needs change and because of the spirit of interdependence—as well as independence from the commercial insurance market—that mutuals and reciprocals typically engender. Furthermore, for any one organization seeking risk financing, a pool or reciprocal is easier to form, enter, or exit than is a stock organization.

Nearly all pools are structured as mutual organizations or reciprocals—very few, if any, begin as stock organizations. Because interdependence is essential to the basic notion of a pool, ownership of the organization by those whom it protects is highly logical; ownership as a stock organization by "outsiders" would tend to counter the basic spirit of the enterprise. Thus, in addition to the preceding advantages, the members of the pool can also "persuade" other members to adopt sound risk control and other proper management techniques.

Domicile An organization or group forming a captive or pool has considerable freedom in choosing the legal jurisdiction that will be its "home" in the sense that the captive or pool (1) is first formed in, (2) is regulated primarily by, and (3) is subject to the tax laws of that jurisdiction. A captive or pool need not conduct the bulk of its activities in its domiciliary jurisdiction as long as it meets the minimum requirements for maintaining a corporate office in that jurisdiction. In a legal sense, such an office need be little more than a mailing address and can, in fact, be maintained by an agent whose primary business is maintaining corporate offices for a large number of captives, pools, or other noninsurance organizations that wish to be domiciled in a given jurisdiction but, in fact, conduct the bulk of their business elsewhere.

The very wide range of domiciles can be broadly classified as *domestic* (located within the United States or other country in which the participants are legally domiciled) and offshore (any jurisdiction that is not domestic). *Offshore domiciles* offer the general advantages of freedom from taxation by the country in which the captive parents or pool participants conduct the bulk of their business (although these offshore sites may have their own special tax and other regulatory requirements). Within the United States several states have enacted statutes designed to encourage formation of captives or pools, both to meet the risk financing needs of their own domestic corporations and to gain the revenue and prestige derived from taxing and/or regulating the captives or pools they might attract from other jurisdictions. During times of rapid captive or pool formation, some jurisdictions appear to be competing to become captive or pool capitals.

Because captives or pools are best conducted as permanent enterprises, not as temporary devices for benefiting from fluctuations in commercial insurance markets, an organization or group should choose a domicile best suited to its long-term needs, regardless of which jurisdictions may temporarily be most popular. Therefore, simply for convenience, an organization or group whose operations are concentrated in a particular jurisdiction often will choose it for a domicile regardless of the regulatory, tax, or other incentives available elsewhere.

Other organizations or groups, especially those whose operations already span several countries, tend to explore a wider range of domiciles in terms of the (1) ease of formation, (2) freedom from regulation, (3) operating convenience, and (4) tax advantages. The first criterion is often heavily (perhaps excessively) emphasized. A particularly attractive jurisdiction is one that offers the following:

- low minimum capital requirements initially and as the underwritings of the captive or pool grow,
- rapid formation with few, if any, mandatory waiting periods or "red tape" delays, and
- permission for one captive or pool to underwrite coverage against a wide range of loss exposures so that the legal structure of the enterprise may remain relatively uncomplicated.

With respect to regulatory freedom, the second important criterion in deciding where to locate a captive or pool, a favorable domicile often is one that does the following:

- permits and recognizes as "insurance" the writing of a wide range of coverages on loss exposures located throughout the world,

- imposes few or no insurance rate regulations or recognizes diverse premium rating plans for individual insureds,
- allows the captive or pool to invest its reserves and other funds in a variety of financial instruments, real property, and other tangible assets,
- places few restrictions on the movement of or convertibility between international currencies, and
- has a tradition of political and liberal regulation of business, thus ensuring that current freedoms are likely to remain.

Operating convenience, the third criterion, is likely to be greatest in a jurisdiction characterized by the following:

- has a strong business infrastructure of insurance, reinsurance, banking, and accounting firms that will be able to supply services or personnel to support the operations of the captive or pool,
- recognizes the economic benefits it derives from and wishes to continue to attract captive and pool operations,
- is linked to reliable internal and international communications networks, especially telephone systems, so that information and funds can be readily exchanged and transferred,
- is accessible to convenient transportation, and
- has a suitable economic and legal environment and culture.

In terms of the tax climate, an attractive domicile is one that does the following:

- levies little or no premium tax on captives or pools,
- requires no, or only a small, annual licensing or other business privilege fee, and
- imposes little or no state income tax on captive and pool earnings from underwriting or investment operations.

Although a captive or pool should be formed only as a long-term risk financing technique, those responsible for the initial venture should recognize that time may require changes. Economic and regulatory conditions may some day require that the domicile be moved. Such a move may technically require only a few changes in legal forms, addresses, and similar details. Nevertheless, moving a captive may require shifting financial assets from one jurisdiction to another and satisfying various security and other regulations of the jurisdiction from which the move is being made. Therefore, to allow for a possible change in domicile, those choosing the initial home should be sure that it does not unduly restrict the portability of the enterprise.

Initial and Continuing Capitalization Any risk financing mechanism should have access from its inception to financial resources from which (1) to pay the initial costs of launching the enterprise and (2) to absorb unexpectedly high losses, especially during the first few years of operation. Access to ample financial resources greatly increases the likelihood that the enterprise will succeed, and therefore substantially enhances the financial security enjoyed by its "clients."

It is for these reasons that the insurance codes of all jurisdictions require an organization that seeks to be recognized as an insurer to begin operations with at least the minimum amounts of paid-in surplus (or for a stock organization, capital and surplus) specified in the applicable code for the kinds and amounts of insurance to be offered. Beyond this initial capitalization, these codes specify minimums below which paid-in surplus must never fall. (If these minimums are not met, the insurance regulator usually has the authority to place the insurer in financial rehabilitation or receivership.) These initial and continuing capital and surplus requirements vary widely from one jurisdiction to another, and within any one jurisdiction the code often specifies different minimums for different types of insurance. Many jurisdictions also establish different minimums for stock insurers, mutuals, and reciprocals, while still other jurisdictions specify separate sets of capitalization requirements for captives as well as for organizations wishing to qualify as "self-insurers" of workers compensation or other loss exposures.

These capital requirements can greatly influence an organization's choice of domiciles. Some organizations may not have or be able to raise the capital they would need to qualify as an insurer in a jurisdiction in which they would prefer to be domiciled. (Even for a single-parent captive or other risk financing mechanism that does not seek the status of an insurer, the capital and surplus requirements of a jurisdiction are one indication of the resources that will be needed, according to sound risk financing, to operate even such a captive.)

The types and timing of funding to meet initial and continuing capital requirements also vary. Some jurisdictions require cash, certificates of deposit, or other liquid assets, while others will accept letters of credit or financial guarantee bonds. Some jurisdictions require the entire amount of the initial capital to be deposited with regulatory authorities before a new insurer is authorized to issue its first policy; other jurisdictions establish a schedule that permits particular types of insurers (especially captives and small pools) to begin operations before collecting the minimum capital or surplus that will eventually be required.

In addition to initial and continuing capital, many jurisdictions also impose other financial and investment restrictions on insurers to ensure that they remain able to meet obligations to policyholders; and a related requirement is that authorized insurers follow certain auditing and reporting procedures and document their continuing financial solvency for the insurance regulator. For example, most jurisdictions mandate that the permanent minimums of capital and surplus be maintained in specified classes of particularly conservative investments. Each jurisdiction also is likely to establish guidelines for maximum permissible ratios of premiums written to policyholders' surplus, of particular classes of an insurer's investments to its total assets, and of the insurer's net retentions (after deduction of ceded reinsurance) in the aggregate and for any given loss exposure. Moreover, each insurer must follow specified auditing and reporting practices so that the insurance regulator can confirm that each licensed insurer is operating within these guidelines and other strictures.

The form of organization chosen for a captive or pool influences how it can best raise its initial and continuing capital. Stock organizations typically obtain their beginning capital and surplus from their owners (as distinct from those to whom they provide risk financing); these funds are generated on any basis the owners choose. The additions to surplus generated from such a stock organization's risk financing activities are determined by the dividends paid to stockholders—the lower the portion of earnings distributed as dividends, the more earned surplus remains to support risk financing operations. In a mutual or reciprocal organization the initial surplus is generated through individual assessments against participants. Thereafter, the annual contribution from each parent or participant to the organization's financial reservoir from which losses and operating expenses are paid is affected by its loss exposures, the extent to which these exposures are insured through the captive or pool, the premium rates charged each parent or participant, and any dividend returned to that parent or participant.

For a captive or pool operating as a mutual or reciprocal, premium and dividend rate structures followed during its initial years should be designed to generate and retain surplus by using rate structures that are relatively simple. As the captive or pool matures, its senior management often will choose more refined rating and/or dividend schedules that reflect each participant's individual loss control efforts.

Premium rates often reflect the extent to which various participants retain loss exposures through different deductibles. The net cost of insurance for organizations that retain more of their exposures can be reduced by a premium rate structure or a dividend scale that rewards a greater retention. Because fundamental fairness and shared interests are so essential to the success of a captive or pool organized as a mutual or reciprocal, and because organizations using captives or pools tend to be directly involved in their management, it is crucial that the formulas for raising initial capital, developing premium rates, and distributing dividends appear equitable to all participants.

Method of Providing Coverage A captive or pool may function as a primary insurer, a reinsurer, or as a combination of both in helping its parents or participants meet their risk financing needs. As a primary insurer, the captive or pool receives payments (premiums if the arrangement qualifies as an insurance) from its parents or participants. In return, it issues policies that obligate the captive or pool to pay each parent's or participant's losses as would any commercial insurer. Also functioning as a primary insurer, a captive or pool may reinsure a substantial portion of its primary insurance obligations, again much as any commercial insurer would.

As a reinsurer, a captive or pool may negotiate an agreement with one or more commercial insurers (*fronting insurers*) to issue policies in each fronting company's name to parents or participants. As shown in Exhibit 8-2, the fronting company then cedes all or most of its primary insurance obligations back to the captive or pool, which thus retains both control of and investment earnings from the bulk of the premium and/or reserve dollars initially paid for the primary coverage. If the captive or pool as a reinsurer is not able to retain the loss exposures of the parents or participants obtained through such fronting arrangements, the captive or pool may—as indicated by the broken lines of Exhibit 8-2—enter into additional reinsurance arrangements to further distribute these exposures throughout the reinsurance market. Because only the fronting insurer and not the captive reinsurer needs to be licensed in a jurisdiction where the parent's or participant's loss exposures are located, fronting arrangements have the additional advantage of permitting a captive or pool to generate underwriting earnings without being licensed in a variety of jurisdictions.

Finally, a captive or pool may act as a primary insurer for some exposures and as a reinsurer for others, thus giving it more flexibility in dealing with the loss exposures of parents or participants. It also has many more strategic options for generating underwriting and investment income from various segments of the primary insurance and reinsurance markets.

Types of Coverage Most captives or pools provide the types of insurance their parents or participants cannot otherwise easily obtain. Thus, most captives and pools have recently provided liability coverages, particularly for medical and other professional malpractice exposures, workers compensation obligations, and products liability losses. Concurrently, many municipalities and other public entities have experienced serious price and availability problems with coverage for

Exhibit 8-2

Typical Relationships of Captive or Pool, Parent or Participant, Fronting Insurer and Reinsurer*

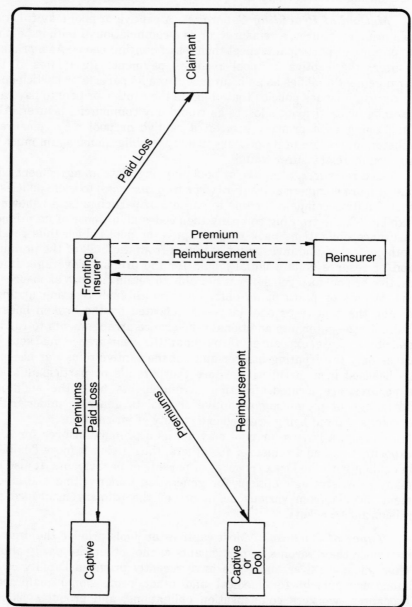

* Reprinted with permission from V.M. Stephens, et al., eds. *Risk Financing*, (Dallas, TX: International Risk Management Institute, Inc., looseleaf revised and updated periodically), October 1983, p. IV.D.16.

their general liability exposures, which often encompass police, fire, and other activities that tend to generate many large liability claims.

Beyond meeting their parents' risk financing needs, a growing number of captives (as distinct from pools) have shifted their focus to generating positive underwriting profits by gaining more complete control of investable funds for their parents. In this new focus, liability coverages have again proven attractive for captives because of the long periods during which funds in loss and unearned premium reserves can be held as investments.

Captives and pools also frequently have provided life and health coverages to support parents' or participants' employee benefit plans, again because of the opportunities for long-term investment income. However, the federal Employee Retirement Income Security Act (ERISA) places rather strict limitations on the extent to which a captive or pool can act as a fiduciary of funds held for the ultimate benefit of parents' or participants' employees. These restrictions are designed to protect the interests of these employees. They are also designed to prevent a captive or pool from facing conflicts of interest or engaging in "self-dealing" when carrying out its dual responsibilities to these employees and their respective employers.

Again, using fronting arrangements, captives and pools frequently have offered coverages of exposures that are required by insurance codes in various jurisdictions to be underwritten by an insurer domiciled in that jurisdiction. Workers compensation and automobile liability exposures often are subject to such regulations in states that want to ensure that their residents injured on the job or in highway accidents are adequately compensated. One method of meeting these local insurance requirements through a domestic insurer in such a jurisdiction is to front coverage through that domestic insurer with the understanding that the fronting company will reinsure this primary coverage through the captive or pool. The net result is that the parents or participants in the captive or pool can both meet the requirements of the local statute and achieve many of the investment and other benefits they could derive from retaining these exposures.

Operating a Captive or Pool

Having established a captive or pool, the founders must decide on a general management framework within which the captive or pool can efficiently conduct its marketing, underwriting and rating, reinsurance, claims management, loss control, and financial management activities. They also must ensure that these daily operations generate data for evaluating the actuarial, financial, and general management performance of the captive or pool. Those who wish to operate a successful captive or pool must establish regular procedures for performing each of the same functions on which the success of any insurer depends. For some of these functions, the captive or pool will need to rely primarily on its own in-house personnel because of their unique understanding of the captive's or pool's operations. For other activities, outside experts may be indispensable, at least initially. A third set of activities may be jointly performed by internal and external personnel, who are retained as consultants or on some temporary basis. As a preview for much of the following discussion, Exhibit 8-3 indicates how many essential functions within a captive or pool are performed by internal personnel, by outside experts, and by both.

General Management Framework   Organized as a stock, mutual, or reciprocal organization, every captive or pool must have a structure of executive and support personnel to conduct its activities.

General Captive Management.   A captive insurer can be managed by its own executives and personnel or through a contract with an outside management firm. Some single-parent captives are administered through or guided by the parent's insurance department; the parent's risk management professional often is appointed chief executive officer of the captive. In this capacity, the professional may manage the captive on behalf of the parent. For association and group captives, executives and operating staff are often chosen from outside the ranks of a parent's employees, although the overall governing board of such a captive is likely to include risk management professionals from several of the parents.

For many new captives, as well as for those that remain relatively small and informal, the popularity of external management principally stems from the fact that the captive's operations can be conducted more economically by an outside management company. In addition, the presence of an independent management team, none of whom are employed by a parent, has been offered as evidence to the Internal Revenue Service that an association or group captive is an independent entity to which the parents have transferred loss exposures, thus qualifying for income tax deductions for insurance premiums. Such independent management, indicating that the parents are "dealing at arm's length" with the captive, also has been useful in demonstrating to other insurers and reinsurers in the United States and abroad that the captive is a true insuring organization worthy of status as a peer.

Captive management services are quite readily available from many large insurance brokerage and consulting organizations and from the risk management service departments of major commercial insurers. Captive management services usually are provided on a fee basis, according to the amount of the work performed. Some captive

Exhibit 8-3
Typical Allocation of Captive or Pool Functions Among Internal, External, and Shared Expertise*

Function	Internal	External	Shared
Marketing	X		
Data Collection	X		
Underwriting		X	
Reinsurance & Insurance Brokerage		X	
Contract Insurance/Coverage Plan Administration			X
Billing/Collections	X		
Claims Handling		X	
Loss Control/Prevention			X
Management Information Systems		X	
Payroll/Premium Audits		X	
Accounting			X
Investment Management			X
Financial Audit		X	
Actuarial Review		X	
Performance Audit		X	
Legal Counsel		X	

* Reprinted with permission from V.M. Stephens, et al., eds. *Risk Financing*, (Dallas, TX: International Risk Management Institute, Inc., looseleaf revised and updated periodically), October 1983, p. IV.F.10.

management organizations, however, charge a fixed monthly or annual fee plus out-of-pocket expenses.

General Pool Management. The governing body of a pool, usually a board appointed by the members, is responsible for the pool's general operations and financial condition. This responsibility includes determining premium rate levels, securing reinsurance, establishing dividends and earnings distribution procedures, selecting any needed outside providers of actuarial and loss control services, and establishing procedures by which new participants can join the pool or existing participants can withdraw from it.

Essential to the success of any pool is every participant's understanding of the mutuality of this risk-sharing arrangement. No participant's risk financing costs can be guaranteed; the possibility of post-loss assessments against all members (or any class of them) because of some members' unusually adverse loss experience needs to be appreciated by all, especially by those who may be more accustomed to the guaranteed-cost insurance customarily provided by commercial insurers. While hoping for reduced cost and greater premium stability, the participants must be prepared for the possibility of adverse loss experience and fluctuating cost. This commitment to shared risk is particularly vital when many of the participants in a pool are small or medium-sized organizations or persons who are members of a trade or professional association who are not used to underwriting others' loss exposures. (While a group or association captive also entails such mutuality, the parents of a captive typically are more prepared for this responsibility than are most participants of most pools.)

For those unusual situations where extremely adverse insured losses or very poor investment results may render a pool's initial capital inadequate, the governing body of a pool must be prepared to fund any projected deficit. Prompt remedial action may make it possible to levy only small assessments against members over several years to generate funds to restore the financial strength of the pool. This avoids imposing any single, very large assessment at the very time the pool and perhaps many of its participants are in particularly weak financial condition. Therefore, it is vital to establish at the outset how the amount of any such extraordinary assessments will be determined and what, if any, continuing responsibility for such assessments remains the obligation of participants who withdraw from the pool. If participants leaving the pool are no longer subject to assessment, established participants—as well as those who have recently joined the pool—may be responsible for a disproportionate share of the deficit. In short, to minimize possible inequities and misunderstandings, it is vital that the terms for assessments be unambiguous and clearly communicated to all current and incoming participants.

Underwriting and Rating Once a captive or pool has selected the types of coverage it wishes to provide to its parents or participants, it must have access to technical expertise in order to establish the contractual terms for insuring loss exposures and for determining appropriate premiums for this protection. The personnel of the captive or pool may have such underwriting and ratemaking expertise. In most cases, however, it can best be obtained through an insurance brokerage or consulting firm, a risk management service department of a commercial insurer, or from an independent service provider. In addition, the captive or pool must have direct and continuing access to these essential skills.

Any competent outside service provider normally will evaluate the loss exposures of the captive or pool parents or participants, develop policy forms to meet these exposures (while excluding exposures the captive or pool does not wish to undertake), calculate appropriate premium charges, and develop underwriting guides for placing parents or participants in appropriate rating classes (or, if necessary, denying coverage to some applicants). These developmental tasks require some time and effort for which the service provider will charge either an hourly or a flat fee. If internal personnel are performing these tasks, they should have enough time to carefully complete them.

For a captive or pool that does not wish to qualify as an insurer, then the charges it levies against parents or participants may be structured in any way that is mutually acceptable and financially sound. For such an enterprise, few regulations affect the nature or price of the financial protection provided. In contrast, a captive or pool that seeks to qualify as an insurer under the laws of its domicile must follow the regular underwriting and rating practices that comply with the procedures and the standards of adequacy, equity, and reasonableness of that jurisdiction.

The ratemaking procedures of a sound captive or group generally follow those of a traditional, commercially insured policy both because these procedures are sound insurance practice and because they typically are mandated by applicable insurance codes. Thus, a captive or pool may charge manual (guaranteed-cost) premium rates or may establish any of a variety of merit rating or loss-sensitive rating plans authorized by the insurance code by implementing regulations for the type(s) of coverage written within the captive's or pool's domicile or, in some cases, the jurisdiction in which the loss exposure is located. However, because captives and pools heavily emphasize mutuality and loss sharing, rating plans often emphasize dividends based on group experience.

Such dividends both reward favorable loss experience and reduce parents' or participants' ultimate risk financing cost. In a financial and cash flow context, dividends are partial refunds of risk financing funds from "policyholders' surplus" because the sum of their "premiums" and investment income is greater than the total of losses paid, loss reserves, and operating expenses over one or several calendar quarters or years. Further, the amounts returned as dividends are deemed by the management of the captive or pool as no longer needed to support any expansion or diversification of the captive's or pool's activities. (For a captive or pool structured as a stock organization, these dividends are paid to stockholders who usually are not insureds.)

Insurance premium rates must be based on actuarial and financial assumptions regarding at least three factors: parents' or participants' loss experience, the captive's or pool's operating expenses, and investment income. Dividends are generated from favorable deviations—lower losses or operating expenses and/or higher investment income for the captive or pool—from the results projected in premium rate calculations. (Many insurers who wish to pay dividends regularly use loss, expense, and investment income assumptions to determine premium rates so that some minimum dividend will be generated—so that something "extra" will be returned to policyholders. Here, the size, rather than the existence, of dividends depends upon favorable deviations from these assumptions.) As a result of different ratemaking procedures, the following are true:

- Better than average insured loss experience generates savings for the captive or pool, which, if not needed to support expanded operations or diversification into other activities, can be returned to parents or participants.
- Expense savings may result from reduced administrative expenses, more effective loss control, and economies of scale due to collective purchasing from outside service providers.
- The size of dividends generated from investment income depends on the market performance of the captive's or pool's financial assets and the amount of its expenses to support its investment activities.

Once the particular dividend rate for a given quarter or year has been determined by the senior management of the captive or pool, the dollar amount of each parent's or participant's dividend for that period usually is related to its premium volume and/or loss experience.

Dividend policy must address not only the size of periodic dividends but also the parents or participants that may be eligible for them. The charter or bylaws of a multi-parent captive or pool may stipulate that a parent or participant is eligible for dividends that were generated only during its years of membership. Alternatively, each periodic dividend may be based on the cumulative results of the captive or pool since its inception rather than on the loss, expense, or investment experience for individual periods. Also, to encourage continuing membership, the dividend formula for a captive or pool—unlike that of most commercial insurers—may specify that a parent or participant is not eligible for any dividends that become payable after it withdraws—that is, in some captives and pools, dividends are not prorated for the portion of the last dividend period during which a withdrawing parent or participant leaves the captive or pool.

Marketing Because captives and pools exist to meet the risk financing needs of particular organizations or groups, their marketing activities should be correspondingly targeted and their marketing expenses similarly reduced because their potential clients are readily identified and presumably inclined to use their risk financing services. In fact, a captive with only one or a few parents may have essentially no identifiable marketing activities or expenses. In contrast, a captive or pool with a sizable membership must continue its service, educational, and promotional efforts, often in the form of "membership" drives. These and similar activities attract and hold members who might otherwise seek the apparent benefits of commercial insurance or some other form of risk financing. Therefore, the in-house staff of the typical captive or pool devotes a significant degree of effort to developing the loyalty and serving needs of present or prospective parents or participants.

Reinsurance Few captives or pools, like few commercial insurers, have the capital and underwriting capacity to retain completely the full amount of all loss exposures. Consequently, most captives and pools, especially relatively small ones, need reinsurance to support their underwritings in the same way that commercial insurers also need reinsurance (see Chapter 5). In addition to supporting their own risk-bearing activities, some captives or pools may seek reinsurance in order to provide insurance capacity, to sell reinsurance, in national and world insurance and reinsurance markets.

Reinsurers also provide a captive's or pool's senior and technical managers with useful information about insurance and reinsurance management. Moreover, should a captive or pool seek to withdraw from a line of risk financing it has previously been providing, portfolio reinsurance is totally essential. Because the purchase or sale of reinsurance is a very technically intricate process, most captives or pools must use the expertise available from a reinsurer or a reinsurance broker to represent it as a buyer or a seller in reinsurance and retrocession markets.

To achieve these benefits, a captive or pool must have credibility as a buyer and/or seller of reinsurance. Therefore, the management of a captive or pool should focus on the several factors that reinsurers weigh in determining whether and how much coverage to provide to, or reinsurance to seek from, a captive or pool. Among the important factors generally considered by reinsurers are the following:

- The legitimacy of forming a captive or pool—the most ideal reason being to provide cost-effective risk financing to parents or participants (not simply to provide income tax advantages).
- The extent of managerial and financial commitment of the parents or participants to maintaining the captive or pool on a stable, permanent basis regardless of price and availability fluctuations in commercial insurance markets.
- The adequacy of the financing for the captive or pool and how readily available additional capital will be.
- The extent to which the policy forms and underwriting practices of the captive or pool parallel those of the commercial insurance markets (greater similarities typically give reinsurers more faith in the captive or pool).
- The adequacy of the premium rates charged by the captive or pool.
- The adequacy of internal technical expertise or of readily obtainable outside expertise.
- The general caliber and reputation of the captive's or pool's senior management.

A declining number of reinsurers still view captives and pools with the skepticism with which they were first greeted (until perhaps 1975) in the reinsurance and retrocession markets. They were originally considered as interlopers seeking to divert premiums from traditional insurance markets. To counter this skepticism and to build a deserved reputation in these markets, captives and pools have sought to demonstrate that even though they are "newcomers," captives and pools preserve the essentials of sound insurance operation. However, these captives and pools have simultaneously needed to convince their present and potential parents and participants that they are special providers of needed protection—sources of risk financing not readily found in other commercial markets. Thus, captives and pools have simultaneously sought to appear reassuringly traditional to the reinsurance markets and refreshingly innovative to those for whom they provide risk financing.

Claims Management Prompt payment of losses and claims, as well as vigorous control of the amounts of these payments, are extremely important and require broad technical expertise. Therefore, those who are responsible for managing the claims-handling activities of the captive or pool should be as skilled as commercial insurers in coverage analysis, loss and claim evaluation, and negotiating skills. Moreover, the rising standards of professional liability now being imposed on loss and claim adjusters generally imply that the claims management personnel for a captive or pool must also be able to meet these standards, especially when dealing with third-party claimants who may sue the captive or pool if their claims are not handled according to the common law and fair claims practices acts of their jurisdiction. Therefore, all but the largest captives and pools rely almost exclusively on external legal counsel or other service providers to handle loss and claims investigations, litigation, claims payments, and subrogation activities. Effective cooperation among the parents or participants in a captive or pool, the managers of the captive or pool, and the outside service providers is required. In addition, the specific duties and rights of external claims-handling personnel must be detailed in writing and confirmed or clarified as necessary by ongoing discussions so that the claims-handling function is properly performed.

Loss Control On the one hand, reducing loss frequency and severity of parents or pool participants requires as much expertise as does the claims-handling function. On the other hand, a parent's or a participant's own personnel are in the best position to recognize and ideally eliminate the actual hazards associated with their daily work. Therefore, many pools and captives have found that loss control is best performed by outside technical experts and an organization's own personnel. In an ideal setup, outside experts would consult with supervisory and first-line personnel within an organization to develop customized risk control programs. They could also provide ongoing technical assistance in training, thus developing loss control programs that are both tailored to the exposures common to all members of the pool and to the unique features of each member organization. As with outside claims-handling personnel, external loss control experts should have their duties and rights detailed in writing so that they can more completely meet their "clients'" expectations.

Financial Management In one sense, insurance and other risk financing mechanisms are nothing more than complex financial transactions comparable in many ways to banking. Risk financing without adequate management is, therefore, as impractical as trying to conduct banking activities without adequate records. Therefore, a captive or pool and its parents or participants must, to be successful, both maintain good accounting records that will become the basis for financial management. To achieve this, the financial management of a captive or pool typically is shared by the staff and management of a captive or pool and the accounting and financial personnel of each parent or participant. Furthermore, because insurance accounting can be complex, outside service providers, such as insurers or independent firms that serve insurers, are often used. They often help each organization to adapt their accounting software to accommodate detailed ledgers, filing structures, and reports that consistently and accurately reflect the transactions and financial condition of the pool or captive. The staff of the captive or pool or an outside service firm typically furnishes monthly balance sheets and statements of operations to the governing board of the captive or pool. These results are also semiannually or annually reported to all parents and participants. The same personnel also prepare information needed for rate filings with state regulatory officials and for completing tax returns and other documents required by state and federal revenue authorities.

Evaluating Performance   An indispensable step in managing any activity—including the operation of a captive or pool—is controlling its performance. This is done by gathering information on activities, comparing this information with standards for acceptable performance, and where necessary, correcting substandard performance. To ensure proper evaluation and control, the internal management of a captive or pool must have a system for gathering data on performance. It will use this data to review the organization's actuarial, financial, and general management, considering the fact that these activities may be performed by the organization's internal personnel or by outside service providers.

Management Information System (MIS).   A computer-based management information system (MIS) is critical to loss control, claims, and other writing functions for a pool or captive of any size. Only a well-structured MIS can gather and process the data that will be used as a basis for making actuarial, investment, underwriting, and claims management decisions. The MIS then fits into a performance evaluation in the following way: Most standards for measuring captive or pool performance arise from the plans made when the venture was founded; these plans may be revised in strategic long terms or more tactical short terms. In either case, these plans envision certain volumes and patterns of cash flows and rates of return, levels of rates and structures of rating classes, loss ratios and claims adjustment cost percentages, and numbers and types of parents or participants. From these plans, a senior executive can derive, with the help of an MIS, projections, or models, of what the financial statements and operations of the various departments within the captive should show in various monthly or annual periods. These projections, properly made and subject to change for any unforeseen external conditions, can be the performance standards for the captive or pool.

In addition to *performance standards*, against which the results of activity are measured, the captive or pool management and the work of outside service providers should be evaluated by *activity standards*. (Recall from elsewhere in this ARM Program that an activity standard is not used to measure results—which may be subject to chance fluctuations, such as unexpected frequencies or severities of accidental losses—but the efforts put forth to seek these results. Activity standards are premised on a belief that good efforts will produce good results.) Because the successful management of a captive or pool requires cooperation between internal personnel and external service providers, the activity standards that highlight symptoms of inadequate cooperation are extremely important. Exhibits 8-4 and 8-5 summarize the activity standards for evaluating the in-house senior management of a captive or pool and of external service providers. The standards for external providers also may serve indirectly as standards for internal departments performing these same functions: If these critical operating functions are not being performed as cost effectively as they could be by an external service organization, then the possibility of turning to an external provider should at least be evaluated.

SUMMARY

The distinction that exists in principle between risk retention (internal financing of losses) and risk transfer (relying on external sources) is not always totally clear in practice. Between clear retention (such as using current revenues or funding reserves to pay for losses) and clear transfer (such as commercial insurance or the noninsurance contractual arrangements to be analyzed in Chapter 9) there is a relatively narrow but crowded continuum of risk financing techniques that have elements of both retention and transfer. These hybrid techniques have raised questions about the tax and regulatory status of the organizations that use them.

Having briefly touched on the issues of taxation and regulation, this chapter has more thoroughly examined from a managerial and financial perspective a variety of risk financing techniques. It concentrated on captives and pools, but described many types of insured cash flow plans. Close to the traditional forms of retention are single-parent captives—insurance subsidiaries affiliated with individual companies

Exhibit 8-4
Activity Standards for Senior Captive or Pool Management*

- Regular delivery to senior management of financial data and information that is comprehensible, timely, and useful

- Adequate opportunity for senior management to discuss operating trends

- Senior management approval of audit policies and periodic review of their implementation

- Joint participation by senior and operating management in developing annual and other periodic budgets

- Proper cash management and handling in cooperation with bank and investment officials to assure proper accounting, availability of funds, and few if any breaches of security

- Periodic senior management review and approval of investments, underwriting, marketing, and other department plans

- Annual senior management selection or confirmation of external auditors, to provide regular, detailed reports

- Senior management review of competitive bidding processes for selecting external service providers

---

* Reprinted with permission from V.M. Stephens, et al., eds. *Risk Financing* (Dallas, TX: International Risk Management Institute, Inc., looseleaf revised and updated periodically), December 1986, p. IV.D.16,17.

managed primarily to meet that one parent's risk financing needs. Multi-parent captives serve the risk financing needs of many parents who share loss experience. Their existence is quite independent of the wishes of any one particular parent. Because of this, they begin to look like a more traditional risk transfer operation, which is characterized by the mutual sharing of losses and the clear transferring of the financial burden on those losses to a legally and managerially separate entity.

Closer to traditional forms of transfer are pools. They serve only the risk financing needs of the organizations that form them and that participate in their financing and management. Most pool members are within the same industry or geographic territory.

Still closer to (or even entering) the risk financing realm recognized as true transfer are mutual insurers. They are characterized by

Exhibit 8-5
Activity Standards for External Service Providers (or Internal Captive
or Pool Departments)*

Marketing

- New parent/participant solicitation by direct mail, personal visits, etc.
- Number of educational and promotional meetings
- Quality of promotional materials
- Response to service complaints

Underwriting

- Maintenance of underwriting policy manual and supporting rationale
- Timely rating and pricing proposals for prospective parents/participants
- Maintenance of coverage documents
- Timely rerate/renewals to existing parents/participants
- Timely generation of billing source documents
- Management of underwriting support services, such as specialty engineering, underwriting surveys, etc.
- Timely provision of coverage support documents to parents/participants
- Maintenance of exposure summary questionnaire

Reinsurance

- Timely and comprehensive applications for reinsurance
- Advocacy before reinsurance underwriters
- Critical review of reinsurance contracts
- Aggressive reinsurance negotiation on behalf of pool
- Maintenance of reinsurance contracts
- Monitor financial and operating stability of reinsurer/insurers
- Timely placement of commercial insurance policies if not available from the pool

Financial Management

- Maintenance of program budget reporting system
- Maintenance of general ledger and check reconciliation
- Production of monthly balance sheets and statement of operations
- Performance of monthly aging of loss drafts
- Timely filing with state regulatory agencies and Internal Revenue Service
- Having timely and accurate cash flow projects
- Preparation of papers for external auditors
- Management and quality control of field adjusters
- Compliance with procedures and controls
- Ensuring procedures and control of field adjusters
- Compliance with procedures and controls
- Ensuring promptness and expertise of claims handling
- Maintaining adequate file documentation and proper claims verification
- Maintaining accurate reports of payments and reserves
- Adequacy or excessiveness of payments
- Perform periodic loss reserve adequacy analysis
- Aggressive pursuit of subrogation
- Timely claims notice reporting to reinsurers
- Periodic technical review of high amount claims
- Preparation and maintenance of loss control plan of service
- Development and maintenance of training calendar
- Documentation of loss prevention field visits
- Documentation of quality control reviews of field loss control specialists

Actuarial Activities

- Timely production of experience modification factors
- Documented review of rate adequacy
- Quarterly summary of high amount losses
- Annual summary of loss ratios by parent/participant and by line of coverage
- Annual summary of earned premiums by parent/participant by line of coverage
- Annual claims information details by line of coverage to facilitate actuarial rate adequacy tests and experience modification
- Documentation of captive's or pool's expense ratios by type of insured and in comparison with ratios for commercial insurers

* Reprinted with permission of V. M. Stephens et al, eds, *Risk Financing* (Dallas, TX: International Risk Management Institute, Inc., looseleaf revised and updated periodically), December 1986, pp. IV.D.17-20.

management that is almost totally independent of any one participant, a sharing of losses among participants, and the willingness (or even eagerness) to attract more participants from a wide variety of industries. Several of today's most successful mutual insurers began as what were then, in effect, captives with just one or a few parents. The term captive was then not recognized. As these organizations gained their independence, they became pools and often mutuals (sometimes converting to stock insurance organizations) as they expanded their underwritings to new and diverse groups. For regulatory, taxation, and managerial purposes, it is often difficult to define the precise point in this growth process when these risk financing mechanisms ceased being devices for retention and became insurers.

Although it is sometimes difficult to label an enterprise as a true retention or transfer device, pools have been more readily accepted as risk transfer than have captives. This may have been because pools, by definition, provide risk financing for at least two participants (and usually for many more), while most of the first captives began as single-parent organizations. Consequently, the parents of these original captives had difficulty demonstrating that their insurance subsidiaries provided any true transfer of losses beyond their economic family or that there was any genuine sharing of the financial burden of losses.

As the captive concept has been extended from a single-parent enterprise to one that serves the members of associations and then to one that provides risk financing for more diverse groups of unrelated parents, many captives have evolved into pools of mutual insurers. Their management becomes independent of the original parents, and by serving numerous organizations, they have established the sharing of exposures, drawing nearer to the traditional concept of insurance transfer. Precisely when or if they have achieved insurance status has not always been clear. However, those groups that have been formed under the federal Risk Retention Act, which enables manufacturers, professionals, and other groups to form risk retention groups or purchasing groups to obtain or provide their own liability coverages, generally are recognized as insurers (or collective buyers of insurance). As such, they have been favorably regulated and taxed.

Recognizing that captives and pools could divert substantial premium dollars away from traditional insurance markets, many commercial insurers have developed premium payment and ratemaking plans through which their insureds can achieve at least two of the major benefits claimed for captives and pools: (1) lower premiums for favorable loss experience and (2) greater control of, and more investment income from, premium dollars that would otherwise be held by the insurer. Thus, to compete with captives and pools, commercial insurers have offered deferred and lagged premium payment schedules, retrospective rating plans, and discounted (net present value) premium payment plans, as well as compensating balances plans.

In deciding to use commercial insurance or a captive or pool, an organization must weigh the benefits and costs of a captive or pool. The benefits include reduced (or stabilized) risk financing costs, improved net cash flows, broader insurance coverages, improved loss control and claim services, relative freedom from insurance marketing regulations, improved coordination of insurance programs that span numerous jurisdictions, and greater access to the domestic and international insurance and reinsurance markets. The disadvantages of forming and operating a captive or pool include unexpectedly costly or ineffective risk financing and resource commitments to the captive or pool so extensive that it is difficult for an organization to shift to other risk financing alternatives. The decision to form a captive or pool should be based on sound internal financial and managerial considerations, not primarily on income tax benefits.

Even if a captive or pool appears to be beneficial, its parents or participating organizations may not possess or have access to the financial resources and types of expertise needed to make a captive or pool feasible. To a great extent, the feasibility of a captive or pool is determined by basic preliminary decisions that include the organizational form it should take, its jurisdiction of domicile, its initial and continuing capitalization, its method of providing coverage, and the types of coverage it will offer. Any single organization or group that considers launching a captive or pool must be prepared to, in essence, operate an insurance company—to provide the general management framework for an insuring organization, and to secure internally or externally the underwriting, ratemaking, marketing, reinsurance, claims management, loss control, and financial management expertise required of any soundly operated risk financing enterprise.

CHAPTER 9

Contractual Noninsurance Transfers

INTRODUCTION

The law of contracts gives contracting parties many opportunities to decide how to deal with losses that may strike one or more of them as they carry out their agreement. They may agree, for example, that one party will reimburse the other for its loss; or they may agree that one party will undertake an activity (and with it the resulting loss exposures) that the other party normally would perform; or they may agree that one or more of them will waive a right to sue the other either for breach of contract or for some tort related to the activity covered by the contract. This chapter is an analysis of such contracts—contractual transfers in which none of the parties acts as an insurer, and in which exposures to potential loss or the financial burden of paying for actual losses are shifted. As an introduction to this chapter, a short, hypothetical scenario is useful in illustrating the various categories of such contractual transfers. The chapter then goes on to examine some of the elements in this scenario as they illustrate the actual kinds of contracts that fall within these categories.

It should be recognized that the one characteristic shared by the risk-shifting contracts in this chapter is that the transferee does not act as an insurer. Instead, the transferee agrees to perform some action that shifts to it some of the transferor's (1) exposures to loss that may occur in the future or (2) cost of financing recovery from losses that have already occurred. From the transferor's perspective, the first noninsurance transfer is a means of risk control because it rids the transferor of a loss exposure or some *possibility* of loss. The second transfer is risk financing because it provides the transferor with a source of funds to finance recovery from an actual loss.

AN ILLUSTRATIVE SCENARIO

Peter Builder, who for twenty years has successfully bought land near urban areas to develop as shopping centers and shopping malls, is considering purchasing a sixty-acre tract from Ms. Cellar, whose departed husband made his fortune in petroleum. Peter is aware that because the land he wants to buy once was used as a petroleum tank farm, this tract and the aquifer beneath it may be contaminated with petroleum by-products or other hazardous wastes. Because federal law makes anyone who has ever owned land that proves to be contaminated potentially liable for environmental cleanup costs, he is reluctant to purchase this particular tract. Therefore, he creates Terra Corporation—owned by Peter, his wife, and children—to which Ms. Cellar is happy to sell the tract at a favorable price. This land, which is Terra Corporation's principal initial asset, is then mortgaged by Terra Corporation to raise funds that it, in turn, lends to Peter Builder to finance the development of another "Peterbuilt" mall on the land.

Not entirely sure what underground storage tanks or piping for petroleum or other potential toxic materials might be encountered when landscaping the tract for the mall, Peter Builder subcontracts this work to Digger Phelps, Inc., an earth-moving contractor, specifying that only Digger's employees will perform this work. Their contract also provides that Digger Phelps will reimburse Terra for the cost of replacing or repairing any Terra structures damaged by Digger's equipment or personnel during the landscaping or excavating. Because Peter Builder is less than fully confident of Digger's reliability or even ability to do the excavation work, Peter asks Digger's father, an old friend who preceded Digger in the business, to guarantee that the father will complete the excavation if Digger does not.

As the shopping mall is developed, the newly constructed buildings become the property of Terra, which leases them to various merchants, including Lester E. Hassle, principal stockholder of Less Hassle Bank, which has seven state-chartered branches. Because many entrepreneurs and other merchants like Mr. Hassle (known to his associates as "Les E.") are eager to become tenants in Peterbuilt Mall, they willingly pay premium rents, agree in their leases not to sue Terra or the members of the Builder family for any harm they may suffer because of toxic or polluting substances in the ground on which the mall is built, and commit themselves to hold harmless both Terra and the Builder family from any such claims by customers, employees, occupants, or other users of their respective leased premises. Peter Builder also leases from Terra an office for himself and his staff, but Peter does not explicitly agree to hold Terra, himself, and his family harmless from others' claims. Just as an organization cannot properly be said to self-insure itself, so no individual or organization can hold itself harmless.

Each tenant also agrees to have a *waiver of subrogation* clause inserted in each of its insurance contracts "wherever possible" for the benefit of Terra and the Builder family. Because of these waivers, no tenant's insurer is likely to sue Terra or the family for reimbursement of funds that the insurer has paid as indemnity for losses for which Terra or the family may be responsible.

Illustrations in the Scenario

The Peterbuilt Mall scenario introduces a number of risk control and risk financing contractual transfers, not involving insurance, that will be analyzed throughout this chapter. The risk control transfers shift an exposure from the transferor to transferee before the loss occurs. As will be explained, any loss from such an exposure is the responsibility of the transferee. As mentioned, risk financing contractual transfers shift to the transferee the financial burden of restoring losses that have already struck the transferor. If the transferee fails to provide the compensation called for by the contract, the burden of the loss remains with the transferor and has not been effectively transferred.

The preceding scenario illustrates the following contractual transfers for risk control.

- *Incorporation.* The law considers a corporation to be a legal person distinct from its shareholders and, in the absence of fraud or overriding concerns for social justice, solely responsible for its own wrongs (including those of its agents). As a result, by acting through Terra rather than as an individual, Peter Builder has shifted to this corporation many of the liabilities that would otherwise fall upon him and his family. Furthermore, acting through Terra insulates the family's assets from claims arising from any wrongs for which the corporation may be liable.
- *Leases.* The owner of real or personal property may be held liable for any harm done to others because of the unsafe general condition of that property, but a lessee or tenant normally cannot be held liable to those harmed unless the harm arises from a condition the tenant has brought about on the leased portion of the property. Thus, the owner of property

usually can shift loss exposures inherent in that ownership, such as potential liability for environmental pollution or toxic harm to others, by selling the property to another and by leasing it back from the "new" owner. In the preceding scenario Peter Builder (1) avoided personal liability as an owner of the possibly polluted tract by having Terra buy the ground and (2) by renting his office space in the mall. Similarly, Lester E. Hassle and the other merchant-occupants of the mall are only lessees and are, therefore, insulated from the statutory liability that attaches to ownership of polluted lands. Just as "ownership has its special rewards," so does it carry its special loss exposures. These exposures can be shifted by shifting ownership.

- *Subcontracts.* All activities have associated loss exposures that fall upon those who perform these activities. Peter Builder, recognizing that the initial landscaping and excavation work could be particularly hazardous because of the pollution potential, contracted with Digger Phelps to do this work. Consequently, Digger's employees (not Peter's) are exposed to toxic harm, and Digger (not Peter) is the one who may be held primarily liable for the effects of any pollutants released into the environment by the excavation activity. Unless Peter was somehow negligent or otherwise at fault in selecting Digger or supervising his work, he would incur no liability from the excavating.

- *Surety Agreements and Guaranty Agreements.* A surety is a person or organization that guarantees to one party of a contract that another party to that contract will perform as promised. The surety normally is not a party to the contract. In the scenario, Digger Phelps' father acted as a surety in guaranteeing Peter Builder that Digger would complete the excavation work as promised in the contract. In the language of suretyship Digger is the *principal* or *obligor* (the person obligated), and Peter Builder is the *beneficiary* or *obligee* (the person to whom the contractual obligation guaranteed by the surety is owed). The surety promises to fulfill the obligor's promise if the obligor is not able or willing to do so; that is, it protects the obligee by assuming the burden for a potential loss by taking some action other than paying money to the obligee. For this reason, suretyship agreements and guaranty agreements are classified as contractual transfers for risk control. In practice, the surety usually carries out its guarantee by paying to have yet another party perform the obligor's promise. For example, because Digger's father is now retired, he would be more likely to hire some younger landscaper to finish Digger's work than finish it himself. Whatever payment the father as surety may make to hire another is made for the benefit of the surety. It is not a payment to or on behalf of the obligee and thus is not risk financing for the obligee. The father's right as surety to complete Digger's unfinished work would not be jeopardized by the original contract provision that only Digger's employees would work on the land. A major purpose of the original limitation was to preclude Digger from subcontracting to someone even less competent—a limit designed to protect Terra. However, once Digger had breached his promise to perform, the only real protection for Terra is to have the surety or someone equally competent complete the work.

● *Waiver Agreements.* A waiver is an informed relinquishing of a known legal right. Through the waiver in Les Hassle's and the other mall tenants' contracts, the merchants gave up their rights to sue Peter Builder, his family, and Terra. Waivers remove a potential liability from those who could be held responsible for harm. Because of their waivers, the mall tenants excuse Peter Builder and the others from potential liability for pollution-related harm.

The scenario illustrates the following contractual transfers for risk financing:

● *Indemnity Agreements.* By an indemnity agreement, one party to a contract agrees to pay another if the latter suffers a specified type of loss. For example, Digger Phelps in its landscaping contract with Terra agreed to pay the corporation the replacement cost of restoring any structural damage caused by Phelps' machinery or employees while landscaping or excavating.

● *Hold Harmless Agreements.* A hold harmless agreement is a commitment that one contracting party makes to another to hold the latter harmless from specified types of legal claims that may be brought against the latter because of activities covered by the contract. For example, as part of their lease contracts, the mall tenants agreed to hold Terra and the Builder family harmless from suits that might be brought against them by persons using each tenant's leased premises. In this context, holding harmless normally entails both providing legal defense for and paying any settlement or verdicts on behalf of the transferor—here, Terra or the Builders. Hold harmless agreements can be viewed as a special type of indemnity agreement dealing only with the transferor's liability losses from specified activities.

Through the four contractual transfers for risk control—incorporation, leases, subcontracts, and waiver agreement—the shifting of a loss exposure from a transferor to a transferee (1) rids the transferor of virtually all possibility of suffering any loss from the transferred exposure and (2) creates a duty for the transferee to protect the transferor from loss by doing something other than paying money to (or on behalf of) the transferor.

In contrast, in the two contractual transfers for risk financing—indemnity agreements and hold harmless agreements—the loss exposure is not shifted from the transferor to the transferee; only the financial burden of losses is shifted. Second, the transferee's duty is to pay money to (or on behalf of) the transferor after the transferor has suffered some loss. Thus, while a contractual transfer for risk control makes it very unlikely that the transferor will suffer any loss, a contractual transfer for risk financing becomes operative only after the transferee has suffered loss. The transferor then is entitled to receive, or have paid on its behalf, money that indemnifies the transferor for the loss. If the transferee is unable or unwilling to provide the required funds, the financial burden of the loss remains with the transferor.

Generalizing from the Scenario

The Peterbuilt Mall scenario illustrates the general truth that activity implies risk. Even a seemingly passive activity such as owning the properties on which Terra builds necessarily exposes the owner to loss. Recall from ARM 54 that an organization's choice of activity or assets it owns or uses also forces it to assume, at least initially, the exposures to accidental loss that inherently accompany that asset or activity. How an organization should deal with these loss exposures so that it (or those it serves) can benefit from its activities is a central challenge to sound risk management.

One obvious option is to avoid completely assets or activities that are too risky in the sense that the associated accidental or business losses (also called *pure* or *speculative* losses) probably will outweigh the benefits. However, two significant difficulties in this approach are that first, losses and benefits from untried projects can be extremely difficult to forecast; and second, some exposures (such as those associated with natural disasters, hiring employees, or using motor vehicles) may be very difficult to avoid completely.

When avoiding activities is neither advisable nor feasible, the creative use of contracts provides an organization with many options for coping with the loss exposures inherent in the activities and assets. The different types of contracts and how they are used are described in the following two subsections.

Insurance Versus Noninsurance Transfers Insurance contracts allow an organization to transfer many of the financial consequences of accidental losses. Under such an insurance transfer, the insurer/transferee is the indemnitor (the provider of indemnity or other benefits), and the insured/transferor is the indemnitee (the recipient of such benefits). An insurance contract thus obligates an insurer to pay money or other benefits to or on behalf of an insured under circumstances specified in the contract. (As shown in Chapters 4 and 5, these circumstances generally relate to the occurrence of an accidental loss that qualifies as an insured event and fulfilling the policy conditions that must be met to perfect the insured's right to protection under the policy.) Corresponding to this contractual obligation or duty of the insurer, the insured has the contractual right to receive (or to have provided on its behalf) indemnity or other benefits under the same circumstances that the insurer has the duty to provide them.

The usual insurance policy therefore creates certain conditional duties for one contracting party and correlative conditional rights for the other. Because these duties and rights pertain to financing recovery from accidental losses, and because exercising these rights and duties usually transfers the financial burden of loss, an insurance policy can be called a contractual transfer for risk financing. Because the transferee here is an insurer, this transfer also could be called a contractual insurance transfer. In practice, this last term is redundant; insurance is more convenient and usually adequately descriptive.

All *noninsurance transfers* differ from insurance in that under a noninsurance transfer the transferee is not acting as an insurer; that is, the transferee is not pooling others' loss exposures and becoming a transferee in order to make a profit. Under a noninsurance transfer the transferee is accepting the exposure to loss or the financial burden of the transferor's actual losses as a quite incidental aspect of another business transaction. It is from this transaction that the transferee expects to profit, not from the risk transfer. (Insurers can be parties to noninsurance contractual transfers. For example, an insurer could be managing the construction of the malls that Peter Builder is erecting, and this insurer could be a transferor just as Peter is in the preceding scenario. In such a situation, however, the fact that the building owner is an insurer would be only coincidental to the owner's status as a transferor.)

Risk Control Transfers Versus Risk Financing Transfers As shown by the various agreements in the Peter Builder scenario, a contract can effectively (1) create rights and duties that relate to risk control and risk financing and (2) establish transferees other than insurers. The rest of this chapter focuses on contracts involving transferees who are not insurers and deals with the full range of noninsurance risk transferring contracts. Because of (1) the common law freedom to devise and enter into contracts, (2) the contract-drafting skill of risk management professionals and other business executives, and (3) constant changes in business practices, there can be no permanent catalog of all types of noninsurance contracts and contract provisions. It is possible, however, to classify such agreements into the following two large families as mentioned earlier:

- Risk control transfers—like incorporation, leases, subcontracts, surety agreements, and waivers—shift from the transferor an exposure to some potential loss by requiring the transferee to perform some activity other than the payment of money that rids the transferor of the exposure.
- Risk financing transfers—like indemnity agreements and hold harmless agreements—shift to the transferee the financial burden of a loss by obligating the transferee to pay money after a loss has occurred to or on behalf of the transferor.

Exhibit 9-1 summarizes the significant differences between these two families of contractual transfers.

In noninsurance contractual transfers for risk control and risk financing, and in insurance, the contract generally is formed before any loss occurs. However, because risk control transfers shift exposures to loss rather than the financial burdens of an actual loss, a risk control transfer becomes effective when the transferee actually performs the action that rids the transferor of a loss exposure. For example, as soon as Digger Phelps' employees began the landscaping and excavation work they subcontracted from Builder, Terra no longer faced any workers compensation liability. The workers compensation exposure had thus been shifted to Digger Phelps after the contract was made and before anyone was injured.

In contrast, a risk financing transfer provides the transferor with protection only after the funds to restore a loss are received. Until the actual loss has occurred, the transferor cannot know that the transferee will pay. If the transferee fails to provide the expected funds, the transferor receives no protection and has never truly transferred the financial burden of the loss to the transferee. For example, Peter Builder and Terra have Digger Phelps' promise of reimbursement for any damage Phelps' activities may do to Terra's structures, but they cannot be sure of this protection until Phelps' employees have damaged a Terra building and Phelps has actually paid for the damage.

Exhibit 9-1

Families of Contractual Transfers; Risk Control and Risk Financing

Characteristic	Risk Control Transfer	Risk Financing Transfer
Subject of Transfer	Exposure to Loss (Possibility of Loss)	Financial Burden of Actual Loss
Timing of Transfer	Before Transferor's Loss	After Transferor's Loss
Effect of Transferee's Nonperformance	Loss Falls on Transferee	Loss Falls on Transferor (Never Truly Transferred)
Frequent Examples	Incorporation Lease Subcontract Waivers Exculpatory Agreements Surety Agreements	Indemnity Agreements (including insurance) Hold Harmless Agreements

Another critical difference between a risk control and a risk financing transfer becomes apparent when a transferee is bankrupt or otherwise unable to perform the terms of the contractual transfer. In a risk financing transfer a bankrupt transferee provides no protection to the transferor, who must therefore pay for its own accidental loss. In a risk control transfer, however, a bankrupt or uncooperative transferee remains responsible for its own accidental losses, leaving the transferor's protection intact.

The next major section in this chapter examines the more frequent examples of each of the risk control and risk financing contractual transfers listed at the bottom of Exhibit 9-1. This chapter treats commercial insurance only in passing in order to make clear how other transfer mechanisms differ from it.

TYPES OF CONTRACTUAL TRANSFERS

In the absence of transfers for risk control or risk financing, common law and state and federal statutes apportion risks of loss among the parties to a business transaction. In very broad terms, an organization or individual that owns property must bear the losses that arise from that ownership; similarly, an organization or individual that engages in an activity must bear the losses generated by that activity for which it is legally responsible. However, common law and many state and federal statutes also permit the parties to a business agreement to make different contractual arrangements for dealing with exposures to loss or the financial burden of actual losses. These agreements change the otherwise applicable apportionments of loss exposures or actual losses generally by law.

As stated in the preceding section, the two general types, or families, of contractual transfers are risk control transfers and risk financing transfers. Risk control transfers include incorporation, leasing, subcontracting, suretyship, and waivers. Risk financing transfers include insurance, indemnity agreements among noninsurers, and hold harmless agreements. (Although insurance is a contractual transfer for risk financing, the focus of this chapter is on contractual transfers that do not involve insurers.)

Risk Control Transfers—Commitments to Act, Not Pay

Many risk management professionals are experienced in insurance and/or financial management, and they are thus quite accustomed to dealing with contracts for restoring actual losses. Perhaps because of this background, they often find challenging the concept that another large group of contracts—by which parties shift exposures to possible losses by committing themselves to actions rather than money to rectify a potential loss—are equally valid risk management techniques. These risk management professionals also may find that risk control transfer contracts are somewhat unusual because most of the documents, particularly leases and subcontracts, traditionally have been handled by departments in their organization not directly involved in risk management. Nonetheless, noninsurance contractual transfers for risk control have long been important, if not fully recognized, risk management tools. These contracts are described in the following text.

Incorporation[1] The corporation as a form of business organization originated in the fourteenth and fifteenth centuries when England and various European countries enacted statutes permitting individuals to establish private businesses. The corporate form of enterprise allowed business leaders to accumulate large amounts of capital by taking relatively small amounts from many individuals or firms in exchange for a number of shares in the corporation proportional to each contribution. Incorporation thus permitted a group of individuals to undertake business enterprises that otherwise would have required more capital or entailed more risk than any single executive or small group of partners would have been willing or able to venture. Examples of such activities include exploring unknown territories, developing new technologies, and founding very large financial institutions. To encourage individuals and small businesses to participate in corporate activities, the statutes authorizing private corporations included a crucial provision limiting each stockholder's potential loss: no stockholder could lose more than the value of the shares that stockholder owned. Thus, each stockholder's personal assets or holdings in other businesses were insulated from any possible losses in a corporate venture.

Modern incorporation statutes in most western countries, the U.S. federal government, and all the states provide similar stockholder protection. In the absence of fraud or other intentional wrongs by a corporation or its officers or employees, the most a corporation can lose in either a business venture or because of an accident or lawsuit is the value of that corporation's assets. Consequently, any one stockholder's maximum financial loss is the value of that stockholder's shares. If the corporation has relatively little capital, the amount the corporation (and thus any one of its stockholders) can lose is correspondingly limited.

The principle of incorporation thus allows an executive to organize various business enterprises so that each is conducted by a separate corporation. In doing so, the risk control technique of segregation is applied—the "divisions" between exposure units become the legal boundaries of separate corporations. In this way, a business executive can limit loss potentials arising from business risks, accidental losses, or liability claims. Limiting potential liability losses is an important reason why, for instance, an owner of several taxicabs or trucks often forms a separate corporation according to the activities of each vehicle. The individual entrepreneur thus shifts to the corporation exposures that otherwise would threaten personal finances, while the corporation itself is exposed to loss no greater than its assets. Similarly, stockholders can largely control the total value of a corporation's assets by contributing or withdrawing capital to or from the enterprise. The corporation, as legally separate from any of its stockholders, can serve as a transferee for exposures that individual stockholders might otherwise face. As a transferee, and in exchange for the capital contributed by one or more stockholders, every corporation agrees to carry out the business activities for which it has been organized.

While the legal barrier between a corporation's assets and activities and those of each of its stockholders is quite clear—particularly with respect to accidental physical damage to the corporation's assets or net income losses from interruption of its business—this barrier sometimes can be penetrated. For example, courts may seek to "pierce the corporate veil" by attacking a major managing stockholder's personal assets. This can be done in cases involving liability claims against the corporation where (1) corporate assets appear to have been manipulated to frustrate creditors of a corporation seeking bankruptcy protection or (2) the corporate form seems to mask the personal wrongs of a predominant stockholder or major executive. In these cases the courts often place more importance on compensating those harmed by the corporation than on maintaining the normal separation between corporate property and stockholders' personal assets.

Those who do business with small corporations, and thus regularly become their creditors, are aware of the limited personal liability of a corporation's owners. Therefore, to preserve their access to the personal assets of these stockholders, creditors frequently require that the corporate owners personally cosign with the corporation all contracts, notes, and other credit obligations. In effect, this action "desegregates" corporate and personal finances and liability; and in doing so, it undercuts the protection normally afforded an owner by the risk transfer mechanism of incorporation. It also undercuts the protection normally afforded a corporation by statutes that provide that, as stated, the most a corporation can lose is the value of its assets. The corporation thus becomes equivalent to a partner or proprietor with respect to owners' personal liability. However, these types of arrangements with creditors do not defeat the advantages of corporate liability with respect to obligations arising out of tort claims.

Leasing The law separates ownership of property—that collection of rights and duties of those who are said to "own" property—into many separate "bundles." One important bundle is the right to occupy or use real or personal property for a period between two specified points in time. This right is a portion of an owner's right to occupy and use this property without a time limit. This more limited right is known as a *leasehold,* under which the lessee may occupy or use the real or personal property for the period specified in the contract establishing the leasehold. This contract is commonly called a *lease.* Before and after a leasehold is in effect, the right to occupy or use the property remains with the owner.

Certain obligations and exposures to loss accompany the ownership of property but not its use or occupancy. Some of these obligations are taxes, loss from physical destruction of the property or its obsolescence, and liability for dangerous conditions of or on the property. A *tenant* (or lessee) occupying or using the property does not incur any of these obligations; nor does the tenant suffer any of these losses unless (1) the lease obligates the lessee to return the property to its owner, the *lessor,* in the same condition at the end of the lease as at its beginning or (2) the lessee alone has caused a dangerous condition that has harmed others. If the property being occupied or used by a lessee is damaged or destroyed during the term of a lease, the lessee's only loss may well be (depending on the lease provisions) nothing more than the use of the property for the remaining term of the lease. This loss often can be recovered by both parties by simply leasing other substitute property.

By leasing property rather than owning it, a lessee consequently eliminates the exposure to loss of the value of the entire property and much of the potential liability for harm to others resulting from dangerous property conditions. By never owning but using a particular item of property under a lease, an organization can leave these exposures with the owner. If an organization already owns some property, it can shift the associated exposures by selling the property while retaining the right to occupy or use the property under a lease with the new owner. This transaction is known as a sale-and-lease-back arrangement, which also allows the former owner of property to convert its equity into cash. The new owner often is a corporation or other organization created or selected by the former property owner primarily for these risk-shifting and financing purposes. The new owner may even be a real estate management firm, more able than the former owner to control and/or retain losses related to property ownership. If fraud is not involved, such a transfer normally will be upheld by the courts (except when there were dangerous conditions on the property that were apparent before the property was sold and leased back). If the assets of the new owner are relatively small, any claimant's opportunities to collect a substantial judgment due to injury arising from the condition of the property are correspondingly limited.

Because the basic law of leaseholds leaves with the lessor (and permanent property owner) obligations and loss exposures related to property ownership, the lease agreement need not specify that the lessee is relieved of these obligations and exposures. This arrangement is implicit in common law. Thus, many leases are silent with respect to exposures to accidental loss. In fact, most lease provisions that do mention loss exposures refer to obligations the lessee would not otherwise have with respect to preventing or paying for accidental losses. For example, lease agreements for real property often specify that the lessee will return the property to the lessor in its pre-lease condition with only "fire, flood, and ordinary wear and tear excepted." This wording transfers to the lessee the exposure to and financial responsibility for damage or destruction of the property by all perils other than those excepted. The lessor therefore retains or agrees to otherwise finance losses from fire, flood, and ordinary wear and tear.

A lease of all or part of a building may give the tenant the right to alter the leased space for personal or business purposes such as conducting a manufacturing operation or displaying merchandise for retail sale. Such a lease should specify whether the alterations made by the tenant, often called *improvements and betterments*, become the property of the lessor or remain the property of the lessee. If the lease agreement does not stipulate otherwise, permanently attached improvements and betterments made by the lessee, *irremovable improvements* such as display windows or wide doorways, become the property of the lessor. Improvement and betterments not permanently attached, *removable improvements* such as display cases, carpets, and many lighting fixtures, remain the property of the lessee, who may remove them at any time. A lease often obligates a lessor to repair or replace permanently attached improvements and betterments if they are damaged or destroyed during the leasehold of the lessee who installed them. Otherwise, it is usual for the lessor and the lessee to bear any losses to those improvements and betterments that are their respective property.

The test for removability is not whether the improvements and betterments in question are attached to the structure, but whether they can be taken out of the structure without significantly and permanently damaging it. This test differs from the usual criterion in insurance that considers any property attached to a structure to be part of that stucture and not part of its contents. For example, in insurance contract interpretation, wall-to-wall carpeting is part of a structure because it is normally attached at the carpet's edge. Under a lease, however, such carpeting would typically be a removable improvement because it can be taken up without damaging the underlying floor. In contrast, a solid stone mosaic floor typically would be a permanent part of a building for insurance and lease purposes because it would be so difficult to remove.

Subcontracting An individual or organization that performs a particular activity generally is held primarily responsible for any losses generated by that activity. Thus, an organization that does not wish to undertake the loss exposures associated with any given activity often can contract with another organization to perform it. For example, Peter Builder may well have contracted the excavation and landscaping work with Digger Phelps so that Digger's machinery and employees, not Terra's, would be exposed to any damage and injury from this work. In general, any property, net income, or personnel loss exposure associated with an activity can be successfully transferred in this way. Furthermore, if the bargaining power of the parties to such a contract does not enable the subcontractor/transferee to require the transferor to hold the transferee harmless from the financial consequences of any actual property, net income, or personnel losses from this activity, both the exposure to these losses and the burden of financing recovery from them will rest on the subcontractor/transferee.

The situation is somewhat different with the liability exposures associated with a particular activity. They are not so easily transferred, especially with respect to harm to third parties. For example, if Digger's employees' negligence created a hazard (perhaps a large, unguarded hole) that causes injury to a pedestrian, that employee and Digger would clearly be primarily liable. However, the injured person would almost certainly sue Terra as the responsible party for the general condition of the land it owned. Because the law seeks to provide compensation to those who are injured, courts tend to ignore contractual "side agreements" that would frustrate the otherwise valid claims brought by outside parties. For example, a pedestrian falling into a hole left by Digger's employees probably would be able to gain at least a court hearing for the contention that Terra had been negligent in selecting Phelps as a subcontractor or in failing to properly supervise the subcontractor's work. Furthermore, quite aside from any contracts between Terra and Digger, this claimant almost certainly could sue Terra for having failed to maintain its land in safe condition.

Despite the difficulty of "subcontracting away" liability exposures, this method is very frequently used to shift exposures to organizations better able to prevent or to finance recovery from losses generated by particular activities. Thus, many organizations normally contract with specialty firms not only for building construction projects, but also for maintenance activities, waste disposal, and transportation of raw materials and finished products. Another innovative use of subcontracting for shifting loss exposures is the currently widespread practice of contracting for temporary employees from agencies who are the direct employers of the temporary workers. This technique allows the contractor to leave with the agency the loss exposures associated with personnel such as injuries, resignation, and retirement. The contracting organization receives thus most of the benefits of temporary labor without assuming the associated employee benefits exposures.

The performance of each of these subcontracted activities requires machinery or skills typically unrelated to an organization's primary productive activities, equipment, and expertise. The organization can therefore obtain such services more cheaply and reliably through an outside source, the subcontractor, whose special skills and resources also help to perform specified tasks more safely. In addition, because these activities are the subcontractor's primary business, a competent subcontractor should be able to arrange more reliable and less expensive risk financing for the losses arising from its particular activity than could other organizations not so focused on these activities.

Although this particular contractual transfer for risk control often is called subcontracting, it is not necessary that the transferor be an independent contractor and the transferee technically a subcontractor. Any contract engaging another party to perform a particular service and, implicitly, to assume the loss exposures associated with that service can be a valid application of this technique. Historically, however, this shifting of exposures was pioneered principally by general construction contractors who, not wishing to assume the exposures involved in such activities as excavation or electrical wiring, hired subcontractors for this work. The general contractor thus became the transferor and the subcontractor, the transferee. Thus, by common practice, the transferee became known as a subcontractor.

Suretyship and Guaranty Agreements[2] A suretyship agreement is a contract among three parties in which one, the *surety*, agrees to be answerable for the promise or debt that a second party, the *obligor*, owes to the third party, the *obligee*. The surety's commitment is to perform or to hire an outside party to perform in the obligor's stead as soon as the obligor's failure or inability to perform becomes clear and the obligee demands performance from the surety. A *surety agreement* thus protects the obligee by providing a second source of performance—if the obligor does not perform or pay as promised, the surety presumably will.

Similarly, under a *guaranty contract,* an obligee to whom a promise has been made also can look to a *guarantor* for performance. However, in contrast to a surety, a guarantor becomes obligated to perform only after the obligee has made every reasonable and legal effort to compel the obligor's performance. In contrast, a surety agreement permits the obligee to demand performance of the surety as soon as the obligor's first substantial failure to perform becomes apparent. Thus, a guaranty contract provides the obligee with a second alternative for the performance of a promise; a surety agreement provides the first alternative.

Both agreements allow the obligee to practice a form of segregating exposures that is somewhat comparable to having standby machinery: if the obligor does not perform, the obligee may turn to the surety or guarantor for performance.

Another important difference between the two agreements is that a guaranty contract is a two-party agreement between the guarantor and the obligee. It is separate from the agreement between the obligee and the obligor. Under a surety agreement, the original promise of the obligor is also the promise of the surety; under a guaranty agreement the guarantor's promise should parallel, but may differ in some details from, the obligor's promise to the obligee. As a consequence, a guarantor is not as precisely bound by the terms of the contract containing the promise of the obligor to the obligee. By suretyship law, if the obligor may rightfully refuse to perform—perhaps because the underlying promise was secured through fraud or the basic contract between the obligor and obligee was otherwise defective—the surety is also released from performance. Whether a guarantor is released under similar circumstances depends upon the wording of the separate guaranty contract. Thus, unlike a surety, a guarantor may not be released from its promise to the obligee by any rule of contract law that might release an obligor and a surety from a promise to the obligee. As mentioned below, the surety may have some further independent defenses relieving the surety of the obligation to perform.

Like other types of noninsurance contractual transfers, a surety agreement also differs from most insurance contracts in two ways: (1) the surety's primary obligation is to perform as promised for the obligee, not to pay money to compensate the obligee for the obligor's breach of contract; and (2) a surety agreement is a three-party contract, while virtually all insurance policies are two-party contracts. Some insurers routinely function as (and even make a specialty of being) a surety. These insurers are examples of corporate rather than personal suretyship from which most of the laws of suretyship and guaranty originated. Insurers that issue performance bonds are, in fact, acting as sureties, not as insurers. However, insurance against employee dishonesty—even though often termed a *fidelity bond*—is a two-party contract between the employer and the insurer; dishonest employees of the insured are not direct parties to this insurance arrangement.

A surety has a number of rights to protect it against sustaining loss from the obligor's misconduct or collusion between the obligor and the obligee to the surety's detriment. These rights include *exoneration, subrogation, indemnity,* and *contribution.* The doctrine of exoneration applies if the obligee does not protect its rights against the obligor but passively relies upon the surety. For example, if the obligor falls behind schedule or indicates an intention not to perform as promised, and if the obligee then fails to preserve its rights against the obligor, the surety is released or exonerated from liability to the extent that the surety can show that the obligee's inaction increased the surety's loss or otherwise harmed the surety. As previously explained, an obligee is entitled to the surety's protection as soon as the obligor stands in breach, but the obligee must not then release the obligor from the consequences of its nonperformance.

The right of subrogation works in that a surety that fulfills an obligor's promise to an obligee is entitled to the same payment the obligor would have received. Thus, if a surety completes construction of a building on which an obligor has defaulted, then the obligee (the building owner) must pay the surety for the portion of the work completed on the same basis that the defaulting contractor would have been paid. The initial contractor's failure to carry out its promise does not relieve the obligee of paying for the work because this would be an undue benefit to the obligee. The obligee's payment to the surety at the contracted price thus promotes equity and provides a good example of a risk control transfer in that it involves a commitment to *act* not to pay.

Indemnity applies when a surety puts forth effort or money to fulfill the obligor's promise to the obligee. Under such circumstances the surety has the right to proceed directly against the obligor to recover the fair price of its effort and/or any funds it has paid to the obligee as compensation for the obligor's inaction. The obligor then becomes bound to indemnify the surety for the costs of fulfilling the promise.

Contribution comes into play if there are two or more sureties. The basic law of suretyship obligates each surety to perform in full on the obligor's behalf. If necessary, each must carry out the entire promise to the obligee. Between themselves, however, each surety is liable only for a proportionate share of the cost of carrying out the promise. Accordingly, any one surety is entitled to compensation from each of the others so that each surety ultimately shares a prorated portion of the total cost of fulfilling the obligor's promise.

As mentioned, because a surety's contractual commitment is the same as the obligor's, any justification (or legal defense) for nonperformance that releases the obligor from the underlying contract also releases the surety. The surety also can be legally released under the following three circumstances: (1) the suretyship agreement can be invalid. This can occur, for example, if the surety's promise was obtained by fraud or if the surety did not receive adequate legal consideration (anything of value) in exchange for its promise. (2) The obligee can release the obligor from the contract. If this happens, the surety also is released because to hold the surety while excusing the obligee clearly can lead to collusion against the surety. (3) The original contract is modified without the surety's consent. Because the surety's promise is the same as the obligor's promise, any attempt by the obligee and obligor to alter—especially make more demanding—the commitments of the obligor releases the surety from its original commitment.

The law of suretyship and guaranty agreements is much more complex than this summary can adequately suggest. The portions of the preceding discussion that have been limited for convenience to a suretyship also have their counterparts for guaranty contracts, which are appropriately adjusted for the fact that a guaranty agreement is a two-party contract and separate from the contract between the obligor and obligee. Because many organizations often become involved in surety and guaranty agreements, a risk management professional should be aware of the opportunities these contracts provide in terms of additional support for promises, which thus reduces the likelihood that one party to a contract will suffer loss because of another's breach of the agreement.

While most suretyship and guaranty situations can be understood through a careful analysis of what is equitable, in each case competent legal counsel should be consulted before making any business commitments involving a surety or guaranty situation. Here, as with many other cases in which the law becomes intertwined with exposures to loss, a risk management professional's primary responsibility is to remain alert to situations that require special legal knowledge. Properly used, suretyship and guaranty contracts offer valuable protection; misunderstood or misused, they can become exposures to loss for all involved parties.

Waivers Every individual and organization is subject to being sued (1) for breach of contract by any of the other parties with whom they have entered into contracts, (2) in tort by anyone against whom that individual or organization may have committed a civil noncontractual wrong, and (3) by the local, state, or federal government for having committed a crime. Conversely, every individual or organization has the right to sue (1) those with whom they have entered into contract for having breached that contract and (2) those who may have committed torts against them. (Only government bodies that enforce the law have the power to seek a criminal indictment against an individual or organization.) This right to sue under contract or tort law does not guarantee that the plaintiff will win, but being subject to civil suits does create loss exposures for virtually every organization and individual. Even if a civil suit is groundless, the defendant will incur costs of investigation and legal defense.

Any individual or organization having the power to sue under contract or in tort also may *waive*, that is, knowingly relinquish, that right. After such a waiver has been given, the organization or individual subject to being sued no longer faces a liability exposure to those who have waived this right. For example, common law gives a lessee of real property the right to sue a lessor for failing to maintain habitable premises; as long as the lessee maintains this right, the lessor is exposed to liability losses if the lessee should sue and win in court. If, however, a lessee waives its right to sue, the lessor no longer faces this liability exposure from this particular lessee. Consider, for example, a lease provision that reads as follows:

> Lessee, as a material part of the consideration to be rendered to the
> Lessor hereby, waives all claims against the Lessor for damages to

the goods, wares, and merchandise in, upon, or about said premises and for injuries to Lessee, his agents, or invitees in or about said premises.

Unless improperly obtained, this provision relieves the landlord of any concern that the tenant will sue to collect for damage to any "goods, wares, and merchandise" or for any injuries to the tenant or persons who may be on the premises at the tenant's request. As worded, the clause is quite broad, seemingly excusing the lessor from liability for even intentional harm to the lessee. The lessor simply is not exposed to and does not face the possibility of loss from liability to the lessee for claims falling within the scope of this provision. If the lessee should seek to sue the lessor, the lessor should be able to have the claim summarily rejected by any court made aware of this waiver.

When an organization obtains valid waivers, it essentially rids itself of liability loss exposures. Thus, waivers function as effective risk control mechanisms. For example, the preceding lease provision severely limits the landlord's exposures to suits from the lessee. (It can be argued that this provision totally eliminates this exposure depending on the interpretation of "injuries to Lessee"). Such a provision does not, however, prevent others such as the lessee's employees, other agents, guests, or other invitees from directly suing the landlord. (Notice that this particular provision does not obligate the lessee to hold the lessor harmless from such suits, that is, to provide the lessor with legal defense and to pay any verdicts or judgments levied against the lessor.)

To be effective, however, a waiver must be fairly bargained—that is, not obtained by coercion, deceit, or concealment—and may need to be supported by specific legal consideration paid to lessee by the lessor. As long as such a waiver does not seem unreasonable to the court having jurisdiction and does not contravene any applicable statute, such a waiver can be a most effective shield against potential liability. Although this particular example is drawn from a lease, virtually any contract may contain one or more waivers. Some contracts contain a single provision granting *mutual reciprocal waivers*, but the courts generally do not require balanced reciprocity as long as there is some evidence of fair bargaining and reasonable disclosure regarding any waiver.

Waivers generally are embodied in original contracts signed before the parties begin their contractual dealings and before any of them has suffered harm for which it might sue and for which a waiver might become relevant. It is possible, however, for an organization or individual to waive its rights to sue after it has suffered some harm for which it might bring a claim. When such a waiver is made, thus intended to operate retroactively, it is sometimes referred to as an *exculpatory* or *excusing agreement*. In this context, an exculpatory agreement is a particular type of waiver. In less precise usage exculpatory agreement may be a general synonym for waiver.

Risk Financing Transfers—Commitments to Pay

A risk financing transfer is a contract, or provision of a contract, by which the transferee agrees to pay money to or on behalf of the transferor after the transferor has suffered some specified loss. If the transferee is an insurance company, this contractual transfer for risk financing typically is termed *commercial insurance,* or even more simply *insurance.* If the transferee is not an insurer, these contracts typically are called *indemnity agreements* or *hold harmless agreements* if the losses being paid relate to the transferor's liability losses.

In all types of such contractual transfers, the transferor/indemnitee's protection is only as reliable as the transferee/indemnitor's ability and willingness to pay money when needed to restore the loss. For example, in the Peter Builder scenario, Terra presumably could have purchased general property insurance to protect it against the financial consequences of damage to mall buildings. However, for protection against liability claims that mall customers might bring against Terra for pollution-related harm, Terra required each mall tenant to hold Terra and the Builder family harmless from any such claims. This achieved a noninsurance contractual transfer for risk financing from Terra to these tenants for this type of loss.

Insurance Because commercial insurance has been examined at length elsewhere, it is here sufficient to say that commercial insurance typically provides more reliable financial protection than do most hold harmless agreements. The greater reliability or financial security, to recall a term introduced in ARM 54, provided by insurance stems from the following:

- Greater financial resources, structured primarily for the purpose of indemnifying others for loss rather than for conducting some other business of the transferee.
- Need to maintain an impeccable reputation for leaving no properly transferred loss uncompensated.
- Greater attention to the wordings of contract provisions describing precisely the nature and extent of duty to pay for losses.
- More stringent regulation of contractual provisions and of procedures for paying losses when due.

In some very significant cases, however, a risk financing transfer to a noninsurer may be more reliable. Such a transfer is likely to provide more dependable protection for a transferor when the following are true:

- Some characteristic of the loss (for example, the peril causing it or the valuation standard for measuring the transferee's loss and the transferor's financial obligations) puts it outside the scope of typical insurance contracts. For example, newspaper publishers and airlines, typically unable to obtain insurance for their net income losses resulting from labor union strikes, have developed quite elaborate and precise contracts for combining these exposures and paying resulting losses among themselves.
- The transferee's degree of commitment to fulfilling all the terms of its general business contracts with the transferor motivates the transferee to provide full indemnity when an insurer might question the indemnitee's right to payment.

Indemnity Agreements   In general, any party to a contract has the right by common law to agree to pay or indemnify the other party for any losses the latter may suffer in carrying out the terms of the contract. Thus, the range of transactions in which such noninsurance contractual transfers appear is extremely broad. However, the common law of contracts and the statutes of some jurisdictions do limit a given party's right to agree to pay another's loss. Indemnity agreements are therefore classified in terms of both (1) the types of transactions in which they are likely to appear and (2) the extent to which they obligate the transferee, who would otherwise be excused by common law.

Hold Harmless Agreements   Indemnity agreements may provide a transferor with funds for restoring any type of accidental loss to property, net income, liability claims, or the loss of the services of the transferor's key personnel. The group of indemnity agreements that cover the transferor's liability losses growing out of the activities under the contract between the transferor and transferee has become extremely large and diverse. Therefore, these indemnity agreements have been given the special, somewhat colloquial label of hold harmless agreements. As mentioned, under a hold harmless provision the transferee agrees to hold the transferor harmless from specified classes of liability claims by providing the transferor with funds to pay (or paying on the transferor's behalf) for legal defense, verdicts and settlements, court costs, and other expenses related to the types of claims encompassed by the agreement. Hold harmless agreements typically are classified in terms of the degree of responsibility the transferee assumes for claims against the transferor. The following section provides detailed examples of these types of agreements.

NONINSURANCE CONTRACTUAL TRANSFERS FOR RISK FINANCING

Because the wording and use of noninsurance contractual transfers for risk financing are largely unregulated, there are no standard forms for indemnity and hold harmless provisions in a contract and no truly uniform practices for when they should be used or for which party should be the transferor or the transferee. In general, one party transfers the financial burden of specified types of losses whenever (1) that party has the bargaining power to require the other party to be its transferee, (2) such a transfer is standard practice for the type of transaction or industry involved, or (3) the transaction calls for a risk financing transfer by the criteria described in the section Factors Affecting Appropriate Use of Risk Financing Transfers later in this chapter.

The following discussion classifies indemnity and hold harmless provisions according to the types of transactions in which they appear and by the extent to which they alter liabilities for losses as established by common law.

Agreements/Provisions Classified by Type of Transaction[3]

Any written contract may contain a noninsurance contractual transfer for risk control or risk financing. For example, the ticket a garage owner normally gives those who park their cars contains a very broad waiver of the car owner's common law right to bring claims against the garage owner for damage to the vehicle and its contents. As another example, automobile rental agreements require the lessee to purchase insurance for, or otherwise bear the financial burden of, damage to the vehicle for which the rental company, as the vehicle owner, would have responsibility under common law in virtually all circumstances except when the vehicle is rented. Finally, it is possible and quite likely that two organizations exchanging documents for the sale, rental, or maintenance of a product or piece of equipment will each insert into their document a provision that makes the other party an indemnitor. These provisions may be so enmeshed in the document that neither party realizes that there is a mutual promise to indemnify the other. This often creates almost insoluble problems of contract interpretation. Such conflicts can effectively render both provisions— and both parties' attempts to collect indemnity from the other—

virtually meaningless. To avoid such difficulties, each organization's risk management professional, legal counsel, and key managers should recognize where to look for the more common forms of indemnity and hold harmless agreements.

Construction Agreements A building contractor's work creates a number of loss exposures, principally liability exposures, for the owner of the land and the building under construction. For example, the contractor's activities may harm pedestrians, owners of adjoining properties, or even the entire community through the release of toxic substances into the environment. As a landowner, the individual or organization for which the building is being constructed is ultimately liable for all such harm. The owner also is liable for any breaches of building permit provisions or building codes that may result from the contractor's or the architect's decisions and other efforts.

For protection against liability losses related to such exposures, landowners normally require that they be held harmless by the building contractor and/or the architect from specified types of claims related to the construction. Contractors and architects normally do not have enough bargaining power to remove such hold harmless provisions from a contract because the landowner can almost always find another contractor or architect who will agree to the hold harmless provisions.

The exact extent of the claims against which the contractor and/or architect agrees to hold the landowner harmless can be determined only by a very careful reading of the indemnity or hold harmless provision. Even this may leave unanswered some questions about the scope of the losses for which the contractor agrees to pay. The following is a fairly typical example of a hold harmless agreement pertaining to liability claims against the building owner:

> The Contractor shall indemnify and hold harmless the Owner and its agents and employees from and against all claims, including attorneys' fees, arising out of or resulting from the performance of the Work, provided that any such claim (1) is attributable to bodily injury, sickness, disease or death, or to injury to or destruction of tangible property (other than the Work itself) including the loss of use resulting therefrom, and (2) is caused in whole or in part by any negligent act or omission of the Contractor, any Subcontractor, anyone directly or indirectly employed by any of them or anyone for whose acts any of them may be liable, regardless of whether or not it is caused in part by a party indemnified hereunder.
>
> In any and all claims against the Owner or any of its agents or employees by any employee of the Contractor, any Subcontractor, anyone directly or indirectly employed by any of them, or anyone for whose acts any of them may be liable, the indemnification obligation under this Paragraph shall not be limited in any way by any limitation on the amount or type of damages, compensation or benefits payable

by or for the Contractor or any Subcontractor under workmen's compensation acts, disability benefit acts, or other employee benefit acts.

The obligations of the Contractor under this Paragraph shall not extend to the liability of the Architect, his agents or employees arising out of (1) the preparation or approval of maps, drawings, opinions, reports, surveys, change orders, designs, or specifications, or (2) the giving of or the failure to give directions or instructions by the Architect, his agents or employees, provided such giving or failure to give is the primary cause of the injury or damage.

This type of provision can be as difficult for laypersons to understand as an insurance contract. Those familiar with insurance, however, should apply the framework for interpreting an insurance policy to the analysis of such provisions. For instance, a careful reading will reveal that (1) the contractor is obligated to pay only for claims against the owner (and persons affiliated with the owner), not for any property damage, loss of income, or extra expenses the owner may incur and (2) the contractor's financial obligation to respond to such claims is unlimited, and (3) there is no gauge for measuring the maximum dollar value of the claims to which the contractor must respond, even though virtually all insurance policies specify such a maximum. In addition, this provision does not indicate whether the transferee/indemnitor is obligated to pay any punitive damages for which the transferor/indemnitee may become liable or whether bankruptcy of the transferee/indemnitor will relieve it of any further liability. The impact of punitive damages and bankruptcy on both hold harmless and other indemnity agreements varies greatly among jurisdictions. In some, the payment of punitive damages by the transferee/indemnitor is automatically included within a hold harmless agreement; in others, they are included only if specified; and in still others, contractual transfer of the obligation to pay punitive damages is illegal. Bankruptcy excuses a transferee/indemnitor in some jurisdictions, often depending on the nature of the harm suffered by the claimant who brings suit against the transferor/indemnitee.

Service Agreements Constructing a building can be viewed as a highly specialized type of service that results in a tangible product, which, when finished, ends the contractor's services. Other services including maintenance and transportation, however, frequently are purchased on a continuing basis. The providers of such services often agree to a generic type of hold harmless agreement such as the following provision in a contract under which a college (Owner) purchases continuing bus transportation for its students:

The Contractor shall be responsible from the time of the beginning of operations, for all injury or damage of any kind resulting from said operations, to persons or property regardless of who may be the owner of the property. In addition to the liability imposed upon the Contractor on account of personal injury (including death) or property damage suffered through the Contractor's negligence, which liability is not impaired or otherwise affected hereunder, the Contractor assumes the obligation to save the Owner harmless and to indemnify the Owner from every expense, liability, or payment arising out of or through injury (including death) to any person or persons or damage to property (regardless of who may be the owner of the property) of any place in which work is located, arising out of or suffered through any act or omission of the Contractor or any Subcontractor, or anyone directly or indirectly employed by or under the supervision of any of them in the prosecution of the operations included in this contract.

The contractor's obligation under this provision is markedly broad because (1) the contractor agrees to hold the owner harmless from virtually all property, liability, and other losses (except probably revenue losses) that the owner may suffer because of the contractor's errors and (2) the contractor agrees to be responsible for even those claims brought against the owner because of the owner's sole negligence. Comparing this provision with the preceding one illustrates the range over which contractual transfers for risk financing may vary.

Purchase Order Agreements The raw materials, components, and supplies purchased by manufacturer, wholesaler, or retailer from another person or organization (a vendor) for use in a product the purchaser sells to others may be the basis for a products liability claim against the purchaser. The items purchased from the vendor may prove defective, or they may be the wrong type or grade for use in the product. In such a situation, common law gives the ultimate buyer or other user of the product the right to sue everyone involved in the production or sale of that product, ranging from the supplier of the raw materials to the retailer. Any organization in this chain also has the right to ask any other party in the chain to provide it with protection against any products liability claims. The traditional practice is for each organization to seek hold harmless indemnity from its immediate supplier or vendor through a provision such as the following:

The Vendor agrees to indemnify and save harmless the Purchaser and its agents, representatives, and employees from any and all charges, claims, and causes of action by third persons, including but not limited to agents, representatives, and employees of the Vendor and of the Purchaser based upon or arising out of any damages, losses, expenses, charges, costs, injuries, or illness sustained or incurred by such person or persons resulting from or in any way, directly or indirectly, connected with the performance or nonperformance of this Agreement, of the vending services provided for hereunder, or the performance of or failure to perform any work or other activity related to such vending services, provided, however, that notwithstanding the foregoing, the Vendor does not agree to indemnify and save harmless the Purchaser, its agents, representatives and employees from any charges, claims, or actions based upon or arising out of any damages, losses, claims, expenses, charges, costs, injuries, or illness sustained or incurred as the sole result of the negligence of the Purchaser, its agents, representatives, or employees. In the event a claim is filed against the Purchaser for which the Vendor is to be held liable under the terms of this agreement, the Purchaser will promptly notify the Vendor of such claim and will not settle such claim without the prior written consent of the Vendor.

Like an insurance contract, this provision also has some "exclusions" and "conditions." For example, the provision exempts the indemnifying vendor from responding to claims brought against the purchaser based entirely on the purchaser's "sole negligence" without any fault of the vendor. This provision also makes the vendor's promise conditional upon the purchaser immediately notifying the vendor of any claim; the vendor has authority to manage claims, while the purchaser is barred from making any separate settlement with a claimant. However, notice that, unlike an insurance contract, this provision does not obligate the purchaser/indemnitee to cooperate with the vendor/indemnitor in the vendor's management of any claim.

This provision also protects the purchaser, suggesting that the purchaser has enough bargaining power to obtain a promise of indemnity from the vendor and that the vendor's eagerness to contract with the purchaser made the agreement at least tolerable to the vendor. These relationships may be reversed. A vendor who is the exclusive national manufacturer of a very popular product may be able to require each wholesale and/or retail purchaser to agree to hold the manufacturer harmless from products liability or other claims (or even from losses not involving liability that the manufacturer may suffer). Marketers throughout the distribution chain may have no choice but to provide the manufacturer with this promise of protection if they wish to carry the product.

When several parties in the production-marketing chain enter into a series of indemnity or hold harmless agreements, considerable confusion can result. If all agreements shift the financial burden of losses one "link" back along the chain, then the original manufacturer (or even raw material supplier) may become obligated to finance the losses of all claims against other parties. In the opposite case, when the financial burden is shifted forward, then the retailer may become burdened with the losses of all the parties in the chain. In a yet more complicated situation in which the agreement provides for indemnity from purchasers and from vendors, the aggregate liability of all the producers and marketers may accumulate at various points along the chain. To guard against such confusion and to ensure that financial responsibility is equitably and efficiently distributed, the agreements should be planned so that exposures fall on those who are most qualified to prevent losses or so that losses that do occur fall on those who are qualified to finance their recovery. These concerns are addressed in the section Management of Noninsurance Contractual Transfers later in this chapter.

Lease of Premises Agreements Even though leases of real or personal property may contain no explicit risk transfer provisions, they are inherently contractual transfers for risk control. As explained, a lease by nature allows a lessee to enjoy the use of property for a specified period without having to assume many of the loss exposures that are inherent in property ownership. While such *exposures* remain with the lessor, a lessor can attempt to shift the financial burden of some *actual losses* to the lessee, particularly if the lessor has superior bargaining power. Thus, a lease may also contain elements of risk financing transfers. This illustrates a frequent but little-noticed aspect of noninsurance contractual transfers: a single agreement, even a single contract provision, can embody transfers for both risk control and risk financing.

A lessee of all or part of another's premises typically must accept the entire lease agreement as prepared by the lessor. Most lease agreements consequently are written so that they substantially favor the lessor; furthermore, unlike insurance contracts, which courts often interpret in an insured's favor, leases are usually read by the courts as if the parties had roughly equal bargaining power, particularly if the lessee is an organization renting business space rather than an individual or family renting "personal" space. Finally, a lessee wishing to do business in a particular location often has a limited choice regarding the number of properties that are available for rent. Therefore, a lessee may have to agree to a hold harmless provision such as the following, which is common in mall and shopping center properties:

> Lessee shall indemnify and save harmless Lessor from and against any and all loss, cost (including attorneys' fees), damages, expense, and liability (including statutory liability and liability under workers compensation laws) in connection with claims for damages as a result of injury or death of any person or damage to any property sustained by...Lessee and...all other persons...which arise from or in any manner grow out of any act or neglect on or about the Shopping Center by Lessee, Lessee's partners, agents, employees, customers, invitees, contractors, and subcontractors.

This provision obligates the lessee to respond only to liability claims that may be brought against the lessor, not to the lessor's property damage, net income, or other losses. This clause is quite broad in the sense that the lessee's financial responsibility extends not only to the lessor's common law liabilities but also its statutory liabilities, including workers compensation claims. In numerous states such an attempt to shift workers compensation and other statutory liability would be highly vulnerable to a court challenge by an injured employee of the lessor or by some third party injured in the shopping center. Both could claim that the financial security of their statutory protection had been significantly jeopardized by an attempted contractual shift from the lessor to the presumably less financially able lessee.

Equipment Lease Agreements An individual or organization who obtains the use of major items of equipment by leasing them usually must promise to return the equipment in its original condition, often subject to certain exceptions. Such a promise protects the lessor against loss to the equipment, which often is out of the lessor's direct control or supervision for substantial periods. Such a promise is exemplified by the following indemnity provision in a lease agreement for machine tools:

> The Lessee covenants that it will in respect of the Equipment
> * pay the rentals promptly when due,
> * assume responsibility for them, at current values, against fire and loss or damage from whatever cause arising,
> * employ them only on work carried out on the Lessee's premises,
> * permit the Lessor to inspect them at all reasonable times, and
> * on termination of this agreement, return them to the Lessor at the expense and risk of the Lessee.

This clause is not especially burdensome for the lessee because (1) the lessee does not assume any financial responsibility for liability claims against the lessor that may arise from the lessee's possession or use of the equipment and (2) the lessee is responsible only for the property value of the leased equipment, not for the revenue the lessor could have earned on the equipment had it remained undamaged and available for another rental.

Other equipment leases, however, obligate the lessee to hold the lessor harmless from liability claims related to the equipment while it is in the lessee's possession. The lessee may even be required to maintain insurance that provides the lessor with liability (and often other) protection. An example of such a broader commitment for the lessee is the following provision in a lease for trucks and trailers, referred to as equipment:

> Lessee shall maintain Public Liability and Property Damage Insurance as well as Workers Compensation Insurance and agrees to hold Lessor harmless from any such claim while said equipment is in the actual service of the Lessee; however, Lessor shall maintain at his own expense Public Liability and Property Damage Insurance which

shall be effective while the equipment is parked, deadheading, bobtailing, or otherwise being operated in any manner other than under or pursuant to specific dispatch instructions from the Lessee; and the Lessor will save Lessee harmless from any loss, claim, or liability while the equipment, or either unit thereof, is so used or employed. This shall be construed to mean that the Lessee will not be responsible for Public Liability, Property Damage, Workers Compensation or Cargo Insurance when the equipment is being used other than in connection with the transportation of freight under the authority and with the authorization of the Lessee, or when the same is being used in any manner except under or pursuant to dispatch instructions of the Lessee.

This provision attempts to distinguish sharply between the exposures to the equipment when in normal use by the lessee and exposures at all other times. It obligates the lessee to provide indemnity (through insurance) only when the equipment is in normal use.

Bailment Contracts Many business transactions involve placing personal property (property other than real estate) in the custody of some other party, such as for repair, transportation, or safe keeping. This temporary transfer of the custody of property is known as a bailment; the party having temporary custody is a *bailee,* and the owner to whom the property is to be returned is the *bailor.* For example, when one of Terra's vehicles is at the Goodridge Garage where Peter Builder normally has the company's vehicles serviced and repaired, the garage is the bailee and Terra is the bailor. Similarly, when the quarry from which Terra purchases building stone places a shipment in the hands of an independent trucker for delivery to a Terra building site, the trucker is a bailee. The owner of the stone—which could be either the quarry or Terra, depending upon the terms of their contract of sale—is the bailor.

Like most bailments in business situations, both these arrangements are known as *compensated bailments* rather than as *gratuitous bailments.* (The latter occurs when, say, one friend loans an umbrella or a book to another friend.) In a compensated bailment the bailor normally pays the bailee for work or service related to the bailed property. Such bailments also are said to be *mutual benefit bailments* in the sense that both the bailee and bailor expect to benefit from their business transaction. For example, Goodridge Garage receives money for maintaining Terra's vehicles, and Terra gains reliable repairs and maintenance in exchange.

Under the common law of compensated mutual benefit bailments, the bailee must exercise great care for the safety of the bailor's property in contrast to the degree of care required of a bailee in a gratuitous bailment or a bailment that benefits only the bailee (the friend who borrows a book). The common law normally requires a compensated mutual benefit bailee to return the property to the bailor in its original condition, excusing the bailee only for damage caused by acts of God and normal wear and tear. A special class of compensated mutual benefit bailees consists of common carrier transporters of others' goods—that is, carriers who stand ready to transport anyone's cargo in accordance with an established schedule and set of fees. A common carrier is responsible for any damage to a bailor shipper's cargo except that caused by (1) acts of God, (2) warlike activities (usually described as involving acts of a public enemy, but not including rioting or terrorism), (3) exercise of public authority (as when police block the access to a particular neighborhood, thus depriving a business located there of its normal profits), (4) fault or neglect by the shipper (such as poor packaging or labeling), and (5) any *inherent vice* of the cargo (that is, any potential for the shipper's goods to destroy themselves, as when ice melts or explosives explode because of improper packaging or labeling).

A compensated mutual benefit bailee normally is held responsible for damage to a bailor's property and must not only replace it with comparable property but also must compensate the bailor for any loss of profits, continuing expenses, and other financial harm that the bailor has suffered as a consequence of damaged property.

By a contract, a bailor and bailee may alter the common law apportionment of their respective loss exposures. For example, in many business situations bailees seek to limit their liability through posted notices or contract provisions stating that the bailee is not responsible for damage to the bailor's goods or that the bailee's liability is limited to a specified amount per item or only to the value of the property (that is, excluding any profits or loss of use the bailor would have earned from the property). In contrast, a bailor may seek to increase a bailee's liability by, for example, holding the bailee responsible for specified acts of God (such as fire or windstorm).

Either party to a bailment contract may have business reasons for undertaking loss exposures that the common law normally places on the other party. While respecting each party's freedom of contract to fairly bargain apportionments of loss exposures, the courts have been reluctant to enforce exposure-shifting bailment contract provisions that are contrary to practice within the particular industry, not equitably negotiated, or less than adequately disclosed. For example, a "Not Responsible For Damage To Vehicles" statement on the back of tickets given to customers of a public parking garage normally is ignored by the courts as an inadequately disclosed and unbargained attempt to shift the garagekeeper's liability contrary to the bailor's reasonable expectation.

Contracts of Sale and Supply[4] Contracts pertaining to marketing goods and services offer innumerable opportunities for transferring loss exposures between the buyer and the seller. The transfer normally favors the party with the greater bargaining power. For example, in order to maintain firmer control of their products as they move through marketing channels, some manufacturers and processors sell their goods on consignment. This arrangement leaves title to the property in the hands of the manufacturer or processor until the distributor sells the goods to the retailer or ultimate consumer. This arrangement also means that the distributor, having never taken title to the goods, never is exposed to loss from their damage or destruction. Ownership, and thus the loss exposure, moves directly from the manufacturer or processor to the retailer or consumer, allowing the distributor to earn revenue only from its distribution.

Another type of contract related to property ownership is a service or maintenance agreement under which a sales or maintenance organization promises to protect the buyer or other owner of substantial personal property against specified types of losses to or arising from that property. (Notice that service and maintenance agreements, under which a property owner is a transferor of some exposures, differs from a lease agreement, under which the transferor never faces ownership-related exposures while having the right to use the leased property.) If the service or maintenance firm promises to provide services only but does not also agree to indemnify the property owner for losses, the agreement is one of risk control, not risk financing. If, in contrast, the maintenance or service firm agrees to "hold [the owner] harmless" from liability claims against the owner, then the agreement—because it calls for payment of money rather than simply provision of services—becomes a risk financing transfer.

Service and maintenance firms become transferees under the following types of sale and supply agreements:

- Agreements to deliver fuel to the customer/transferor so that the customer never runs out of fuel. The fuel dealer becomes obligated to pay for any frozen pipes and other specified losses if the customer is ever without fuel.
- Purchase agreements for data processing equipment, air conditioners, vehicles, or similar items with guarantees of maintenance and replacement as necessary.
- Service contracts under which real estate agents undertake the maintenance of specified items of equipment, such as heating systems, in homes they sell.

Such service and supply contracts can border on insurance if they go beyond guarantees of the quality of the goods or the reliability of the supplier's performance and extend to other causes of loss. For example, sales and supply firms have been held to be engaged in the business of insurance, thus making them subject to the provisions of the applicable state insurance code in the following situations:

- A tire dealer has agreed to give an allowance for unused mileage if a tire that it sold is damaged by road hazards.
- A glazier has promised to replace plate glass windows broken by any cause.
- A fuel oil dealer has agreed to deliver oil for the next ten years at a lower price per BTU than any other energy firm serving the same area (exposing this dealer to a substantial business risk if, for example, hydroelectric or nuclear power becomes cost-effective in its area).

Inadvertently becoming subject to an insurance code can be very restrictive, burdensome, and costly for a sales or supply organization. In effect, the firm can be forced to withdraw from the ambitious service or maintenance agreements through which it sought to attract customers by becoming the transferee of exposures that customers normally bear.

Sales and service contracts may substantially modify the common law doctrines that normally distribute loss exposures between buyers and sellers of property. The fundamental common law is that risk of loss—both to property itself and from loss of use of that property—moves with the title to property, with the owner always bearing these exposures. Therefore, special risk transfer provisions aside, the time when ownership changes is important in identifying and managing an organization's loss exposures. For example, when Company S sells a product to Company B in another city, specifying when Company B acquires ownership is essential. (This is also good practice even if Company S and Company B are neighbors because accidents may occur even in seemingly safe areas.)

To highlight some crucial points in the more extended ARM 54 discussion of transfers of title to property, Company S may provide in its standard sales contract that each sale is "F.O.B. Detroit," where Company S is located. The abbreviation *F.O.B.* stands for *free on board*, meaning that the seller is free of responsibility for the goods once they have reached the designated location. Regardless of whether Company S delivers its products in its own vehicles or by common or contract carrier, this provision means that Company B acquires the goods (and the related loss exposures) as soon as they are aboard a carrier in Detroit. If, however, the specification is "F.O.B. Des Moines," which may be the location of Company B's warehouse or perhaps some central distribution point, then Company B owns and is responsible for the loss of the goods when they reach Des Moines and are ready to be unloaded.

However, an alternative sales contract—particularly a contract of sale for permanently installed equipment—may provide that Company B does not become the owner until the property has been unloaded, installed, and has passed a series of operational tests in the buyer's facility. Such an arrangement allows the seller to maintain control of the property and to ensure that it has been properly placed in service. If, in contrast, Company S wishes Company B to be responsible for damage to the property throughout its transport, Company S may require that Company B take title to the property at Company S's shipping dock. The bargaining power of the buyer and seller, as well as industry custom, is likely to influence these allocations of loss exposures.

Responsibilities for ownership exposures may be divided, different responsibilities being transferred at different times. Thus, if the shipment between Company S and Company B is under *C.I.F.* terms (meaning that the basic cost of the goods plus insurance and freight charges are included in the quoted price), Company B normally acquires ownership as soon as the goods are on board a carrier, but Company S is required to purchase sufficient insurance and to pay for the freight. If the insurance is less than the amount established by the custom of the trade or the specifications of the sales contract, Company S, because it has failed to fulfill the C.I.F. conditions, must compensate the buyer, Company B, for its loss. Such an arrangement illustrates how it is often possible to combine risk control transfers (pertaining to the shifting of title and consequent exposure to loss) with risk financing transfers, here obligating the seller to provide insurance for, or to directly indemnify, the buyer.

Another frequent allocation of exposures in sales of property occurs in *installment or conditional sales contracts* under which the seller commonly reserves ownership rights until all the conditions of the contract (most notably, the buyer's final installment payment) have been met. Although the seller usually retains title, exposure to loss because of damage to the property may be transferred by the sales contract immediately to the buyer. This can be achieved by a contract provision obligating the buyer to complete the contract by continuing installment payments even though the property may be lost or damaged before the buyer has made the final payment. Such an arrangement preserves the seller's right under an installment contract to either receive the full purchase price or, if the buyer defaults, to repossess the property. Here, the buyer also may secure insurance or other risk financing to protect its interests and obligations arising out of the property. During the time between the first and last installment payment, therefore, both the buyer and the seller are exposed to loss from damage to and have an insurable interest in the property.

A final frequent arrangement is that property that has been sold remains in the hands of the seller for later delivery to the buyer. Valuable items of personal property as well as substantial quantities of fungible goods (commodities or bulk goods, all parts of which are presumed to be uniform) often are sold in this way. The contract of sale becomes effective as soon as the buyer and seller have agreed on the particular items or quantity to be sold, the price, and the delivery date; the sales contract commonly specifies that ownership of the property transfers to the buyer at that time. While the ownership-related exposure to damage thus passes to the buyer, the seller having custody of it still has a bailee's responsibility for its safety. In such cases, therefore, both the bailor's ownership interest and the bailee's liability for damage may expose each to loss and support each party's purchase of appropriate insurance or other risk financing arrangements.

Agreements Classified by Extent of Responsibility Transferred

All contractual transfers of exposures to loss or of the financial responsibility for an actual loss define the obligations of the transferor and the transferee under common law. These agreements may also define these obligations in a way that modifies each party's responsibility under common law. Classified in terms of the extent to which these agreements modify common law, they can be grouped according to whether they (1) restate existing common or statutory law, (2) shift responsibility for joint fault to one party based on stated conditions, (3) shift all responsibility to one party except for losses that are the transferor's sole fault, to (4) shift all responsibility. While these four types of provisions can be applied to any property, net income, liability, or personnel loss, most pertain to a transferor's potential or actual liability losses.

Restating Law By embodying in their contract the essential provisions of the existing law as they understand it to govern their transactions, the parties to a contract may eliminate much uncertainty about how the law will apportion legal or financial responsibility for losses that either of them may suffer in carrying out their contract. Such contracts eliminate, or at least greatly reduce, any likelihood that (1) a court may misinterpret their intentions, (2) some future court case or statute may affect their respective rights, or (3) an accident occurring in, or otherwise involving, some other jurisdiction may bring that jurisdiction's laws into play under the general doctrines of "conflict of laws" that apply when parties in different jurisdictions sue one another.

Each of these three sources of uncertainty is a cause of what has been termed *juridical risk,* the possibility that a court will reach a decision that differs from the parties' expectations, that is, that the court will change what the parties thought they understood to be the law.[5] In applying a fairly bargained contract in which the parties have clearly expressed their intent, courts generally enforce the contract, allowing the parties to "make their own law" as far as equity allows. A clause that merely restates existing law may just name the appropriate provisions of an existing statute or cite relevant court cases, may identify the jurisdiction by whose laws at a given date the parties intend to be bound, or may recite the substance of their understanding of the current law. The third alternative is exemplified in the following provision for the sale and delivery of construction equipment from a seller to a buyer, both of which are business organizations:

> *Application of Law.* The Buyer and Seller agree that each shall bear any loss resulting from physical damage to the Equipment that occurs during the time each party, respectively, holds title to the Equipment. Title to the Equipment shall pass in accordance with the customary trade interpretation of the conditions of sale specified at the top of this agreement. "Loss" here means any damage to the Equipment, loss of income to the owner from its use, and liability for harm to others arising from the ownership, use of, or defects in the Equipment. This provision shall be interpreted in accordance with the common law and statutes of the State of Illinois (wherein both parties are situate), as enacted or interpreted as of the date of this agreement. Except as provided in these statutes or court rulings, neither the Buyer nor the Seller shall be responsible for indemnifying the other for any loss relating to the ownership, maintenance, or use of, or defect in, this Equipment.

Shifting Responsibility for Joint Fault   Two or more individuals or organizations working together to carry out their contract may jointly harm some third party, or at least be joined as defendants in a civil suit charging them both with fault for a breach of contract or a tort. The facts of the situation may not make clear which party is at fault or their relative proportions of fault. Determining who is responsible and to what extent may be a very difficult, time consuming, contentious process.

Such difficulties can be largely eliminated, and one contracting party's common law responsibility for joint civil wrongs can be shifted to the other contracting party, if the one to which such joint responsibility is shifted (the transferee) agrees to hold the other party (the transferor) harmless from claims arising from their joint fault. Such a transfer is embodied in the italicized portion of the following clause from a lease for an entire commercial building:

> Lessee shall repair partitions, all structural and window glass, electric and plumbing fixtures, and all machinery installed in the leased premises. Lessee shall be liable for, and shall hold the Lessor harmless with respect to, all claims relating to damage or injury to the property or persons of others alleged to have occurred on or to have been caused by the condition of the leased premises, if such injury or damage is alleged to have been caused by an act or neglect of the Lessee (including anyone in the Lessee's control or employ) *or the joint act or neglect of the Lessee and Lessor.* The Lessee shall at once report in writing to the Lessor any defective condition known which the Lessor is required to repair, and failure to so report shall make the Lessee responsible for damages resulting from such defective condition.

This provision is noteworthy because the italicized words pertaining to joint responsibility are surrounded by many other provisions describing the lessee's responsibility not only for liability claims but also for damage to the premises. The ten or eleven words are designed to shift the otherwise joint responsibilities for harm to others, making what once was joint the *sole* responsibility of the transferee. This responsibility could easily be overlooked by the lessee (or even mistakenly omitted by a hurried lessor), especially if such a provision is typed or otherwise individually prepared for each agreement and not made a part of the preprinted form. In short, both the transferor and the transferee must be sure that the provisions express their shared intent.

Shifting All Responsibility Except the Transferor's Sole Fault The preceding provision arguably would not apply if the two contracting parties and some outside third party all were named defendants in a civil suit: the clause does not mention the third party's fault. Nor does it refer to claims arising from more complex chains of causation like suits for bodily injury or property damage involving the fault of the transferor coupled with some slight fault of the plaintiff or the wrongful acts of a civil authority or other entity immune from suit. In these more complex cases a transferee (such as the above lessee) could maintain—with some reasonable chance of success—that it was not obligated to hold the transferor harmless from the claims of others.

A hold harmless provision that would protect the transferor in such cases would be phrased to apply to all claims except those arising from the transferor's sole fault. The following is an example of such a provision in a contract for the construction of a building:

> The Contractor shall indemnify and hold harmless the Owner from and against all claims ... attributable to bodily injury ... unless caused entirely by the Owner's act or omission.

Under this provision the contractor would not be obligated to respond to a suit against the owner if the contractor could show that, regardless of any allegations, the injury to the plaintiff was caused solely by the owner. If the concluding words of the above clause read "... alleged to have been caused entirely by ..." the wording of the plaintiff's complaint, rather than the actual facts of the case, arguably would determine whether the contractor was obliged to hold the owner harmless. To further illustrate the importance of carefully phrasing hold harmless provisions, assume the clause read:

> The Contractor shall indemnify and hold harmless the Owner from and against all claims ... attributable to bodily injury ... whether or not caused in part by the Owner.

The words following "whether" do not limit the contractor's duty to respond—in fact, the provision seeks to make the contractor financially responsible for all claims regarding bodily injury against the owner. However, the reference to bodily injury is itself a limitation, excluding other sorts of claims.

Shifting All Responsibility Beginning with a relatively simple restatement of common law, the three preceding indemnity and hold harmless provisions have progressively worked on behalf of the transferor/indemnitee, shifting ever greater financial burdens to the transferee/indemnitor. A yet more extreme provision and an example of its associated difficulties appears in a contract that a municipality requires of the owner of a building that was to be demolished by explosives. The parties to the contract are the municipality, the general contractor for the entire project, and the explosives subcontractor chosen by the general contractor.

Because work with explosives is inherently dangerous and imposes strict liability without fault on those who engage in or direct it, the municipality wants to hold the parties involved financially responsible for all claims that might be lodged against the city or its personnel because of this project. The permit for the demolition therefore includes the following provision:

> The undersigned owner, general contractor, and subcontractor (hereinafter collectively referred to as "Indemnitors") for and in consideration of the undertaking of the municipality to provide regular police, fire, and other assistance during the Activity, and for other good and valuable consideration, the receipt and sufficiency whereof is hereby acknowledged by Indemnitors, do hereby jointly and severally covenant, undertake, and agree that they, and each of them, will indemnify and hold harmless (without limits as to amount) the

municipality and its officials, officers, employees, and servants in their official capacity (hereinafter collectively referred to as "Indemnitees"), and any of them, from and against all loss, all risk of loss, and all damage (including expense) sustained or incurred because of or by reason of any and all claims, demands, suits, actions, judgments, and executions for damages of any and every kind and by whomever and wherever made or obtained, alleged caused by, arising out of, or relating in any manner to the Activity, and to protect and defend Indemnitees, and any of them, with respect thereto.

The owner of the structure to be demolished, once aware of his potential personal liability under the above provision, required to be held harmless by the general contractor under the following provision:

Indemnification. General Contractor warrants that it is an independent contractor and agrees to indemnify and save harmless the Owner from and against any loss or expense by reason of any liability imposed by law on the Owner and from and against claims against Owner for damages because of bodily injuries, including death, at any time resulting therefrom, accidents sustained by any person or persons on account of damage to property rising out of or in consequence of the performance of this Agreement, whether such injuries to persons or damage to property are due or claimed to be due to any negligence of general contractor, the Owner, their agents, servants, or employees, or of any other person.

As a result of this provision, the general contractor demands to be indemnified by the subcontractor under the following very similar provision:

Indemnification. Subcontractor warrants that it is an independent contractor and agrees to indemnify and save harmless the Owner and General Contractor from and against any loss or expense by reason of any liability imposed by law upon the Owner and General Contractor and from and against claims against Owner and General contractor for damages because of bodily injuries, including death, at any time resulting therefrom, accidents sustained by any person or persons on account of damage to property rising out of or in consequence of the performance of the Agreement, whether such injuries to persons or damage to property are due or claimed to be due to any negligence of General Contractor, the Owner, their agents, servants, or employees, or any other person.

These three provisions together would place the financial burden of all claims on the subcontractor. The municipality, once sued, could turn to the owner for protection, the owner could turn to the general contractor, and the general contractor could turn to the subcontractor. The city, the owner, and the primary contractor may not have fully considered (1) whether the subcontractor was financially able to provide the protection provided for in the hold harmless provisions, (2) whether placing the entire financial burden of potential losses on the subcontractor was economically the most efficient allocation of risk control and risk financing responsibilities for all the parties, or even (3) whether the courts would uphold each attempted transfer.

In fact, the court that eventually considered these matters refused to enforce the provisions against the subcontractor. Instead, the owner, the primary contractor, and even the city were held liable when some of the subcontractor's blasting activities damaged nearby properties. The court found that, for the reasons suggested in much of the following discussion, these provisions were "guilty" of the following:

- They were fairly negotiated but resulted from inappropriate use of the transferors' economic power.
- They sought to transfer a legal duty (here, conducting blasting operations safely) that is so fundamental that the law will not recognize an attempted transfer without its prior consent through legislation or court order.
- They improperly tried to deprive members of the public exposed to harm of the compensation (from the owner and the primary contractor) to which the public was entitled, thus harming the public interest and violating public policy.

A fundamental theme of much of the following discussion is that noninsurance contractual transfers, especially for risk financing, constitute sound risk management only when the transfers properly apply the legal and managerial principles that determine when and to what extent individuals and organizations should alter the responsibilities for managing loss exposures and for financing recovery from actual losses that are set forth in both common and statutory law. So, much as contracts can modify common law, so does the law check noninsurance contractual transfers.

LEGAL PRINCIPLES UNDERLYING
NONINSURANCE CONTRACTUAL TRANSFERS

The great diversity in the wording and application of noninsurance contractual transfers for risk control and risk financing illustrates the importance of freedom of contract as a principle in English and American common law. Yet the limitations on this freedom to contractually transfer loss exposures and financial burdens of losses, which are imposed both by common law and by statutes in many jurisdictions, are important because they seek to prevent unconscionable behavior in the parties to a contract and to protect the public.

Freedom of Contract

Under the legal doctrine of freedom of contract, legally competent parties are generally free to bargain as long as the bargaining does not unreasonably interfere with the rights of others. Contracting parties thus have the right to mutually bind one another to carry out the bargain, and the courts generally will enforce a contract against any contracting party who may later decide not to abide by its terms. Some of those terms may be the contract provisions assigning responsibility for risk control or risk financing to various parties. As part of enforcing the provisions of valid contracts, the court generally will require compliance with these risk-shifting provisions.

Limitations on This Freedom

Despite the latitude historically enjoyed by the parties to a contract, courts now increasingly refuse to enforce noninsurance transfers that (1) manifestly have not been fairly bargained (that is, are "unconscionable" because they are so drastically unfair to the transferee) or (2) unreasonably interfere with the rights of others who are not parties to the contract, thus making the transfer against public policy or contrary to the public interest. Furthermore, statutes in many states attempt to preserve fairness and to foster economically appropriate allocations of loss exposures and actual losses that are consistent with public policy by such legislative strategies as (1) prohibiting certain types of transfers (particularly hold harmless agreements) in some contracts, (2) prohibiting certain wording in some types of contractual transfers, or (3) prescribing precisely the wording of transfer provisions.

Limitations Under Common Law A fundamental objective of common law is to balance the interests of individuals and groups whose actions, if based only on self-interest, can be expected to bring them into conflict, often infringing on others' rights. With respect to contractual transfers of loss exposures or of the cost of losses, this objective requires balancing (1) the potentially competing interests of contracting parties and (2) the collective rights of contracting parties as a group against those of society and the economy. *Unconscionability* is the key concept on which competing interests between contracting parties are balanced; *public policy* or *public interest* is the key point of balance between contracting parties and the community as a whole.

Unconscionability. When enforcing contracts, the courts generally assume that because they are carrying out the original intentions of the contracting parties, it is appropriate to hold each party to the original, freely made promises. As a result, the true consent of the parties is an essential prerequisite of any valid contract. Without it, the courts have little basis for requiring a party to fulfill a promise.

In some extreme circumstances the courts will infer from the terms of the contract itself an absence of true consent. A court will conclude that no party would have voluntarily agreed to a contract so unfavorable to its interests. Therefore, that party must have been physically, psychologically, or economically coerced into signing the contract, and it would now be unconscionable to hold that party to such an unfair bargain even though the contract appears to be valid. For example, assume that an employee were to waive all rights to workers compensation benefits shortly after suffering a seriously disabling injury and that employee had not reclaimed in common law rights to sue the employer for negligence or other cause for the injury, a court would almost surely refuse to enforce this waiver. It would instead allow the employee to pursue statutory workers compensation benefits. The court would likely reason that the employee would only have agreed to such a waiver by being misled or coerced, and thus, that the waiver agreement did not rest on true meeting of the minds of the employer and the employee. Having deduced the absence of mutual consent from the inequity of the waiver, a court would almost certainly ignore it.

Public Policy. Questions about the unconscionability of a contract provision require a court to examine the bargaining relationships between the parties to that contract. On the other hand, in terms of public policy the implications of a contract provision demand that a court consider the economic and social consequences of a particular contract provision if entire groups of people or organizations, situated similarly to the specific parties who bring their dispute to court, were to enter into contracts like the one the court happens to be considering.

Many contracts between parties considered by the courts to be unconscionable would also be found to be contrary to public policy. For example, the same injured employee's waiver of workers compensation benefits described as unconscionable also could be found to be contrary to the public policy objectives of workers compensation statutes. One of the goals of these laws, part of public policy as to how recovery from work injury losses should be financed, is to relieve the government—and ultimately taxpayers—of the burden of financing medical care and living expenses for an employee disabled on the job and his or her family. Given this objective, any agreement between an employer and an employee waiving the employee's statutory right to workers compensation benefits (without receiving in return some alternative compensation) probably would not be honored by the courts because it puts the burden of the loss on society rather than the employer. As such, the contract is contrary to public policy.

Another example of how an improper risk control transfer can be limited through unconscionability or public policy reasons is an agreement between a common carrier and a cargo shipper who excuses the carrier from liability for damage to the cargo due to the carrier's negligence. The Federal Interstate Commerce Act makes a common carrier liable for all damage to goods except for specified causes, therefore, any dilution of this liability by a private risk transfer agreement would be contrary to the act's objective of protecting the public by encouraging common carriers to carefully transport goods. Moreover, because common law traditionally requires a common carrier to meet to a very high standard of care, a court would be likely to infer that a shipper would have excused a carrier from negligence only if the carrier had coerced the shipper. Such coercion would make the contract unconscionable, thus negating the shipper's waiver.

Statutory Limitations Nearly half the states have inactive statutes that deal with indemnity and hold harmless agreements. The states may prohibit the agreements, forbid the use of certain wording in certain contracts, or specify precise wording of the agreement. These statutes reflect the current legislative questioning of one contracting party's attempt to limit its liability for negligence or other wrongdoing by contractually compelling another party to waive its right to sue or to pay the transferor's losses. This legislation reflects public concerns for (1) preserving incentives for organizations to act carefully to prevent harm to others and (2) the source of adequate compensation for those harmed, especially compensation from financially strong organizations, who may likely be the ones to have the bargaining power to enforce an unconscionable indemnity or hold harmless agreement.

The current statutory limitations on indemnity and hold harmless agreements are noteworthy for their diversity, especially their variations with respect to the following:

- the types of noninsurance contractual transfers to which the statutes apply (generally for risk financing, not risk control),
- the parties the statutes regulate in terms of who can be a transferor or a transferee, and
- the scope of the exposures (particularly liability exposures) whose transfer the statutes seek to regulate.

Each statute must therefore be read carefully to determine how it treats these variables. For example, consider the following statute:

A covenant, promise, agreement, or understanding in, or in connection with, or collateral to, a contract or agreement relative to the construction, alteration, repair, or maintenance of a building structure, appurtenances, and appliances including moving, demolition, and excavating connected therewith, purporting to indemnify or hold harmless the promisee against liability for damage arising out of bodily injury to persons or damage to property caused by or resulting from the sole negligence of the promisee, his agents or employees, or the indemnitee, is against public policy and is void and unenforceable; provided, that this section shall not affect the validity of any insurance contract, workers compensation agreement, or other agreement issued by an admitted insurer.

This statute applies only to (1) indemnity and hold harmless agreements, (2) relating to building construction/demolition, (3) seeking to transfer the promisee/indemnitee's sole negligence, and applying only if (4) the transferee/indemnitor is not an insurance company admitted to this state. It does not make explicit whether it excludes insurers only when conducting an insurance business or, more broadly, with respect to any noninsurance contract into which an insurer may enter as an ordinary indemnitor or indemnitee. Thus, this statute would not be relevant to any indemnity or hold harmless agreement in which any one or more of the following conditions prevailed:

- the agreement did not pertain to building construction/demolition,
- the agreement applied to losses other than those "caused by or resulting from the sole negligence of the promisee" (such as the joint negligence of the promisee/indemnitee and the promisor, or the joint fault of the promisee and some third party not involved in the contract, or even the wilful misconduct of the promisee), and
- the promisor/indemnitor is an insurer admitted in the jurisdiction.

Given the extremely broad range of circumstances for which executives and their legal counsel or risk management professionals may draft creative indemnity or hold harmless agreements, it would be a legislative challenge to draft a statute that applied equitably and unambiguously to certain contracts and not to others. For example, with regard to the preceding provision, statutes in other states refer not only to the building structure, appurtenances, and appliances, but also to roads, highways, and bridges. It is not clear whether the statute in the example applies to contracts involving highway, road, or bridge construction—the term building structure arguably is quite vague.

Despite these difficulties, the statutes that apply to hold harmless and indemnity agreements can be classified into those that prohibit transfer, those that prohibit particular wording, and those that prescribe the exact wording in any clause the contracting parties choose to include in their agreement.

Prohibitive Statutes. A statute that appears to be designed to prohibit virtually all indemnity and hold harmless agreements protecting certain classes of persons reads as follows:

> *Indemnification Agreements Prohibited.* Any agreement or provision whereby an architect, engineer, surveyor or his agents or employees is sought to be held harmless or indemnified for damages and claims arising out of circumstances giving rise to legal liability therefore on the part of any said persons shall be against public policy, void, and wholly unenforceable.

This statute is very broad in that it bars both hold harmless and indemnity agreements that might be applicable in "circumstances giving rise to legal liability" regardless of the nature of the wrongdoing or the sole or joint fault of any specified or unspecified party. Perhaps significantly, the statute also is very narrow in denying hold harmless or indemnity protection only to architects, engineers, surveyors, and their associates. Any hold harmless or indemnity agreement in which, for example, a building owner, contractor, or subcontractor is involved presumably is valid in this jurisdiction. Like most statutes generally dealing with noninsurance contractual transfers or specifically with indemnity and hold harmless agreements, the scope of this statute—broad in some respects, narrow in others—probably reflects the legislative concerns prevailing when the statute was enacted more than it represents a thorough attempt to respond to the public interest.

Statutes Prohibiting Particular Wording. In a very important sense, statutes that prohibit a narrowly defined class of hold harmless or indemnity agreements—such as those defined in terms of the transferor's "sole negligence"—effectively forbid the use of such wording in these provisions. An alert business executive, attorney, or risk management professional concerned with contracts drafted or carried out in jurisdictions having such statutes will take care that these specific words do not appear. To validate their contracts, they will instead ensure that the hold harmless and indemnity agreements protecting them are phrased in terms of, say, the transferee/indemnitor's "joint fault," or "shared legal responsibility." In short, the key words of a statute prohibiting a certain type of risk transfer agreement are the very words that ought to be avoided in a risk-shifting provision that the drafter hopes will prove enforceable.

Other statutes more directly address the wording of risk control and risk financing transfers. For example, a statute of one jurisdiction provides:

No agency of this state nor any political subdivision, municipal corporation, or district, nor any public officer or person charged with the letting of contracts for the construction, alteration, or repair of public works shall draft or cause to be drafted specifications for bids, in connection with the construction, alteration, or repair of public works:

- in such a manner as to limit the bidding, directly or indirectly, to any one specific concern, or . . .
- in such a manner as to hold the bidder to whom such contract is awarded responsible for extra costs incurred as a result of errors or omissions by the public agency in the contract documents.

This statute notably prohibits (1) only public entities and their officials and agents from drafting bids for contracts that hold the bidder "responsible for extra costs incurred as a result of errors or omissions by the public agency *in the contract documents,*" not other errors or omissions, and (2) then only in building/demolition contracts for public works. This statute appears to have been drafted in response to a particular legislative concern rather than as a general statement of public policy toward holding others "responsible for . . . errors and omissions" of another contracting party. The statute has no application to private organizations or individuals, public contracts unrelated to public works, or errors and omissions of the public agency that are not reflected in the contract documents.

Statutes prohibiting particular wording in risk transfer agreements generally have very narrow targets; compliance with these statutes involves primarily avoiding the prohibited words and other related phrases. Creative draftsmanship and contract design usually can achieve the contracting parties' intentions almost as fully as if this particular kind of prohibitory statute did not exist.

Prescribing Wording. Attempting to prevent a transferee/indemnitor from undertaking overly burdensome commitments in an indemnity or hold harmless agreement, some states specify that if a particular type of contract does contain any such provision, the wording of the provision must incorporate certain phrases. The following statute illustrates this limitation.

any portion of any agreement or contract for or in connection with any construction, alteration, repair, or demolition of a building structure, appurtenance, or appliance including moving and excavating connected with it or any guarantee of, or in connection with any of them, between an owner of real property and an architect, engineer, general contractor, subcontractor, sub-subcontractor, materials man, or between any combination thereof, wherein any party referred to herein obtains indemnification from liability for damages to persons or property caused in whole or in part by any act, omission, or default shall be void and unenforceable unless

- the contract contains monetary limitation on the extent of the indemnification and shall be a part of the project specification or bid documents, if any; or
- the person indemnified by the contract gives a specific consideration to the indemnitor for the indemnification that shall be provided for in this contract....

The legislature here appears to have reasoned that an indemnity or hold harmless agreement for building construction/demolition has been fairly bargained if (1) the indemnitor's obligation has some monetary limit and (2) the transferor gives specific legal consideration to the transferee for the promise of protection. Again, notice that this entire provision applies only to construction/demolition projects, not to any bailment, equipment lease, sales or service contract, or any other contractual transfers for risk financing or risk control. Nor does this statute require that even every construction contract contain these provisions; the statute only demands that if a hold harmless or indemnity agreement is included, it shall contain the specified wording.

As another illustration, one state has enacted the following requirements with respect to all "construction contracts" that contain indemnity provisions:

Section 1. Construction contracts, plans and specifications which contain indemnification provisions shall include the following provisions:

The obligations of the contractor shall not extend to the liability of the architect or engineer, his agents or employees arising out of (1) the preparation or approval of maps, drawings, opinions, reports, surveys, change orders, designs, or specifications, or (2) the giving of or the failure to give directions or instructions by the architect, or engineer, his agents or employees, provided such giving or failure to give is the primary cause of the injury or damage.

Section 2. Any indemnification provision in a construction contract in conflict with the above provision shall be unlawful and unenforceable.

This statute does not require an indemnification provision in every construction contract; it does demand, however, that any party—public or private—excuse the contractor and its associates from indemnifying an architectural or engineering firm and its associates from claims arising out of specified situations. Notice that the precise wording of the required provision is specified for this type of contract but for no others.

MANAGEMENT OF NONINSURANCE CONTRACTUAL TRANSFERS

Faced with the variety of uses for noninsurance contractual

transfers for both risk control and risk financing, yet aware of the legal restrictions on their use, an organization's risk management professional must work to develop a consistent, feasible program for managing such contractual transfers—for becoming a transferee or transferor where appropriate, but always with a clear understanding of the nature, scope, and direction of each transfer. In some situations the organization will not seek to be a transferor or a transferee, but will strive to let the common or statutory law work as intended to apportion exposures to and the financial burden of losses. Consistent and effective control of noninsurance contractual transfers requires, first, careful attention to the factors affecting the appropriate uses of such transfers from the standpoint of both the organization and society, and second, a clearly written and widely disseminated organization policy with general administrative controls and specific control measures for managing noninsurance contractual transfers.

Factors Affecting Appropriate Use of Risk Transfers[6]

Many executives and even some risk management professionals tend to view noninsurance contractual transfers—especially those for risk financing—as a contest between themselves and their counterparts in the opposing organization: "Try to beat the opposition before they beat you." The contest can be a serious and important one: the use and wording of contract provisions, especially liability-related hold harmless agreements not connected with construction contracts, is largely unregulated. Many organizations concerned about their rising liability insurance costs often look upon waivers and hold harmless agreements as clever ways to reduce their liability exposures and loss costs, often at others' expense, and the drafting of provisions for shifting exposures and risk financing obligations can be a means to this end.

Yet the "goring of oxen"—safeguarding one's own while attacking others'—is neither the object of nor the proper perspective on drafting a transfer. In the perspective of sound risk management, the goal is to employ noninsurance contractual transfers for risk control and risk financing in ways that efficiently apportion loss exposures and the cost of losses for both the transferor, the transferee, and the economy as a whole. *Efficiency* here refers to both organizational and economy-wide cost of risk; so the most efficient transfer will lower the cost of risk for each contracting organization.

Because the drafting and use of noninsurance contractual transfers can become a game, a risk management professional should participate not as a contestant but as a referee, seeking fairness and mutual benefit for all participants. As such, this person should consider the following three factors that are particularly relevant to the fairness of the contract and the mutual benefit of the contracting parties: (1) the legal enforceability of these provisions, (2) the relative abilities of the parties to manage risk (*i.e.*, to keep losses from happening and to pay for those that do), and (3) the price or other legal consideration the transferor has explicitly or implicitly given to the transferee.

Enforceability Legal enforceability is one of the factors that determines the appropriate use of a contract—in fact, it can determine whether or not that contract can be used at all. As discussed under the heading, Limitations Under Common Law, a contract is not enforceable if it is found to be unconscionable and/or in violation of public policy or statutes. Second, it can be difficult to enforce a contract if the transfer provisions do not restate the law as it is understood by the parties to a contract. The result is that the transfer as interpreted by the courts often will differ from what the parties had in mind (see material under the heading, Restating Law). Third, as discussed under the heading, Purchase Order Agreements, attempts by the parties to a contract to rid themselves of the same or related exposures or financial burdens can make it difficult to enforce the contract because risks have been transferred and retransferred to the extent that it can be almost impossible to tell who has agreed to accept what.

Ability to Manage Risk Another factor to be considered in determining the appropriateness of a contract is the ability of the transferee to pay major losses when they occur. Has the transferee accepted in this and other contracts more responsibility than it can handle? Construction companies, in particular, are a common target for hold harmless clauses; yet, as a group, they are also subject to sudden and severe financial strains in the ordinary conduct of their own business. It can be questioned whether there is always wisdom in such extensive pyramiding of responsibilities.

As a general practice, transferees must receive enough benefits from their contracts to cover the obligations assumed under them. However, what are fair benefits for the transferee may not always be reasonable for the transferor to offer. Noninsurance transfer, therefore, may not be the most efficient method for handling a given exposure. Moreover, transfers may render impracticable, or even preclude, handling of an exposure in a more efficient way. Not only may the transferee be unable to pay for large losses, but it may also be unable to do anything effective about reducing the losses.

These limitations on the efficacy of transfer apply particularly when the negligence exposure is transferred. This may violate the fundamental general management principle of keeping responsibility and authority in the same hands. That is, when liability for the negligence of one's own employees is transferred, the incentive to control such negligence is divorced from the authority to do so: the transferor retains the authority, whereas the transferee acquires the responsibility and thus the incentive.

Price/Consideration Paid   The third factor that is related to the fairness of a contract is the price or other consideration given by the transferor to the transferee. With respect to cost, the greatest efficiency commonly will be achieved when the responsibility for the financing of losses and the authority for the practical control of the hazards involved are lodged with the same party. This proposition requires such arrangements as having manufacturers rather than distributors assume the full financial responsibility for losses arising from faulty products and for defective materials used in the manufacturing process. It also calls for manufacturers to assume full responsibility for claims arising out of statements in their advertising. But distributors should have full financial responsibility for claims arising out of their own statements in selling and advertising and for their own acts of assembling, disassembling, mixing, storing, and packing of products. Similarly, a contractor should have full financial responsibility for the activities of his employees and agents and the condition of the premises, equipment, and materials under his active control or supervision, or to which his expertise applies. On the other hand, his principal, the building owner, should have full responsibility for losses arising out of such items as his specifications and from any use the owner makes of the premises on which the contractor is working. Since these dividing lines between responsibilities are not clear in all instances, the underlying contract, in the interests of economy and the ease of enforcement, should be specific and carefully worded.

In determining who can best manage exposures and pay for losses, it is important that the contractual transfer not be considered by itself. How one transfer relates to another should be considered. This sometimes leads to exceptions to the general rule of merging responsibility and authority. Consider the responsibility of a single tenant in a large office building for damage to the entire building. The general rule would require this tenant to assume liability for all damage arising from the small portion of the premises it actively controls. But this rule would make it necessary for the tenant to buy insurance against its possible liability for severe fire damage to the building, duplicating the owner's insurance covering the same property.

Once a risk management professional or other executive has considered these factors in determining the fairness of a contract, risk management efforts should concentrate on establishing an effective program for controlling noninsurance transfers.

Elements of a Noninsurance Transfer Control Program[7]

The first and most essential step in establishing a sound program for controlling an organization's use of and liability exposures under the various noninsurance contractual transfers is to develop a consistent transfer strategy. This ensures that the organization (1) is a transferor when this role serves both the organization and the general economy, (2) is a transferee where this role is similarly appropriate, and (3) is neither a transferor nor transferee when neither role is appropriate.

Much of the material in this chapter has been directed at protecting an organization from inadvertently becoming a transferee. This protective stance can be regarded as the *defensive strategy* toward noninsurance contractual transfers—trying to avoid becoming the "victim" of such a transfer. A defensive strategy should reflect a proper understanding of the conditions under which it is dangerous for an organization, and thus economically inefficient for society to become a transferee. Such a strategy also may reflect a negative, distrustful attitude toward noninsurance transfers as a risk management technique; for some, this attitude may be justified by experience.

The opposite position, the *aggressive strategy* of trying to take advantage of other organizations by using economic power to impose transfers, also frequently is inappropriate for an organization and society; indeed, unwavering pursuit of an *aggressive strategy* is regarded by many risk management professionals as unethical. It is quite possible that an unduly aggressive strategy has prompted others to consistently follow a defensive strategy and for legislatures and the courts to look with suspicion upon transfers that are effected under such circumstances.

A more balanced and productive strategy is neither consistently defensive nor aggressive. Instead, it will be developed out of an examination of the implications of alternative noninsurance transfer arrangements for the contracting organizations and the economy. As a result, transfers are used only when they benefit all the contracting parties without, at the very least, harming the general economy. Therefore, a sound policy rests both on a good general administrative program and on specific controls to secure appropriate transfers while avoiding inappropriate ones.

General Administrative Controls Regardless of the size of the organization, it is important that there is an organized administrative program for controlling contractual transfers. The risk management professional needs to cultivate an understanding with everyone who is involved with contracts, including those who draw up as well as those who accept contracts. These people also should be encouraged to stay in close touch with the risk management department regularly and inform it of the status of all contracts.

The initial objective of these controls should be to give all contracts-related personnel a clear understanding of the exposure which may be hidden in the most "simple" contracts and the need to submit such documents for review by experienced personnel. In practically every organization a large number of the contracts will be more or less routine. The control system can be readily tailored to this situation. To illustrate, some weeks or months of careful scrutiny will probably indicate that purchase orders, service contracts, and various other more or less common contracts will contain only a standard indemnity agreement, if any. Once the responsible executives have discerned this pattern, appropriate decisions can be made about dealing with the liability involved; these contracts can then be left to periodic auditing.

The more dangerous areas relate to contracts that cannot be classified as "routine." With these contracts the proper guidance for all responsible personnel is of manifest importance. It cannot be stressed enough that risk transfer agreements are not easy to spot, are less easy to evaluate, and can be inordinately hazardous. The risk manager or other official with responsibility for controlling these transfers must be given an adequate opportunity to perform the difficult function of reading and interpreting each contract. Unlike routine contracts, these types of agreements need more attention than periodic auditing.

Even the most imaginative and thorough administrative program for controlling contractual transfers should be periodically reviewed. It is quite possible, for instance, that procedures that were "always used" can become unnecessarily cumbersome or not sufficiently precise. Similarly, the cost of administering the program must be known and watched. Control, which depends upon knowledge of the facts, is the key objective.

Specific Control Measures Having identified and evaluated the exposure in the contractual transfer provisions, the person responsible for risk management must make decisions about the treatment of these exposures or must present recommendations to management. If the risk manager can establish the proper authority, he or she should be able to review all contacts before they are finally executed. This provides a basic opportunity for rejecting inappropriate contracts. If this authority is not established, it is possible that a department head so preoccupied with the benefits of a contract for that department may not be sensitive to a provision such as "paragraph XXVII, Indemnity." Too often this apparently insignificant clause can adversely affect the financial stability of the entire organization.

Assuming that the risk manager does review a contract and recommends that it be endorsed, as it most often must be, the relevant considerations then generally are as follows:

- To what extent can the assumption of exposure be reduced?
- What exposure can the organization afford to assume?
- To what extent should contractually assumed exposures be transferred by insurance?
- Can specific provisions of contracts be deleted, particularly those that involve exposures that can be neither safely retained nor transferred?
- Is it possible to negotiate clearer contract language—especially to clarify the intentions of the parties on all points that seem likely to present problems?

Reduction of Exposures Assumed. Reducing the exposures assumed is a specific and a general matter. For example, both parties to a contract may wish to consider cutting the scope of the transfer clause in a *specific* contract to that which can be effectively and economically handled by the transferee's insurance. The contract drafters on both sides should clearly understand insurance, especially its applications and shortcomings in contractual liability coverage. In addition, they cannot overlook the uncertainty of a court's interpretation of this coverage and of the contractual transfer agreement itself.

In general terms, risk management professionals should be cautious about the number of contractual transfers that are simultaneously in effect. Numerous transfers have not only complicated business relationships but have raised costs as well. Wherever the use of a contractual transfer can be eliminated, the exposures must be assumed or otherwise managed.

Retention of Exposures. A given agreement or group of agreements may present exposures that the organization is willing to assume without insurance. These usually will involve only minor and remote hazards, free of any element of catastrophe. However, if the risk management professional determines that exposures introduced by the contract are dangerously severe, retention is likely to be unwise.

Transfer Through Insurance. For exposures to be covered by insurance the risk management professional must be as completely certain as reasonably possible of the available coverage. The insurance protection, if any, of the other contracting party also must be examined. There are not only questions of arranging needed coverage but also of obtaining from the insurer a clear explanation of its coverage and legal defense obligations.

Dealing With "Unmanageable" Provisions. Even the best use of loss reduction, retention, and insurance may fall short of helping to control contractual transfers. Rather than avoid such a contract, management can seek to remove some of the provisions. Examples might include eliminating transfers of liability related to acts of God, contingencies for which no insurance can be obtained, and sole negligence. The ability to make such changes depends on the bargaining strengths of the parties and how important their contractual relationship is.

Clarity of Contract Language. Wherever possible—and it may be possible more often than is at first supposed—the contract language should be revised for clarity. Definitions are very important, yet often omitted.

Fundamental Guidelines

The following are the most basic guidelines for the proper use by all parties of noninsurance contractual transfers for risk control or risk financing:

- *Make sure the indemnitor is financially able to stand behind its commitment.* In view of the outcome of some court decisions, it is almost imperative that this commitment be backed by insurance of at least $1,000,000 per occurrence. Department managers may complain that this coverage is excessive; the risk management professional should explain that every responsible organization should carry at least these limits.
- *Require a certificate of insurance for contractual liability coverage before contract operations begin.* The certificate should clearly state that the insurer must provide at least 30 days' notice of cancellation or of material change in coverage.
- *Be named as an additional insured in addition to obtaining a waiver of subrogation.* Although being added as an additional insured can pose some problems—such as an obligation to pay premiums or to comply with certain policy conditions after the loss, the advantages far outweigh the disadvantages.
- *Avoid being too severe.* If a contractual transfer is too extreme, it may be construed by the courts as invalid because it is unconscionable or contrary to public policy. The farther apart the two parties are in their bargaining power and knowledge of the terms of the contract, the more chance there is of an unenforceable agreement.

- *Avoid ambiguity.* The courts do not favor agreements that indemnify an individual or organization against the consequences of its own negligence or intentional wrongdoing. If the contract language is ambiguous, courts generally construe an indemnity agreement to make it consistent with common law doctrine and public policy. Generally this will mean that a person or organization is indemnified for liability even if it was only passively negligent in causing loss or injury.
- *Become more actively involved in legislation.* Many of the present statutes limiting noninsurance indemnification are the products of lobbying efforts by special interest groups. Risk management professionals have an obligation to their organizations and the public to present at least equal reasons for laws that can benefit an organization and the economy.

SUMMARY

Two or more individuals or organizations may contract with one another to shift either loss exposures or the financial burden of actual losses. A contract provision shifting loss exposures obligates the transferee to act instead of or on behalf of a transferor; no payment is required. This arrangement achieves risk control for the transferor because there is no longer any possibility of loss from a transferred exposure—even if the transferee should become bankrupt. In contrast, a contract provision for risk financing obligates the transferee to pay losses to or on behalf of the transferor, thus providing the transferor with protection only when the transferee is able and willing to provide the promised funds. For both transfers to be effective, they must be enforceable in the courts.

Contractual transfers for risk control are achieved through such mechanisms as incorporation, leases, subcontracts, surety agreements, and waivers. All contractual transfers for risk financing can be described as indemnity agreements, but agreements that pertain to the transferor's liability claims are known as hold harmless agreements. One useful way of classifying indemnity agreements is in terms of the transactions with which they are associated—such as construction agreements, purchase order agreements, leases of premises and equipments, bailment contracts, and sale and service agreements. In addition, hold harmless agreements may be further classified as those that (1) restate the law, (2) obligate the transferee to finance liability claims involving the joint fault of the transferor and the transferee, (3) require the transferee to respond even to claims alleging the transferor's sole fault, and (4) require the transferee to pay all the transferor's liability losses of any sort.

Organizations and individuals have a general right, frequently described as the freedom of contract, to transfer exposures and the financial burden of actual losses as they wish, provided that these transfers violate no rights of the contracting parties or society. Freedom of contract, however, is limited by common law and statutes. Thus, on the basis of common law, any attempted risk control or risk financing transfer that is undisclosed to the transferee or is improperly obtained through coercion or deception is likely to be rejected. Similarly, courts generally refuse to enforce attempted transfers that would be contrary to the public interest on the basis that these transfers contravene public policy. Statutes in about half the states further limit freedom of contract by (1) entirely prohibiting certain transfers, (2) prohibiting specified wording in particular types of transfers, or (3) mandating a particular wording of any transfer agreement the parties may chose to include in their contract.

The managers of an organization's noninsurance contractual transfers should allocate exposures to loss and financial burdens of actual losses in ways that minimize the cost of risk for all concerned, and that respect all parties' rights and responsibilities. To achieve this objective, managers should draft, approve, and monitor all contracts with the following guidelines in mind:

- The transfer is fairly bargained and fully understood by all contracting parties, that is, the allocation of responsibilities between transferees and transferors should be as exhaustive and unambiguous as possible.
- The transfer agreement deals explicitly with all aspects of the loss exposure or of the actual losses (including all the property, net income, liability, and personnel losses that can stem from any particular accident).
- The agreement details or gives procedures for how it will be implemented.
- Exposures and losses should be transferred on a basis that is at least as efficient (that is, as inexpensive or as profitable) as other equally reliable risk management techniques.
- Transferees should be able and willing to meet their risk control and risk financing obligations.
- Each transferee should have significant ability and authority to apply risk control to the losses for which it is financially responsible.

- The price or other legal consideration a transferor gives a transferee should make the transfer financially attractive to both parties.
- The parties anticipate and make provisions for changes in the nature of their activities, and the resulting impact of these changes on their risk transfer agreement, over the life of the contract.

Chapter Notes

1. For documentation of the historical aspects of this discussion see *Cambridge Economic History of Europe* (London: Cambridge University Press, 1977), vol. 5: *The Economic Organization of Early Modern Europe*, ed. E. E. Richard and C. H. Wilson, pp. 439–447.

2. The material under this heading is derived from two sources. The first is G. W. Crist, Jr., *Corporate Suretyship*, 2nd ed. (New York: McGraw-Hill Book Company, 1950), pp. 3–8. The second is Robert I. Mehr and Bob A. Hedges, *Risk Management: Concepts and Applications* (Homewood, IL: Richard D. Irwin, Inc., 1974), pp. 142–144.

3. The specimen contract provisions cited under this heading are drawn or adapted from Georgia Chapter of the Society of Chartered Property Casualty Underwriters, *The Hold Harmless Agreement*, 3rd ed. (Cincinnati, OH: The National Underwriter Company, 1977), pp. 57–103 or Robert L. Mehr and Bob A. Hedges, *Risk Management: Concepts and Applications*, pp. 136–145.

4. The discussion under this heading is drawn substantially from Robert I. Mehr and Bob A. Hedges, *Risk Management: Concepts and Applications*, pp. 138–140.

5. The term juridical risk in a risk management context appears to have originated in Robert I. Mehr and Bob A. Hedges, *Risk Management in the Business Enterprise* (Homewood, IL: Richard D. Irwin, Inc., 1963), pp. 439–444.

6. Portions of the discussion under this heading are reproduced with permission from Robert I. Mehr and Bob A. Hedges, *Risk Management: Concepts and Applications*, pp. 147–150, 414–416.

7. The material under this heading is reproduced with permission from two sources. The first is Georgia Chapter of the Society of Chartered Property and Casualty Underwriters, *The Hold Harmless Agreement*, pp. 105–115. The second is Alan M. Pearce, "Legal Prohibitions Against Use of Hold Harmless Agreements," *Risk Management*, April 1977, pp. 32–34, 36, 38.

CHAPTER 10

Financing Employee Benefits

INTRODUCTION

Financing employee benefits—arranging the sources and directing and controlling the uses of the funds an organization devotes to meeting its employees' personnel loss exposures—illustrates two of the basic themes that unite an organization's risk financing with its general management. The first is that sound risk financing, like all good management, strives to make the best use of funds in meeting organizational objectives. The second is that conflicting goals (here, the somewhat divergent goals of an organization and of its employees in designing and using employee benefit plans) require optimizing, rather than maximizing, managerial decisions.

Employee benefit plans focus on helping an organization's employees finance recovery from their personal and family losses from death, disability, retirement, and unemployment (and not the organization's own exposures to the loss of the services of key personnel). Employee benefit plans also serve an organization's need to attract and hold valuable employees who are satisfied with their overall compensation (wages plus benefits) and thus remain productive. Nonetheless, conflicts between employees' and the organization's goals can arise: for example, when employees' wishes for greater protection or other benefits become too costly for the organization, thus depriving it of funds which might be used for other purposes. As another illustration of potential goal conflict, financing employee benefits may impose on the organization financial uncertainties which restrict its capacity to undertake potentially profitable or otherwise beneficial projects. Thus, employees' needs for protection must be balanced against the employer's other needs for funds. Decisions about employee benefits financing that achieve this balance are likely to be optimizing, not maximizing, decisions because both the employees and the organization's goals will be partially, not fully, met.

Once these divergent needs have been recognized and expressed as projected costs, designing employee benefit plans provides many opportunities for an organization to make the best feasible use of the funds it does devote to employee benefits. These opportunities arise from the fact that employee benefit costs, in the aggregate over the long run, are among the most predictable of risk financing costs. Even though individual disabilities or deaths may be difficult to predict, employee benefit plans automatically generate a pooling of the personnel loss experience of an organization's workforce. Therefore, the cash outflows needed to pay for these losses can be projected with considerable accuracy. Consequently, the sources of these funds, such as insurance or the investments of a funded trust, also can be planned with considerable precision so that cash availabilities can be matched with cash needs. Here, typically more than elsewhere, the risk management professional involved in employee benefits design and administration can apply the basic principles of financial and general management that "cash flows count" and "cash availabilities should match cash needs."

Because financing employee benefits is quite comparable to other financial management decisions outside the traditional scope of risk management, not all risk management professionals yet have direct responsibility for employee benefit financing. However, the trend toward integration of risk financing with general managerial finance and of risk management with overall organization management suggests that all risk management professionals should have a basic understanding of employee benefit financing and should at least recognize how an organization's use of funds to finance employee benefits can affect its overall sources and uses of funds for any purpose, including other risk financing needs.

This chapter emphasizes the planning and design of employee benefits and the related financing techniques. To better enable the risk management professional to participate in this planning and design, this chapter examines (1) such fundamental concepts as employers' reasons for establishing employee benefit plans and the relative strengths and weaknesses of group insurance and trust fund mechanisms for accumulating and disbursing funds for employee benefits; (2) the factors that need to be considered in designing employee benefit plans and funding mechanisms in ways which best balance employees' needs with employers' objectives; and (3) how employee benefit funding mechanisms can be arranged so that the timing of cash outflows for benefits tends to match cash availabilities for these needs.

FUNDAMENTAL CONCEPTS IN EMPLOYEE BENEFIT PLANNING[1]

Employee benefits are a rapidly growing and increasingly important form of employee compensation. Employers and unions have increased and liberalized the coverage and amounts of benefits under what might be called the "traditional" forms of employee benefits, while at the same time they are adding new forms of benefits. The result is that the number, complexity, and cost of employee benefits are constantly increasing. On the other hand, there has been an important trend in recent years toward attempting to contain increasing costs, particularly in the medical expense area. This has led to increased emphasis on planning and achieving cost-effective benefits. Further, the loss of tax revenue due to the tax-favored status of many employee benefits has caused the taxing authorities at the federal level to reconsider some of the tax advantages granted to certain employee benefits.

Definitions of Employee Benefits

This seems like a comparatively simple question. Most people who use the term *employee benefits* probably have a general idea of what they mean by it. And yet there are variations among organizations and authors in the field as to what they include as employee benefits.

Broad Approach Some sources take a broad approach to the definition of employee benefits and include virtually any form of compensation other than direct wages. For example, the Chamber of Commerce of the United States in its annual surveys of employee benefits includes the kinds of nonwage payments and benefits shown in Exhibit 10-1 in its overall category of "employee benefits." This table shows that employee benefits, defined in this fashion, represent a large portion of the total compensation costs of employers. This broad kind of definition is also frequently used by those concerned with the personnel management function in business.[2]

The percentage of payroll represented by these employee benefits varied widely among the 1,454 reporting companies in the survey, ranging from less than 18 percent to over 65 percent of payroll. So it appears that individual companies may follow quite different strategies with respect to the benefits component of their total compensation package. The average percentages also varied by industry, and, as

Exhibit 10-1

Employee Benefits as Percentages of Payroll for 1,454 Reporting Employers in 1983 by Type of Benefit*

I. Employer's share of legally required payments:		
A. Old-Age, Survivors, Disability, and		
Health Insurance (OASDHI)	6.3%	
B. Unemployment compensation	1.4	
C. Worker's compensation	1.2	
D. Compulsory temporary nonoccupational disability		
insurance and other special plans	0.1	
Total		9.0%
II. Employer's share of pension and other agreed-upon payments:		
A. Pensions	5.0%	
B. Life insurance premiums, death benefits, and medical		
care expenses	7.0	
C. Short-term disability	0.3	
D. Salary continuation or long-term disability	0.3	
E. Dental insurance premiums	0.5	
F. Miscellaneous payments to employees	0.5	
Total		13.6%
III. Payments for nonproduction time while on the job		
(e.g., rest periods, lunch periods, wash-up time, etc.)		2.3%
IV. Payments for time not worked (e.g., paid sick leave, vacations,		
holidays, voting time, National Guard duty, jury and witness duty,		
time off for personal reasons, etc.)		9.4%
V. Other items:		
A. Profit-sharing payments	1.0%	
B. Contributions to employee thrift plans	0.5	
C. Special bonuses and awards	0.3	
D. Employee education expenditures, special wage		
payments, etc.	0.5	
Total		2.3%
Total Employee Benefit Payments as a Percentage of Payroll		36.6%
Summary of Employee Benefits in survey as:		
Percentage of payroll (as shown above)		36.6%
Cost per payroll hour		$3.69 per hour
Cost per hour per employee		$7,582 per hour

* Reprinted with permission from Chamber of Commerce of the United States, *Employee Benefits 1983* (Washington, DC 1984).

might be expected, larger companies tended to pay higher benefits than smaller ones.

At one time employee benefits were popularly referred to as "fringe benefits," and this term is still used today, even in the Internal Revenue Code. However, as Exhibit 10-1 demonstrates, these benefits have grown to the point where they are far more than "fringes." That term really has become a misnomer when applied to them. In fact, employee benefits have become so important to most employers, both as a cost of doing business and as part of their total compensation package, that careful planning and handling of these benefits have become vital to the employer's success.

Narrower View Other observers take a more narrow view in defining employee benefits. An example is the following definition used by the Social Security Administration in its periodic studies of employee benefit plans:

> An "employee-benefit plan," as defined here, is any type of plan sponsored or initiated unilaterally or jointly by employers or employees and providing benefits that stem from the employment relationship and that are not underwritten or paid directly by government (Federal, State, or local). In general, the intent is to include plans that provide in an orderly predetermined fashion for (1) income maintenance during periods when regular earnings are cut off because of death, accident, sickness, retirement, or unemployment and (2) benefits to meet medical expenses associated with illness or injury.[3]

This definition focuses on plans designed to maintain an employee's income in the face of certain personal losses, as well as on plans providing benefits for medical expenses incurred by employees and the dependents.

Employee Benefits as Part of the Total Compensation Package Another way to view employee benefits is to consider them as an important part of an employer's total compensation package for employees. This *total compensation package* represents all the ways, direct and indirect, that an employer uses to remunerate or benefit its employees. Such a package normally consists of a variety of elements that have different characteristics and purposes. These elements can be classified in various ways; one possible system is shown in Exhibit 10-2, which should be reviewed at this point.

In a very broad sense, all these possible elements of an employer's total compensation system could be considered employee benefits in that they benefit employees. In defining the scope of employee benefits, however, we generally cover only those plans listed as "Indirect and Deferred Compensation Plans" in Exhibit 10-2. The plans included in this group are more extensive than the narrow definition given above, but they are less extensive than the Chamber of Commerce's broader definition. As such, these employee benefits seem to represent a logical grouping of most of the plans and programs that are included whenever employee benefits are discussed as part of a total compensation package. For example, in its survey of "How Major Industrial Corporations View Employee Benefit Programs," *Fortune* showed the coverages and benefits then provided by the top 500 and the second 500 U.S. industrial corporations (the *Fortune* 1,000 Corporations). See Exhibit 10-3. While these data are now somewhat dated, they are

Exhibit 10-2
Elements of Total Employee Compensation

I. *Base Compensation:* This consists of direct cash wage or salary payments. It is the amount of the employee's regular wage or salary and is the core of any compensation system.

II. *Personnel Practices and Other Employee Payments Related to Base Compensation, including:*
   A. vacation time,
   B. paid holidays,
   C. paid funeral leave,
   D. tuition refund plans for employees (and their dependents),
   E. moving allowances,
   F. recreation plans,
   G. time off for personal reasons,
   H. employer paid physical examinations, and like benefits.

III. *Current Incentive Compensation:*
   A. annual bonuses,
   B. current profit-sharing payments in cash, company stock, or both, and
   C. similar current compensation based on individual or company performance.

IV. *Indirect and Deferred Compensation Plans:* This category encompasses a diverse group of plans; however, they generally can be characterized as plans providing benefits to employees or their dependents in the event of certain *personal* losses (that is, security-type plans), as plans for *deferring compensation or benefits into the future,* as plans involving certain tax advantages for the covered employees, as capital accumulation plans, or as some *combination of these ideas.* They generally do not provide currently available compensation for employees. However, some of these plans may overlap to some degree into one or more of the other categories of compensation given above. For example, employee stock plans also can be regarded as incentive compensation plans in the sense that they give eligible employees a direct ownership stake in the future success of the corporation.

These indirect and deferred compensation plans can be classified as follows:
A. Life and accident insurance coverages:
   1. group term life insurance,
   2. survivor income benefits,
   3. postretirement death benefits,
   4. group whole life insurance,
   5. accidental death and dismemberment insurance,
   6. travel accident insurance,
   7. split dollar life insurance,
   8. wholesale life insurance,
   9. salary savings life insurance, and
   10. other death benefits.
B. Medical expense benefits:
   1. "basic" hospital, surgical, and regular medical coverages,
   2. major medical and comprehensive medical expense coverages,
   3. dental expense benefits,
   4. health maintenance organization (HMO) coverage,
   5. prescription drugs, and
   6. other medical expense benefits.

continued on next page

C. Disability income benefits:
   1. short-term disability benefits,
   2. long-term disability benefits,
   3. franchise health insurance, and
   4. other disability benefits.
D. Retirement programs:
   1. pension plans,
   2. deferred profit-sharing plans,
   3. employee thrift/savings plans,
   4. cash or deferred arrangements (Section 401(k) plans),
   5. nonqualified deferred compensation,
   6. postemployment contracts,
   7. retirement plans for the self-employed (HR-10 plans),
   8. individual retirement accounts and annuities (IRA plans),
   9. simplified employee pension (SEP) plans,
   10. tax-sheltered annuities,
   11. preretirement counseling, and
   12. continuation of other employee benefits into retirement.
E. Stock plans:
   1. stock purchase plans,
   2. incentive stock options,
   3. nonqualified stock options,
   4. restricted stock plans,
   5. nonqualified stock bonus plans,
   6. employee stock ownership plans (ESOPs and PAYSOPs), and
   7. other stock and performance plans.
F. Property and liability insurance coverages:
   1. workers' compensation, and
   2. "collectively merchandised" personal property and liability insurance coverages.
G. Unemployment plans
H. Other benefit plans:
   1. personal financial counseling,
   2. prepaid legal service plans, and
   3. tax-sheltered investment for executives.

V. *Executive Perquisites,* that is, special benefits for executives such as:
A. supplemental retirement income (ERISA excess plans),
B. supplemental executive retirement plans (SERPs),
C. supplemental death and/or medical benefits,
D. company cars,
E. executive dining room,
F. club memberships,
G. physical examinations,
H. vacation expenses, and
I. company loans and similar special benefits.

included here to show the kinds of benefits that commonly are considered as employee benefits.

Reasons for Employee Benefit Plans

Given the growth in employee benefit plans, it is logical to ask why employers should want to establish such plans as a way of compensating their employees. What reasons encourage the establishment of

Exhibit 10-3

Extent of Various Employee Benefit Plans Among the Fortune 1,000 U.S. Industrial Corporations*

Type of Benefit	Percentage of Top 500 Firms Providing the Benefit[1]	Percentage of Second 500 Firms Providing the Benefit[1]
Group term life insurance	96%	91%
Survivor income	23	17
Group whole life	7	19
Group accidental death and dismemberment	56	64
Group travel accident	76	69
"Basic" group hospital, surgical and regular medical	95	97
Group major medical	99	99
Prescription drugs	62	64
Vision care	3	8
Group dental	20	18
Short-term disability income	87	77
Long-term disability income	86	84
Pension plan	96	91
Profit-sharing	29	36
Thrift/savings program	38	23
Company stock purchase	45	37
Group automobile	11	4
Group homeowner's	3	1
Personal financial counseling for executives	29	11
Group legal	—	1

[1] There were 245 of the top companies included in the Survey of which 157 (64%) responded and 299 of the second 500 companies, of which 180 (60%) responded.

*Reprinted with permission from Fortune, *How Major Industrial Corporations View Employee Benefit Programs* (New York: Fortune Market Research, 1975).

these plans rather than, say, simply giving employees larger cash wages instead? The reasons are generally as follows:

1. concern for employees' welfare,
2. improved corporate efficiency,
3. attracting and holding capable employees,
4. favorable tax laws,
5. demands in labor negotiations,
6. social and indirect governmental pressures, and
7. inherent advantages of group insurance.

Concern for Employees' Welfare Most employers are truly concerned for the welfare of their employees. While they may be showing an element of paternalism, employers also demonstrate a social consciousness in this regard.

Further, as a practical matter, when an employee dies, becomes disabled, has heavy medical expenses, or retires without adequate resources, either the employer or the unfortunate employee's fellow workers often have been more or less expected to "do something" for the employee in the absence of a formal benefit program. Prior to the existence of employee benefit plans, "doing something" in many cases involved "passing the hat" among other employees or putting pressure on the employer. But these approaches often were uncertain, inefficient, time-consuming, and perhaps inequitable. A formalized employee benefit program can meet employee losses in a much more consistent, certain, efficient, and fair way.

Improved Corporate Efficiency As a practical matter, it is virtually impossible to show the precise dollars-and-cents bottom-line results of an employee benefit program, of a particular proposed benefit, or of an increase in benefits. Nevertheless, most authorities believe that efficiency and business profits are enhanced in a number of ways by the adoption of a sound employee benefit program.

Morale. First, employee morale should be improved by the existence of a well-planned and effectively communicated employee benefit program. Employees may feel the employer "cares" about them. In any event, such a program *relieves employees of the worry and fear* they or their families may have over the possibly devastating financial effects of certain personal losses they may suffer. Employer-provided benefits also relieve employees—at least to some extent—of having to pay for their own insurance out of their after-tax paychecks. At the very least, the employer avoids the potentially poor morale among employees that would result from not having an adequate benefit program.

Chance for Promotion. Employee benefits, particularly retirement plans, can also serve the important management function of *keeping channels of promotion open.* Benefits can be used to facilitate the systematic retirement of older employees, particularly executive personnel, thereby opening up opportunities for able, younger employees to move ahead in the firm. Otherwise, such younger employees may leave the firm for better opportunities elsewhere.

Facilitate Work Force Reduction. In a somewhat related manner, retirement plans, perhaps supplemented in various ways, can be used to *encourage voluntary early retirements when a reduction in work force is necessary.* Such an approach may avoid or reduce the necessity of laying off younger workers who may have less seniority or service with the employer. Such plans might also provide a way to *solve some management-level personnel problems* through retirement or early retirement in a graceful and acceptable manner.

Employee Identification with Profits. Some types of employee benefits, such as deferred profit-sharing plans and employee stock plans, can *give employees in general an identification with, and an interest in, the efficiency and profits of the firm.* In addition, certain selective plans designed for those persons who are expected to have the greatest personal impact on corporate profits are intended to stimulate improved corporate bottom-line results.

Attracting and Holding Capable Employees Improving the quality of personnel is a classic reason for adopting and improving employee benefits, one that is closely related to improving corporate efficiency. When competing for employees in a labor market in which most employers have a reasonable or even attractive employee benefit program, the firm without such benefits or with an inadequate benefit program may find itself at a competitive disadvantage in recruiting and retaining the employees it wants.

An employee benefit program may really represent more of a "maintenance factor" in motivating employees than a positive inducement to join or to stay with an employer. In other words, the absence of an adequate benefit program may cause employee dissatisfaction, but, on the other hand, the presence of such a program may not be a strong motivator for better employee productivity and overall performance. This, however, is a subjective issue. The effects of an employee benefit program on employees probably depend in large measure on the kind of benefit involved; on how well it is communicated to and understood by employees; and on the ages, positions, attitudes, and other personal characteristics of the employees involved.

How well a firm's employee benefit program is *communicated* to employees has a considerable bearing on its impact on their morale and productivity. Furthermore, as employee benefits assume a larger relative position in a firm's total compensation package, their overall impact on employee recruitment, retention, attitudes, and productivity probably increases.

Favorable Tax Laws A number of tax advantages have been permitted as a matter of public policy to apply to employee benefit plans and to their participants. This relatively favorable tax treatment has become an important reason for employers to provide such benefits for their employees rather than simply paying them higher wages. Employee benefits, in effect, provide greater after-tax value to employees than a wage or salary increase, assuming the employees need and want the benefits. This sort of benefit is particularly valuable to the higher paid, and hence more highly taxed, managerial and executive personnel who are often the very ones making the decisions for a company regarding its employee benefit program.

As far as a corporate employer is concerned, its contributions to employee benefit plans normally are deductible for federal income tax purposes as a business expense.[4] In effect, a corporate employer in the 46 percent corporate income tax bracket saves about one-half of its tax-deductible contributions to employee benefit plans because it reduces its corporate income taxes. For example, the after-tax cost to a corporation of annual tax-deductible contributions to employee benefit plans of $1,000,000 is about $540,000 [$1,000,000 before-tax cost—($1,000,000×the .46 top corporate tax rate)=$540,000]. Yet the same can be said for a straight wage or salary increase, which is also income tax deductible for the corporation.

What, then, makes employee benefits more attractive than a simple wage or salary increase from a tax standpoint? The answer lies in the favorable tax treatment of employee benefits to the covered employees. This combination of tax-deductible contributions by the employer, along with the favorable tax treatment to the covered employees, gives employee benefits their tax attractiveness relative to direct wage or salary increases.

There are several possible kinds of tax advantages to covered employees, depending on the employee benefit involved. Some employee benefits provide employees with an economic benefit (such as limited group term life insurance and medical expense coverage) for which the employee is not taxed at all. Assume, for example, the value of employer-provided group term life insurance for an employee is $500. The value of this insurance coverage is not taxable income to the employee, unless the face amount exceeds $50,000. If the covered employee is in a 25-percent personal income tax bracket, the employer would have to pay him or her approximately $667 more in salary for the employee to have the same $500 after taxes [$667—($667×.25)] with which to buy life insurance protection for himself or herself and his or her family.[5]

Other employee benefits, such as "qualified" pension or profit-sharing plans, provide income that will ultimately be taxable to the employee or his or her dependents. Yet the taxable income is deferred to some future time (such as retirement), when presumably the employee's personal income tax bracket will be lower. In the meantime, the employer's contributions to the plan and the plan's investment earnings are not currently taxed as income to the covered employees.

Some employee benefits may also provide capital gains and certain income averaging advantages. This may be true for "qualified" retirement plan benefits payable in a lump sum.

Demands in Labor Negotiations Since employee benefits are within the scope of collective bargaining, the employer is legally obligated to bargain in good faith with the union over such demands, if presented. Of course, the employer does not have to grant the union's demands, but labor negotiations frequently result in compromises leading to granting at least some of a union's demands. Thus, labor union pressure in collective bargaining negotiations must be counted as an important reason for the establishment or improvement of employee benefit plans.

Social and Indirect Governmental Pressures Subtle social pressures in employers' communities can compel them to do something to take care of their employees when they suffer certain personal losses or become too old to work. At least in some degree, employers may adopt employee benefit plans in the spirit of meeting social responsibilities as good corporate citizens. Further, some employers may feel that if they do not provide adequate employee benefits for their employees, the government will step into the breach with government or social insurance programs.

Inherent Advantages of Group Insurance Employee benefits are frequently provided through group insurance or some similar group plan. Certain cost savings and other advantages usually arise from providing coverage under a group plan, as compared with buying similar coverage individually. These inherent advantages should therefore be counted as a motivation for providing group insurance coverages to employees as employee benefits.

Group Insurance Technique for Providing Employee Benefits

Let's take a closer look at the inherent advantages of the group insurance technique.

Group insurance is difficult to define. But it can be viewed as an arrangement for insuring a group of persons under a single contract made by an insurer or by another carrier with an entity, such as an employer, that acts as the policyholder. Thus the group is the essential unit for insurance purposes rather than any individual in the group. In most cases, the individuals in the group are insured without requiring any of the individual evidence of insurability that would normally be required in underwriting individual insurance policies.

Basic Characteristics of Group Selection The group itself, rather than the individuals within the group, is underwritten in group insurance. This arrangement is possible because certain basic characteristics of the group insurance technique make group selection, rather than individual selection, feasible. These characteristics apply primarily to group life and health insurance, although other employee benefits, such as group annuities (pensions), are also provided through the group mechanism. These characteristics are:

1. eligible groups,
2. minimum number of persons,
3. minimum proportion of the insured group,
4. eligibility requirements for covered persons,
5. employer sharing of cost (normally),
6. efficiency of administration, and
7. maximum limits on any one life.

Eligible Groups. Not all groups are acceptable for group underwriting. Theoretically, the most desirable groups have the following fundamental characteristics.

First, the group should be formed for a purpose other than obtaining low-cost, nonindividually underwritten group insurance. In other words, *obtaining group insurance should be incidental to the major purpose of the group.* If insurance is not incidental, then those joining the group could possibly create an adverse selection situation against the insurance plan. *Adverse selection* is the tendency of those most exposed to a potential loss to attempt to secure insurance against the loss. Due to human nature, adverse selection is probably always present in insurance plans to at least some degree, but insurers and other insuring organizations seek to minimize its effect by following certain principles of group selection.[6] An employer-employee group (the employees of a single employer) clearly exists for a purpose other than obtaining group insurance. Obtaining group insurance is normally just an incidental part of securing employment in such a group.

Second, there should ideally be a constant flow of lives through the group. In this way, younger persons come into the group while older lives leave it, thus keeping the rates of mortality and morbidity for the group as a whole more or less constant. Again, the employer-employee type group meets this criterion well because younger workers are constantly being hired while older workers retire.[7]

Third, membership or participation in certain groups may indirectly mean that the members have to have certain health standards. Active employees of an employer, for example, must of necessity be healthy enough to be actively on the job when their group insurance commences.

Actually, the groups that can be covered by group insurance are determined mainly by state insurance laws and insurance company underwriting rules and practices. The acceptable groups have expanded over the years. Perhaps the most desirable kind of eligible group is the employer-employee group. Yet other eligible groups include multiple-employer groups, labor union groups, creditor-debtor groups, and a variety of miscellaneous kinds of groups (such as members of professional associations, fraternal groups, college alumni societies, and the like).

Minimum Number of Persons. Frequently, a minimum number of lives must be in the group for the plan to be written as group insurance. The most common minimum size requirement in group life and health insurance probably is ten lives, although as few as two or three persons may be written under certain conditions.

The two basic reasons for a minimum size requirement are:

1. to reduce the likelihood that impaired (unhealthy) lives will form a disproportionately large part of the group (that is, to avoid adverse selection) and
2. to spread the fixed expenses of the insurance plan over more lives and thus reduce administrative costs per insured life.

A common misconception is that a minimum size requirement in group insurance exists to enable an insurer to cover a large enough number of lives in each group so that the insurer can predict a particular group's own loss experience on the basis of the law of large numbers and then charge the group a premium based on its own losses. This idea is not correct. While the loss portion of the premium for larger groups, say 500 or more lives, may be based entirely on the group's own loss experience, and many other groups are experience-rated to some extent, the actual minimum size requirement in group insurance of, say, 10 or fewer lives is far too small to assure than the law of large numbers would operate with *each* group. Rather, the basic reasons for the minimum size requirement are to reduce adverse selection and to control administrative costs as explained above.

Minimum Proportion of the Group Insured. This is commonly called a *participation requirement.* In group life and health insurance plans, when the covered employees pay part of the cost (contributory plans), it is usually required that at least 75 percent of the eligible employees elect to participate in the plan. Where the employer pays the entire cost of the group insurance (contributory plans,) 100 percent participation by the eligible employees is normally required. The reasons for a participation requirement in group insurance are essentially the same as those for a minimum size group—to avoid adverse selection and to spread fixed expenses.

Automatic Determination of Benefits. The benefit amounts in group insurance often must either be the same for all covered persons or be determined automatically on some basis that precludes individual selection by covered persons or by their employers. Benefits may be based on salary, position, service, or some combination of these factors. The reason again is to avoid adverse selection. In the absence of such automatic determination, impaired lives in the group may tend to select larger amounts of benefits, while the healthier lives probably will not be so inclined.

In recent years, however, there has been a distinct tendency to allow employees more latitude of choice with respect to their benefits and benefit amounts under employee benefit plans. Plans that allow employees to elect optional, additional amounts of life insurance under a group life plan are an example. Furthermore, the adoption of "cafeteria" compensation plans, or flexible benefits, in which the essence of the plan is to allow employees considerable choice in selecting their own benefit programs, clearly compromises this characteristic to some degree. Cafeteria plans, therefore, must be concerned with the resulting adverse selection, and they do employ certain limits and devices to attempt to deal with it.

Eligibility Requirements for Covered Persons. In group plans, employees must meet certain eligibility requirements for coverage. For example, in contributory plans employees must enroll in the group plan within a certain period (such as 31 days) after becoming eligible, or else they must show evidence of individual insurability if they join at a later time (other than during certain specified open enrollment periods in some cases). Also, group plans normally require covered persons to be active, full-time employees when their coverage commences. Such eligibility requirements are aimed at avoiding adverse selection. They also seek to avoid the administrative expense of covering short-term or transitory employees.

Employer Sharing of Cost. Group insurance written on employer-employee groups usually involves some contribution to the premium by the employer. Of course, in noncontributory plans the employer pays the entire cost. By sharing at least some of the cost, the employer can make the group coverage attractive to most employees, including the younger, healthier lives who otherwise might be able to purchase individual insurance at lower rates. Some employer-employee group plans, however, are written on an employee-pay-all basis or with a layer of benefits on an employee-pay-all basis.

Efficiency of Administration. Group insurance should have a centralized, efficient administrative unit to handle plan administration and to keep administrative expenses down. In employer-employee groups, employers assist insurers or other carriers in administering plans, and, in some cases usually involving larger groups, they handle almost all plan administration, including the paying of claims. The employer is almost the ideal administrative unit because it already maintains payroll and other employee records needed for group insurance purposes.

Maximum Limits on Any One Life. Depending on the size of the group, there are maximum limits placed on the amount of group life, accident, and disability income insurance on any one life without showing individual evidence of insurability. This proviso helps avoid a disproportionate amount of insurance on any one impaired life in the group.

Advantages of the Group Insurance Technique Certain advantages are inherent in the group insurance technique:

1. low cost,
2. automatic coverage of impaired lives,
3. flexible and advanced benefits, and
4. ease and convenience of purchase.

Low Cost. Perhaps foremost among the advantages of the group technique is a generally *lower cost per unit of protection* compared with individually sold insurance. This cost advantage arises primarily from the lower administrative and servicing costs per unit of protection involved in selling, installing, and servicing one plan covering many lives as opposed to many individual policies.

The employer also performs at least some, and in some cases most, of the administration of a group plan and thus absorbs this part of the administrative expenses of the plan. Of course, this part of the arrangement may represent a hidden cost to the employer. But to the extent that the employer is already set up to handle these administrative functions (such as through its existing payroll records), greater efficiency and lower total costs may result.

Further, as far as the covered employees are concerned, the employer's contribution in a contributory plan, or its total financing in a noncontributory plan, reduces or eliminates the cost of the plan to them. Yet the employer must bear the cost.

The group insurance technique, however, does not necessarily reduce the loss or claim cost per unit of protection. In fact, losses or benefits per unit of protection may be somewhat higher under group plans, as compared with individual policies, because the opportunity to underwrite (select) individuals is generally absent in group insurance.

On the other hand, those groups that have better-than-average claims or loss experience and that are also large enough so that their individual claim or loss experience counts significantly in determining their final premiums will have lower group plan benefit costs than other less desirable groups. The reason is that the claim or loss experience of a particular group may be considered in determining the final cost of group protection for the group through the technique of experience rating.

Automatic Coverage of Impaired Lives. Some persons turn out to be uninsurable when they have to show evidence of individual insurability in the process of purchasing coverage on an individual basis (like life and health insurance, for example). Normally such people are automatically covered by group insurance up to the plan's regular limits, even though they could not obtain individual insurance at any price or only on a "substandard" basis.[8] Group coverage can therefore be a substantial advantage for such persons. They also have the right to convert their group term life insurance to individual permanent life insurance contracts, without showing individual evidence of insurability, upon termination of employment. Many times they can also similarly convert group medical expense insurance upon termination. These conversion privileges can also be very valuable to impaired lives when they leave the insured group.

Flexible and Advanced Benefits. Group insurance can often be designed to fit the specific needs and circumstances of particular groups, so more flexible, innovative, and sometimes more extensive benefits may be provided under group insurance than under individual policies. Also, advanced forms of benefits are often offered first as group benefits, such as in the case of major medical expense insurance and dental benefits. So employees may have newer, more advanced, and possibly more liberal benefits available to them as group coverage, which might not be as readily available to them under individual policies.

Remember, however, that many individuals should not rely completely on group coverage. They usually also need individual insurance against at least some risks that is tailored to their own circumstances. They can purchase the amounts and kinds of available individual insurance as their needs and objectives dictate. Also, employees own and control their individual insurance protection regardless of changes in employers or even temporary unemployment. Viewed in terms of individual needs and possible changes in an employment situation, individual insurance also provides elements of flexibility and control for the individual. Thus the flexibility argument really can be made both ways.

Ease and Convenience of Purchase. The whole concept of the group insurance technique, particularly as applied to employer-employee groups, provides a convenient and more-or-less automatic way for employees to secure coverages that most of them sorely need. Without the group technique and the employer participation and approval involved, many employees would probably be without such protection.

Limitations of Employee Benefit Plans

While there are many good reasons for employers to adopt or expand employee benefit plans, there are certain limitations on the adoption of such plans by employers. There are limitations on too great a reliance on employee benefits by employees in their personal financial planning.

An alternative to the adoption or expansion of employee benefits is to increase direct base compensation or perhaps current incentive compensation for all, or a group of, the employees. Depending on the circumstances and the nature of the employee group, some employees may prefer more current compensation to indirect and deferred benefit plans. This alternative could also be more advantageous to the employer under some conditions. (However, it must be recognized that employees today generally expect a "good" benefits program from their employer as part of their total compensation package.)

The following are some limitations or constraints that employers might want to consider when deciding whether to adopt or expand an employee benefit program:

1. *Additions to or increases in employee benefit programs obviously increase employers' compensation costs.* Whether employers are willing to bear these increased costs depends on many factors, including their financial and profit position, their competitive situation, and the cost/benefit relationship they see in adopting or expanding the plan. The stability and growth of corporate earnings clearly are important factors in this decision. A corporation with fluctuating or uncertain earnings may be hesitant to adopt, say, a pension plan that imposes relatively fixed costs on the company. Such a corporation might be willing to consider instead a deferred profit-sharing plan whose cost to the employer is not fixed but based on the firm's future profits.

2. *The costs of some employee benefits may tend to increase over time or to be uncertain.* The rapid inflation of medical care costs, for example, has resulted in dramatic increases in the cost of medical expense coverages in employee benefit plans. Employers are very concerned with such cost increases and are involved in overall efforts to control the rising cost of medical care.

   Similarly, legislative changes may result in unexpected cost increases for certain employee benefits. The requirements of the *Employee Retirement Income Security Act of 1974* (ERISA), for example, may have increased the pension costs and funding requirements for many firms.

3. *Once a benefit is given, it is hard to take it back.* Many employers feel it is difficult from an employee relations viewpoint (quite aside from collective bargaining consider- ations, which are another matter) to drop or modify an employee benefit once it has been provided to employees.

4. *If employees are unionized, any benefit plan proposed for them by management is subject to collective bargaining.* Employers may be hesitant to bring up a plan or plan improvement that might simply be added to the union's demands at the bargaining table.

5. *Some employers may feel that employees generally do not understand or appreciate employee benefits or their cost.* Such employers may favor direct wage increases to motivate their employees.

6. *Finally, at some point, employees may prefer direct wage increases to additional indirect or deferred employee benefits.* This issue really deals with the most appropriate "mix" in a firm's total compensation package. Unfortunately, the most appropriate "mix" is very difficult to determine objectively. Even if it could be measured objectively at any point in time, it probably varies over time and almost certainly is not the same for different employees at different levels in the organization and at different stages of their lives or careers.

These limitations must be balanced against the reasons for adopting employee benefit plans. As we have seen, the long-term trend has been toward increasing the relative role of employee benefits as a part of the total compensation package.

Objectives of Plan Design

There are a number of possible objectives in the design or redesign of an employee benefit plan. Some of these may also be characterized as general employer compensation objectives. Obviously, some objectives are more important than others, and not all employers attach the same order of priorities to them. So we shall start this discussion by noting that employee benefit plan design should fit into an organization's total employee compensation objectives or strategy. Then, within this general context, we shall consider the specific objectives that may shape the design of an organization's employee benefit plan.

Employer Total Compensation Objectives Total compensation is the combination of all forms of direct and indirect compensation utilized by an employer. One of management's important functions is the development of a total compensation strategy that reflects the employer's objectives, the needs and desires of employees, and the competitive framework within which management is operating.

General Compensation Strategy and Employer Characteristics. Employers may adopt different business strategies with respect to employee compensation in general. Many employers want to compensate their employees at a level about in line with that which generally prevails in their industry and/or geographic area. They strive toward a middle or average compensation level in their general employment market and often want an employee benefit program that also meets these characteristics. Other employers may follow a high wage or salary philosophy, thereby attempting to attract the better management, technical, and general employee talent. Still other employers may frankly follow a low wage or salary policy, thereby keeping their payroll costs down and tacitly accepting the resultant turnover and other possible inefficiencies. Such employers may also want to adopt modest employee benefit programs.

The characteristics of the particular employer or industry also have an impact on employee benefit plan design, as well as on general compensation strategy. A large, well-established employer in a growing or mature industry may take a relatively liberal approach to employee benefits. On the other hand, in industries that are highly competitive or beset with cyclical fluctuations, employers may not be willing to add to their fixed costs by adopting liberal and costly employee benefit programs. Further, young, growing firms that may have heavy needs for capital may not be able to take on the relatively large, fixed-cost commitments of certain types of employee benefits. They may prefer to rely more heavily on incentive types of compensation, for example.

In its overall compensation strategy, an employer must decide, either explicitly or implicitly, on the balance to be struck among direct pay, incentive pay, and indirect benefits (employee benefits) for its work force. This decision, of course, reflects the circumstances and philosophy of the firm, as well as the needs and desires of its employees (and union if its employees are organized).

Compensation-Oriented Benefit Philosophy. With respect to employee benefits themselves, many firms have what may be termed a "compensation-oriented" philosophy in designing their benefit plan. This phrase means that the firm tends to relate employee benefits primarily to compensation, with the level of benefits tending to follow the level of compensation.

Benefit- ("Needs"-) Oriented Philosophy. The other general philosophy toward employee benefits is a benefit- or needs-oriented approach. This approach tends to focus primarily on the needs of employees rather than on compensation.

In practice, employee benefit plans tend to be a compromise between these two philosophies. Group life insurance and pension benefits, for example, are customarily related primarily to compensation, at least for nonunion employees. On the other hand, medical expense benefits tend to be primarily benefit- or needs-oriented. However, the balance struck between these two philosophies will affect plan design.

Specific Employee Benefit Plan Design Objectives Bear in mind that the specific objectives of employee benefit plan design are affected by an employer's total compensation philosophy, as already discussed. Thus, employee benefit plan design should complement the employer's total compensation strategy.

Benefit Adequacy. An important goal in the design of most employee benefits is to maintain an appropriate level of benefit adequacy for covered employees. Having said this, the important questions remain as to what is an "appropriate level" and which employees should be benefited. The goal of benefit adequacy relates more to a benefit or needs philosophy for plan design. Examples of efforts to evaluate benefit adequacy, as noted previously in this book, include:

1. attempting to determine replacement ratios of total requirement benefits in relation to earnings for pension and other requirement plans,
2. providing disability benefits up to a reasonable percentage of an employee's predisability earnings, and
3. evaluating an employer's medical expense benefits in terms of the overall proportion of employee medical expenses paid for by the plan, and so forth.

Competitive with Other Plans. As noted previously, most organizations seek to have an employee benefit plan that they regard as competitive with other firms in their industry and/or with other firms in their local labor market. This goal is part of the general competition for an adequate and efficient labor supply. Employers sometimes express this objective quite specifically. For example, a company may have a written policy indicating that the organization's employee benefits will be compared each year with the programs of certain leading employers in the industry and/or in the geographic area involved. It might then specify that the overall value of the organization's employee benefits (or some other comparative measure) will be maintained at a certain level, say within the top 50 percent of this sample of employers. This kind of formalized comparison and evaluation can be facilitated through several of the specific approaches to plan design discussed later in this chapter, such as comparison of plan specifications, illustrations of benefits, benefit value comparisons, benefit level comparisons, and the like. There is growing interest in making such organized and consistent comparisons with respect to benefit design and evaluation. Some employee benefit plan consultants have developed rather sophisticated techniques for making such comparisons with comparable or competitive organizations.

Consistency. Another design goal is to provide consistency or balance among benefits within the employee benefit plan or plans, as distinguished from competitiveness with the plans of other organizations. An employer may want to maintain a reasonable balance, in terms of benefit adequacy and cost, among the various kinds of employee benefits in its plan. For example, the employer may not wish to provide very extensive death benefits through various sources while at the same time offering rather "skimpy" disability benefits. The same might be true for retirement benefits: An employer might provide benefits for employees at retirement or close to retirement from a variety of sources, often on a favorable preretirement tax basis, that will equal or even actually exceed their preretirement earnings. This may encourage early retirement, which the employer may regard as desirable. Yet it may also produce undesirable results, such as the loss of skilled employees, inadequate benefits in other areas, and a lack of balance between direct cash compensation and deferred compensation in the form of retirement benefits. Further, it may indicate a lack of coordination among various plans that the employer may maintain to provide retirement benefits. Benefit programs may easily get out of balance. Some of the approaches to employee benefit plan design, discussed later, may be helpful in maintaining balance among different kinds of benefits.

Similarly, employers may wish to maintain consistency of benefits among different categories of employees (such as union and nonunion, or hourly rated and salaried), among different plant locations, and within different components of the corporate structure, such as among subsidiaries and between subsidiaries and the parent company.

Proper Coordination (Nonduplication). It is becoming increasing clear that employee benefits should be coordinated with each other, as well as with government-mandated plans, so as to provide an effective total benefit program without wasteful duplication. In the case of government-mandated plans, such coordination is sometimes necessary to avoid excessive total benefits in relation to the losses incurred. Such is the case, for example, with respect to the integration of medical expense benefits with Medicare for covered retirees. In other cases, the coordination of private and public plans is designed to help achieve equity in total benefits. Such is the case, for example, with respect to the integration of private pension benefits with Social Security retirement benefits.

Contribution to Employee Morale. It is almost a truism that employers hope their employee benefit plans will contribute to employee morale. The extent to which this aim is actually accomplished, however, often depends not only on the quality of plan design but also on how effective management is in communicating the benefits to employees.

Employee Incentives (Encouragement of Productivity). The extent to which this often stated objective is actually achieved may depend on a number of factors, such as the quality of the plan itself, the degree to which it is understood by employees, and the relative emphasis on certain incentive-type components within the plan. With respect to incentive components, some elements of the typical employee benefit plan probably are primarily "maintenance-type" benefits. In other words, they would have a negative impact upon employee morale, and perhaps on productivity, if they were absent, but they probably do not have a strong positive impact on employee productivity when they are present. Such elements may include, for example, medical expense, death, and disability benefits. On the other hand, some types of benefits, such as profit-sharing plans, stock purchase plans, and ESOPs and TRASOPs, are more likely to stimulate employees to help make the employer's operation more profitable or efficient.

Support for Employer Personnel and Recruitment Objectives. This objective is similar in concept to the two preceding. Clearly, employers want an employee benefit plan that will help them retain and recruit personnel to meet their personnel and recruitment objectives. Here again, relative emphasis on different components of an employee benefit plan may be relevant to the types of employees the employer is particularly anxious to recruit. An attractive medical expense plan, for example, may be helpful in attracting clerical or hourly rated employees; to executive or professional employees, pension and profit-sharing plans, stock ownership plans, and other forms of incentive compensation may be more important. This objective may be particular important if an employer is attempting to attract established executive talent from other companies.

An illustration of how employee benefit plan design can affect the recruitment of executives can be shown in an example. Assume that

Company X would like to recruit a proven and competent forty-five-year-old executive, Ms. Able, from Company Y. Ms. Able likes Company X's prospects and management philosophy, and the terms of employment offered by Company X seem attractive to her until she considers the impact of the change on her potential pension benefits. Suppose (for simplicity of illustration) that both Company X and Company Y have defined benefit pension plans with benefit formulas providing a percentage of pay unit benefit of 1 percent of her final five-year average pay for each year of service. Further suppose Ms. Able has 20 years of service with Company Y and average annual compensation for pension purposes of $40,000 for the last five years. Also suppose that, based on her reasonable salary expectations for the future, she can expect to have an average annual compensation of $90,000 for the five years preceding her normal retirement age of sixty-five. If Ms. Able remains with Company Y, and if her assumptions are realized, she will have a pension beginning at age sixty-five of $36,000 per year (40 years × 1 percent of final average pay of $90,000 = $36,000 per year). (For purposes of simplicity, this illustration ignores any social security integration.)

On the other hand, if Ms. Able accepts Company X's offer, her combined pension benefits from Company Y (being fully vested) and from Company X would be reduced to $26,000 per year at age sixty-five. She would receive $8,000 per year from Company Y's plan (20 years × 1 percent of 5-year pay of $40,000 per year as of her termination from Company Y = $8,000) and $18,000 per year from Company X's plan (20 years × 1 percent of final average pay of $90,000 = $18,000 per year). For the sake of simplicity, we have used the same salary figures for both companies. As a practical matter, of course, it is probable that Company X's compensation would be higher than Company Y's in order for its job-offer to be attractive to Ms. Able.

As things stand in this illustration, if Ms. Able were to take the more attractive job offer with Company X, she faces a substantial decline in her potential pension benefit. There are possible alternatives to avoid this result. For example, Company X might offer Ms. Able an unfunded, nonqualified supplemental executive retirement plan to make up for her lost potential pension benefits. Or Company X may have other attractive benefits that may make up for this potential loss of pension benefits.

Cost Control. Cost control will clearly impact on most of, if not all, the general decision factors in plan design to be considered in the next section. Obviously, employers are concerned with the level of costs for given benefits. The various ways of expressing overall employee benefit plan costs are described later in this chapter. Employers are also concerned with the predictability of costs. One aspect of this factor may be to avoid adopting or increasing benefits whose costs tend to be uncertain or constantly increasing; this may be one factor holding down the development of group property and liability insurance, for example. Possible abuses arising from poor plan design have obvious cost implications. Proper structuring of disability benefits is a clear example. Further, the objective of proper benefits coordination has an impact on cost control. Excessive or duplicative benefits may have an adverse impact on employee incentives. They may encourage absenteeism and result in higher plan costs because employees can collect more in benefits than the losses they incur.

Administrative Convenience (and Cost) to the Employer. This design objective may be particularly significant for smaller or moderate-sized employers. Administrative problems tend to grow, in any event, as employee benefit plans themselves become more complex and as there are increasing legal, regulatory, and tax requirements for such plans.

Satisfaction of Legal Requirements. Naturally, the design of an employee benefit plan must meet the various tax, regulatory, employment discrimination, and labor law requirements for such plans.

Satisfaction of Employee Needs and Wishes. In designing and evaluating employee benefit plans, employers often spend a great deal of time and effort in attempting to determine the employees' wishes with respect to benefits. Different categories of employees may have different needs and wishes. This variety may be a reason for the use of different employee benefit plans for different categories of employees and for the development of "cafeteria compensation plans," discussed later in this chapter. Employers should recognize that employees will have different needs and wishes depending on the stages of their life cycles.

General Decision Factors in Plan Design

Given general and specific objectives, certain factors should or may be considered in employee benefit plan design:

What Benefits Should Be Provided? This question is the crux of employee benefit plan design. Although many alternatives have been discussed, many of the decision factors that follow relate back to this basic question. An employer may also want to set certain cost parameters on benefit plan design.

Who Should Be Protected or Benefited? This factor has many aspects and varies among different employee benefits. For example, whether to provide dependents group life insurance is an entirely different question from the almost universal provision of medical expense coverage for the dependents of active employees. The various considerations involved in deciding this question have been discussed in previous chapters; however, the following is a brief summary of some of the issues that might be considered in this area:

1. What probationary periods (for eligibility for benefits) should be used for various types of benefits? Does the employer want to cover employees and their dependents more or less immediately upon employment, or to provide coverage only for employees and their dependents who have established more or less "permanent" employment with the employer? Is there a rationale for different probationary periods for different benefits?
2. Which dependents of active employees should be covered?
3. Should retirees (as well as their spouses and perhaps other dependents) be covered, and for which benefits?
4. Should survivors of deceased active employees (and/or retirees) be covered? And if so, for which benefits?
5. What coverage, if any, should be extended to persons on disability?
6. What coverage, if any, should be extended to employees during layoff, leaves of absence, strikes, and so forth?
7. Should coverage be limited to full-time employees?

What Options (Choices) Should Employees Have? This decision factor is becoming more important in employee benefit planning. There has been a distinct trend toward giving employees more flexibility in choosing their benefit patterns under an employee benefit plan. The concept has been growing that employee benefit plan design should make employee benefits more relevant to the individual needs of employees and their families, rather than being designed with the hypothetical "average" employee in mind, with few modifications possible from this basic plan.

On the other hand, it must be recognized that individual employee choice and flexibility can violate or compromise some of the basic characteristics of group selection. For example, if employees have a choice of benefit amounts or options, or choices among benefits, this flexibility may compromise certain group selection characteristics, such as the automatic determination of benefits, the eligibility for benefits on the basis of employment status rather than individual selection, and perhaps a minimum proportion of the group insured requirement for group insurance underwriting purposes. To the extent that flexibility in plan design introduces increased administrative complexity and hence costs for the employer, the group selection characteristic of administrative efficiency may be compromised, at least in part. So striking some balance between these fundamental characteristics of group selection and the desirable goal of increased flexibility may be necessary.

In the area of employee choice, the kinds of fundamental design patterns might be classified as follows:

1. traditional design with minimal employee choice,
2. traditional design with certain employee options, and
3. "cafeteria" compensation.

Traditional Plan Design with Minimal Employee Choice. This has been a common approach toward employee benefit plan design, in which a fixed pattern of benefits is provided to all eligible employees without their having much choice concerning benefit levels or composition. The benefit package is designed largely on the basis of what management, or management and a union in collective bargaining, thinks would best satisfy the needs of the "average" employee. There is little or no room for variation on the basis of individual employee needs or desires.

Traditional Plan Design with Certain Employee Options Built into Existing Benefits. Probably reflecting the approach of most major employers today, this method essentially provides a fixed pattern of benefits but allows employees a certain measure of choice within the established benefits. It is actually a modification and extension of the previous category. Under this approach, employees are given certain choices with respect to the types and levels of benefits within the existing employee benefit programs that the employer pays for, in whole or in part. Since employees can make these choices without having employer contributions to the plan taxed as income to them, they are sometimes referred to as "before-tax" choices. Many of these choices have been noted in previous chapters; they might include, for example:

1. optional levels of supplementary group term life insurance,
2. the availability of death or disability benefits under pension or profit-sharing plans,
3. choices of covering dependents under group medical expense coverages,
4. an HMO option,
5. a Section 401(k) cash or deferred election, and
6. a variety of participation, cash distribution, and investment options under profit-sharing, thrift, and capital accumulation plans.

Another approach to providing flexibility under traditional plans is to allow employees to purchase additional benefits, on an employee-pay-all basis, over and above those provided through the employer's regular plan. This method actually involves the employer's making such benefits available to employees on a more favorable group basis for their individual purchase. Since benefits are purchased by employees from their incomes after paying federal income taxes, this approach may be referred to as buying such benefits on an "after-tax" basis.

Cafeteria Compensation. "Cafeteria compensation," or "flexible compensation," is one of those much-discussed concepts that may mean different things to different people. However, cafeteria compensation generally refers to a flexible benefits program under which employees have the opportunity to choose, on a before-tax basis, among various levels and forms of certain nontaxable benefits and cash compensation, subject to an overall maximum amount. Thus, the essence of a cafeteria plan is a trade-off among different benefit plans and among different benefit plans and cash (cash must be an available choice). For tax purposes, the Internal Revenue Code defines a "cafeteria plan" as follows:[9]

(A) all participants are employees, and
(B) the participants may choose among two or more benefits consisting of cash and statutory nontaxable benefits.

Cafeteria compensation is mentioned at this point because it exemplifies the highest level of flexibility in employee benefit plan design.

Advantages and Limitations of Employee Choice. A number of advantages have been suggested for providing greater employee choice with respect to employee benefit plans. When carried to their logical end, these advantages are basically the same as may be cited for the cafeteria compensation concept. They are as follows:

1. Employees are given an opportunity to tailor, to the degree permitted, their employee benefits in a way most relevant to their own particular needs.
2. Similarly, employees can change the structure of their benefits to meet their changing needs over their life cycles.
3. Greater flexibility of choice will increase the value of employee benefit programs to employees and hence result in greater appreciation of these plans by the employees.
4. As a result, it is suggested that there will be improved employee morale and performance.
5. There will be an improvement in the economic efficiency of the allocation of employer compensation expenditures as a result of greater employee choice.

6. With particular reference to cafeteria compensation, it is suggested that the involvement of employees and their families in the selection of benefits increases their understanding and appreciation of the benefits and their cost.
7. It is also argued that cafeteria compensation may provide the potential for the control of future benefit costs.

On the other hand, a number of limitations on the extent of individual employee choice in the fashioning of their own benefit programs have been suggested. These limitations include the following:

1. Some of the desires or perceived needs of employees may vary from their actual needs. In other words, it is suggested that some employees may make bad choices among benefits when given the chance.
2. It is suggested that an employer may be subject to employee morale problems and to community public relations problems in the event that certain employees or their families suffer uncovered losses due to their opting against appropriate coverages. As we shall see later, this argument may lead to the formation of a mandatory "core" of benefits for all eligible employees, even under a cafeteria compensation plan.
3. Greater flexibility of employee choice almost invariably results in increased complexity of plan administration and increased administrative expenses.
4. Greater employee choice may lead to increased benefit costs, particularly with reference to cafeteria compensation; there may also be substantial developmental costs in implementing such a plan.
5. Increased flexibility with respect to employee choice may bring greater "adverse selection" by employees.
6. Increased employee choice may create some problems with respect to insurance company group underwriting requirements and practices.
7. Finally, it is suggested that some employees may be unable or unwilling to make the proper choices. This could also give rise to legal liability on the part of the employer for inadequate, inaccurate, or incomplete information given to employees.

How Should Benefits Be Financed? An important decision factor in employee benefit plan design is who should pay for the benefits. Benefits can be financed on several bases:

1. noncontributory (employer-pay-all),
2. contributory (employer and employee sharing cost), and
3. (sometimes) employee-pay-all.

In most cases, the real decision is between noncontributory and contributory financing.

Arguments for Noncontributory Financing. The following advantages have been cited for the noncontributory approach:

1. *All eligible employees are covered.* Under a noncontributory plan, all eligible employees who have completed the probationary period, if any, are covered by the plan. This feature can avoid employee and public relations problems that might arise under a contributory plan. For example, otherwise eligible employees may not elect coverage under a contributory plan, and hence they and/or their dependents may not be covered when a loss or retirement occurs. Despite the logical justification for noncoverage, it can prevent employee relations and public relations problems after the fact.

   Coverage of all eligible employees also avoids possible adverse selection under contributory plans, since those employees who are most subject to a potential loss will often elect to contribute and be covered under a contributory plan, while those employees less subject to the loss may decline to contribute and be covered.

   Further, coverage of all eligibles avoids difficulties in meeting participation requirements of the underwriting rules of insurance companies or under state group insurance laws.

2. *Tax efficiency.* Noncontributory employee benefits frequently provide the most effective form of employee compensation from a tax point of view. In most cases, employer contributions to an employee benefit plan do not result in current gross income to the covered employees for federal income tax purposes, even though these contributions are normally deductible by the employer as a reasonable and necessary business expense. Thus, the coverage or protection currently provided under employee benefit plans through employer contributions are available to employees without current income taxation on their value (or, as has been referred to previously, on a "before-tax basis").

   On the other hand, most employee contributions to employee benefit plans are not deductible by the employee for income tax purposes. Such contributions are made by the employees out of income that has already been taxed (or on what has been referred to previously as an "after-tax basis"). The precise tax impact depends on the type of employee benefit involved. As a general proposition, however, noncontributory employee benefits are more tax efficient as a way of compensating employees than are contributory plans. Of course, it must be noted that benefits paid under employee benefit plans financed through employer contributions may constitute taxable income to the employees when received, or they may serve to eliminate an otherwise available income tax deduction for the employee. Yet even in the case of benefits that are taxable when received, there still may be certain income tax advantages for benefits payable under employee benefit plans.

3. *Group purchasing advantages.* To the extent that all eligible employees are covered, as opposed to less than all under a contributory plan, the employer may be able to secure more favorable group rates or other conditions of coverage than would otherwise be the case.

4. *Avoiding employee dissatisfaction with payroll deductions.* Employees dislike payroll deductions, and this may work at cross purposes to the overall goal of enhancing employee morale and good will. Further, employees may want more in the way of direct cash compensation to offset payroll deductions.

5. *Union or collective bargaining pressures.* Labor unions generally favor noncontributory plans in their collective bargaining with respect to the workers they represent. To the extent that an employer extends the benefits won by unionized workers to nonunion workers as well, collective bargaining may also result in noncontributory plans for them. Further, if an employer is seeking to avoid the organization of its employees, the employer may prefer to eliminate or minimize employee contributions to benefit plans in order to help maintain its nonunion status.

6. *Ease and economy of administration.* Since payroll deduction is not necessary under a noncontributory plan, benefit and accounting records are easier to maintain. Also, it is not necessary for the employer or insurer periodically to solicit employees who are not covered under a contributory plan to determine if they now wish to participate.

7. *Possibility of greater employer control of plan.* It is sometimes suggested that an employer may be justified in exercising more control over a noncontributory plan than a contributory plan.

Arguments for Contributory Financing. On the other hand, the following are among the advantages frequently cited for the contributory principle in financing employee benefits:

1. *More coverage and/or higher benefits possible.* Given a certain level of employer contribution toward the cost of an employee

benefit plan, employee contributions may make possible a more adequate plan, or they may enable a plan to be installed in the first place.

2. *Possible greater employee appreciation of the plan.* It is argued that when employees contribute to a plan, they will have greater appreciation for the benefits that they are helping to finance. They will not take such benefits for granted.

3. *Possible lessening of abuses of benefits.* In a similar vein to the previous argument, it is suggested that employees will be less likely to abuse an employee benefit plan if they know that such abuses may increase their own contribution rates.

4. *More effective utilization of employee benefits.* In this more subtle argument for contributory plans, it is suggested that those employees who have greater needs for particular employee benefits, and perhaps who are more likely to be career employees of the employer, will be the ones most likely to elect to participate in a contributory plan. On the other hand, the employees who elect not to participate in a contributory plan are most likely to be those who actually have few needs for the plan and who may also be shorter-service employees. In effect, a contributory plan tends to allocate the coverage more nearly among those who have the most need for it, since they are the ones most likely to be willing to contribute to the cost of their coverage. Thus employer contributions (as well as employee contributions) are used more effectively.

5. *Plans providing employee options or supplementary coverages must be contributory.* When an employee benefit plan allows covered employees to elect supplementary coverages or options, it necessarily involves the employees' paying at least part of the cost of the supplementary coverage. Otherwise, the coverage would simply be a part of the basic plan.

6. *Encourages greater employee self-reliance.* It is suggested by some that contributory plans make employees more responsible for their own financial security and hence less dependent on the employer.

7. *Possibility of greater employee control of plan.* Employee control is the other side of the coin; that is, the counterpart of the argument regarding greater employer control of noncontributory plans.

Employee-Pay-All Financing. This approach is less common and tends to be supplementary when used. One of the characteristics of group selection is that the employer should share in the cost of the plan. Sharing the cost helps to make the plan attractive to employees, avoid adverse selection, keep costs from rising, and maintain greater employer interest in the plan.

Nonetheless, employee-pay-all plans do operate successfully in some situations. The following arguments might be made for employee-pay-all financing:

1. *Separate optional plans may be offered.* Some employers offer employees the opportunity of purchasing additional coverages at group rates, without individual underwriting, which supplement the benefits of the regular employee benefit plan. These might include, for example, additional accident insurance, life insurance, hospital indemnity coverage to supplement Medicare, and so forth. These additional coverages are normally on an employee-pay-all basis.
2. *Benefits not otherwise available.* Employee-pay-all financing may be the only basis on which an employer feels it can offer the coverage. In the future, such a plan might be shifted to a contributory or even to a noncontributory basis.
3. *Possible favorable circumstances for the plan.* Some of the circumstances that produced financial problems for employee-pay-all group insurance in the past may be avoided in some modern situations. For example, if employees are able to afford the coverage, if the group rates are attractive to employees, if employees perceive the coverage as desirable, and if a regular flow of younger lives into the group can be maintained, employee-pay-all coverage can operate successfully, assuming some or all of these factors operate to produce satisfactory claim experience under the plan.

Employer Philosophy Concerning Benefit Financing. It would seem desirable for employers to have a consistent philosophy for their employee benefit financing approach. Sometimes it appears that whether a plan is financed on a noncontributory, contributory, or employee-pay-all basis depends largely on whatever was done when the plan was originally installed—without any currently consistent philosophy. Applying a contributory philosophy or a noncontributory philosophy across the board for all employee benefit plans is, of course, possible. Yet the approach generally followed is to vary the financing approach among plans because of differences in plan characteristics and costs. Some of the rational bases for financing decisions might include the following:

1. The employer may pay all the cost of employee coverage, but it may require employee contributions for some or all of the cost of dependent coverage (primarily under medical expense plans).

2. The employer may provide what are considered as "basic" or essential employee benefits on a noncontributory basis, while requiring employees to pay part or all of the cost of additional, supplementary coverages. It might be argued that this rationale really reflects the efficiency in the use of employer contributions argument that was mentioned already for contributory plans.

3. Labor unions tend to favor noncontributory benefits, so under negotiated plans, or under plans for nonunion employees that reflect trends in negotiated plans, employers may adopt the noncontributory approach.

4. The employer may determine the maximum financial commitment it can make to the plan and then require employee contributions for costs above that level.

Recognition of Employee Service Employee service can be recognized in a variety of ways in employee benefit plan design. One such way is in the benefit formula for certain types of benefits—for example, for pension, profit-sharing, group life, and disability income benefits. On the other hand, some types of benefits, such as medical expense benefits, rarely reflect employee service.

Another area in which service may be reflected is the length of the probationary period, if any, that employees must serve before they become eligible for specified types of benefits. Such probationary periods often vary among the specific benefits comprising an employee benefit plan. As an illustration, Exhibit 10-4 is a listing of the probationary periods in the various benefit plans of a large chemical corporation.

Like financing arrangements, the use of probationary periods in plan design should be based on a reasonably consistent employer philosophy. In other words, why should there be, for example, no probationary period—or a relatively short one—for medical expense benefits but, on the other hand, a relatively long probationary period for pension, capital accumulation, or LTD benefits? One reason for the use of relatively long probationary periods is to restrict benefits or certain types of benefits to employees who may be considered "presumptively permanent," as opposed to relatively short-service employees. Another reason for probationary periods is to avoid the administrative cost of setting up records for short-service employees. On the other hand, some types of benefits, such as medical expense benefits, are more or less expected to be made available by the employer to its employees and their dependents.

One possible philosophy with respect to the use of probationary periods is to divide employee benefits into "protection-oriented"

Exhibit 10-4

Illustrative Listings of Probationary Periods for Specified Types of Benefits for a Corporation

Name of Plan	Eligibility for Participation
Health care plan	Fifteenth of the month following date of hire
Disability income protection program	
Basic disability allowance	After probationary period of employment
Extended disability allowance	1 year of service
Long-term disability allowance	1 year of service
Primary life insurance plan	3 months of service
Basic life insurance plan	3 months of service
Travel accident plan	First day of active employment
Pension plan	1 year of service
Savings plan	First anniversary of date of hire or rehire
Workers' compensation	First day of active employment
Supplemental workers' compensation plan	First day of active employment
Social Security	First day of active employment

benefits and "accumulation-oriented" benefits. "Protection-oriented" benefits consist of medical expense benefits, life insurance benefits, short- and long-term disability benefits, and so forth—benefits that protect employees against a serious loss that could spell immediate financial disaster for them or for their dependents. For such benefits, there could be no probationary period or a relatively short one, because the need for immediate coverage might be regarded as outweighing the reasons for using probationary periods. On the other hand, "accumulation-oriented" benefits consist of pension benefits, profit-sharing plans, thrift plans, stock bonus plans, and so forth. An employee who stays with the employer would normally have a relatively long period in which to accumulate such benefits, and so a reasonably long probationary period could be justified.

Employers often want to reflect service to some degree in their benefit design decisions in order to reward long and faithful service, to retain productive employees, to build morale, and to help avoid unwanted turnover. On the other hand, benefit plans may also need to be structured to attract needed employees in the labor market. Also, some plans, like medical expense plans, may not lend themselves well to recognizing service. Finally, if service is recognized in the benefit formulas for some types of plans, such as disability or life insurance plans, relatively high benefit levels may be provided for older, generally longer-service employees. This may result in higher costs and possible adverse selection.

Possible Use of Employee Benefits to Encourage Early (or Normal) Retirement The previous section dealt with how employee benefit plan design might help encourage longer employee service. The other side of this coin is structuring employee benefits so as to accommodate employee retirement at a time that is beneficial to the organization as well as to the employees involved. The ADEA amendments of 1978, raising the maximum age for mandatory retirement in private employment to seventy, and the need in many industries to pare their work forces in order to cut costs, have brought this question into sharper focus for employers. Some employers may want to structure their employee benefits to permit or to encourage employees to retire at the normal retirement age (frequently age sixty-five) or even earlier. Employee benefit plan design features that may help accomplish this goal include the following:

1. nonaccrual of pension benefits beyond normal retirement age,
2. maximum age-based reductions in employee benefits for active employees to the extent permitted by ADEA after normal retirement age, and
3. provision of relatively liberal total retiree benefits.

Similarly, early retirement may be encouraged by the following:

1. liberal retirement benefits in general,
2. liberal pension plan early retirement provisions,
3. adoption of other capital accumulation programs, and
4. payment of supplemental separation allowances (in other words, "open window" early retirement plans).

On the other hand, the employer who wishes to have employees delay their retirement might follow the reverse of some or all of these suggestions.

Relationship of Benefits to Employer Profits Essentially, the question is: How much should benefits depend on employer profits—or, perhaps, on the performance of the employer corporation's stock? A fundamental decision in this area is whether the firm should adopt a pension plan, a profit-sharing plan, or both. (If both, the question is then: With what relative emphasis?) An employer can also adopt other types of employee benefits that place relatively greater emphasis on employer profits or stock performance, such as stock bonus plans, incentive stock options (ISOs), other kinds of stock or performance plans, thrift plans, ESOPs and TRASOPs, and the like.

A compensation objective of employers is often to give employees an identification with the employer's profit goals and thus to improve employee productivity. Profit-oriented benefits tend to help accomplish this goal. On the other hand, there may be disadvantages in relying heavily on profit-oriented benefits. Benefits will be less assured for employees, and, in some cases, they may not be adequate. Also, in the face of declining profits or stock performance, these plans may actually have an adverse impact on employee morale and productivity.

Separate or Uniform Benefits Another decision for employers is whether employee benefits should be geared to categories or groups of employees, perhaps with separate plans for different categories. Or should the same benefits be provided for all employees? Many factors may affect this decision. If the employees are represented by one union, or a number of unions, the employer may negotiate separate plans with one or more of these unions. Also, in the case of employers for whom labor negotiations are conducted on an industry-wide basis, benefit plans may be determined through industry-wide labor negotiations. When an employer has both union-represented and nonrepresented employees at the same location or locations, it may have separate plans for each group. Sometimes, as a matter of policy, an employer will extend the benefits negotiated for unionized employees, or at least benefits representing the same level of employer contributions, automatically to its nonrepresented employees. Larger employers commonly have separate employee benefit plans for hourly rated (or unionized) employees, salaried employees, and perhaps other exempt employees. On the other hand, employers may opt to have the same benefits apply to all employees.

How Should Benefits Be Funded? This important decision has cost, financing, and operational efficiency implications. The funding vehicles available for employee welfare plans can range from fixed-premium group insurance contracts to complete self-funding. For pension plans, the vehicles range from fully insured plans to self-funded trusteed plans.

PENSION COSTS AND FUNDING REQUIREMENTS

The following sections will discuss pension costs and how and when they are recognized, particularly for pension funding purposes. Plan costs are, of course, a major determinant of what employers will contribute to fund a pension plan. Then, we shall consider the regulatory requirements and constraints imposed by the *Employee Retirement Income Security Act of 1974* (ERISA) and the tax laws that relate to pension fundings.

Nature of Pension Costs

Pension costs often represent a large component of the overall costs of an employee benefit plan, frequently second only to health care costs. Thus, the approaches used in estimating, recognizing, and funding these costs have important implications for the employer in terms of its costs of doing business, its financial condition, and in terms of meeting tax and regulatory requirements. Also, in the event of certain special situations, such as mergers and acquisitions, the extent of a firm's accrued pension obligations can be quite important in valuing the firm.

The nature and complexity of funding pension costs depend to a great extent on the fundamental nature of the pension plan involved. For defined contribution plans (money purchase pension plans, for example), the pension cost obligation of an employer is the fixed factor, while the benefits to participants are the variable factor. Thus, there is no problem in knowing the costs to be funded under a money purchase plan; the cost is fixed by the pension benefit formula. For example, if an employer has a money purchase pension plan providing that the employer will contribute 10 percent of a covered employee's basic compensation to the plan if the employee contributes 4 percent of his or her compensation, the cost to the employer that must be funded each year is 10 percent of compensation (less nonvested forfeitures in the case of a defined contribution *pension* plan). Of course, the employer will still have to decide what pension funding instrument to use in accumulating these pension funds for the benefit of the participants and their beneficiaries.

In the case of a defined benefit plan, however, the pension benefit to be provided to participants is determinable through the benefit formula, and the cost of the plan to the employer is the variable factor. In fact, this ultimate cost will not be known until all benefits under the pension plan have been paid, which will be many years, or indefinitely. Therefore, to fund defined benefit pension costs in advance, it is necessary to estimate what such costs will be (using actuarial assumptions as explained later), and then to allocate such costs to appropriate accounting periods (using an actuarial cost method as explained later) over the years the plan is in operation. Clearly then, the pension costs under a defined benefit plan cannot be known in advance, and it would only be by chance that actual plan costs would be the same as those estimated in advance. This need for estimating and allocating costs for funding purposes, and the consequent need for actuarial certification, present complications in the use of defined benefit pension plans that do not exist for defined contribution plans. Therefore, most of the remaining discussion in this chapter will relate to defined benefit plans.

Over the long period of time that a pension plan will typically be in existence, the ultimate costs of the plan will equal the benefits paid to participants and their beneficiaries plus the expenses incurred in administering the plan and less the investment return on accumulated plan assets. Actually, this fundamental equation applies to any kind of employee benefit plan. It is particularly pertinent to pensions, however, because they represent such a long-term undertaking, and because they involve the accumulation of substantial assets whose investment return becomes a very important determinant of ultimate pension costs.

There are several aspects or components of the costs of a defined benefit pension plan that should be explained at this point. First, given appropriate actuarial assumptions and a selected actuarial cost method, the *normal cost* of a plan is the estimated current cost of the pension benefits accrued by the plan participants for the particular year under consideration. It may also be referred to as the *current cost* or *running cost* for benefits earned that year by the covered employees.

The *actuarial liability* of a pension plan is the cumulative liability for accrued benefits as of any given point in time. It may also be referred to as the *accrued actuarial liability, accrued liability* or *actuarial accrued liability*. When defined retrospectively, it is the accumulation of all prior normal costs for the plan, adjusted for interest, benefit payments, expenses, and actuarial gains and losses. When defined prospectively, it is the estimated present value of future benefits under the plan less the estimated present value of future normal costs under the plan. It also represents the amount of pension reserves that should be on hand at a particular valuation date to meet the total accrued benefits under the plan as of that date. If the pension assets actually on hand for the plan are less than the actuarial liability as of any point in time, the plan has an *unfunded actuarial liability* to the extent of the deficiency. On the other hand, if the pension assets actually accumulated for the plan exceed the actuarial liability, the plan is said to have an *actuarial surplus* to the extent of the excess. The percentage of the actuarial liability for a pension plan that is matched by plan assets at any point in time is referred to as the *funded ratio* of the plan.

A pension plan also may have an *initial past service liability*, which is the liability for benefits credited to plan participants for their service before the plan came into existence. It may also be referred to as the *initial actuarial liability*. This actuarial liability arises because defined benefit plans customarily give credit in their benefit formulas for service rendered by covered employees before the plan became effective. *Past service liability* may also arise from benefit increases that are applied retroactively to employee service rendered prior to the increases. The cost of a plan's past service liability is normally amortized over a period of years and is charged to the plan year by year.

The vast majority of pension plans use the approach of advance funding of the plans' future pension liabilities. *Advance funding* is the setting aside of assets to meet pension obligations before the plan participants actually retire or otherwise become entitled to receive benefits under the plan. Advance funding, in effect, is required for plans that are subject to the minimum funding standards of ERISA. Therefore, it is actually those plans that are not subject to ERISA's funding standards that may be funded in some manner other than advance funding. Also, from accounting and financial management standpoints, advance funding recognizes pension costs as they are being incurred. Further, advance funding of qualified plans permits employers to take advantage of the tax-favored build-up of pension assets permitted by the tax law to meet their future pension liabilities.

Pay-as-you-go funding involves the paying of actual pension benefits as they become due out of the employer's current income and/or assets. It does not involve the advance accumulation of funds to meet pension liabilities. Aside from certain governmental programs, pay-as-you-go funding is generally used only for certain executive retirement plans that are specifically exempted from ERISA's minimum funding standards. These include excess benefit plans and supplemental executive retirement (top-hat) plans. These plans are unfunded and hence operate on a pay-as-you-go basis as far as pension funding is concerned. However, employers frequently carry life insurance policies on the executives' lives, and these policies are owned by and payable to the employer to aid the employer in financing benefits under supplemental executive retirement plans.

Another general approach toward pension funding is *terminal funding*. Terminal funding involves the funding of a participant's retirement benefits when he or she reaches retirement age but not before. This approach also would not meet the minimum funding standards of ERISA.

Employer Contributions to Defined Benefit Plans

We shall now consider the factors that will affect the amount of an employer's contributions to fund a defined benefit pension plan on an advanced funding basis. These factors basically involve making appropriate actuarial assumptions, selecting an actuarial cost method, valuing plan assets, meeting certain regulatory and tax requirements concerning contributions, and developing an employer's policy concerning funding the plan.

Actuarial Valuations Defined benefit pension plans periodically (usually annually) have prepared an actuarial valuation involving the estimation of plan actuarial liabilities and a reporting of the assets available to meet those liabilities. Actuarial valuations serve a number of purposes, but basically they are intended to indicate the level of contributions the employer may make to fund the plan during the year; to show the plan's current funding status; to provide information for meeting various regulatory requirements, such as the funding standard account (described later in this chapter), and the limits on tax-deductible pension contributions; to provide information to plan participants; and for other purposes. ERISA requires that actuarial reports under the law be signed by *enrolled actuaries*. These are actuaries who are enrolled with the Joint Board for the Enrollment of Actuaries established by the Secretary of Labor and the Secretary of the Treasury under the provisions of ERISA. Thus, an enrolled actuary normally performs the actuarial services for a defined benefit pension plan. ERISA also requires that an actuarial valuation of a defined benefit plan be made at least every three years.

Making Actuarial Assumptions Since the established benefits under a defined benefit plan normally will be paid many years in the future, it is necessary to estimate the future costs and liabilities under such a plan. In making these future estimates, the actuary must make certain assumptions as to what the various factors that will determine plan costs and liabilities will be in the future. The following are the major actuarial assumptions that must be made in estimating pension costs and liabilities for a defined benefit plan.

Mortality. Mortality is obviously an important cost factor for a pension plan. The ultimate cost of a plan will be affected by the longevity of retired participants, the probability that a participant will survive until normal retirement age, and the cost of any survivorship features (such as qualified preretirement survivorship annuities) and other ancillary death benefits under the plan. In most cases, mortality is estimated from published mortality tables, often with some adjustments. In some cases, a plan's own mortality experience may be used. Finally, some tables are now available with combined mortality experience for male and female lives (so-called unisex tables). A unisex table does not state separate mortality rates for male participants and for female participants, as most tables do.

Turnover. Another actuarial cost factor is employee turnover or withdrawal rates. Depending upon the vesting provisions of a plan, turnover will reduce pension costs. Actuaries often estimate turnover from a turnover table. Turnover varies widely among employers and may be affected by such factors as age, sex, and length of service.

Salary Changes. Since many defined benefit plans base their pension benefit formulas at least partly on earnings, an important cost factor for these plans is the estimated future changes in such earnings. For this purpose, actuaries use *salary scales* that show expected increases in earnings as a single percentage rate of increase, such as 6 percent per year, or as varying percentages based on employees' ages,

Pay-related pension benefit formulas may be on a career-average basis or on a final-pay-average basis. Since the pension benefit in final-average benefit formulas will be directly related to future salary, salary projections will be more important as an actuarial cost factor for these plans than for career-average-type formulas.

Retirement Ages. The normal retirement age for a pension plan is the earliest age at which the plan's benefit formula will produce the full benefits contemplated by the formula for a retiring participant. It is thus the retirement age contemplated in the actuarial assumptions for the plan.

In the United States, this normal retirement age has traditionally been sixty-five. Many pension plans, however, permit retirement before the normal retirement date (that is, early retirement), and under the ADEA requirements plans must permit most employees to work until age seventy, which generally would be beyond normal retirement age. If a plan provides for full actuarial reduction in the event of early retirement (i.e., payment of an early retirement benefit that is the actuarial equivalent of the early retiree's accrued pension as of his or her early retirement age), then this would actuarially make allowance for the beginning of pension payments before normal retirement age. However, there is a distinct tendency for pension plans to allow early retirement at certain ages and/or with certain service without imposing actuarial reductions or without imposing full actuarial reductions on the early retirement benefits. In this case, to reflect pension costs accurately, additional actuarial assumptions are needed to reflect the estimated actual ages at which participants will retire. Thus, for example, plans may assume an average retirement age, or that certain percentages of employees will retire at different ages. Since subsidized early retirement provisions (those without full actuarial reduction) can be expensive for an employer, assumptions concerning actual retirement ages can be an important actuarial cost factor. Employers may also wish to consider the impact of retirements delayed beyond normal retirement age, depending upon how such delayed retirements affect pension benefit payments under the plan.

Investment Earnings. In terms of its potential long-term effect on pension costs, the assumption concerning the investment return that will be earned on pension assets is perhaps the most significant of the actuarial assumptions. The investment earnings assumption is commonly called the *valuation rate of interest.* Normally, this assumption represents the total estimated return on pension assets, including interest, dividends, rents, and capital appreciation. The relative importance of these components of total return depends, of course, upon the composition of a pension fund's investments.

Estimated plan costs vary inversely with the valuation rate of interest assumed. Thus, the higher the valuation rate, the lower the estimated future pension costs. However, because of the long-term nature of pension liabilities and the consequent long-term nature of pension investments, it is common to be relatively conservative in selecting a valuation rate of interest in setting actuarial cost assumptions. On the other hand, when actual investment yields in the securities and capital markets are relatively high, there may be pressure to use less conservative investment earnings assumptions in actuarial cost calculations.

Disability. If a pension plan provides a separate disability benefit or benefits, an assumption concerning disability rates is needed to estimate the cost of such benefits. Also, an estimate of disability will be needed to determine the number of participants who will become disabled and hence will not receive their regular retirement benefits.

Social Security Increases. For pension plans that are integrated with Social Security, assumptions should be made concerning future increases in Social Security benefits, including the Social Security wage base and cost-of-living adjustments.

Other Assumptions. Other assumptions may also be made in valuing pension costs and liabilities. Some examples include the actuarial reduction factors (if any) for optional annuity forms (other than the normal annuity form), the marital status of participants in connection with joint and survivor annuities and preretirement joint-and-survivor annuities, and the actuarial value of lump-sum distributions that plans may make available to participants instead of periodic pension payments.

Considerations Involved in Setting Actuarial Assumptions. The setting of appropriate actuarial assumptions involves considerable judgment. Pension plans are long-term undertakings; thus, the factors affecting their costs can change substantially over time. Hence, actuarial assumptions are only estimates for the future. They can be changed periodically as actual experience shows them to be too conservative or too liberal.

As a matter of management policy, employers should consider how conservative they want the actuarial assumptions to be. Relatively conservative assumptions will produce currently higher estimated pension costs and liabilities. On the other hand, if experience in the future should turn against the plan, future cost estimates would not increase, or would not increase as much, as they would if less conservative assumptions had previously been used. As a regulatory matter, ERISA and the tax law require the pension actuary to use assumptions that in the aggregate are reasonably related to the plan's experience and reasonable expectations under the plan, and that offer the actuary's best estimate of anticipated experience under the plan. This standard, however, provides reasonably wide latitude in making appropriate actuarial assumptions.

Selecting Actuarial Cost Method

An actuarial cost method, or actuarial funding method or valuation method, is essentially a mathematical system for allocating the costs of a defined benefit pension plan to particular years. It determines the pattern of funding these costs over the years. Thus, the pension costs applicable to each year are determined by the actuarial cost method used, the actuarial assumptions adopted, and the actual experience of the plan.

There are two broad groupings of actuarial cost methods: methods based on *accrued benefits*, and methods based on *projected benefits*. A detailed analysis of the different types of actuarial cost methods within each of these broad groupings is beyond the scope of this text; however, the nature of these basic approaches will be summarized next.

Accrued Benefits Methods. The accrued benefits actuarial cost methods involve the determination of the pension benefit earned (or accrued) in each particular year for each employee, and then the calculation of the actuarial present value of these benefits as determined for all participants for that year. This results in the normal cost, or current service cost, for the year. The actuarial liability for the plan, then, would be the present value of all benefits accrued under the plan to the valuation date.

An example of an accrued benefits actuarial cost method is the so-called *unit credit method.* To illustrate this method, assume that a pension plan's benefit formula calls for a pension benefit of 1½ percent per year of each year's compensation on a career-average basis for each year of service up to a maximum of thirty years of service starting at a normal retirement age of sixty-five. Thus, for a fifty-year-old participant who earns $20,000 in a year, the normal cost for the participant for that year would be the present value (using the plan's actuarial assumptions) at age fifty of a pension benefit of $300 per year ($20,000×1½ percent) beginning at age sixty-five. There also would usually be amortization of past service liability over a period of years under this approach.

Projected Benefits Methods.   Under this second general category of actuarial cost methods, the approach is to determine the pension benefit estimated to be payable at the expected retirement age, and then to calculate the present value at retirement of this projected benefit. The annual cost is then a future stream of contributions that will be necessary to fund the present value of the projected benefit.

An example of a projected benefits actuarial cost method is the *entry-age normal cost method.* Under this method, the normal or current cost each year for a participant is the level annual contribution necessary to provide the projected pension benefit at retirement age, assuming that the contribution was paid from the participant's entry age into the plan (age of eligibility) until his or her retirement date. Since a participant may receive credit for service prior to the effective date of the plan, and hence have an entry age prior to the effective date of the plan, a plan will normally have a past service liability under this method that will be amortized over a period of years.

Considerations Affecting Choice of Actuarial Cost Method.   The various actuarial cost methods that may be chosen will produce different patterns of pension costs over the years. This obviously will affect an employer's choice of funding method. Other factors that may affect the actuarial cost method include employer funding objectives, employer financial strength, desired flexibility in funding, actuarial assumptions, and pension plan design. As a regulatory matter, the actuarial cost method used must be acceptable to the IRS, and a change in method normally requires prior IRS approval.

Valuing Plan Assets   The valuation of plan assets is important in helping to determine the level of employer contributions to a pension plan and in assessing the plan's funding status. Naturally, the value of plan assets also directly affects the measurement of plan investment performance and is necessary for making investment decisions.

The following methods of asset valuation either have been used or may be used in valuing pension assets.

1. Market Value. This approach is almost self-explanatory. Assets are valued at their market values as of a particular date. This method is gaining increasing use, particularly since the passage of ERISA.

2. Valuing Bonds and Other Evidence of Indebtedness at Amortized Cost. ERISA permits employers to value bonds at cost, with the amortization of any premium of discount from the date of purchase to the date of the bonds' maturity or date of call, whichever is earlier. This option permits an element of stability in valuing a plan's bond portfolio.

3. Formula Methods. There are a number of formulas that are used to value pension assets. Their purpose is usually to avoid undue fluctuations in asset values, but still basically to track with the underlying market values of the assets.

4. Original Cost. This approach involves valuing securities at their original cost, or book value, regardless of subsequent market value. In its pure form (that is, without some formula adjustment), this method probably does not meet the ERISA regulatory standard described next.

For purposes of meeting the minimum funding standards prescribed by ERISA, the law requires that pension assets be valued on the basis of any reasonable actuarial method that takes into account fair market value.[10] Further, before a change in valuation method may be made, prior IRS approval is required.

Once plan assets are valued for actuarial purposes, the plan's actuarial liability may be compared with its assets to determine its funding ratio. If the actuarial liability exceeds assets, the difference is the unfunded actuarial liability. If the plan assets exceed the actuarial liability, the excess is the actuarial surplus.

Funding Standards

Minimum Funding Standards. One of the significant regulatory requirements added by ERISA is the minimum funding standards for defined benefit pension plans, money purchase pension plans, and target benefit pension plans. While money purchase pension plans technically are subject to ERISA's minimum funding standards, the law's funding requirements are met with respect to such plans if the amount called for in the plan's contribution formula is contributed each year. Similarly, the required contribution for target benefit plans is the amount called for in the plan document that is based on the participants' compensation, ages, and an assumed interest rate. Therefore, the remainder of this discussion will deal with the minimum funding standards for defined benefit pension plans.

The minimum annual funding requirements under ERISA require employers to contribute to defined benefit plans an amount that is sufficient to fund the normal cost for the year and to amortize the plan's past service liability and experience gains and losses over certain maximum periods of time. The amortization is to be in equal annual installments, including principal and interest. Thus, the minimum annual employer contribution required by ERISA would equal the sum of the following:

1. *Normal cost* for current service for the year.
2. *Amortization of initial unfunded past service liability* (costs relating to participants' service before establishment of the plan). For plans adopted after January 1, 1974, this amount must be amortized over not more than thirty years from the date the plan was adopted. In the case of plans in existence on January 1, 1974, amortization of the past service liability as of the plan year beginning after December 31, 1975, must be over not more than forty years. Forty-year amortization also applies to multi-employer plans.
3. *Amortization of increases or decreases in past service liability* due to plan amendments over not more than thirty years from the time each amendment is effective. Forty-year amortization applies to multiemployer plans.
4. *Amortization of experience gains and/or losses* (in other words, situations in which the plan's actual experience is better (gains) or worse (losses) than the actuarial assumptions used) over not more than fifteen years from the time the gain or loss is determined. Twenty-year amortization applies to multiemployer plans.
5. *Amortization of gains and/or losses from changes in actuarial assumptions* over not more than thirty years.
6. *Amortization of any waived contributions* (see discussion following) for any prior year over not more than fifteen years.
7. Amortization of certain other amounts.

If an employer fails to meet these minimum funding requirements, and as a result the plan has an "accumulated funding deficiency," a 5-percent excise tax is imposed on the deficiency if it is not contributed within specified time periods after the end of the plan year. In addition, if the accumulated funding deficiency is not corrected within ninety days after a notice of deficiency, an additional excise tax of 100 percent of the deficiency is imposed.

Funding Standard Account. Whether a plan meets ERISA's minimum funding requirements is determined or accounted for through the annual preparation of a "funding standard account" for the plan to record its funding status. This account is credited with employer contributions for the year and with the amortization of gains resulting from reductions in plan liabilities (such as experience gains). It is charged with the plan's normal cost for the year and the amortization of plan liabilities needed to satisfy the minimum funding standards described in the preceding section.

As an illustration of the calculation of the funding standard account for a defined benefit plan, assume that a single employer plan is established on January 1, 1976, with a calendar plan year. The plan uses a unit credit actuarial cost method with a valuation interest rate of 6 percent. A valuation is performed as of January 1, 1976, with a calendar plan year. The plan uses a unit credit actuarial cost method with a valuation interest rate of 6 percent. A valuation is performed as of January 1, 1986, to determine costs and funding status for the 1986 plan year. The normal cost for the 1986 plan year was $152,000, and the annual charge for the amortization over 30 years of the plan's initial past service liability was $137,074. In 1979, the plan had an experience gain, and the annual credit resulting from the amortization of this gain over 15 years was $972. Finally, the 1986 employer contribution was $300,000. The funding standard account reflecting these data is shown in Exhibit 10-5 shows a credit balance that is improved at 6 percent interest for the year involved. Since a plan must meet the minimum funding standards on a cumulative basis, this net credit balance will be carried forward as a credit on next year's funding standard account. Thus, such a credit balance may serve to offset otherwise-required employer contributions in future years.

Full Funding Limitation. The law also contains a provision that, in effect, would not require further funding for ERISA minimum funding purposes when a plan becomes fully funded according to the law. This full funding limitation for a plan year is the excess, if any, of the actuarial liability plus the normal cost for the plan year over the value of the plan's assets. The employer's contribution for minimum funding standards purposes does not have to exceed this excess amount. Further, no deduction for tax purposes is permitted for a contribution that exceeds this amount.

Relief from Funding Standards. In appropriate circumstances, the IRS, as an administrative matter, may grant an employer certain relief from ERISA's minimum funding standards. One of these forms of relief is the waiver of minimum funding standards for an employer in any years in which the employer is unable to meet the standards without unusual and substantial business hardship and in which the employer can show that the application of the minimum funding standards would harm the interests of the plan participants. Under these circumstances, the IRS can waive all or part of a plan year's minimum funding requirement, but not for more than five years in any fifteen consecutive years. Also, the amount waived must be amortized over not more than fifteen years. This waiver relief is intended to avoid

Exhibit 10-5
Illustration of Funding Standard Account for Defined Benefit Pension Plan

Credits:	
Employer contribution for year	$300,000
Amortization (over 15 years) of a 1979 experience gain	972
Total credits	$300,972
Charges:	
Normal cost (for cost of benefits earned during the year)	$152,000
Amortization (over 30 years) of initial past-service liability (for cost of benefits earned for participants' services before the plan was adopted)	137,074
Total charges	$289,074
Credit Balance	$ 11,898
Interest in Balance (at 6%)	714
Net Credit for the future	$ 12,612

plan terminations in the face of an employer's temporary business hardship.

The IRS may also grant an employer an extension of amortization periods for past service costs or experience losses. Such an extension will not be granted unless the employer shows that application of the minimum funding standards would be adverse to the interests of the plan participants or would result in a substantial risk of plan termination or reduction of benefits.

Plans Not Subject to ERISA Funding Standards. As explained earlier in this chapter, all pension plans are subject to the ERISA minimum funding standards unless they are specifically exempted by the law. This applies to both qualified and nonqualified pension plans.

Some of the important categories of retirement and/or capital accumulation plans that are exempted from the ERISA minimum funding standards include the following:

1. Profit-sharing, stock bonus, and employee stock ownership plans,
2. Pension plans funded exclusively by the purchase of certain individual insurance contracts or group insurance contracts that have the same characteristics as these individual insurance

contracts. The following are requirements for this exemption: an individual insurance contract plan must provide for level annual premiums from the time the employee begins plan participation until his or her retirement, plan benefits must be the same as those provided under the insurance contracts, the benefits must be guaranteed by an insurance company, premiums must have been paid on time or the contract reinstated, the rights under the contracts must not be subject to a security interest, and there must be no outstanding policy loans during the plan year. Thus, certain individual policy pension plans and group permanent pension plans may qualify under this exemption.

3. Unfunded nonqualified plans maintained by an employer primarily to provide deferred compensation for a select group of managerial or highly compensated employees. These would be the traditional nonqualified deferred compensation plans.

4. Unfunded excess benefit plans established to provide benefits in excess of the contribution and/or benefit limitations of Section 415 of the IRC.

5. Plans that have not provided for employer contributions after September 2, 1974 (that is, employee-pay-all plans).

6. Welfare-benefit plans.

7. Individual retirement account or annuity plans (IRAs).

8. Various other plans, including governmental plans, church plans, and partnership buy-out plans.

Limits on Employer Tax Deductions The IRC provides certain limits on annual employer contributions to defined benefit pension plans that are deductible for federal income tax purposes by the employer in that year. There are two basic alternative limitations on tax-deductible employer contributions to defined benefit plans. One is the so-called normal cost method. Under this alternative, the tax deduction is limited to the normal cost for the year plus the amortization of past service costs over no less than a ten-year period. The other alternative is the so-called level cost method. Under this approach, an employer may deduct the level amount needed to fund each employee's benefits (including those from both past and current service) as a level amount over the participant's remaining years until his or her retirement date. However, there is a special rule if the costs attributable to three or fewer employees are more than 50 percent of the remaining pension costs, as might be the case for smaller closely held employers. In this event, the unfunded costs for these three or fewer employees must be amortized over a period of at least five years.

If it were to happen, however, that the employer contribution necessary to meet the ERISA minimum funding standards previously described would exceed whichever of these alternative methods applied, the limit for federal income tax deductibility would become the ERISA minimum funding requirement. Finally, as previously noted in this chapter, the tax-deductible limit cannot exceed the full funding limitation.

If an employer were to contribute more to a defined benefit plan than the deductible limits just described, any excess contribution may be carried over and deducted in later tax years. As a practical matter, however, employers usually do not want to contribute more than they can take as an income tax deduction in the current year.

Employer Funding Policy As a minimum, employers must annually fund their pension obligations in an amount at least equal to that required by the ERISA minimum funding standards. On the other hand, employers normally do not wish to fund their pension obligations in an amount greater than they can deduct that year for federal income tax purposes. Within these parameters, however, employers have a considerable degree of discretion as to the pension funding policy they wish to follow. The following are some factors that may affect employer decisions in this regard:

1. Cash Flow Considerations. Employers may want to maintain reasonable stability in the cash flow required to fund their pension plans. This factor depends, in part, on the financial strength and stability of the employer.
2. Nature of Plan. This will naturally have an impact on employer funding decisions. The extent of plan costs, in relation to payroll for example, will have an important impact on how rapidly an employer can afford to fund the plan.
3. Nature of the Industry and Competitive Conditions. An employer's funding policy will naturally be influenced by the competitive conditions under which it must operate. If profit margins in a particular industry are quite narrow, for example, it may be important for an employer to keep its pension expense as low as possible. Of course, the reverse may be true in more affluent industries.
4. The Employer's Internal Rate of Return. If the after-tax rate of return the employer can earn on funds within its own business is relatively high compared with the tax-free return from qualified pension fund investments, the employer may be inclined toward funding its pension obligations around the minimum permitted level.
5. Matching Contributions to Accrued Benefits. Employers may establish certain goals for funding plans, such as funding an

amount at least equal to the total present value of accrued benefits or of accrued vested benefits.

6. Accounting Considerations. In accounting for pension costs on its financial statements, an employer may need to follow a consistent expense policy with respect to pension costs.

FUNDING EMPLOYEE WELFARE BENEFIT PLANS

Important decision factors in the employee benefit planning process are how the benefits are to be financed and what financing instruments or mechanisms are to be used. As the costs of employee benefits have increased, both absolutely and as a component of overall compensation, the issue of how these plans are to be funded has become a more and more important business decision. The funding methods used have budgeting, accounting, solvency, tax, and cost implications for the employer.

Employers are naturally interested in controlling the overall costs of employee benefit plans. When viewed broadly, the approaches available to employers to control or reduce overall plan costs fall into the following general categories:

- Improved plan design (including possible benefit cutbacks where warranted or necessary).
- Adoption of specific cost containment programs, such as discussed previously for health care cost containment.
- Improved administration of benefit plans by the employer and/or third parties.
- Adoption of more cost-effective funding and/or servicing arrangements.
- Consolidation of carriers (and perhaps changing carriers) that serve as funding agencies for benefit plans.

This chapter is basically concerned with the last two methods just enumerated with regard to employee benefit plans other than retirement plans.

The term "welfare benefit plans" as used here refers to most of the kinds of employee benefits discussed in this book, other than pension, profit-sharing, and other capital accumulation plans. It thus includes medical expense benefits, disability income benefits, group term life insurance, supplemental unemployment benefits, severance pay, dependent care assistance benefits, group legal service benefits, and others. The term is perhaps somewhat vague, but it is used here because it is finding increasing acceptance in practice. For example, it is the term employed in the Internal Revenue Code (IRC) for the provision added by the Tax Reform Act portion of DEFRA concerning funding limits on "funded welfare benefit plans."

Insured Plans

Group insurance, or group benefits in the case of the "Blues" and HMOs, is an important instrument for funding certain employee benefits. An *insured plan* for this purpose means one with the following characteristics: the benefit is funded through an insurance company or other carrier, the employer pays a premium to the insurer, the plan is administered by the insurer, and the insurer provides substantial guarantees for the payment of promised plan benefits. As so defined, insured plans may be on a *fixed-cost (or "pooled") basis* (using the insurer's manual rates) or may be *experience rated.* These were the traditional ways of funding employee benefits in the past, but there has been a distinct trend in recent years toward *modified insurance arrangements* (discussed later in this chapter) and/or use of *self-funding* of employee benefits.

Class or Manual Rating This approach involves determining the premium a group is charged for a particular benefit on the basis of the overall claims experience and expenses of the insurer or from overall insurance industry data for that class of business. The insurer thus charges all similarly situated groups a fixed premium that is sufficient to cover the insurer's overall claims or losses, administrative expenses, commissions and other acquisitions costs, taxes, an amount for contingencies, and an amount for profit or a contribution to the insurer's surplus. As has been noted, class or manual rates are sometimes referred to as "pooled rates" or "fixed rates."

Class or manual rates are used in group insurance mainly for smaller groups that because of their lack of credibility for experience rating purposes are not eligible for the insurer's experience rating plan. They are also used for determining initial premiums for groups that are experience rated when the group is first insured, or when the group is transferred from another carrier and its past experience with that carrier cannot be obtained. Depending upon the credibility of the group (as explained next), some combination of a group's own claims experience and the insurer's manual or expected claims may be used to calculate the group's claims charge for experience rating purposes. Finally, even though a group is eligible for experience rating, the employer may find it financially advantageous to use a fixed cost insurance arrangement in some cases.

Community Rating Blue Cross-Blue Shield may use community rating for the hospital and/or medical benefits they provide. Community rating involves charging the same rate for a uniform benefit program to the subscribers or to a class of subscribers within a given geographical area. These uniform rates are based on the average cost of the benefits for the subscribers or class of subscribers as a whole within the geographical area (or community). Traditionally, the Blues applied community rating to all groups and did not use experience rating. This philosophy basically resulted in "pooling" the experience of all groups, good and bad, within the community and produced uniform community rates for all groups.

However, competition with the insurance companies forced the Blues to abandon this traditional community rating philosophy with respect to many groups and to adopt experience rating for those groups to compete effectively with the insurers. The Blues still use community rating, however, for individual subscribers and for smaller groups that are not eligible for experience rating. HMOs also use community rating.

Experience Rating *Experience rating* means that the premium that is ultimately paid for group insurance will be based in whole or in part upon the group's own claims experience, and perhaps also upon the insurer's actual expenses incurred in administering the particular group's plan. The basic concept is that, from an actuarial or statistical point of view, if a group is large enough, its own claims experience will be sufficiently reliable or predictable for the insurer to use that experience (and perhaps the group's own administrative expenses as well) to determine the final premium for the group.

Experience rating thus helps produce rate equity among groups that are large enough so that their own claims experience, in whole or in part, is sufficiently statistically reliable to make the group eligible for experience rating. Further, group insurance is highly competitive and groups may have the option of self-funding rather than purchasing group insurance. Thus, there would be a natural tendency for the groups with better experience either to seek insurers that offered experience rating or to self-fund. From a competitive point of view, therefore, experience rating permits insurers (and the Blues) to compete effectively among themselves for the better groups and to compete effectively with self-funding as an alternative. Experience rating is commonly employed in most forms of group insurance, including medical expense, dental, group term life, short-term disability, and long-term disability.

Experience rating is applied retrospectively and prospectively. When applied *retrospectively*, the insurer's experience rating system operates at the end of a group's experience period, commonly one year, to determine what the experience of the group was during that period and whether the group is entitled to any refund (dividend or retrospective rate credit) of the original premium paid for the experience period. Thus, the system is looking backward at the group's actual experience over the past experience period to determine whether any refund is due based upon the group's actual experience as compared with its expected experience. In summary form, experience rating used retrospectively applies the following general formula to a group's experience during the experience period:

Premiums Earned
—Benefit Charges (based on the group's incurred and/or expected claims)
—Retention Charges (to cover administrative expenses and other charges)
—Dividend or Retrospective Rate Credit Payable (or Deficit to be Carried Forward)

When applied *prospectively,* experience rating is used as part of the renewal rating process, whereby any change in the group's renewal premium for the next succeeding experience period is based at least in part upon the group's actual experience during the previous period. Thus, prospective experience rating is used to determine a group's premium for a future period which, in turn, will be subject to retrospective experience rating at the end of that period. Prospective experience rating may also be used to develop initial premiums for groups that are eligible for experience rating and that change insurers or other carriers when their previous experience is available.

Self-Funding

General Characteristics Self-funding, as its name implies, means that an employer pays employee benefits from its own assets without shifting any risk or liability for benefit payments to an insurer or other carrier, other than through the possible use of stop-loss coverage. (Self-funding is sometimes referred to as "self-insuring" employee benefits, but in this text the term "self-funding" will be used as the more descriptive and proper term.) Some employers, particularly larger employers, will self-fund employee benefits entirely from their own resources without any use of stop-loss insurance. For most benefits, however, a completely self-funded approach can typically be used only by very large employers. Most employers purchase various types of stop-loss insurance to protect them against unexpectedly adverse claims experience from their self-funded programs. When such stop loss insurance is used, a self-funded program is sometimes referred to as a "split-funded plan."

Employers may provide self-funded employee benefits directly from their own current income and/or assets without any other intermediary to provide the benefits. For tax and possibly investment reasons, however, many employers utilize one or more *Voluntary Employees' Beneficiary Associations* (VEBAs), which are commonly referred to as Section 501(c)(9) trusts, as a vehicle for self-funding certain types of employee benefits. Employer contributions to a VEBA are normally tax deductible by the employer in the year contributed as ordinary and necessary business expenses, and the investment income of the VEBA is not taxable income (in other words, it accumulates tax free) because of the tax-exempt status of a VEBA under Section 501(c)(9) of the IRC. However, a trust or other arrangement must meet certain tax law requirements, as described next, to qualify as a VEBA under the Code. In addition, the Tax Reform Act of 1984 portion of DEFRA established limits on the current income tax deduction an employer can take for contributions to "funded welfare benefit plans," which include VEBAs.

As has been noted, there has been a considerable increase in self-funding of employee benefits, particularly through VEBAs. During the 1950s and 1960s, employee benefits were usually insured on either a fixed-cost or an experience rated basis. Larger employers, however, increasingly utilized self-funding to save costs and for other reasons. In recent years, many employers have utilized self-funding for at least some of their employee benefits.

The subject of self-funding is taken up at this point in the chapter so that it can be compared more easily with the insurance approach (especially experience rating) of funding employee benefits. In addition, the rationale for some of the modified insurance arrangements to be discussed later in the chapter will be better appreciated if self-funding is considered first. These modified insurance arrangements are intended in large measure as a response to some of the advantages alleged for the self-funding of employee benefits.

Rationale for Self-Funding The nature, characteristics, and limits of self-funding have been considered in the preceding discussion. This discussion, along with that about traditional experience-rated group insurance, provides a good background for analyzing the rationale for self-funding. Later in this chapter we shall consider certain modified insurance arrangements that may respond to the arguments for self-funding.

The following are the main motives or reasons that may cause employers to consider self-funding their employee welfare benefit plans. These reasons will be analyzed in relation to traditional experience-rated group insurance.

Savings in Plan Costs. The costs of an employee benefit plan can be broadly classified into benefit charges and expenses of administration. In analyzing how self-funding may or may not save plan costs, it will be helpful to consider the costs under experience-rated group insurance and then to observe what effect, if any, self-funding may have on each cost element.

Self-funding normally is not considered to have an important effect upon the benefit charges (the claims) component of plan costs. Assuming a group is large enough to be 100-percent credible for experience rating purposes, the group would generally pay its own loss costs whether it is funded through a group insurance contract with full experience rating or is self-funded. Under these circumstances, the group's loss costs will essentially depend upon the benefits provided, the plan design, the characteristics of the group, and the use of appropriate cost containment measures. The timing of the payment of loss costs and the issue of who holds the reserves for future claim payments will differ as between experience-rated group insurance and self-funding, but this point actually pertains to the cash flow issue, which is discussed in the next section.

If a group is not large enough to be 100-percent credible for experience rating purposes, then the question of whether it would save on loss costs by self-funding depends upon whether its experience is significantly better or worse than the average experience assumed by the issuer in determining expected losses for the group in the experience rating process. For smaller groups that are not 100-percent credible, however, the possibility of chance fluctuations in claims experience and the consequent financial risk to the employer should also be considered in evaluating group insurance as compared with self-funding. Of course, to the extent that an employer could secure more effective claims administration or claims cost control through either insurance or self-funding, there would be a loss cost advantage for one approach or the other. However, there is nothing inherent in either an insured arrangement or a self-funded arrangement (with, say, an ASO contract or an independent firm administering the claims) that would necessarily produce better claims administration or cost control.

Finally, in experience-rated group insurance, a pooling, or stop-loss, charge may be included as part of the benefit charges assessed against the group's experience. This is the cost of limiting the employer's liability under experience rating. As noted previously, however, this pooling charge should logically be compared with the cost of stop-loss insurance for a comparable self-funded group. The employer may want to make such a cost comparison for its particular group.

With respect to potential savings in plans costs, most attention has focused on possible savings in administrative expenses (the retention in experience-rated group insurance) by adopting the self-funding alternative. If we review the changes normally included in an insurer's retention, it might be argued that savings could be achieved through self-funding in the areas of commissions and other acquisition costs, the charge for risks or contingencies (the risk charge), premium taxes, and any contribution to the insurer's profit or surplus.

The extent of any savings in commissions and other acquisition costs would seem to depend upon the nature of the services performed by the agent or broker and upon whether those services would have to be performed by the employer or by another party on a fee basis if the plan were self-funded. Pure sales charges probably could be avoided by self-funding. Sometimes group insurance cases are written without commissions or on a fee basis. It may be argued that the risk charge could be saved by self-funding, to the extent that it is intended to protect the insurer against losses if a group with an experience rating deficit changes insurers. To the extent that a portion of the risk charge is intended for contingencies, however, a self-funded plan might want to make a similar provision. Any contribution to an insurer's profit or surplus would be saved by self-funding. In most cases, though, this would be quite small.

Perhaps the most important area of potential cost savings through self-funding would be the avoidance of state premium taxes. Depending upon the state or states involved, these taxes could be as high as 4 percent of premiums, but they probably average around 2 percent for larger groups. Premium taxes can generally be avoided by self-funding. Whether experience-rated group insurance or self-funding is used, the other expenses of administering a group plan, including cost of claims administration, generally apply. In the final analysis, then, with respect to the expense element, an employer or its advisors should evaluate the expected amount of the retention of one or probably more insurers in relation to the expenses expected to be incurred (including additional internal expenses of the employer's own staff) if self-funding is used. Naturally, such a comparison should be made on a consistent basis among insurers and between insurance and self-funding.

Improved Cash Flow. The concept behind this motive for self-funding is that the employer, or a VEBA established by the employer, can have the use of the reserves established for future benefit costs rather than having those claim reserves held by an insurance company. Thus, it is argued that, either directly or indirectly through its contributions to a VEBA, the employer (rather than the insurance company) would have the advantage of the time value on these reserves. In the case of contributions to a VEBA, the reserves for future claim payments accumulate income tax free, which further enhances the time value of these claim reserves for the employer on an after-tax basis.

This cash flow argument is a complex one. Insurers do maintain sizable claim reserves for their experience-rated group contracts, but they usually also credit the policy holder with interest on these reserves, either as part of the retention or separately in the experience rating process. However, it is sometimes argued that policyholders do not know precisely how this interest factor is calculated or applied. Assuming that interest is credited by an insurer on the claim reserves it holds for a group contract, the issue then becomes whether the after-tax return that the employer can earn on these reserves if they are retained in its own business, or the before-tax return that can be earned if they are accumulated tax-free in a VEBA, will be better than the return credited to the group for experience rating purposes by the insurer. This, in turn, would seem to depend upon the interest rate and method of calculation used by an insurer for interest credited on claim reserves, as compared with the after-tax rate of return the employer can generate within its business, or the before-tax rate of return that can be generated by investments in a VEBA.

On balance, the alleged cash flow advantages of self-funding have been an important reason for employers to choose this alternative. Thus, various modified insurance arrangements, discussed next in this chapter, are aimed at reducing in various ways the amount of employer money that will be held by the insurer. Further, the reserving practices followed by insurers in their experience rating will have a bearing upon this rationale for self-funding. Thus, employers should investigate and evaluate the reserving practices of insurers in choosing among insurers or in choosing between insurance and self-funding. It is also possible that the statutory funding limits for "funded welfare benefit plans," discussed earlier, may reduce to some degree the cash flow attractiveness of such plans.

Benefits To Be Provided. Certain kinds of benefits that are provided by employers on a self-funded basis are not available through the insurance mechanism. Some examples are supplemental unemployment benefits, severance pay, and vacation benefits.

In other cases, an employer may prefer broader benefits or more liberal underwriting than may be available from insurance companies. On the other hand, employers may not want to provide certain benefits that might be required under group insurance contracts. Under some circumstances, employers may feel that the insurance market for a particular benefit is too limited, or too costly, or that reserving standards are too high, and they will therefore consider self-funding for that benefit.

Desire for Greater Control Over the Plan. Employers may be inclined toward self-funding in order to have maximum control over their plans. This might involve a desire for greater control over claims administration, investment policy with respect to reserves, or the timing of contributions to the plan. This factor naturally depends upon the benefits, compensation, and management philosophies of the employer.

Modified Insurance Arrangements

The insurance industry has developed a number of arrangements that modify traditional experience-rated group insurance and usually result in either greater cash flow to the employer or savings in premium taxes or both. Thus, they tend to address the forces that may cause employers to consider self-funding.

Minimum Premium Plans An early modified insurance arrangement was the minimum premium plan, sometimes referred to as the "MET-CAT Plan" because of an early minimum premium plan entered into between the Metropolitan Life Insurance Company and the Caterpillar Tractor Company. As its name implies, this plan is designed to reduce the premium paid by a policyholder to the insurance company to a minimum and, thus, to reduce premium taxes. These plans are typically used for larger employers for whom the premium tax is a relatively large percentage of their group insurance retentions and whose claims experience is 100-percent credible for experience rating purposes.

Under a typical minimum premium plan, the insurer becomes liable for claims only after the aggregate claims paid during a particular period, such as a policy year, exceed a specific level, commonly 90 percent of expected claims or the normal premium. The employer self-funds claims up to the level at which the insurer becomes liable. For this coverage, the insurer charges only a fraction of the premium it would normally have charged for traditional experience-rated group insurance. This "minimum premium," for example, might be approximately 10 percent of its normal premium in a situation in which the employer is paying claims up to 90 percent of the premium normally charged. Also, under minimum premium plans, the insurer remains ultimately liable for future claim payments and must therefore maintain claim reserves for the group contract. Thus, these plans are primarily intended to reduce premium taxes rather than to improve employer cash flow.

Retrospective Premium Arrangements A commonly used modified insurance arrangement is the so-called retrospective premium arrangement, or "retro plan," under which the insurer charges the employer an initial group insurance premium that is less than would normally be charged, but in return the employer agrees to pay an additional premium at the end of the experience period if incurred claims plus the insured's retention exceed the initial prospective premium. There is usually a limit on this additional premium so that the total premium paid by the employer during the experience period cannot exceed some percentage, such as 125 percent, of the initial prospective premium. Any claims in excess of this limiting percentage are borne by the insurance company. Thus, for example, a group medical expense plan, might charge an initial prospective premium of, say, 10 percent less than would be called for under the insurer's regular experience rating formula, but with a provision requiring the employer to pay an additional premium at the end of the experience period of up to 15 percent more than the initial premium if incurred claims and the insurer's retention exceed the initial paid premium.

The effect of retrospective premium arrangements is that the employer is allowed to retain part of the premium which otherwise would have been paid to the insurer. It thus improves the employer's cash flow. On the other hand, the employer's potential liability for adverse claims fluctuations in the group's experience may be increased, because the employer assumes a limited potential liability if incurred claims plus the insurer's retention exceed the initial premium, which the employer would not do under traditional experience-rated group insurance.

Premium-Lag Arrangements Another modified insurance arrangement is the so-called premium-lag or premium-delay arrangement; it is designed to allow the policyholder to retain more of the funds that otherwise would be paid to the insurance company, and hence to improve the employer's cash flow. Under this approach, the plan allows an employer to defer payment on monthly group insurance premiums for a specified period of time beyond the normal 30-day grace period. The most common delay periods for this purpose are 60 to 90 days. Assuming a 90-day lag in premium payments, this, in effect, allows the employer to have the use of approximately 25 percent of the annual premium on the group contract. Thus, this kind of arrangement is intended to answer the cash flow argument for self-funding. However, insurers may offset the cost of such premium-lag arrangements by increasing their retention or by charging interest on the delayed premiums.

Reserve-Reduction Arrangements This modified insurance arrangement is similar in purpose to the premium-lag arrangement just discussed; it allows the policyholder to retain that portion of the annual group insurance premium that is equal to the claim reserves which the insurance company would otherwise retain. Thus it is another answer to the cash flow argument for self-funding.

Under both this arrangement and the premium-lag arrangement, the group policyholder remains liable to the insurer for the amount of the premium retained by the policyholder. Thus, in the event of the termination of the group insurance contract, the funds retained by the policyholder must be paid to the insurer.

Cost-Plus Arrangements In discussing modified insurance arrangements, the term "cost-plus" may be used by practitioners in several contexts. However, a cost-plus arrangement can be thought of as one in which the group policyholder pays for claims incurred up to a specified maximum amount and also pays to the insurer a specified retention for plan administration. Depending upon their terms, these plans may amount to the employer's paying its own claims plus a retention to the insurance company.

Factors To Consider in the Funding Decision

The decision among funding vehicles—fixed premium group insurance; experience-rated group insurance, with or without modified insurance arrangements; or self-funding—is not an easy one. In practice, employers will often use several or all of these funding approaches for the various benefits in their employee benefit plan. For example, an employer might use fixed premium group insurance for its long-term disability plan, travel accident plan, and accidental death and dismemberment plan, experience-rated group insurance for its group term life plan; self-funding with aggregate and specific stop-loss insurance and an ASO contract or other contract for claims administration for its medical expense plan; and self-funding without other arrangements for its severance pay and sick pay plans.

The following are some of the factors an employer should consider in deciding upon the appropriate funding vehicles for the various benefits in its employee benefit plan:

1. The cost and cash flow considerations discussed previously in this chapter.
2. The kinds of benefits involved. Self-funding may be most appropriate for benefits involving high-frequency and low-severity claims. For certain benefits under certain circumstances, carriers may have natural advantages that would be hard for

the employer to duplicate through self-funding. For example, Blue Cross coverage has a cost advantage in certain areas because of the "hospital discount" available to them; HMOs may have an advantage because of their method of providing health care services.

3. The size of the group involved and the credibility of its loss experience.

4. The financial strength of the employer. This will affect the employer's ability to absorb unexpected fluctuations in claims experience under self-funding or under some forms of modified insurance arrangements. However, the availability and cost of aggregate and/or specific stop-loss insurance for self-funded plans would have an important effect upon an employer's ability to assume financial risk under such plans. The financial strength of an employer might also affect its willingness to recognize future claim liabilities under self-funded plans.

5. The availability and cost of administrative arrangements (including claims administration) for self-funded plans.

6. The availability and cost of funding vehicles for self-funded plans, such as VEBAs. In this respect, the employer should also assess the impact, if any, of the funding limits on the deductibility of employer contributions to "funded welfare benefit plans" (including VEBAs).

7. The employer's philosophy concerning compensation and benefits for its employees, and its willingness to assume financial risks in this regard.

8. There may be certain tax factors that will affect the decision. For example, death benefits in the employee benefit plan are generally provided through group term life insurance and are not self-funded. An important reason for this is that the federal income tax exclusion for life insurance proceeds paid by reason of the insured's death is clear when death benefits are funded through group term life insurance. However, there is substantial question as to whether this life insurance exclusion would apply to death benefits paid on a self-funded basis, other than for the $5,000 employer-paid death benefit. Therefore, this important tax factor strongly inclines employers toward insuring the death benefit rather than attempting to provide it on a self-funded basis. Of course, a VEBA could purchase a group term life insurance contract from an insurer to cover its members, and the life insurance exclusion would be available. In this case, however, group term life insurance is still the funding vehicle. As previously noted, the funding limits on

employer contributions to "funded welfare benefit plans" may affect the employer's decision in this area.

Obviously, it is clear that the decision concerning the appropriate funding vehicle or vehicles for an employer's welfare benefits is a complex one and has important financial implications for the employer.

SUMMARY

Risk management professionals clearly have an interest in, and often share or have sole responsibility for, the planning and design of employee benefit programs that fulfill an employer's commitment to providing employees funds for financing recovery from their own and their families' personnel losses.

Planning these programs—both the benefits provided and the funding mechanisms—requires recognizing the reasons for such plans and the relative strengths and weaknesses of funding mechanisms based on insurance and trust funds. In evaluating these objectives, it is important to distinguish between those which are truly altruistic in serving only employees and those which partially (or even primarily) are in the employer's self-interest. In designing the mechanisms to fund various employee benefits, it is important to consider: (1) the timing of cash flows into and out of each funding vehicle, (2) the extent to which the employer earns investment income on funds held to pay future benefits, and (3) the degree of uncertainty to which the employer is exposed because of the variability in loss experience or unexpected fluctuations in investment results.

Employee benefit financing presents many planning and design choices—among them what benefits to provide, whether they should be funded on a contributory or noncontributory basis, whether funds should be accumulated through insurance or a funded trust, or (if through insurance) whether on a group or an individual-policy basis. In making these decisions, it is important not to confront them as simply "either/or" choices—for example, using either an insured or a trusteed plan. For most of the factors involved in employee benefit financing, there is a wide range of choices between the "either" and the "or" extremes. This range provides opportunities for rather precise initial tailoring of employee benefits and of funding arrangements and for considerable latitude in later adjusting these plans to reflect changing workforce characteristics, loss experience, and investment results. Sound management of employee benefit financing, like all risk financing decisions, can contribute substantially to an organization's financial strength and operational success.

Chapter Notes

1. This chapter consists primarily of material reprinted with permission from Chapters 1, 13, 19, and 20 of Jerry S. Rosenbloom and G. Victor Hallman, *Employee Benefit Planning*, 2nd ed. (Englewood Cliffs, NJ: Prentice-Hall, 1986).
2. See, for example, George Strauss and L. R. Sayles, *Personnel—The Human Problems of Management*, 4th ed. (Englewood Cliffs, N.J.: Prentice-Hall, Inc., 1980), Chap. 26.
3. See Martha Remy Yohalem, "Employee-Benefit Plan" 1975, *Social Security Bulletin*, Vol. 40, No. 11 (November 1977), p. 19.
4. There are some exceptions to this overall statement that should be noted. In general, an employer's contributions on behalf of an employee's *total* compensation (including employee benefits) is reasonable and necessary for the business. Also, various rules must be met for employer contributions to "qualified" retirement plans, Section 501(c)(9) trusts, and certain other benefit plans to be income tax deductible.
5. An added factor is that the employer would normally be able to buy the group coverage at lower group rates than the employee would have to pay for individually purchased insurance. See the discussion of the inherent advantages of group insurance later in this chapter.
6. In individual insurance, insurers seek to minimize adverse selection by underwriting the individual applicants for insurance and by rejecting, increasing the rates for, or modifying the coverage for those who do not meet the insurer's underwriting standards.
7. Note, however, that when group insurance is continued on retired lives, and the flow of lives out of the group is thus delayed, the costs of the group plan increase, and some approach must be adopted to finance the benefits on retired lives.
8. "Substandard" policies in individual insurance are written on lives that do not qualify for standard coverage according to the insurer's underwriting rules. They are written with a higher premium and/or with restricted coverage to compensate for the extra risk.
9. I.R.C. Sec. 125(d). However, a cafeteria plan under the IRC does not include any plan that provides for deferred compensation, other than a Section 401(k) cash or deferred arrangement.
10. In applying this standard, IRS regulations specify that an actuarial method properly takes into account fair market value if the actuarial value of the assets falls within a "corridor" of between 80 percent and 120 percent of the fair market value of the assets, or if a five-year average value of the assets falls within a corridor of between 85 percent and 115 percent of average fair market values.

CHAPTER 11

Dealing with Insurers and Other Providers

INTRODUCTION

This chapter draws on the chronology of the actual renewal of an insurance program for a real, but "disguised," medium-sized retailer. It presents ideas and procedures that should be useful to risk management professionals in making and renewing contracts with insurers and other providers of risk financing. It also discusses other services upon which risk management programs draw for both financial protection and the expertise that the organization itself cannot cost effectively provide. One case study cannot illustrate all the diverse circumstances for which an organization needs to approach various "markets" for the insurance and other resources its risk management program requires. The case approach is, however, most instructive for examining the principles, procedures, and ethics that should prevail in all such dealings with every source of protection or service.

CHRONOLOGY OF AN INSURANCE RENEWAL

The company renewing its insurance was a regional supermarket chain located in the southwestern United States. The company no longer exists, but its demise was unrelated to risk management matters. With approximately 125 stores in a three-state area, it maintained its own warehouse distribution facilities and truck fleet operations. It employed more than 6,000 full- and part-time employees and had annual gross revenues in excess of $700 million. This chain,

205

whose stock was publicly held but family controlled, had been in business since the early 1900s.

Internal Preparations and Discussions

The company had a July 1 expiration of its combined retrospectively rated insurance program covering workers compensation, general liability, real and personal property, and automobile physical damage and liability exposures. With this in mind, shortly after the first of the year, the chain's risk management professional approached his immediate superior and the chief financial officer of the company. The risk management professional explained that although the incumbent broker was performing adequately and there were no serious problems with the insurer, he felt that it was his responsibility to see what else the insurance marketplace had to offer.

The risk management professional recommended and gained senior management's approval of a marketing process known as *closed (or selective) bidding*. The supermarket chain would ask a number of insurers' marketing representatives, who the risk manager believed were particularly qualified, to submit competitive bids on the chain's insurance program. Selective bidding contrasts with *open competitive bidding* in which the organization seeking insurance essentially "publishes" the specifications for the insurance program it desires, allowing any insurer or insurance marketing representative to submit a bid. Because this chain's risk management professional was confident he knew the insurance market, he and the company's senior executives agreed that full open bidding would be unnecessarily time consuming.

The risk management professional then approached the following eight sources of coverage because of their particular expertise or niche in the insurance marketplace:

1. The incumbent brokerage organization was asked because of its quality work and the fine job the account representative servicing this chain had done during the preceding two and one-half years.
2. The agency that was used immediately before the incumbent was contacted and asked if it was interested in again looking at the account. Because no "bridges had been burned," this agency was most willing.
3. A newer agency in the city was approached because among their staff was a former account executive who had handled the chain's insurance several years earlier for the incumbent broker. Because of his knowledge of the account, he might have a competitive edge with underwriters.

4. An out-of-state brokerage organization was asked to participate because of the risk management professional's previous contact with this firm. In addition, over the years one of the principals of this firm had developed a rather unique business relationship with the senior vice president of underwriting for one of the major insurers in the country. It was hoped that this direct contact also might provide an advantage to the chain in securing coverage.

5. A major "alphabet house" brokerage was contacted because of the tenacity their sales personnel had displayed during the previous two years. Their continued contact with the risk management professional, keeping him abreast of items of interest and aware of their obvious willingness to participate in the renewal process, made inviting them advisable.

6. The sixth candidate, another brokerage, also was from another state and was contacted primarily because of its expertise with supermarkets, particularly with risk retention programs for medium-sized and large supermarkets. The risk management professional had heard many good things about this particular firm.

7. This participant was an out-of-state brokerage that was in the process of opening a local office. The head of this new office was a former risk management professional with one of the country's largest supermarket chains. Therefore, the brokerage was invited because of the imagination and expertise that this one individual had to offer.

8. The eighth candidate was one of the country's three top direct writers—an insurer whose salaried employees dealt directly with insureds rather than through independent agents or brokers as marketing representatives. To make sure that all avenues would be explored, the chain's risk management professional felt that he would have been remiss had direct writers not been included.

Invitation to the Marketplace

During the middle of January, these eight firms were asked if they were interested in informally discussing a July 1 renewal. All eight responded positively. Over the next ten days, the risk management professional met with representatives from each firm for preliminary discussions of the procedures that would be followed. From these meetings each learned that there was no dissatisfaction with the incumbent brokerage, its account executive, or the present insurer. The eight firms also were told that although price was important, no change would be made for merely marginal premium savings. During these early informal meetings, discussions ranged from the history of the grocery chain, its philosophy toward risk retention, and its approach to claims handling to the level of service that was expected from the agent or broker and the insurer.

With the exception of the direct writer (which would provide all the insurance for which it successfully bid), all participating agents and brokers were asked to submit within ten days their first, second, and third choices of insurers, giving their reasons for selecting these companies and briefly describing their experience with them.

Because of the number of candidates, there could easily have been an embarrassing or awkward overlap in which more than one agent or broker contacted a single insurer for a coverage quotation. To preclude any resulting confusion or concern in the marketplace, each candidate's choice of insurers was controlled by the risk management professional. Where possible, first choices were assigned, but where there was an overlap each involved candidate was given its second or third choice. It was also agreed that the incumbent brokerage would be able to deal with the present insurer and would also be allowed its first choice of an alternative. These special arrangements for the incumbent recognized the importance of loyalty and continuity in insurance dealings.

Although insurance contracts generally provide coverage for only one year, no renewal scenario can be annually repeated. Underwriters are reluctant to entertain quotations for accounts that are "shopped" every year. They are justified in their unwillingness to make price concessions or coverage improvements if they feel that price is the primary decision-making factor. A longer relationship between insurer and insured allows for (1) advantageous pricing for loss experience that has been favorable over a period of time and (2) a reduced likelihood that an underwriter will view a single adverse year as a reason for discontinuing or substantially raising premiums on the entire account.

Development of Specifications and Underwriting Data

Specifications At this point in the process one major question faced the risk management professional: should highly detailed specifications be developed, or should the candidate firms be given free rein to develop their own programs? The advantages of developing precise specifications are like those of standardized insurance policies, such as the comprehensive general liability policy form recommended by most state insurance rating bureaus. Through such specifications, the risk management professional can be reasonably certain that all proposals will be uniform. However, highly particular specifications limit the creativity of account executives and underwriters.

To develop either highly specific or very general insurance specifications, a risk management professional must take the first step in the risk management decision process: identifying and analyzing the organization's property, net income, liability, and personnel loss exposures using standardized survey questionnaires, financial statements, flow charts, and personal inspections of the organization's premises and operations. Second, the risk management professional also must classify possible insurance coverages into one of the following categories:

- mandatory (required by law, such as compulsory automobile liability or workers compensation insurance),
- desirable (such as high limits of liability insurance, replacement cost coverage on buildings and personal property, and appropriate business interruption insurance), and
- available (such as robbery and burglary coverage for an organization that does not have substantial amounts of money or other highly portable valuables on premises or medical malpractice coverage for an organization not engaged in the business of providing medical care).

Any organization must purchase mandatory coverages, probably will want to obtain desirable coverages, and should at least consider available coverages. The policies in this third category can be accepted or rejected according to the extent of the organization's exposures, its financial position, and the concerns of its owners and/or senior executives.

Once these exposures and coverages have been identified, a risk management professional can then develop in narrative or outline form (or a combination of both) a summary of the organization's exposures and insurance requirements (or wishes). When given to the candidate firms, this summary provides the prospective underwriters with a first impression of the organization as an insurance account. It also serves as a foundation for the more detailed insurance specifications underlying the request for proposal (RFP) that will be given to each candidate. A carefully designed and complete presentation of the organization's insurance needs brings it closer to the goal of obtaining optimum coverage at a reasonable price.

The final specifications should be sufficiently detailed so that the underwriters have enough information to develop specific quotations for the coverages that the organization considers essential or desirable. It is important, however, that the specifications are broad enough to allow the underwriters and their marketing representatives to be somewhat innovative in designing insurance coverages and packages to meet the organization's needs. By allowing insurers this flexibility, an organization's risk management specialist also creates opportunities for exploring alternative methods of financing that otherwise probably would not be considered.

Underwriting Information The task for the supermarket chain's risk management professional now became one of developing the necessary information and data for agents/brokers and underwriters so that the most meaningful insurance quotations could be obtained. Good, professional underwriting information can result in convincing an insurer to take an organization's account at a fair price. In addition to providing the participating candidates with all the necessary information, the risk management professional must ensure that his time is not drained by answering the same questions for each participant.

Although an insurance renewal is a most important part of a risk management professional's activities, the day-to-day operations of the risk management department must continue. One way of achieving both goals is to provide the representatives of prospective insurers with as much information as possible about an account in a format that is also useful in the organization's own routine risk management activities. Therefore, this supermarket chain presented to each of the eight candidates a copy of a manual that it had previously developed and maintained. It contained the following eight sections:

- *Locations.* In this section each store was listed showing whether it was owned or leased, its square footage, whether it was a freestanding facility or located within a mall or shopping center, its address and adjoining properties, whether the facility contained an automatic sprinkler system, and last, the gross sales for the past fiscal year. This section also listed, in like manner, all other locations where the chain conducted normal operations, including stamp redemption centers, retail drug stores, garden shops, poultry plants and farms, warehouses, and miscellaneous locations.
- *Payroll.* Payroll audits for the four preceding years were provided by state and by workers compensation payroll code.
- *Vehicles.* Each vehicle owned, leased by, or regularly used by the company was listed in the company's records by its vehicle number, body type, make and model, vehicle identification number, and license plate number. Garaging location and predominant use also were indicated.
- *Operating Revenues.* This section included both annual sales for the past ten years and projected sales for the next five, as well as sources of miscellaneous income as from investments and some minor house and garden equipment rental activities.

- *Personnel.* This section included biographies of the company's key risk management personnel and other senior managers with whom the selected insurer and its representatives would be expected to work. Insurance being a business of "utmost good faith," the character of these individuals was of some underwriting significance.
- *Safety Activities.* So that the underwriters would see the company in the best possible light and would be aware of its efforts in loss prevention, a complete section on safety was included. It especially focused on (1) schedules of monthly safety meetings and the agenda for each and (2) copies of plant emergency organizations and members of the response teams.
- *Losses.* The past five years' loss experience was summarized in this section to give the underwriters an idea of the chain's direction in risk management. The loss experience was categorized by type of coverage (property, business interruption, workers compensation, general liability, product liability, and automobile physical damage and liability). Computerized printouts of all incurred claims by location were made available and included specific notations on any claim whose value was reserved for more than five thousand dollars.
- *Present Insurance.* Because the chain's current insurance contracts were largely in manuscript form, it was decided to make a copy of these contracts—one for property and net income and the other for liability, exposures—available to all the candidate firms, although the copies did not include information on the premium rates the chain currently was paying. If, by some chance, the existing policies had a gap, making them available to all participants would reveal that flaw so that it could be corrected in the renewal policy.

One of the underlying goals of the chain's risk management professional in sketching the outlines of the desired insurance program was to guide each candidate firm toward recommending a loss-sensitive insurance program rather than a *guaranteed-cost program* based on premium rates published in an insurance manual. The risk management professional specifically requested retrospectively rated coverage, thus giving up some of the advantages of guaranteed-cost insurance in order to make the chain's insurance costs more responsive to its actual loss experience.

The primary advantage of *guaranteed-cost coverage* is that it provides a measure of stability in insurance expenses, generally a budgetable cost that pleases most finance and accounting departments. A major disadvantage of guaranteed-cost coverage is that an insured who has excellent loss experience receives no prompt reward through lower insurance costs. A *loss-sensitive program*, such as *retrospective rating*, makes the ultimate net cost of an insured's coverage highly dependent on its own loss experience. Under any retrospective rating plan the insured must pay a minimum periodic premium, but is guaranteed that the premium for any given coverage period will not exceed a predetermined dollar maximum. The insured's actual premium becomes the minimum premium plus incurred losses and the insurer's administrative cost of paying these losses.

Since it is impossible to determine what the actual incurred losses will be until sometime after the close of a coverage period, retrospective rating plans call for an estimated premium to be paid during each coverage period; this premium is accordingly adjusted as the insured's actual loss experience becomes known and matures. Hence, a primary advantage of retrospective rating is that good loss experience results in lower premiums, which in turn become an incentive for even greater risk control effort throughout the organization.

Schedule for Receiving Proposals

Before the last week in February, the information manuals were completed and distributed to the involved parties. Although somewhat time-consuming to read and digest, they were reviewed with the candidates in case there were any major omissions in the specifications or descriptive material and so that all parties had an opportunity to understand the information. The equity of the bidding process was of primary importance. The risk management professional's integrity and the chain's reputation could not afford to be tarnished or impugned by an impropriety or favoritism toward any of the candidate firms.

Since the decision had been made to allow the candidates considerable freedom to innovate within the specifications, substantial time would be needed to review and analyze the eight quotations. All candidates were reminded that their presentations had to be made during the last week in May. This would allow the risk management professional and his staff the first two weeks in June to compare and evaluate the proposals, the third week in June to make a presentation to top management, and the fourth week in June to implement a new program, if necessary.

In late March one of the eight candidate firms reported that it would be unable to submit a quotation. This candidate, one of the world's largest brokerages, found that it would not be permitted to place coverage with either its first or second preferred insurer and consequently felt that it could not be competitive. Rather than submit a proposal that was felt to be beneath its professional standards and that

Exhibit 11-1

Key Features of Retrospectively Rated Insurance Proposals

Proposal	Fixed Cost	Loss Conversion Factor	Maximum Chargeable Losses	Maximum Possible Total Cost Col.2+[Col. 4 x (1+Col. 3)]
(1)	(2)	(3)	(4)	(5)
A	$424,322	16%	$1,780,715	$2,489,951
B	325,000	13.5%	1,021,500	1,484,402
C	313,416	$85,000	1,000,000	1,398,416
D	414,661	14.28%	2,126,270	2,844,562
E	356,159	11.4%	1,541,872	2,073,084
F	538,619	11.4%	2,230,000	3,022,839
G	318,600	9%	1,100,000	1,517,600

had no reasonable chance of being selected, this candidate chose to withdraw from the bidding process.

Evaluation of Proposals

On June 10, slightly ahead of schedule, a comparison of the seven remaining renewal proposals was put on a spreadsheet by the risk management professional. The characteristics of retrospective rating generate a number of objective factors that can be portrayed and compared on a spreadsheet much as in Exhibit 11-1. These factors are explained as follows:

- *Fixed Costs.* If the chain had no insured losses, what would be the cost for the "pure insurance" portion of the program—the minimum retrospective premium? The minimum fixed cost for each proposal appears in Column 2 of Exhibit 11-1.
- *Loss Conversion Factor (LCF).* What dollar amount or percentage of losses would be charged for the handling and settlement of claims? Column 3 of the Exhibits gives these figures. Notice that six of the seven presentations quoted claims administration costs on a percentage basis. Proposal C, which happened to have the lowest maximum total cost, quoted claims administration costs as a fixed dollar amount. Pricing claims administration services as a percentage of claims paid can lead to questions about the incentive an insurer's claims department has to settle claims for the lowest reasonable amounts.
- *Maximum Chargeable Losses.* This figure, appearing in Column 4 of the Exhibit, represents the maximum aggregate amount of insured losses for which the chain would have to pay

a retrospective premium. If losses were to exceed this maximum in a given coverage period, the insurer would continue to provide indemnity (up to the aggregate coverage ceiling), but the insured would not have to pay any additional premium for that coverage period. Instead, the retrospective rating formula would raise future premiums to cover past losses.

- *Maximum Possible Total Cost.* This figure, shown in Column 5 of the Exhibit, represents the maximum the chain might have to pay for insurance in a given coverage period: the minimum premium plus the product of the maximum chargeable losses times the sum of 1 and the loss conversion factor, which is expressed as a percentage.
- *Financial Rating.* Giving due attention to the five most recent annual overall ratings of each prospective insurer as reported by the A. M. Best Company, a widely respected, reliable source of financial data on many insurers, would ensure that each proposal was backed by financially sound insurers.

After carefully reviewing the factors involved, the risk management professional recommended to senior management that the chain accept not the lowest but the second lowest bid, Proposal B. The reasons for this selection will be discussed later in the chapter.

Implementation of the New Program

After the risk management professional's recommendation was made to and accepted by top management, there was still much work to be done so that an orderly transition to the new insurer would take place on July 1. Some of the paperwork included new certificates of the chain's insurance to be given to vendors and lenders. In addition, identification cards for each of the vehicles had to be prepared and a new accident investigation kit placed in the glove compartment of each vehicle. Store managers and supervisors had to be given the name of the new insurer and its policy numbers so that appropriate first reports of accidents and of claim situations could promptly be made to the insurer's nearest claims representative. For this purpose, orientation meetings were arranged with the new insurer's regional claims manager and the various adjusters being assigned to the chain's account.

FUNDAMENTAL INSURANCE MARKETING CONSIDERATIONS[1]

The preceding chronology properly reflects some basic considerations a risk management professional should keep in mind when placing or renewing insurance. These considerations include the basic nature of marketing in an insurance context, preparing insurance specifications, and deciding how best—through commissions, fees, or some combination of the two—to compensate the insurance intermediary(ies) that cooperate with the organization in its marketing efforts.

Nature of Marketing in an Insurance Context

The American Marketing Association generically defines marketing as "the performance of business activities that direct the flow of goods and services from producer to consumer."[2] This implies that marketing is a seller-initiated activity: sellers initiate the marketing of goods and services that buyers accept. However, the definition of marketing in the context of insurance sometimes says something different about the flow of goods and/or services. The insurance marketing with which a risk management professional deals typically is not the activity of insurers producing policies to be sold at "retail" by insurance agents or brokers to risk management professionals or their organizations. Instead, the typical commodity in business insurance markets is the exposures to accidental loss that organizations attempt to "sell" to underwriters. The idea is to make this transaction for the lowest price consistent with the reliability of the insurers' commitments to provide indemnity when these exposures become actual losses.

Thus, more often than not, the initiative for business insurance transactions comes from insureds seeking protection, not insurers competing to provide it. Insurance agents, brokers, and other marketing intermediaries quite typically act as "sales agents" for organizations seeking to sell their exposures to insurers. These intermediaries normally are compensated through percentage commissions paid by insurers, but the cost ultimately is borne by insureds.

In some situations, especially when "cash flow underwriting" prevails in certain phases of the underwriting cycle, the impetus for insurance marketing may be reversed so that insurers do take the lead in striving to sell policies in order to gain more investable funds. In these circumstances a risk management professional's efforts to make an account attractive to underwriters essentially become an effort to qualify for lower premium rates or broader coverage, not an attempt to obtain the basic "product" (insurance) from the insurer and its underwriters.

In any case, most of the activities of a risk management professional in marketing an organization's *insurance account* (the entire set of insurance policies protecting the organization at any one time) focus on making the organization's insurance needs attractive to underwriters. In doing so the risk management professional will combine efforts with agents, brokers, or other insurance marketing intermediaries. This team should direct its marketing effort toward communicating the nature of the organization's exposures in the most favorable, yet truthful, light. In this effort a risk management professional should do the following:

- Play an active role rather than simply accepting coverage that is offered. In most cases it is the risk management professional who is the primary "salesperson" for the account, ideally situated to seize the initiative in the transaction.
- Establish criteria for selecting insurers, insurance marketing intermediaries, and these intermediaries' account executives as well as providers of other risk management services.
- Analyze or assist insurance marketing intermediaries and others in determining the organization's loss exposures and identifying which insurance contracts can best cover them (if insurance is desired).
- Assisting, when requested by an insurance intermediary (or where otherwise appropriate), an insurance marketing account executive in making oral and/or written presentations to selected underwriters about the organization's exposures and insurance requirements.
- Negotiating, when requested by an insurance marketing intermediary (or when otherwise appropriate), the final terms of each insurance contract the organization purchases and the premium rates it will pay.

While the concept of marketing an organization's loss exposures to underwriters has much merit, there are phases of underwriting cycles, especially during tight "markets," when underwriters rather than risk managers appear to be "in charge" of a "seller's market." These times are the cyclical opposite of "cash flow" underwriting markets. During such times, an organization and its risk management professional may feel fortunate to have obtained any reasonably adequate insurance at anything approaching an affordable premium. Yet even in such insurer-dominated markets, the "marketing" of an organization's insurance account is critically important: when underwriters believe they can provide only very limited coverage, they are most likely to insure first those accounts that promise the greatest underwriting profit (or the least underwriting loss).

Marketing Timing Considerations

Unless substantial changes have occurred from one policy period to the next (as in an organization's loss exposures or in the products or premium rates offered by insurers), a risk management professional normally does not market an organization's account at every renewal of an annual policy. A risk management professional's marketing efforts for a given account typically occur less frequently than once a year. In addition, when active marketing is planned, it should be scheduled far enough in advance of the expiry of the existing insurance.

Frequency Marketing its insurance account can be expensive for an organization, costing tens or hundreds of thousands of dollars for each major marketing effort. The principal cost is salary expense for the risk management professional, support personnel in the organization's risk management department, and fees paid to outside consultants. Marketing should, therefore, not be overly frequent. Moreover, continuous exposure in the insurance marketplace gives an organization an unfavorable reputation as a "shopper," an image which greatly inhibits future effective marketing efforts.

Even when there is no "active" marketing, a prudent risk management professional will continuously keep in contact with insurance markets. Given no specific reason to change "suppliers," most risk management professionals choose to market their accounts no more than every three to six years. Just short of such a full-fledged effort, most risk management professionals conduct brief monthly or quarterly marketing reviews without preparing full-scale specifications or contacting numerous insurance marketing representatives. Through such reviews, a risk management professional can learn of significant changes in available coverages, in the pricing of these coverages, and of any recent, innovative risk financing techniques.

Scheduling Although small accounts may be marketed in approximately one month, the routine marketing of a large account—or that of a smaller organization with particular risk financing challenges—normally requires four to six months, roughly scheduled as follows:

- six weeks to prepare insurance specifications,
- eight to twelve weeks to negotiate with intermediaries and underwriters, and
- two to four weeks to complete any transition to new insurers.

In rare "emergency" situations this process can be somewhat shortened, but insurance intermediaries typically function more effectively in an organization's interests and maintain a more favorable impression of an organization when allowed the normal four to six months. Some additional time should be allowed for renewals occurring near the end of a calendar year (or in June or July for public organizations that use other fiscal years) because of the high volume of renewals at these times. Still more time should be allowed when markets are tight and insurance is particularly scarce or costly.

When an organization wishes to secure quotations through more than one insurance marketing intermediary, its risk management professional should begin informal discussions at least six months before the earliest insurance policy expiration even under the best of circumstances. Dealing with several candidate intermediaries rather than one preselected intermediary is more time-consuming. The candidates must be acquainted with the organization's account and must be told which of its preferred insurers it may approach (*assigning markets*). In addition, the organization needs time to evaluate the substantial number of proposals this process is likely to generate. Because of the complexity of this process, few risk management professionals simultaneously seek quotations from more than four intermediaries, and two or three is more common.

Preparing Insurance Specifications

Preparing written insurance specifications is the joint effort of an organization's risk management professional and its incumbent insurance marketing intermediary, usually with the risk management professional taking the lead. Although this process is costly and time-consuming, it should generate specifications whose major features can be reused for future renewals by updating them and by correcting any errors that may have crept into the original version. To develop sound, enduring, basic specifications, the professionals preparing them should give careful attention to their format and specific content.

Format Properly prepared, the specifications in a format should allow an underwriter to read as little or as much about an account as the underwriter wishes. An underwriter favorably inclined toward an account ideally should be able to find all the essential, decision-making information summarized on the first page, while another underwriter seeking highly detailed information also should be able to find it throughout the text of the document, in exhibits, or through appendices. As a whole, the specifications should be both as brief and as complete as possible.

For this dual purpose, it is usually wise to arrange the specifications so that the information supporting them moves from the general to the specific. For example, the specifications could begin with aggregate losses incurred by line of insurance, followed by tabulations of individual losses, more detailed analyses of particularly large losses, and measures to prevent their recurrence. An efficient format often is enhanced by developing separate sections describing the organization's structure, its financial statements, operation, and risk financing philosophy. These "standardized" sections should be written without any particular reference to specific lines of insurance so that they can be used in different combinations as parts of specifications for various lines of insurance. This process ensures that only relevant information will be included in the specifications for each particular type of insurance. It also reduces the likelihood of factual inconsistencies in the background information accompanying each set of specifications.

To avoid errors in specifications and thus to minimize coverage gaps, overlaps, or other later emerging mistakes, it is good practice to have specifications edited by persons who are competent in risk management and who do not participate in the original drafting. In those frequent situations in which an oral presentation to the underwriters is to accompany the written specifications, it is wise to rehearse at least the broad outline of the oral presentation with these editors to make sure that the ideas and facts orally presented are consistent with the written specifications.

Proper formatting also has its strictly mechanical aspects. For example, a neat and attractive presentation of the insurance account—in effect, a presentation of the organization itself—often can be made in a binder marked with the organization's name and corporate logo. This name and symbol should appear not only on the cover but also on the spine so that an underwriter can find it in a pile of other submissions. The first item in this notebook, usually preceding even the table of contents, typically should be a short note about the contents, for whom and from whom it is being sent, and the names, addresses, and telephone numbers of the risk manager (or other representatives) who is marketing the account. It is also wise to number all the pages in the binder either in one consecutive series or according to each lettered or numbered section for ease of reference and to facilitate updating. Each set of specifications also should be accompanied by a cover letter that does the following:

- Identifies a desired time schedule for receiving proposals for, negotiating the terms of, and implementing any new insurance program.
- Specifies any unusual circumstances underlying requests for especially high limits of desired coverage and appropriate reinsurance.
- Explains the existing insurance program and possibly gives the present premium—if (1) the underwriter or the insurance marketing intermediary has indicated the underwriter's desire for this information and (2) the risk management professional

can provide current premium information comfortably to all underwriters from whom quotations are being sought.

• Lists additional sources of technical information for the underwriter. These may include quality control manuals, product warranties and users' manuals, manufacturers' procedural manuals for their materials or equipment used within the insured organization, and in-house safety records.

• Offers the underwriter an opportunity to visit the organization's facilities and to talk with its risk manager and other relevant executives and personnel.

Content The general contents of insurance specifications should follow a logical order as shown in Exhibit 11-2. While this particular ordering is fairly standard, it may need to be tailored to the insurance needs of a given organization and to any given insurer's or underwriter's preferences regarding the type and sequence of information considered in deciding whether, and on what terms, to accept an insurance account or line of coverage. For example, virtually all property underwriters want information on the maximum loss an insured property may suffer. However, some underwriters emphasize maximum probable loss (MPL, the largest loss from a given peril considered at all likely to occur) at each location, while others stress the amount subject (AS, the total value exposed to loss by a given peril) at each site as the appropriate measure of maximum loss.[3]

The section of the specifications called Insuring Forms Desired (F in Exhibit 11-2) normally will be structured first in terms of types of exposures and second for each type of exposure, whether the organization seeks a *standardized bureau,* a less standard *modified-bureau,* or a tailored *manuscript policy.* Making the organization's contract expectations clear helps avoid misunderstandings and minimizes the need for negotiations after it seemed that agreement had been reached. Experienced risk management professionals here try to provide as much specific detail as possible, specifying policy form numbers if readily available or even attaching sample policies (especially of manuscript policies).

Use of Bidding Processes[4]

As suggested by the marketing experience of the supermarket chain discussed at the beginning of this chapter, bids may be sought either to select a new insurance marketing intermediary or to control the cost of insurance (not necessarily to choose the least expensive insurance).

There are two broad categories of bidding, open and closed. In

Exhibit 11-2
Table of Contents for Liability Underwriting Specifications

A. Description of Operations
1. Overview of operations by subsidiaries, divisions, and branches
2. Financial statement
3. SEC Form 10K and most recent 10Q
4. Annual report

B. Description of Risk Management Department
1. Philosophy
2. Organization and structure
3. Functions provided—cost allocation, claims handling, loss prevention, etc.
4. Services contracted with external vendors

C. Property Exposure Analysis
1. Basis of values: replacement, market or actual cash value, plus date of valuation
2. Total values by location and by line of coverage
3. Source of valuations — who made them and when
*4. Maximum probable loss and the amount subject (maximum possible loss) by location
5. Individual fire protection reports, pictures, and diagrams for large locations
6. Values for property in transit and unscheduled locations
7. Business interruption worksheets
8. Other time element value estimates

D. Liability Exposure Analysis
1. Quantified underwriting data: revenues, payrolls, advertising expenditures, etc.
2. Products which develop exposures
3. Incidental or umbrella exposures
a. Care, custody and control situations
b. Professional liability
c. Potential liability under specified federal statutes
d. Watercraft and aircraft
e. Other perceived exposures

E. Loss Analysis
1. Description of claims handling: insurer, contract adjuster or in-house.
2. Total incurred losses by line of coverage.
3. Description and analysis of all large (say, over $10,000) losses, even if not yet paid.
4. Loss stratification by line of coverage and in total. Exhibit should show losses at varying levels depending on size of risk; for example, losses from 0 to $10,000, $10,001 to $50,000, $50,0001 to $100,000, and over $100,000.
5. Loss forecasting and retention analysis. Trend future losses or use regression analysis to project probable future loss levels.

F. Insuring Forms Desired
1. For property exposures
2. Net income exposures
3. Liability exposures

*See accompanying text for definitions for maximum probable loss and amount subject.

open bidding advertisements are placed in appropriate newspapers or other insurance-related publications asking all intermediaries who meet given qualifications to secure a copy of the specifications and to submit bids. Qualifications for bidding often include a specified minimum number of years of operation for the intermediary, certain staff size, minimum premium volume requirements, service facilities in appropriate cities, and other pertinent criteria. Open bidding can become quite unwieldy unless these qualifications for eligibility are rigorous. While open bidding is not the norm among profit-seeking organizations, it is used most frequently by public organizations whose insurance placement procedures and costs are subject to public scrutiny. Exhibit 11-3 illustrates an open bidding request for insurance proposals. Closed bidding, often called selective bidding, is "by invitation only" to selected intermediaries whose reputations and qualifications are known to the risk management professional and/or the senior management of the insured organization.

Compensating Intermediaries—Commissions or Fees?[5]

Insurance marketing intermediaries such as agencies and brokerages traditionally have been compensated by the insurers through whom they place coverage on the basis of commissions. These are computed as a percentage of the premiums collected by the insurers. This percentage commission system has long been viewed as an equitable means of (1) adequately compensating intermediaries for the services they provide, (2) motivating intermediaries to place greater marketing emphasis on accounts and types of insurance insurers wish to underwrite (and for which they are therefore willing to pay higher commission rates), and (3) permitting intermediaries to share in insurers' growth as reflected in higher premium writings and therefore greater commission income to their marketing representatives. The percentages often vary from one insurer to the next and by line of insurance.

However, the increasing emphasis on the total range of risk management services, only one of which is placing insurance, has broadened many insurance intermediaries' activities to areas such as designing risk retention programs, providing safety and actuarial services, and administering claims. These activities are of considerable value to their business clients but are not directly related to the volume of premiums that are generated. Therefore, an increasing number of intermediaries and many risk management professionals have come to consider fees a more appropriate compensation system than commissions. Such fees are directly paid by clients, reflect the value of the

Exhibit 11-3
Typical "Open Bidding" Notice*

_____ , _____ , invites you to submit sealed proposals for the insurance indicated in the attached specifications. Quotations will be received at the office of Mr. _____ , Treasurer, until 12:00 noon on _____ , 1970.

All proposals will be opened at the time stated above by the Treasurer or his representative, but will not be read aloud. Persons submitting proposals may attend, and may examine the proposals received. There will be no discussion of the proposals permitted at that time.

_____ reserves the right to reject any and all quotations, and also to waive any informalities in any quotation. While price will be a factor in consideration of the bids, it is not the sole criterion, and _____ reserves the right to the use of other criteria in making its decision.

If any of the coverages cannot be furnished, or cannot be furnished in the manner requested, please attach an explanatory note describing any variations between the specifications and your quotation.

Specific locations of buildings, clarification of any items and permission for inspection may be obtained from Mr. _____ .

Quotations must be made on the attached forms except for any supplementary data you may submit.

All carriers must be licensed to do business in the State of _____ , and must maintain an office in the state.

---

*Reprinted with permission from "Marketing," Section 8 of _The Risk Management Manual_ (Santa Monica, CA: The Merritt Company, loose-leaf, revised and supplemented periodically), May 1981, p. 7.

intermediaries' services and are negotiated between the client and the intermediary.

Moreover, eliminating intermediaries' commissions from premiums paid by insureds and instead compensating intermediaries with more clearly identifiable fees allows many organizations to account more accurately for the true cost of the protection they receive from the insurance they buy. Such a system fairly and clearly compensates intermediaries; and because this compensation is not simply a function of a premium, intermediaries can be more objective in recommending and providing noninsurance risk management techniques when these best serve the client.

Some intermediaries receive compensation through commissions and fees. In this case, commissions are usually earned at a lower percentage than if the intermediary's total compensation is through commissions. Fees may be charged by the hour or monthly; or there may be annual retainers or specific fees for particular projects, such as surveys of the client's exposures or setting up a captive insurance subsidiary. Receiving fees from client organizations rather than commissions from insurers often is said to give intermediaries greater loyalty to their clients and to provide these clients with stronger risk management programs and greater control over their total risk management costs.

There is no universally accepted or correct resolution of the "fees versus commissions" dispute. The question certainly becomes more difficult to answer especially if it is viewed in terms of strict black/white, either/or alternatives. To negotiate the appropriate type of compensation for intermediaries in different situations, a risk management professional should be aware of the ways in which each system has been supported.

The following arguments support commissions:

- Insurance marketing intermediaries perform many services that are not directly related to any one insured's account and for which, therefore, no particular insured should be charged. The commission system generates revenue to support these services by averaging their cost over an intermediary's clientele as a whole; without this compensation through commissions intermediaries could not afford to perform these services.
- The effort expected of an intermediary in securing and servicing a larger and more highly rated (more "risky") account is greater than for a smaller, less risky account—especially in view of the added risk analysis, rating, and claims administration activities required by the former. Percentage commissions do, therefore, tend to provide the intermediary with compensation commensurate with its efforts and the value of the services it provides, both to insurers and to insureds.

The following arguments, particularly by risk managers buying insurance for their organizations, support the negotiated fee approach to compensation:

- The fee-for-service system minimizes the conflicts of interest that insurance marketing intermediaries may experience when a sound risk management recommendation would reduce their commission income. For example, recommending that a client adopt higher deductibles or improved risk control measures, which would both lower the client's cost of risk and make the client's account more attractive to underwriters, would reduce the intermediary's commission income by either lowering premium rates or lessening the amount of coverage the client purchases. However, if a fee were provided, the intermediary would not have to sacrifice personal gain for the clients' welfare.

● Intermediaries' traditional percentage commission income from a given account is not proportional to their efforts on that account. Particularly for property insurance (if not for liability coverages with their typically more complex rating systems and higher claims frequency) an intermediary's insurance placement activities are not related to the amount of insurance written on that account: placing and servicing a five million dollar property insurance policy normally does not require five times the effort needed for a one million dollar policy on the same type of exposure. However, the traditional percentage compensation system pays the intermediary five times more for the former account than for the latter. A fee for such activities would more equitably and "evenly" compensate the intermediary.

Both proponents and opponents of the commission system recognize that it has a significantly destabilizing effect on an intermediary's income. If percentage commission rates remain fixed, an intermediary's aggregate annual (or other periodic) commission income tends to rise during the expansive phase of an underwriting cycle (when insurers are seeking more business and their revenues increase) and to decline in tight markets when insurers are reluctant to write coverage on any but the best accounts. Thus, it is during these expansive, liberal underwriting phases when insurance is relatively easy to place that intermediaries enjoy their greatest incomes while having the least real burden of challenging marketing activities. Conversely, during restrictive, more difficult underwriting times—when insureds are likely to be most demanding on intermediaries to place coverage for them—the typical intermediary's commission income from actual insurance sales tends to be lowest because the amount of insurance that is sold is the least.

This cyclical effect on an intermediary's total commission income is somewhat dampened by the fact that commission *rates* tend to fall during the expansive phase of an underwriting cycle, while they tend to rise during the more restrictive phase. This inverse relationship between commission rates and amounts of insurance written implies that an intermediary's total income—which is proportional to the multiplicative product of both amount of insurance written and premium rates for that coverage—tends to be somewhat more stable than insurers' underwriting profits.

Recognizing at least potential deficiencies in the pure commission and the pure fee systems of compensation, some insurers and their intermediaries have explored alternatives that combine elements of both systems. For example, numerous insurers use sliding-scale commission rates, particularly for property coverages, apparently recognizing that an intermediary's work is not wholly proportional to the amount of insurance written. In the sliding-scale system commission rates drop for larger policies, thus generating lower total commissions for larger policies than would fixed-rate commission schedules.

Another example, introduced by intermediaries, is the *management fee* compensation system. This system is largely the result of intermediaries' awareness of their business client's concern that commissions generate conflicts of interest and foster mediocrity because an agency or brokerage can raise its income by merely selling clients more insurance without full regard for their other risk management needs.

The intermediaries waive their normal percentage commissions (where state law permits such waivers) and negotiate with each insured client a *minimum* annual fee, which the client and the intermediary agree represents the total annual revenue the intermediary needs to properly service the account and to generate a reasonable profit. The commissions received by the intermediary from insurers by placing insurance for this client are then credited against (deducted from) the negotiated fee, and the insured client is only responsible for paying the fee remaining at the end of the year. If the year-end total commissions exceed the negotiated fee, the client owes no further fee for that year. If commissions fall short of the fee, no refund is payable to the client because it was agreed at the beginning of the year that the intermediary was entitled to at least that fee. The client also cannot receive any refund of any deposits or installments on the negotiated payment made to the intermediary—such returns would be contrary to the "antirebating" statutes in most jurisdictions. Moreover, under this system commissions and management fees often can be averaged over a period of several years to account for annual variations in premium payment schedules, changes in commission and premium rates, and the insured's loss experience under loss-sensitive premium rating plans.

INSURANCE MARKETING CHANNELS

An organization seeking to buy commercial insurance typically approaches the insurance market through various channels. The most typical is an agent or broker, who may be associated with a large international organization, a smaller regional firm, or an independent local agency or brokerage having offices in only one city. An organization seeking commercial coverage also may choose to deal with an insurer that is a direct writer or to work with an underwriting association cooperative. Collectively speaking, these marketing channels often are termed *intermediaries*.

Some commercial insurers market coverage through several types of intermediaries; some only use one or a few. Therefore, the choice of an insurer and an intermediary often are closely linked. An organization wishing to deal with a particular insurer often has a limited choice of intermediaries; one wishing to buy its insurance through a particular intermediary may have a rather restricted choice of insurers. Moreover, regardless of the type of intermediary chosen by a risk management professional, the qualifications and character of the individual account executive representing that intermediary is of paramount importance. Therefore, in dealing with insurance markets a risk management professional must both understand the generic characteristics of different types of intermediaries and have a clear set of criteria for selecting the individual account executive through which the firm will place its coverages.

Types of Intermediaries

International "Alphabet House" Organizations When a risk management professional first thinks about the ways of buying insurance, it is not surprising that thoughts turn immediately to the fifteen or twenty large brokerages with offices throughout the world, simply because of their size. Their names have become so familiar that they are widely known by their initials alone, hence the term alphabet house. However, size does not guarantee the risk management professional that any one such house can satisfy all of an organization's coverage needs, render exemplary service, or locate all insurers whose premiums are competitive. Still, because no company grows to rank among the top twenty in any industry or type of service without having provided consistently for the needs of its clients on a competitive basis, such large brokerage organizations clearly have many strong features.

The large international firms have specialized departments that can offer services to a client whose activities occasionally range beyond its usual sphere of business. These specialized departments might include, but are not limited to, marine, aviation, or energy-related operations as well as safety, actuarial, and general risk management services. Also of importance is the "clout" that these international brokerages have in the insurance marketplace. Because of the premium volume these brokerages can direct to various insurers, these brokerages often are able to negotiate highly favorable coverage terms and conditions as well as premium levels for their clients. In addition, the vertical integration of many brokerages, which often own or manage insurers or other facilities, allow them a particularly high degree of flexibility.

Regional Firms Regional brokerage firms are smaller and less expansive than the international brokerages. Although the level of service and expertise provided by these firms is notable, they differ primarily from the alphabet houses in the number of offices and other locations they maintain to serve clients. As regional implies, such firms may operate in a particular location, such as within a state or in several contiguous states.

Independents Independent agents and brokers, who generally center their activities in a particular city, stress their ability to provide personalized service. Because of longstanding, face-to-face relationships with their clients and insight into their operations, they can be expected to remain a major marketing channel for clients in the small-to-medium-sized range. The independent agent or broker is able to provide a high comfort level for clients that is difficult for larger competitors to match.

Direct Writers The risk management professional can also look forward to being contacted by direct writing insurers. Although responsible for a sizable percentage of property and liability insurance written for business organizations in the United States, these insurers are unique in marketing their coverages solely through their own employees. Such agents may offer only the policies provided by their one employer. Therefore, the quality of the coverage available through direct writers' "agents" depends almost entirely on the extent to which that insurer has specialized technical capabilities or underwriting capacity for each particular line of insurance. Some direct writers' more streamlined marketing organizations allows them to pass some operating expense savings on to insureds through lower premiums than can be offered by insurers in the more traditional channels.

Association Cooperatives Relative newcomers to the insurance marketplace are association cooperatives. They are independent agencies and/or brokerages that have banded together to pool their resources in selling insurance (in contrast to the insurance-buying cooperatives and risk purchasing groups described in Chapter 8). Although they continue to be independently owned, the members of these cooperatives have joined to combat competition from the large international firms and larger regional marketing organizations. Because of their affiliation, these cooperatives hope to gain greater marketplace visibility, more "clout" with insurance underwriters, and greater ability to serve clients at some distance from the office of any one member agency or brokerage.

Insurance Representatives

When an organization is selecting a person or organization from whom or which to purchase insurance or any other product or service, a number of general characteristics of this seller become relevant:

- Technical expertise—familiarity with the client's needs, operations, and goals,
- Communication skills—ability to present the client's insurance or other needs as effectively and as favorably as possible to insurers, their underwriters, or providers of other risk management services,
- Imagination—creativity not only to see things as they are but also as they might best be, and
- Integrity—insurance transactions having a tradition of "utmost good faith," a basic honesty and willingness to share confidential information, the ability to act as if the client's interests were their own in a manner that exemplifies fiduciary relationships.

The executive making or researching this selection must give careful attention to both the specific characteristics of the insurers' representatives chosen to act as marketing intermediaries and the sharing of a consistent approach to claims administration between the insured organization and the chosen intermediary.

Specific Characteristics of Insurers' Representatives Especially important in selecting an insurance intermediary is the marketing ability of the account representative whom that intermediary assigns to the organization's account. Although there is some overlap between the representative's marketing ability and his or her technical expertise and communication skills, it is important to evaluate how effective a particular individual has been in presenting accounts of a size and complexity comparable to those of the organization seeking insurance.

Careful consideration also must be given to the ancillary services provided by that executive's agency, brokerage, or other organization. Because no two insurance marketing organizations or insurers are totally alike, an effective account representative should be able in any marketing environment to design a risk management program that fits the needs of any given organization at reasonable cost while assisting the organization in claims management and loss prevention activities. The account representative must also stay abreast of market availability, especially when considering specialized coverages. Although he or she may not have complete expertise in dealing with all exposures, someone in the intermediary's organization should be well versed in all the coverages required by the organization seeking protection.

The financial strength of an intermediary, apart from that of the particular insurers it represents, is also an important consideration. Will the intermediary organization continue to function effectively in the future? What is the scope of its business and does it handle exposures associated with various industries, especially like those of the organization now seeking coverage? These questions are particularly important in light of the fact that risk management professionals occasionally have placed "moratoriums" on new business with insurance marketing intermediaries suspected of being in financial difficulty.

The organization structure of the intermediary also can have an important impact on the selection process. The capabilities of an intermediary's top management and the expertise and background of the individual account representative must be melded successfully with the intermediary's risk control services and claims administration facilities.

Another important characteristic of intermediaries is the ability to be more creative. The purchase of guaranteed-cost insurance, as traditionally coupled with a full range of insurer-provided services intended to benefit both the insured and insurer, is not as widespread as it once was. Risk management professionals and their financial managers have recognized that they will eventually "pay for their own losses" whether through insurance or retention. They are therefore now seeking more creativity from intermediaries in designing loss-sensitive plans or other cash flow techniques that will keep corporate funds within an insured organization for an extended period.

The certification of intermediary personnel also is a consideration. It is reasonable to ask prospective brokerages, agencies, or other insurance intermediaries to provide biographical sketches on their key personnel to be involved with the account. Are there Chartered Property Casualty Underwriters (CPCUs), Chartered Life Underwriters (CLUs), Associates in Risk Management (ARMs), Certified Safety Professionals (CSPs), Certified Employee Benefits Specialists (CEBSs), and/or Professional Engineers (PEs), Certified Industrial Hygienists (CIHs), and/or holders of other relevant designations on staff? Do these individuals have practical experience with the needs of organizations like the one now seeking insurance?

Consistent Approach to Claims Administration As discussed in Chapter 12, an insured organization, its insurers, and the insurance agents, brokers, and other intermediaries should agree on a basic philosophy regarding how insured claims should be handled. To determine if such consistency can be developed between an intermediary and an organization, a risk management professional needs to meet with each candidate intermediary (1) to review historical data concerning the organization's loss frequency and severity and (2) to obtain from the intermediary, the claims department of the insurer(s) that intermediary would use, and the indications these insurers' defense attorneys as to how they would have dealt with at least a representative sample of the organization's past claims.

Any organization's basic philosophy on third-party claims—where someone seeks to collect money from the organization for harm they have suffered—can follow one of the three fundamental approaches. The first approach is to settle any third-party claim, regardless of fault, if it can be settled for less than the legal fees for resisting the claim. Although some organizations subscribe to this philosophy, its major disadvantage is that the general public and plaintiff's counsel soon regard the organization as an "easy mark." This can result in many claims for which the organization pays without any true legal liability, thus raising either its cost of retained claims or its liability insurance premiums.

The second approach to third-party claims involves a firmer stand: only claims for which the insured organization clearly was at fault are paid. This approach means denying numerous, possibly justified claims, with the expectation that some injured parties will obtain the advice of an attorney and will sue the organization. Although this philosophy almost surely will generate many lawsuits, attorneys for the public or a plaintiff will understand and respond to the message being sent: this organization will not pay until its liability is made clear. Since a plaintiff's attorney works for a contingency fee, and because the courts are severely crowded, a verdict for the plaintiff—*if* it can be won—will be years in coming.

From the organization's perspective, the risk management professional must recognize that if he chooses "fight instead of flight," some cases will be lost because the organization has been singled out by plaintiffs following a "target defendant" or "deep pocket" strategy. The risk management professional must also recognize that an occasional adverse verdict may become more expensive than making a payment on every claim that occurs. This professional's problem consequently becomes one of selecting which claims to resist (in order to discourage unfounded claims) and which to settle (before they grow to become severely adverse court verdicts). If the insured organization truly is liable to the plaintiff, this second approach to third-party claims indicates that every attempt should be made to settle the claim outside the court system.

The third approach to third-party claims seeks to combine the best elements of the first two. Many organizations have established a policy of *volunteer payments*, paying for initial first-aid or short-term acute medical costs for any injured third party regardless of fault, and then denying any liability unless the organization was manifestly and seriously at fault. Organizations adopting this approach also may volunteer to repair or replace items of personal property damaged or destroyed in accidents involving the organization or its personnel. The voluntary payment of initial medical expenses or restoring personal property can be a good public relations tool and may preclude those harmed from suing.

"UNBUNDLING" THE INSURANCE PACKAGE

Property and liability insurers traditionally have provided at no identifiable additional cost numerous incidental services to their insureds, including exposure analysis surveys, claims administration, actuarial analysis of loss experience, and many others. These services often have been logical adjuncts of insurance protection performed by the insurer for a variety of reasons. For example, some insurers have competed for business on the basis of their expert claims administration and/or loss control services. An insurer may have chosen to provide these services because they are essential to the proper functioning of the insurance mechanism and because they are beyond the capabilities of the typical insured. While no specific charge was made for most of these services, the insurer's cost for providing them was built into the premium structure for all or for each class of insureds. However, major changes in the composition of the insurance market have changed the relationship between the services that are provided and how they are charged.

As both buyers and sellers of insurance for business organizations have become more sophisticated, as rising insurance costs have provided greater incentives for reducing risk financing expenses, and as alternative suppliers of claims, safety, and other insurance-related services have sought marketing niches in traditional insurance markets, the "unbundling" of the insurance policy package has become economically more attractive to many insured businesses. They now often ask that an insurer provide them only with the risk financing protection that is the heart of the insurance transaction, and the indemnity contracts are priced accordingly: with no or a greatly reduced "loading" for the ancillary services that insureds no longer want to purchase from their insurers.

Instead of automatically relying on the insurer for these services, an insured may want to consider the following option: (1) to purchase comparable services from other sources, (2) to provide these services through their own personnel, or (3) to simply do without the services that they believe are no longer needed. As long as insurers are willing to deal with insureds on this basis—that is, as long as the unbundling does not jeopardize the underwriting acceptability of an insured's exposures because the insurer no longer believes the account meets the insurer's standards—then the unbundling of the insurance package can proceed wherever the insured finds it to be cost-effective. In some cases particular insurers will remain the best and most economical providers of some services related to their insurance policies.

Opportunities for Unbundling

Unbundling has given business organizations many more options than the basic "yes/no" choice in the purchase of an insurance policy and the insurer-provided services that traditionally have come with it.

Claims Administration Services Claims handling activities, whose nature and scope will be described in Chapter 12, are a prime candidate for unbundling because many organizations' operations create special types of property, liability, and other claims that require special skills to control, evaluate, and settle. A commercial insurer serving a wide range of insureds may not be expected to keep on staff enough claims administrators (adjusters) to meet the very specific needs of each insurer. Therefore, the organization itself or a firm that specializes in contract claims administration may be a better source for handling claims.

The cost of claims handling services provided by a contract claims administrator is negotiable. Some administrators prefer their compensation to be a percentage of the value of the claims they handle. However, many risk management professionals question paying anyone a percentage of claims to settle them on behalf of the insured. Such a compensation plan would appear to encourage an insurer or administrator to allow claims to rise, thus not acting in the insured's best interests. Fortunately, there are compensation method alternatives.

First, based on an insured organization's loss experience, a contract claims administrator may be willing to charge an annual retainer. This fee reflects expected volume of work regardless of the value of claims handled during the contract period. This pricing method is used particularly by several large international claims management firms in handling an organization whose claims activity occurs domestically and internationally. Such firms will also use this method to handle the geographically remote claims activity for an organization whose activity is typically local. The annual retainer is subject to change from one year to the next (or one contract period to the next) based not only on the volume of work, but also on the types of claims (property, general liability, business interruption, workers compensation, for example) and on the number and types of claims likely to be litigated.

A contract claims administrator may also charge for services on a per-claim basis. This method is more likely to be used when the client organization generates claims related to local business activities. However, an insured who has primarily local but very occasionally remote claims-related activities (as mentioned in the preceding paragraph) may be charged on a per-claim and an annual basis, respectively. Like the charge for an annual retainer, charges on a per-claim basis will vary according to the types of claims and the number and types of claims likely to be litigated.

A contract claims administrator also must be acceptable to the organization's insurer. Settling claims properly, promptly, and cost-effectively requires cooperation between the insurer, the insured, the agent/broker, or other insurance marketing intermediary, and any outside contract claims administrator.

Risk Control Services Although many property and liability insurers provide some risk control services to a wide range of insureds, the growth of technical knowledge about and specialties within risk control have allowed many organizations to establish themselves as specialists in risk control services. In addition, many large industrial organizations, believing that they require specially tailored risk control activities, have developed in-house risk control staffs. Therefore, because risk control has become a cost-effective noninsurance alternative, it is an excellent opportunity to unbundle the insurance package.

Independent risk control specialists can provide assistance in property protection. For example, they can design automatic sprinklers for fire protection, establish and train an in-house fire brigade, coordinate safety training programs, and prepare safety manuals. Comparable expertise in other areas of property protection is available from risk control specialists who deal in vehicle and cargo safety, crime prevention, and crisis management planning.

Risk control specialists also may help a risk management professional to obtain top management support, without which no risk control program will be effective. For example, an outside safety specialist can assist in training supervisors and managers in risk control. Since any on-staff safety specialist can only be in one place at one time and on one shift at one time, it is imperative that all managers and supervisors become not only philosophically committed to safety but also familiar with practical risk control procedures. An external safety consultant often can more effectively convey this need than can an on-staff person regardless of professional competence.

Risk Management Information Services Although many insurers make computerized claim reports available to their larger insureds, these often follow a format not specifically tailored to an organization's risk management needs as its managers perceive them. Independent computer information systems, including both hardware and software, can be tailored to the needs of most organizations' risk management professionals. The procedures for identifying any organization's specific needs for a risk management information system (RMIS) and how such systems can be adapted to these needs are detailed in the ARM 55 text, *Essentials of Risk Control.* These subjects will not be elaborated on here, but it should be pointed out that in the past, delays in receiving the insurers' claims printout were so long that the information could not effectively be used. Risk management professionals for many large organizations have developed comprehensive, state-of-the-art systems through which risk financing and risk control data can be directly tied into the mainframe of an independent risk management information service. The data can thus be promptly processed to generate useful decision-making information. tion service. The data can thus be promptly processed to generate useful decision-making information.

A relatively new concept in the unbundling of the insurance package is the formation of joint ventures between insurers and independent risk management information service firms so that an insurer, not an insured, becomes the "working partner" with an independent service provider. Such joint ventures enable insurers to broaden and deepen their service repertoire and, therefore, their ability to attract and hold insureds. For instance, an insurer can generate for itself the option of whether to provide the service in question—here RMIS applications—for a special fee to those insureds who wish this service or, following the more traditional pattern, to provide this service at no identifiable extra charge to all insureds (with the cost of the service being built into the insurer's premium rate structure). Broader joint-venturing with well-established and widely recognized independent service firms in, say, risk control and claims administration services might also enable some insurers to recapture revenues they may have lost in the unbundling of traditional insurance services.

Financial Management Managing a risk financing program demands many crucial decisions that turn on questions of how many and which exposures to retain, what the appropriate limits and deductibles for primary and excess insurance are, in what financial instruments can any funded loss reserves be invested, and how an organization's captive insurance subsidiary can be managed. Many of these decisions require insight and skills not always found within an organization. (In fact, the management of some organizations may not even recognize that these decisions are required.) Furthermore, some organizations are reluctant to rely solely on their insurers or on the insurers' marketing representatives to keep them abreast of the latest developments in risk financing alternatives to insurance. Several types of independent firms can assist an organization's management in making these decisions.

Numerous agencies and brokerages offer risk financing management services quite apart from their insurance sales activities. They often charge an hourly fee, an annual retainer, or a negotiated fee for each project. Risk management consulting firms also offer a very broad spectrum of such services; they assert that their complete independence from the insurance product heightens their objectivity. Several service firms, including most of the alphabet house brokerages, also specialize in helping organizations establish and operate their own captives or pools. In short, an organization that wants a rather sophisticated risk financing program does not have to manage it in-house or through its insurer. It can contract for risk financing management on particular projects or for a complete "menu" of risk financing services.

A risk management professional should work with the organization's senior management to determine carefully when and to whom it will turn for risk financing advice. Any external source on which an organization depends for this service should (1) thoroughly understand the organization's operations and goals, (2) share the organization's risk financing philosophy, (3) have an established record of reliability and fiduciary responsibility, and (4) maintain excellent communication with the key risk manager and other executives of the organization.

Marketing (Insurance Placement) Services Marketing intermediaries are very likely to have significantly different levels of expertise and means of access to insurers and underwriters for the various kinds of insurance an organization needs. Therefore, in unbundling its insurance package, an organization's risk management professional may decide to place these different coverages through different agents or brokers. It is not at all unusual for an organization to have one agent or broker handle its property coverages, another its liability coverages, a third (perhaps a direct-writing insurer not using an agent or broker) for its workers compensation coverage, and a fourth its employee benefits program. In effect, while any one of these agents or brokers might have the ability "on paper" to place all these coverages, the risk management professional purchases highly specialized insurance placement services from different marketing intermediaries by dividing the organization's insurance program among them.

This method of unbundling is not without its hazards—particularly in the coordination of coverages (minimizing gaps and overlaps), in minimizing disputes as to which insurer covers which loss or claim, and in planning how the various insurers will work together in responding to a major crisis that involves all of them. Recognizing and resolving these potential difficulties requires that the organization's risk management professional take a leadership role in dealing with several intermediaries and insurers. It also requires that these insurers' representatives communicate fully and frankly with this professional and, when necessary, with one another. It should be understood that they should cooperate to serve a common client.

Actuarial Services Organizations that have substantial retention programs need access to much the same expertise that their insurers would draw upon if the retained exposures were commercially insured. Moreover, retained as well as insured losses need to be "adjusted" through appropriate claims administration activities. Thus, both retained and insured losses require that "rates" be established as estimates of the present costs of future losses. These rates may be for insurance premiums or the basis of internal budgetary charges for the organization's own risk management cost allocation system. This type of "financial" activity requires considerable actuarial skill, which few organizations are likely to have on the staff. Therefore, a number of independent service organizations have been developed to provide data-gathering, analytical, and decision-support services to the risk management departments of most organizations. These organizations range from larger agencies or brokerages to actuarial consulting firms and even the mathematics or business departments of many universities. Unbundling the actuarial element from the insurance package is much like separating the above-mentioned financial management services needed for risk financing. Thus, it is important that any actuarial firm or individual expert has qualities comparable to those sought from a financial management service. Moreover, an organization should discuss with each candidate the feasibility of doing actuarial work—whether the candidate can find within the organization's records or elsewhere enough data from which to draw conclusions about loss experience that are useful to the organization.

Advantages of Unbundling Insurance Service

An organization may be able to derive several advantages from unbundling its insurance package. Since insurance premiums generally reflect all of the available services, why should an organization pay for those services that it does not need? Furthermore, is it possible to avoid internally and externally duplicating—and double charges for—the services obtained from another provider?

Although the advantages of unbundling may appear attractive, there is at least one vital caveat. If unbundling is taken too far, the organization's risk management program could become fragmented. The consequent disarray could jeopardize the profitability, if not the survival, of both the client organization and the firms that have committed their resources and futures to servicing this now misman-aged client.

SELECTING A RISK MANAGEMENT CONSULTANT[6]

A risk management consultant is an organization, often a one- or two-person firm that does not sell insurance but provides advice on insurance and other risk management matters for a fee. The essential value of a risk management consultant's service is said to be its expertise and objectivity. A risk management consultant may be hired either for a specific project or on a continuing basis.

A competent risk management consultant should be able to perform, or advise others in performing, virtually any specific task related to the risk management function for any organization. Some consultants specialize in certain activities, such as exposure analysis or claims administration, while others specialize in particular industries, such as building construction or hospitals. The following are some of the most frequent one-time special projects for which an organization may wish to hire a risk management consultant:

- studying an organization's loss exposures and recommending an appropriate risk management program,
- drafting specifications for the bidding of an insurance program and analyzing the proposals received in response,
- auditing all or some portion of an organization's current risk management activities, much the same way an accountant audits financial record-keeping,
- conducting a feasibility study of proposals for establishing a captive insurance affiliate or a pool,
- drafting a risk management procedures manual,

- designing and/or conducting employee safety training programs, and
- confirming the recommendations of an organization's own risk management professional to lend more credence to the essentially completed work of an organization's internal risk management.

A risk management consultant should be hired for a one-time project only when the effort would enable the organization's own risk management professional to maintain or build on the activity or the results of the consultant's work. Any one-time employment of a consultant should be designed to permanently enhance the organization's risk management program, not merely to create a "temporary tempest" of activity that soon ends without any permanent positive effect.

To benefit from a consultant's expertise and objectivity on a continuing basis, some organizations retain a consultant over an extended period. When a consultant is hired on a month-to-month basis or on an annual contract, this consultant may seem to become the risk management "department" of the organization, overseeing its regular safety, insurance, and other risk management activities. A risk management consultant contracted to serve an organization on a long-term basis should have the human relations skills and expertise required to earn the respect not only of the organization's personnel but also of the insurers' marketing intermediaries and others with whom the consultant will need to cooperate to effectively serve their client.

A risk management consultant may be compensated through an hourly or daily fee, on a monthly or annual retainer, or on a per-assignment basis. There is neither an established or approved schedule of fees or other compensation, nor is it always possible to relate a consultant's pay to any specific "savings" in an organization's cost of risk. (In fact, because basing compensation on perceived "savings" could jeopardize a consultant's objectivity and lead to "cut-rate" recommendations, most consultants in risk management—and in other consulting fields—are ethically opposed to such a basis for compensation.) Regardless of the compensation system, it is most important that both the client and the consultant believe that the consultant's service has been worth the fee. This mutual satisfaction through a fair exchange of values provides a firm basis for a continuing working relationship.

Judging the competency of a risk management consultant often is more difficult and subjective than evaluating the qualifications of an agent, broker, or other insurance marketing intermediary. Several states require licensing of risk management consultants, while some states demand only that a risk management consultant register with the state insurance department. A few states have no special regulations on risk management consulting. As in other jobs, education and experience usually are reasonably valid initial indicators of ability, as are references from insurers, their representatives, and the prospective consultant's previous clients. Approximately one-third to one-half of all risk management consultants are members of the Society of Risk Management Consultants, an organization formed through the 1985 merger of the Institute of Risk Management Consultants and the Insurance Consultants' Society. Credentials aside, perhaps the single most important qualification of any risk management consultant is the ability to work and communicate cost-effectively with any given client organization.

Once having decided to hire a consultant, three steps are essential in selecting a particular one. The first is to clarify the purpose and scope of the work the organization wants the consultant to perform. Verifying these matters gives some indication of whether a consultant is needed for a one-time project or on a continuing basis, as well as the particular credentials, experience, and attributes of the consultant the organization should hire.

The second step is to develop and to distribute to apparently qualified consultants a request for proposals (RFP). This RFP should first describe the nature and extent of the work the organization expects the consultant to perform and then give the consultant enough information about the organization to enable a consultant to determine whether it is willing and able to accept the organization as a client. This information should include at least the organization's annual report or other description of its activities, a 10K form or comparable document filed with the federal and state securities regulators, a listing of the organization's loss exposures, actual losses, and its insurance policies and premiums, and a brief summary of the organization's past risk management activities.

The third step in selecting a consultant is to analyze each candidate's written proposal, interview the principals of each candidate, and contact the references that presumably have accompanied each candidate's proposal. The final selection of a consultant should reflect the degree of confidence that the client organization's risk management professional and its senior executives believe they can place in the consulting organization on whose expertise and objectivity they will rely.

MAINTAINING EFFECTIVE WORKING
RELATIONSHIPS

An organization's risk management professional can perform well only by working effectively with others, both within and beyond the organization. Other texts for Associate in Risk Management study have dealt with how a risk management professional's relationships with others within an organization are essential to properly identifying loss exposures, implementing both risk control and risk financing techniques, and gaining acceptance of risk management as an essential job responsibility of everyone within that organization. In contrast, this discussion focuses on the risk management professional's relationships with others outside the organization, particularly with the representatives of the various insurance and other organizations that market the financial protection and services that can be essential to sound risk management.

Every risk manager is an organization's chief point of "personal" contact with all the insurance marketing intermediaries and others whose products or efforts contribute to the organization's risk management program. While the risk manager should be highly aware of this aspect of the relationship, the risk manager also should recognize that the relationship must remain professional and, to some extent, competitive. These relationships are competitive in two senses:

- the risk manager's organization wishes to obtain financial protection and other products or services at a low cost, while all the external providers just as logically wish to enhance their revenues, effectively raising the organization's costs.
- each insurer or other service provider can be replaced by a competitor if its work for the client organization proves unsatisfactory, either to the client or to the provider.

Because these relationships are at once cooperative and competitive, they can be effectively maintained only if the individuals involved meet the following requirements: (1) make a commitment to the risk management program of the client organization, (2) give a full and honest disclosure of relevant information to one another, (3) exercise the ability to surmount their own and others' errors, (4) have an appreciation for the negotiating process, and (5) respect one another as people and as professionals.

Commitment to the Client's Risk Management Program

The central task that brings an organization's risk management professional into contact with representatives of provider firms is the management of the client organization's exposures to accidental loss. A genuine commitment to that task by all concerned is essential to a mutually productive relationship.

For an organization's risk management professional, this commitment affects the ties with representatives of provider firms. If the risk manager has a personal relationship with a firm that would not enhance the organization's risk management program, this professional must be prepared to modify or sever any personal and businesses relationships with these representatives. New relationships with others who can enhance the organization's risk management program should be formed.

The representatives of external providers also must be committed to each of their client organizations' risk management programs—but only as long as this commitment to the client is consistent with the representative's commitment to his or her employer. For example, if the provider asks its employee (representative) to recommend a coverage, product, or service that the employee knows is not beneficial to the client organization's risk management program, this representative must be prepared to either modify this recommendation, release the client, or change employers. In choosing among these alternatives, the representative of an external provider organization should recognize that a competitor will almost surely be better able to serve this client under such circumstances.

Full, Honest Disclosure of Relevant Information

When striving to cooperate, people should be able to openly and truthfully exchange all information relevant to their shared task—in this case, managing an organization's exposures to accidental loss. On one level, this openness only requires that each person be able to recognize others' needs for information and to present it in a mutually convenient form. At another, somewhat deeper level, this honesty requires recognizing the competitive environment in which this information is exchanged. While complete disclosure may be ideal, each party should recognize that the other's loyalty to his or her employer may require withholding some information that an employer considers confidential or proprietary. Here, honesty demands at least a tacit recognition—and sometimes an explicit statement—that "I cannot tell you that." Being honest thus requires that each party acknowledge the obligation to occasionally withhold certain information. Nevertheless, honesty also requires that there be (1) a clear indication that some information is being withheld and (2) no intentional dissemination of false information. Perhaps the best strategy for representatives of organizations that are in some sense competing with one another is for each representative to feel free to ask the other any question—with the understanding that the other may be just as free to decline to respond without being untruthful.

Ability to Surmount Errors

Because everyone makes errors, a risk management professional or a representative of an external provider will confront situations made awkward by their own, a subordinate's, or even a superior's errors. Working relationships must be sufficiently strong and flexible to survive such mistakes and their potentially or actually harmful consequences. A risk management professional or another organization's representative occasionally will have to admit to an error; or it may be necessary to explain someone else's error. At other times a risk management professional or a representative of an external provider may recognize that someone with whom he or she is dealing has made or is about to make an error.

In these cases and possibly others the rapport of the risk management professional with the other individuals must be sufficiently comfortable and open that anyone who has made a mistake does not feel threatened in disclosing it. Similarly, the party not in error should also be able to graciously accept another's admission of error, correction, and any warranted apology. In a sound relationship each party will see that the other is honestly attempting to avoid errors and be truthful. If, however, one party begins to doubt the other's actual honesty and competence, that party should be able to promptly and gracefully withdraw from the business relationship before the other's fault further harms the organizations represented.

Appreciation of the Negotiating Process

Organizations' risk management professionals and those with whom they do business represent different organizations. Therefore, they need to bear in mind that, at times, their obligations to their respective organizations will require them to negotiate—to bargain, even haggle—to support the best interests of their employers. As negotiators, they ought to follow the guidelines for negotiating techniques and strategies set forth in Chapter 12 of this text where these matters are examined in a claim administration context. Negotiators need to understand that it can be perfectly legitimate for one or more of them to change positions, hold some information or alternative positions "in reserve" for later bargaining, and to not reveal one's final position (or one's "bottom line") in the opening negotiating session. At the same time, however, the principles of proper negotiating never allow untruths. There will also be times when good negotiating tactics call for appearing angry at an opponent without actually losing one's temper or perspective.

To maintain effective working relationships, a risk management professional and the representatives of other firms serving an organization's risk management program should be able to truly negotiate with appropriate vigor without allowing their behavior to impair their ability to cooperate after the bargaining has ended. Meeting this dual objective requires some recognition and separation of roles, much as good athletes distinguish between their combative behavior "on the field" and their typically much more friendly and mutually respectful conduct "off the field." Professional athletes in particular recognize that lasting personal relationships away from the game are crucial because, as the seasons change and players are traded, those who were once rivals may find themselves playing on the same team. Much the same is true in risk management for two reasons. A very high level of career mobility in the field of risk management makes it very likely that a person who today is a risk manager for Company A will next year be an account executive for Brokerage B or an underwriter for Insurer C. Therefore to serve their respective firms and to preserve their career opportunities, most risk management professionals in any type of organization need to be able to negotiate effectively as opposing parties and yet respect and cooperate with each other.

Mutual Respect

Perhaps the essence of the preceding requirements for preserving effective working relationships in marketing an organization's insurance can be reduced to one precept: sound relationships require mutual respect from and for all parties. Therefore, every professional in any field should behave towards others in ways that gain and show respect. This may occasionally be difficult because of the personalities or the situations that sometimes confront one in the marketplace. However, most successful risk management professionals have found that their efforts to gain and give are eventually well rewarded.

SUMMARY

For most risk management professionals dealing with the loss exposures of their employers or their client organizations, the marketing of an insurance program is, more often than not, the "selling" of the organization's loss exposures to insurers' underwriters at premium rates acceptable to the development organization. Because of the complexity of this often reversed marketing sequence, an organization seeking to market its entire account often must devote several months and thousands of dollars to (1) developing insurance specifications, (2) selecting appropriate marketing channels, intermediaries, and account executives, and (3) evaluating insurers' coverage proposals.

In light of the effort required and the potentially adverse marketplace response to any annual "shopping" of an organization's insurance account, a risk management professional will want to (1) carefully schedule marketing activities, (2) prepare insurance specifications whose format and contents present the organization's insurance needs in the most favorable, truthful perspective, (3) decide in advance the extent to which the organization wishes, or is willing, to compensate insurance marketing intermediaries for a fee (rather than a commission).

The marketing channels available to an organization are one or more specific intermediaries from the international alphabet house brokerages, regional agency and brokerage organizations, independent (single-city) agents and brokers, association cooperatives, and direct-writing insurers. Having selected one or more channels, an organization then needs to evaluate the candidate intermediaries and, most especially, the specific account executive(s) who are eligible to service the organization's account, request proposals from each candidate, and then make a final choice ("final" until at least it again becomes appropriate to market the organization's insurance account).

While this process of insurance marketing has remained virtually the same, the composition of the market has significantly changed. Two significant trends have led to the unbundling of the various protection and service elements traditionally included in a property and liability insurance policy package. First, risk management has grown both conceptually and practically from simply insurance buying or selling to one means of effectively managing costs. Second, the number of service firms competing for a share of insurers' revenues has substantially increased. Insurers have responded to these developments by allowing insureds to purchase elsewhere (or provide for themselves) such services as claims administration, risk control, risk management information, financial management advice, insurance placement services, and actuarial services. Some insurers also have formed joint ventures with independent service firms so that they may be able to recapture premium dollars lost to unbundling.

These trends and their results have bolstered the importance of the risk management professional. Beyond working with insurers' marketing intermediaries, an organization may choose to employ an independent risk management consultant who sells no insurance but offers for a fee objective and risk management expertise and service. Regardless of whether an organization hires a consultant for a single project or on a long-term basis, the organization should prepare specifications and request proposals from one or more consultants so that both client and consultant understand the other's needs, expectations, and expertise and are reasonably confident they can work together.

Maintaining effective working relationships with representatives of other organizations involved in the insurance marketing process is an important responsibility of an organization's risk management professional. To carry out this responsibility, the professional and all those with whom he or she works must share a commitment to the quality of the client organization's risk management program, provide one another with full and honest disclosure of information relevant to performing this task, be able to surmount their own and other's errors without jeopardizing their own relationships, appreciate and be adept at the negotiating process, and—above all—respect one another.

Chapter Notes

1. The material under this heading is adapted from David Warren and Ros McIntosh, "Marketing a Large Insurance Program," Topic A4 in *Practical Risk Management* (Oakland, CA: Warren, McVeigh, & Griffin), May 1986.
2. Committee on Definitions of the American Marketing Association, *Marketing Definitions* (Chicago: American Marketing Association, 1960), p. 15.
3. The definitions given in parentheses are taken from E.P. Hollingsworth and J.J. Launie, *Commercial Property and Multiple-Lines Underwriting*, 2nd ed. (Malvern, PA: Insurance Institute of America, 1984), pp. 8-9.
4. The material under this heading is adapted from "Marketing," Section 8 of *The Risk Management Manual* (Santa Monica, CA: The Merritt Company, loose-leaf, revised and supplemented periodically), May 1981, pp. 1-7.
5. The material under this heading is adapted from "Marketing," Section 8 of *The Risk Management Manual* (Santa Monica, CA: The Merritt Company, loose-leaf, revised and supplemented periodically), May 1981, pp. 8-15.
6. The material under this heading is drawn from David Warren and Ros McIntosh, "Consultants," Topic H4 in *Practical Risk Management* (Oakland, CA: Warren, McVeigh, & Griffin, loose-leaf, revised and supplemented periodically), January 1985.

CHAPTER 12

Claims Administration

INTRODUCTION

The final step in financing recovery from an accidental loss is *claims administration*. This is the timely payment of proper amounts of funds to restore a loss, whether suffered by an organization itself or by others whom the organization is legally or ethically bound to compensate. This definition of claims administration is intentionally broad. It is designed to encompass payment of (1) legal claims made by others against an organization for losses they have suffered, (2) claims that an organization may make against an insurer, contractual transferee, or wrongdoer legally liable to the organization for its transferred losses, and (3) "claims" the organization makes on its own resources for its losses or the losses claimed by others that the organization has retained.

Thus, categorizing claims into these three groups, an organization may be involved in the payment of a claim in the following three ways:

- By retaining the claim, thus becoming the direct provider of funds to pay for its own or others' losses (ranging from minor vehicle damage within an insurance deductible to a massive uninsured tort judgment against the organization).
- By having transferred the claim by contract, thus becoming the direct recipient of funds (or other compensation) from external sources to pay for its losses (for example, an insured property loss or damage while in a bailee's custody, with the bailment contract obligating the bailee to return the property in good condition).

- As neither a direct provider nor a recipient of funds but as one interested in the sense that the organization is legally or ethically responsible, but has contractually shifted financing this responsibility (through liability insurance or a noninsurance contractual transfer for risk financing under which, for example, a supplier of a component for the organization's product agrees to hold the organization harmless from products liability claims arising from this supplier's component. In effect, the supplier would pay on the organization's behalf).

In principle, the proper amount payable for any given loss and the proper timing of any loss payments are objectively determinable through sound claims administration. The amount and timing of payments should not be affected by the preceding three ways in which an organization is involved in a claim. (To paraphrase Gertrude Stein's famous remark about roses, "A loss is a loss is a loss" having one objective value.)

In practice, the dollar amount of many losses is debatable as is the proper timing of payments to restore that loss. Recipients/indemnitees almost always honestly believe that losses are worth more dollars, and ought to be paid sooner, than do the providers/indemnitors of the funds. In risk financing as in general, receiving money is preferable to paying it. Therefore, claims administration—particularly deciding how much and when to pay for accidental losses—can engender many disputes. It follows that the claims administration process usually must extend beyond the investigation (finding the facts needed to determine the amounts and timing of payments) to negotiations between parties involved in the claim as they seek to resolve their differences, and still further to legal procedures for resolving disputes that cannot otherwise be resolved. This chapter first gives an overview of the claims administration process. It then discusses in more depth the steps in that process: investigation and payment of undisputed claims are explored as are negotiating strategies and dispute resolution techniques.

Moreover, because there is always the possibility, if not the probability, that an organization will have to pay for its own or others' losses, the concluding section of this chapter discusses loss reserving. This discussion of reserves expands on Chapter 2 by describing how the features of a risk financing case influence the amount that ought to be anticipated as the ultimate value of each case. In doing so, this chapter describes the more tangible factors underlying the dollar amounts of reserves, which are "given" in Chapter 2.

Because large amounts of money are often at stake and because assigning responsibility for a loss can be a controversial issue, many parties and their legal representatives frequently are involved in the administration of a claim. An organization usually is represented by its risk management and legal personnel, who may or may not be full-time employees. Each insurer also will be represented by its claims administration personnel, commonly called adjusters, as well as by legal counsel in highly contested cases. Expert witnesses, investigators, and negotiators may also be employed. In short, claims administration may be conducted solely or jointly by (1) the organization's risk management or legal personnel (particularly for retained losses), (2) the claims personnel of the organization's insurers, and/or (3) external claims administrators (or third-party administrators) employed by an organization to represent it in particular types of claims such as employee benefit claims or products or automobile liability claims. This chapter uses the terms *claims administrator* and *claims administrator personnel* as they apply to any of the parties or organizations involved in the administration of a claim.

CLAIMS ADMINISTRATION IN THE RISK MANAGEMENT PROCESS[1]

In terms of the risk financing aspect of risk management, claims administration is the culmination of the risk management decision process. It is the point at which an organization's pre-loss plans for financing losses come into play. Ready funds to restore accidental losses are one of the three major "products" of an organization's risk management efforts—the other two are losses that are prevented or minimized through risk control and management's freedom from the fear of accidental losses. Like all the other goods and/or services from various departments in an organization, the products of risk management activity should be cost-effectively created; that is, they should produce the desired result at the least possible or acceptable cost. The claims administration process described in this chapter defines how to produce funds to finance recovery from a loss in a cost-effective way.

Claims Administration Process

For any loss and for any recipient or provider of funds, the claims administration process consists of the following steps:

- Investigation of the facts of the loss leading to the claim.
- Evaluation by each of the parties involved of the dollar amount that should be paid to finance restoration of the loss.
- Negotiation between the parties to determine the amount and timing of loss payments.

- Legal or other procedures for settling disputes that the parties cannot resolve.
- Payment(s) to finance restoration.
- Monitoring the overall efficiency of the entire claims administration process as part of the risk financing process.

The following section documents the application of the first five steps in the administration of an individual claim. The claim may involve individual property, net income, liability, or personnel. The organization may be involved as a provider or a recipient of funds. The sixth step is handled separately because, as a monitoring function, it applies to the overall claims administration process.

Administration of Individual Claims For many types of losses, particularly those that an organization finances through retention without any outside parties, many of the steps in claims administration can be promptly and almost automatically performed. However, with losses that involve disputes with insurers and third-party claimants, each of these steps may involve a substantial amount of time and money. For either type of loss, effective risk financing requires that each step is carefully performed.

Investigation. After an organization has suffered a property, net income, liability, or personnel loss, an individual from the organization's claim administration personnel should determine the facts and contact the organization's insurer(s), other indemnitors, and/or any person who may have a legal claim against the organization stemming from this loss. If it is impossible for this claims administrator to meet with representatives of all interested parties, telephone calls are often sufficient to gather information and to begin building relationships with others who will be involved in the administration of the claim.

Individuals and organizations who may be entitled to compensation for a loss or who may be obligated to pay for a loss can be confused about the situation. They usually are appreciative and relieved to establish contact with someone who seems able to clarify such a situation. Such assurance can be especially appreciated by an organization's management personnel, who are likely to be extremely concerned about how a given accident will affect the functioning of their department and even the continuation of their jobs.

While such contact thus benefits an organization, it also offers the claims administrator an opportunity to obtain information on the circumstances of the loss from witnesses and potential claimants. A recording device should always be available for this purpose. If statements are recorded shortly after an accident has occurred, the facts of the accident are still fresh in a witness's mind, and the recording becomes an excellent way to preserve these facts for the claim file.

In addition to obtaining statements from witnesses, investigations involve other activities such as fire and police reports. They form an important element of the file and, at first, they may be the only guide to what happened. An organization which is particularly aware of the need for accurate claim reports may well have developed a standardized internal "incident" report form designed to guide the gathering of generally pertinent information. They may also contain other important information, such as names of all parties connected with the accident, the type and extent of injuries, names of witnesses, and names of insurance companies. Photographs and diagrams of an accident scene also can be important. They can provide a good understanding of the accident facts and may even identify a previously unsuspected witness. Some investigations often include inspecting and photographing damaged and undamaged property.

Dealing with injured persons is the major part of many investigations. When first contacting an injured party, the claims administrator should obtain that party's medical authorization so that relevant medical information can be released to the administrator. Without a properly signed authorization, any medical files remain privileged information, thereby increasing the difficulty of evaluating injuries. Authorization forms are also necessary to obtain wage-loss information from employers and other custodians of records. As the investigation progresses, the claims administrator must be prepared to report developments as they occur; incomplete and untimely reporting destroys the value of an investigation.

Evaluation. After completing the initial investigation, and as more information becomes available, the claims administrator should estimate the extent to which involved parties, their respective insurers, or other contractual indemnitors, may be liable for the loss and the amount each may be called upon to pay. The information needed to evaluate a loss varies with the type of claim.

- If there are bodily injuries, they must be valued on the basis of information from the treating physician and/or hospital.
- Evaluating damage to property requires (1) information on the condition of the property before the accident and its use and (2) an exploration of the alternatives for repairing or replacing the property.
- Net income losses must be evaluated on the basis of (1) the organization's or family's pre-loss income, (2) a projection of what its income would have been had the accident in question not occurred, (3) estimates of the length of time its income will

be interrupted or reduced, and (4) the extent to which its income loss may be alleviated from other sources of funds.

Negotiation. Negotiation at its best leads to the mutual determination of a fair settlement for all parties involved in a claim. To be a successful negotiator, a claims administrator also must be a successful salesperson in the sense that an offer must be "sold" to the claimant. The negotiating or selling process can be even more effective when the negotiator knows the person on the other side of the negotiating table; that is, if the claims administrator during the investigation has developed a relationship with the claimant or the claimant's attorney, negotiations will proceed more successfully.

Settlement/Dispute Resolution. A claim can be said to be *settled* when all the parties who are to receive or to provide funds agree on the amount to be paid and the timing of the payments. When an organization is retaining its own losses and no outside claimants are involved, settlement means that an organization's managers agree on which accounts are to be charged and from where the cash will come for the restoration. When an organization is financing others' losses, settlement usually involves broader consent—particularly agreement among the organization, the claimants, and the respective insurers. When a settlement is reached, the claims administrator from each involved organization should be certain that the elements of the settlement are understood and accepted by all parties. This acceptance normally is validated by signatures on releases and/or letters of understanding.

When parties cannot reach settlement themselves or through their attorneys, a lawsuit, arbitration, or mediation becomes necessary. In effect, the court, arbiter, or mediator determines or facilitates the resolution of a dispute. The documents growing out of this process must be signed by the parties involved, thus becoming evidence of their acceptance of the settlement.

Payment. Payment normally follows promptly upon settlement so that the agreement underlying the settlement will not be dissolved by delay. In law and equity a claimant's acceptance of full payment or the first of several scheduled installment payments typically is conclusive evidence of agreement to the settlement. In fact, most checks issued in payment of claims are written so that endorsement, deposit, or cashing of the check constitutes a release by the claimant from any further claims that might arise from the incident that caused the claim. Thus, payment by check reinforced the release a claimant may have signed in the initial settlement.

To support this release, the organization, its insurer, or other indemnitor making payment should obtain and retain receipts, including endorsed checks, and should keep records of lump-sum and installment payments. Once the final payment has been made on a claim, it is *closed.*

Monitoring the Claims Administration Process Monitoring the five-step claims administration process requires an accurate and continuous overview of the claims for which an organization or its insurer is a provider of funds and the claims for which the organization is the recipient of funds. The objective of such monitoring is to ensure that the proper amounts of funds are paid and/or received, and that these payments are made or received at the proper time without undue administrative or legal expense. To achieve this objective, a claims information system and regular claim audits are required.

Claims Information System. Although a manual system may be adequate for a very small program, insurers, contract claim administrators, and most organizations that rely extensively upon risk retention programs require a computerized claims information system. When accurate and timely, the loss experience reports generated by such a system are a valuable tool for tracking claims development and comparing current results with past history and with other organizations' experience. These reports are also helpful in providing an "audit trail" and in reducing opportunities for dishonesty on the part of claimants, insurers, or the claims administration personnel of any other organizations. These reports should contain only information needed to make meaningful claims administration decisions.

To provide the necessary information, a monthly or weekly *claim experience report* should be prepared. This should reflect, for claims pending or closed during the period, the organization's claims payments and claims receipts. This report should be structured on a chronological basis (in terms of when each claim arose), by the type of loss (property, net income, liability, or personnel), or class of claimant (such as employees, product users, and others). While the basic format of each file may be uniform, the types of information or file captions should be tailored to the type of claim and the events that initiated it. For example, on each pending claim arising out of damage to the organization's property, the claim information file should include the following:

- date loss occurred or was reported,
- property and peril involved,
- department, division, or activity in which loss occurred,
- claim payments to date,
- estimated total incurred loss,
- remaining loss reserve,
- identifiable claims administration expense paid to date, and

- claims administrator assigned to case.

Comparable data relevant to a bodily injury liability claim involving a member of the public would include the following:

- date and location of injury,
- date claim reported,
- type of injury (body part affected, instrument causing injury),
- amount paid last month,
- amount paid to date,
- estimated ultimate claim value,
- remaining claim reserve,
- identifiable claims administration expense paid last month,
- identifiable claims administration expenses paid to date, and
- claims administrator assigned to case.

For a public liability claim involving property damage, the same data-gathering format should be used, but the data in the file would reflect the type of claim, the nature of the property damaged, and the peril or force causing that damage.

In addition to the information on individual pending claims, the claim experience report should provide an overview of all claims pending and closed during the month. These should be categorized by type of loss, year incurred, and location within the organization (that is, operating division, geographic location, or some other factor related to the structure of the organization). For each category, for pending and closed claims, the report should provide the following information:

- average (arithmetic mean) incurred loss per claim,
- average identifiable claim administration expense per claim,
- number of pending and closed claims,
- number of claims for each department, division, or activity,
- percentage of number of claims litigated, and
- average number of pending claims per claims administrator.

A series of such claim experience reports enables a risk management professional to identify and focus on any persistent claims administration difficulties, and to compare an organization's current claims administration activity and expense with its own record and with that of other organizations in the same industry.

Claims Audit. While the monthly reports are valuable sources of claims information that are helpful in tracking experience and isolating potential problems, they cannot alone provide a complete assessment of an organization's claims administration. A claims audit is needed. This is an independent, detailed, periodic examination of an organization's claims administration records. It is particularly useful if there are warning signs of difficulty such as the following:

- Failure of an organization's claims administrator to respond promptly to messages from the organization's risk management professional. While this can result from excessive case loads, an administrator who does not make time to respond even within the organization is probably also negligent in responding to others outside the organization.
- Inability of the claims administrator to provide clear and reasonable answers to questions on specific claims. This suggests a lack of adequate investigations, failure to maintain current records, or poorly trained or incompetent claims administration personnel.
- Unexplained fluctuations in reserves. Any rapid changes may be due to changes in personnel whose judgment underlies the evaluation of many claims, shifts in the claims reserving philosophy, persistent clerical inaccuracies, or excessive case loads.
- Sudden increases in the number of litigated claims. Increased litigation may indicate that claims administration personnel are no longer communicating or adequately negotiating with claimants or their attorneys.
- Steady increases in the number or value of pending claims. Such increases may reflect the same problems as increased litigation.
- Substantial increase in the number of seemingly justified complaints related to claims from any responsible source. These complaints require at least a reasonable investigation to determine their validity.

A well-managed organization of any size normally has internal auditors or uses regular external auditors to monitor its claims administering activities. Insurers normally are reluctant to give insureds or their legal representatives access to claims files, frequently asserting that a review of such proprietary information could expose the insurer to liability for invasions of others' privacy. However, most insurers will permit a joint review by an insured and a broker or agent. In this examination the insured or its representative may question a claims representative who physically retains possession of claim files. To the trained claims auditor, this is an unacceptable alternative to a "hands on" claims audit. However, most insurers properly fear that an untrained person may misinterpret information in the claims files and create an unnecessary controversy.

Unless an organization's risk management professional has a

strong claims background or can delegate the assignment to a qualified claims auditor on staff, the services of a qualified expert in claims administration should be retained when the preceding signals suggest the need for a audit. Many risk managers automatically conduct an annual audit. It is often thought not good practice to use an organization's own contract claims administrator (or a competing administration) whose objectivity may be clouded by self-interest. Those who voice this concern believe that objectivity can be gained by a pre-audit agreement that the firm performing the audit will not bid on the claims administration function for a substantial period.

There are a number of qualified independent claims consultants who specialize in claims administration audits. Unless the risk management professional has dealt with and is confident about a particular claims consultant, a *request for proposal* (RFP) should be prepared. This broadly outlines the work required and any areas of concern. The RFP should state the age of the program, the types and frequency of claims, and the number of pending claims. Each applicant receiving the RFP should be asked to provide a general client list and to identify several clients for whom similar audits recently have been performed.

Proposals from claims consultants should clearly outline the scope of the audit, the plan of action, cost, time for completion, and identities and qualifications of the individual auditors assigned to the project. The proposal also should list materials or tasks required from the organization's risk management or other departments in order for the audit to proceed. The largest cost in a claims audit generally is for the consultant's time in reviewing claim files. A representative sample of pending and closed claims draws data from all levels of reserves and payments and all types of litigated and nonlitigated claims.

After an organization and the auditor agree on the scope of work and plan of action, the auditor should be free to explore all areas of the claims administration program. The audit results should then be summarized in a written report. The audit report also should provide a basis for comparing the performance of the organization's claims administrator with industry standards and/or the claims standards specified in the contract for the audit. The audit also provides a basis for comparing the performance of the claims administrator with recommendations from previous audits. The report must identify any problems in the program and offer recommendations for their correction.

Personnel Involved in Claims Administration

For losses incurred and retained by an organization, and that do not involve injuries to others or third-party claimants, only that organization's personnel are typically involved in the claims administration process. In terms of the losses for which the organization or its insurers is likely to provide or receive funds, the organization's claims administration and other risk management personnel can expect to deal with insurers' adjusters, insurance brokers and agents, contract claims administrators, and attorneys. Depending upon the type of claim, each of these persons may represent the interests of the organization or those who have claims against it.

Organization's Personnel As mentioned, sound risk financing requires that each step in the claims administration process must be performed for all claims including (1) the organization's losses, involving no outside claimants, that it pays itself; (2) the organization's loss for which it is entitled to receive compensation from insurers, other indemnitors, or wrongdoers; (3) others' losses for which the organization is legally or ethically responsible and which it pays directly; and (4) others' losses that are the organization's legal or ethical responsibility but for which it has transferred the burden of payment. Thus, regardless of how the organization stands with regard to funds, it needs personnel to handle the responsibilities for a claim and to properly document how these responsibilities have been fulfilled. Such personnel are usually part of the risk management department. A part of their time and that of the organization's risk management professional needs to be devoted to the following:

- Carrying out the five steps of the claims administration process for individual claims.
- Monitoring the claims administration process.
- Ensuring that there are adequate reserves and cash on hand to make claims payments for the organization's retained losses.
- Ensuring that the organization or its transferees has paid others the monies to which they are entitled for their losses that are the organization's responsibility.
- Ensuring that these transferees have paid the organization the monies to which it is entitled for the organization's losses that it has transferred.

An organization with a risk management department with more than one professional often has one or more staff persons to serve as the claims administrators, protecting the organization's risk financing rights and seeing that its risk financing obligations are performed. When there is more than one such specialist, they may divide their duties according to the type of loss (property, net income, liability, or personnel) or according to losses that are retained and transferred. The claims administrators may work not only with the managers of the departments within the organization but also with other people involved in a claim, especially claimants, their attorneys, contract claim administrators, and insurers and their representatives.

Insurers' Adjusters An organization's claims administrator often will negotiate with a representative of the claims department of one of the organization's insurers. Such a representative is commonly called an *adjuster* or *claim representative.* Such titles as *claim supervisor, claim examiner,* and *claim manager* refer to the insurer's supervisory personnel overseeing the work of adjusters and claim representatives.

Because effective negotiating requires knowing as much as possible about the negotiating "opponent," a claims administrator dealing with an adjuster should recognize the differences between *staff adjusters, independent adjusters,* and *public adjusters.* Only the first two *always* represent insurers; the last also *may* represent insureds.

The differences between staff and independent adjusters, and public adjusters have both practical and legal significance. A staff or independent adjuster is legally an agent of the insurer. A public adjuster is legally an agent of the insured. As an agent, this representative is ordinarily empowered to negotiate agreements (binding on their respective principals) regarding the value of a loss and the extent to which that loss is covered by insurance. Each type of adjuster, while properly acting within the scope of his or her apparent agency authority, effectively stands in the shoes of his or her principal. The extent of this *apparent authority* is governed by insurance law and business practice. Should an adjuster go beyond the scope of this apparent authority, that person is potentially liable to its principal for any harm that the principal may suffer as a result. Furthermore, because of the concept of apparent authority, neither an insurer nor an insured is entitled to withdraw from an agreement negotiated by its adjuster/agent merely because of an unusual or undisclosed restriction on the adjuster's apparent authority in the contract through which that adjuster was hired.

Staff Adjuster. A staff adjuster is an employee of an insurer who processes policyholders' claims, usually for a salary. Some adjusters specialize in particular types of insurance or claims, while others are considered qualified by the insurer to deal with any claim. A staff adjuster may work as a *field claim representative* or as an *office claim representative.*

A field claim representative's duties include meeting with insureds, claimants, witnesses, and medical, auto repair, and construction personnel with whom the insurer has contracted to restore a policyholder's or another claimant's covered losses. A field adjuster inspects damage, takes photographs, and makes diagrams of the scene of an accident. A field adjuster also supports office adjusters. Much of a field adjuster's time is spent preparing reports for claim files and conferring with claims supervisors regarding the extent of the insurer's obligations to a particular policyholder or claimant.

Office representatives, or *telephone adjusters* as they sometimes are called, spend virtually all of their time investigating and settling claims from within the office. They typically deal with relatively routine claims whose validity and value can be determined without extensive on-site investigation. While particularly significant in administering many personal lines claims, office representatives also frequently handle many commercial automobile and minor workers compensation claims. The efficiency with which office representatives operate allows them to handle a large volume of uniform claims quite cost-effectively. Insurers usually measure—and an organization administering retained claims also should gauge—the efficiency of their claims management activities in terms of the administrative costs of settling each $1,000 (or $1,000,000) of a given type of claim. Their activities are a good example for an organization's staff claims administrator's handling high-frequency, low-severity claims of the sort that many organizations seek to retain rather than to insure or otherwise transfer.

Many insurers are aware of the expense of maintaining field and office claims personnel. Because these insurer's claims operations must justify this expense by controlling insured losses and by maintaining good policyholder relations, each staff adjuster must handle a substantial volume of claims—either a large number of relatively small claims or a more modest number of higher-value or more complex claims. In any case, the incentives provided by insurers to their staff adjusters often do not motivate claims personnel to spend a great deal of time and/or effort on the settlement of a relatively small claim. These claims personnel often are compensated or otherwise rewarded for focusing their efforts on resolving high-value claims, rather than pursuing precise indemnity or equity for every claim. This "logic of motivation" may apply equally to the claims administration personnel of many organizations that are not insurers.

Independent Adjusters. An independent adjuster is an independent contractor—an individual or a firm—that administers insured claims for one or more insurers. Each insurer is charged for services rendered on each assigned case or on a contract or retainer basis. Independent adjusters provide valuable services on a temporary or emergency basis, or when insurers' claims personnel are not available.

Some insurers do not maintain any staff adjusters, relying only on independent adjusters to process all their claims. These insurers may contract with several independent adjusters in various territories and may even provide them with stationery and report forms to record loss data, make reports to the insurer, and correspond with policyholders and other claimants. The type, volume, and value of the claims an independent adjuster handles are important in determining an independent adjuster's long-term success and acceptance in the insurance community.

Public Adjusters.[2]   Public adjusters also are independent contractors, but they are retained by insureds to represent them in administering claims. These may be very large and complex single claims or a series of more routine claims that require a public adjuster's expertise. A public adjuster performs many of the functions specified by the conditions section of an insurance contract to perfect an insured's legal right to funds (or other protection) under an insurance contract.

A public adjuster may act to protect insured property from further damage, to prepare inventories of damaged and undamaged property, to complete loss reports insurers require of insureds, to assist a client organization in cooperating with an insurer to defend against covered legal claims, and/or in personally negotiating with an insurer's representatives on matters of coverage and loss valuation. Insureds normally compensate public adjusters on the basis of a determined percentage (or sliding scale of percentages) of the amount of the adjusted loss. Public adjusters may also be paid hourly or on a per-case basis. For large, complicated losses, public adjusters can perform services that benefit both insurers and insureds.

Insurance Agents/Brokers   Some insurers routinely empower the same agents who sell their insurance to serve as adjusters in settling certain insured property and liability claims. (A few insurers also similarly authorize brokers to negotiate loss settlements although, under the law of insurance marketing, a broker legally represents the applicant for the purpose of buying insurance.) The agents and brokers usually operate according to rather detailed instructions and limitations as to the types and amounts of claims they can settle. Their claims administration authority often is limited to small and uncomplicated losses and to those situations where a close relationship between an agent and an insured (or between an agent and another claimant) will facilitate a prompt and equitable settlement. When functioning as an adjuster, an agent or broker may receive compensation much like that of an independent adjuster; alternatively, an agent's or broker's adjusting activity may be compensated only by its enhanced status with the insurer.

Contract Claims Administrator   As an insurer may contract with an independent adjuster, so may an insured organization retain a contract claims administrator to negotiate claims or perform other duties in connection with retained, insured, or otherwise transferred losses. For the client organization, a contract claims administrator is a logical extension of the public adjuster. While a public adjuster primarily handles large and especially complex claims, the contract claims administrator handles either diverse types of occasional claims or a large volume of recurrent, more routine claims. In short, the contract claims administrator is particularly useful to an organization that cannot financially or practically justify an in-house claims expert.

Selecting an Administrator. Because claims administration is extremely important to an organization's overall risk financing program, the selection of a contract claims administrator is crucially important. Those making the selection must first be familiar with what qualifies an administrator; second, they must be able to determine that these qualifications are met by each individual or organization who submits a proposal for the job.

As in the process for choosing a claims auditor, the *request for proposal* (RFP) from candidate claims administrators should address each requirement for a qualified administrator. It should also ask for information about the applicant pertaining to each of these requirements. An example of some pertinent requirements and questions is as follows:

- Stature and experience of the applicant and its senior executives.
  - Is the applicant recognized as a competent claims administrator by insurance, risk management, and legal professionals?
  - Does the applicant maintain offices and/or have qualified personnel available throughout the territory in which claims are likely to arise?
  - Is the applicant independently managed or affiliated with an insurer or other organization (and, if affiliated, will this relationship enhance the applicant's ability to meet the client organization's needs)?
  - Is the applicant, as a total organization, qualified to deal with the types of claims to be covered by the administrative contract?
- Applicant's current clients.
  - Has the applicant provided a representative list of its current clients (with names and telephone numbers of personal contacts), and are these clients satisfied with the applicant's service?

- Do the applicant's current clients include firms in the same industry, or with similar claims administration needs, as the prospective client organization?
- Do the applicant's current clients leave it with sufficient resources (especially including competent personnel, files, and equipment) to meet the needs of the client organization?
- Personnel who would serve the prospective client organization.
  - Will the applicant commit specific individuals to serve the organization?
  - Are these people or those who may succeed them experienced with the types of claims for which the organization is seeking assistance?
  - Are these individuals properly certified in areas where certification is legally required?
  - As the client organization grows and diversifies, will the applicant remain able to meet its needs?
- Applicant's business practices.
  - Is the applicant's philosophy of claims handling consistent with that of the client organization?
  - Will the applicant's procedures for claims handling generate the desired results and appropriate documentation for the client organization?
  - Does the applicant have adequate professional liability (errors and omissions) insurance and are applicant's employees appropriately bonded?
  - Will the applicant provide timely special reports and service?
- Applicant's fee structure.
  - Do the applicant's fees reflect charges for number of claims handled or time and expense charges (rather than predetermined percentages for claims settlements)?
  - Does the applicant's fee structure encourage efficient claim settlement by procedures acceptable to the prospective client?
  - Is the overall level of the applicant's fee structure appropriate?

Contract with Administrator. Once a contract claims administrator has been selected, it is good business practice to develop a detailed contract that delineates the rights and duties of the administrator and the client organization. The contract should include such routine matters as the contract period, amount and method of the administrator's compensation, methods of resolving any disputes growing out of the contract, and procedures by which each party may withdraw from the contract. Many claims administration contracts also incorporate, by reference or attachment, the contents of the RFP and of the administrator's written proposal. The RFP and the proposal define the expectations about performance and conduct that presumably were in the minds of the parties when they entered into the contract, and thus it presumably should govern their activities in carrying out the contract. The contract also should include the following:

- The scope of the administrator's authority regarding a settlement, including the types of claims and the maximum dollar amounts of settlements the administrator is expected to settle at its own discretion.
- Details of the services the administrator is to provide the client organization. Such services often include twenty-four hour availability of field personnel, claim investigations, file documentation, periodic status reports, cooperation with insurers (both primary and excess), negotiation with insurers and claimants, and courtroom appearances as necessary.
- The procedures by which the administrator will notify the client organization, its insurers, and legal counsel about claims that are unusual, that are not clearly within the administrator's authority, or that may generate legal proceedings.
- Ownership and access rights to the working files of the client organization and the claims administrator. (Both parties should have reasonable access to the other's information that is vital to cooperation, but many believe that each party should retain exclusive ownership of its proprietary materials and data.)
- The minimum amounts and types of fidelity and surety bonds, and professional liability insurance that the administrator must maintain while the contract is valid.
- Procedures for the final settlement of claims that are pending (or even incurred but not reported) when the claims administration contract is terminated. (Normally, responsibility for the "runoff" of these pending claims is returned to the client organization, which may manage them internally or may transfer them to a new claims administrator; the terminated administrator may have little incentive to effectively manage this "runoff".)
- If the administrator's operating expenses are part of compensation, the types of costs that will be considered as such expenses and how these costs will be computed.

The capacity of any written contract to establish and maintain effective working relationships between any two parties, such as a client organization and its contract claims administrator, is limited; beyond the words of any contract, the parties must have a basic willingness to cooperate for their mutual benefit. Nonetheless, developing and using a fairly detailed claims administration contract is indicative of responsible management by both the client organization and the claims administrator. Their contract can help to avoid many pitfalls on the path toward a mutually beneficial working relationship. It can also protect the rights of others who may be involved as fund recipients, fund providers, or parties at interest in claims administered under this contract.

Attorneys Any party in any way involved in a claim has the right to secure, at its own expense, legal advice and, if desired, legal representation. Thus, any of the several parties involved in a claim may each be represented by one or several lawyers. Any party may seek legal counsel to define and protect its rights, to clarify and work to fulfill its duties, or to negotiate on its behalf. However, the fact that one party retains an attorney does not mean that the other party or parties must do so to "stay even."

The involvement of attorneys in a claim does not necessarily signal that the claim will be litigated. An attorney's knowledge of the law, experience in negotiating, and objectivity in evaluating the interests of and alternatives for the parties to a dispute often enable legal counsel to negotiate a prompt and reasonable settlement much more effectively than the parties could. In fact, one of the prerequisites for successful negotiation is to have competent negotiators for all sides in a dispute.

Nevertheless, although the participation of one or more attorneys can facilitate settlement, the presence of attorneys does not always guarantee an expedient settlement. For this reason a claims administrator must still function as the main overseer of claims negotiations. This person or firm must deal as effectively with the attorneys as with the parties involved in a dispute. The claims administrator must draw on the expertise and other strengths of each of these participants, while attempting to minimize the adverse effects of any participant's negative qualities that a contested claim may elicit.

INVESTIGATION

Investigation is the process of gathering information about an accident, the resulting harm, possible legal liability of any party for having caused that harm, and potential sources of restorative payments owed to or collectible from others to finance recovery from that harm. The purpose of an investigation is to secure these facts so that any resulting claim—any consequent duty to pay, or right to receive, compensatory funds—can be evaluated, settled or, in some cases, resisted.

Insurers routinely investigate every claim brought under any policy they have issued to determine the extent to which they must respond to the claim. In the broader context of risk financing, every organization needs to be able, through its personnel or outside experts, to investigate every claim in which it is involved as a potential provider or recipient of funds or as a party interested in how its insurer or other transferee has compensated another party for harm for which the organization may be responsible. Insurers' claims investigation procedures should, therefore, be part of every risk management professional's repertoire; for these procedures, as elsewhere, insurers' experienced insight can provide many lessons to claims administrators regardless of who employs them or whom they represent in a particular case.

The investigation process involves inquiring about, verifying, and comparing the information relevant to a claim. As mentioned, an investigating claims administrator frequently will find it necessary to observe the scene of an accident; police and fire reports, and medical or hospital records, often can corroborate or disprove a claimant's or witness's account of an accident or the resulting harm. Loss of income, for example, can be verified by a compensation report from an injured person's employer (obtained with the necessary authorization); property damage can be verified by a post-loss appraisal or by comparing pre-loss and post-loss photographs of the property.

A claims administrator conducting an investigation should be continually comparing new with old information so that any conflicts can be immediately recognized. When new information contradicts what was thought to be true, the administrator must reexamine all available information and often further investigate the situation to resolve these conflicts or to determine the most credible version of an accident.

An important objective of all claims administration is to reduce, consistent with legal requirements and proper ethics, an organization's combined cost of claims and claims administration expense, which includes the investigation. Because investigations cost money, a point may be reached at which the additional expense of acquiring more information about an accident is greater than the value of that additional information in reducing ultimate claim payments. Therefore, investigation should cease or should be focused in a new direction or on a new objective when the value of any new information no longer seems to merit its cost.

For instance, an organization may expend great effort and money to prove that another party, not itself, ought to be held legally liable for an entire claim; a relatively small investment in investigation here may save a great many claims dollars. In contrast, investigating the extent of the harm suffered by a particular claimant to which an organization *clearly* is liable, while still justified, may not merit such expensive scrutiny.

Matters To Be Investigated

The investigation of any claim should follow a uniform procedure regardless of whether the organization conducting the investigation stands to be the recipient or the provider of funds to restore any loss. (In fact, until the investigation is complete, it may not always be clear whether an organization will be the payor or payee of any compensatory funds.) In a risk financing context, the facts gathered about an accident should be focused on two essential matters:

1. if any party is entitled to compensation for losses it has suffered in an accident, and
2. the amount of such compensation.

Are Funds Payable? There are four possible answers to this question: no compensation, compensation through insurance, compensation through some other contractual transfer, or compensation under civil law.

First, if no compensation is payable to any party—through insurance, some other contractual risk financing arrangement, or through a civil judgment based on contract or tort law—then each party retains its owns loss.

Second, some compensation may be available through insurance if the facts reveal that (1) an event that falls within the scope of the insurance contract has occurred, and/or (2) the party entitled to insurance protection has fulfilled the conditions needed to perfect its right to insurance recovery.

To demonstrate that an insured event has occurred, the investigation should be designed to disclose that the time, location, peril, person(s), property (or other thing of value) harmed, and type of loss fall within the coverage provisions of the policy. To document that a party entitled to insurance protection has fulfilled all conditions affecting its right to recovery, the investigation should seek facts on (1) whether a valid and applicable insurance contract had been formed, (2) whether the insurance was in force at the time of the loss, (3) whether any circumstance that would have terminated or suspended coverage had occurred without being corrected, and (4) whether the claimant (either the insured or another party to whom the insured is liable) has met all the conditions specified in the insurance policy.

Third, compensation may be available under some other (noninsurance) contractual transfer for risk financing if much the same conditions as above have been fulfilled—that is, that (1) the loss falls within the scope of the transfer agreement, obligating the transferee/indemnitor to indemnify the transferor/indemnitee; and (2) that the transferor/indemnitee has taken the necessary actions before and after the loss to make good its right to compensation from the transferee/indemnitor. An additional, very practical matter for the transferor/indemnitee to investigate is whether the transferee/indemnitor is, in fact, able and willing to provide the stipulated compensation.

Fourth, quite apart from insurance or other contracts that provide restorative funds, civil law may oblige one party to pay damages to another party wronged by a breach of a contract or the commission of a tort (broadly defined as a civil wrong other than breach of a contract). To collect such civil damages, the party alleging that it is entitled to them (a plaintiff) must be able to demonstrate that (1) the defendant has committed all the elements of the contract breach or of the tort in question and (2) the plaintiff is entirely, or at least substantially, without fault.

Amount of Funds Payable   Given that some indemnity payment is due, the investigation should next focus on facts that help determine how much is payable. Regardless of how the compensation will be provided, information on the extent of the loss is universally relevant. How much harm an organization has suffered will largely determine the financial extent of the loss it will need to retain or the amount of indemnity it may be able to collect from its insurers, other transferees/indemnitors, or under civil law. How much harm others have incurred under circumstances that make the organization liable determines, in large part, the compensation the organization (or its insurers) will have to pay to others to help finance their recovery.

Extent of Loss.   Each type of loss—property, net income, liability, and personnel—should be evaluated in the following terms:

- For property losses the initial value of the property, the extent of the damage, and the cost of repairing or replacing the property are crucial.
- For net income losses the particularly relevant factors are the net income that the organization or person harmed would have earned in a given month (or other period) had the accident not occurred, the time required to reestablish preaccident income, and the extent to which the organization or individual entitled to compensation can be expected to mitigate (reduce) its loss.
- For liability losses, the most crucial factors are the extent of the harm suffered by others for which they do not have other

compensation and the extent to which the organization (or other entity) is legally or ethically responsible for that harm.

- For personnel losses, the most important determinants of the amount of the loss are the reduction which the accident has brought about in the net contribution that the person whose services have been lost would have made to the organization or family had the accident not occurred and the period over which that contribution would have been made.

Source of Funds. Beyond the always important question of the extent of the loss to be restored, the focus of the investigation usually varies somewhat, depending upon whether the compensation is to be paid through insurance, other contractual transfers, or under the civil law of torts and contracts.

If insurance applies, two factors should be investigated. The first is the valuation standard used by the insurance policy to measure losses, such as replacement cost, actual cash value, or market value for property; and for net income, reduction of gross earnings or a fixed dollar amount per day or week. The second is any limitation on the insurer's obligation to pay for a particular loss (that is, limits of liability), such as policy limits, retention through deductibles, and policy provisions designed to prevent overcompensation when, for example, more than one policy applies to a particular loss.

If the loss is covered by some other contractual transfer, then the relevant concerns are not only the two insurance-related considerations—valuation standards and limits of liability—but also the indemnitor's ability and willingness to provide the promised compensation.

If compensation is payable because of some civil wrong, then there are three relevant factors to be investigated beyond the always important extent of the claimant's harm. The first is the relative bargaining strength of the claimant and the defendant. The second is the potential courtroom appeal of the plaintiff's position as a result of, for example, the dramatic impact of the plaintiff's harm and the degree of fault or abuse apparent in the defendant's conduct. The third is the type of harm for which the law of torts or contracts in a particular jurisdiction permits recovery—for example, whether a successful plaintiff is entitled to compensation for legal and court costs or for treble damages in certain types of cases.

Amounts that are eventually proven payable or collectible when a claim goes to court—regardless of any underlying insurance or other risk-financing contractual transfer—are almost always less predictable or controllable than when a claim can be resolved out of court. Therefore, the facts revealed in any investigation often help each party to decide if it wants to settle in or out of court. As investigation brings more facts to light throughout the development of a claim, each party may wish to reconsider its decision.

Specific Investigation Procedures[3]

The nature of claims—specifically the type of loss—and whether the organization stands to be the recipient of funds, the provider of funds, or merely a party at interest, will determine the investigation procedure. No one sequence of inquiries is ideally applicable to all situations any more than one risk analysis questionnaire can reveal all significant loss exposures facing all organizations. Nevertheless, experience and logic teach a claims administrator certain patterns of inquiry, much as a risk management professional learns certain thought processes that are especially helpful in identifying and analyzing loss exposures.

To illustrate with a products liability claim that has been brought against a manufacturing, wholesaling, or retailing organization, the claims administrator probably would inquire about the general characteristics of the product line, the item or product involved in the claim, the characteristics of the claimant, the alleged harm to the claimant, and the availability of any insurance or other contractual transfer that might protect the organization against this claim. The following list delineates more specific matters on which the claims administrator might seek information.

- General nature of product line
    - Name, model, and basic description of product
    - Name and address of manufacturer, wholesaler, and/or retailer
    - Names and addresses of other retailers, wholesalers, and distributors of the product and their respective insurers
    - Advertising, any catalog description, and sample of the product together with any instructions to users or dealers and any written product warranties
- Specific item of product/incident allegedly causing harm
    - Present location and condition of particular item of product involved (if reasonably possible, it is best to retrieve or otherwise obtain possession of this item)
    - Name and address of wholesaler, shipper, and/or retailer of this item
    - Exact date item was manufactured, any batch or lot number, and all possible information on specific production of this item

- Results of any tests on this item or other products of the same make and model
- Details of packaging/transport of this item before sold
- Exact date item was purchased, at what price, for cash or charge
- Details of how item was selected such as requested by trade name, selected by buyer, or recommended by dealer
- Any complaints that buyers/users made about this item or any defects or inherently dangerous conditions in this item
- Any evidence of improper use of the item
- Details of accident leading to injury involving the item
- Use and storage of the item between time of purchase and accident causing injury
- Dates of accident and of first report of claim
- Characteristics of claimant
  - Name and address, current and for several past years
  - Educational and employment background, marital status, and economic dependency
  - Total income, assets, and liabilities
  - Account of use of item and of accident
  - Health prior to accident
  - Names and addresses of witnesses provided by claimant
- Extent of organization's liability for harm
  - Details of bodily injury, property damage, personal injury, or other harm alleged by claimant
  - Results of organization's physical examination of claimant and accident scene for other relevant physical evidence (if obtainable)
  - Medical and hospital reports on claimant pertaining to the injury and to medical condition/treatment prior to injury
  - Prognosis for claimant, including evaluation for and cost of rehabilitation
  - Nature of and cost of repairing or replacing any property of claimant allegedly harmed
  - Medical expenses, rehabilitation costs, or outlays for repair/replacement of property claimant (or claimant's insurer) has made to date because of accident
  - Intensity and duration of conscious pain and suffering
  - Extent of any cosmetic disfigurement, loss of marital consortium (the particular benefits characteristic of the marriage relationship), or other unusual harm allegedly resulting from accident
  - All sources of compensation available to claimant to finance restoration of all alleged harm

- Availability of insurance and/or other protection for organization
  - Existence of applicable products liability insurance in effect at time of insured event (which is the accident that caused the injury for occurrence coverage, and both the accident and the filing of the claim if claims-made coverage)
  - Existence of any hold harmless or other contractual transfers for risk financing to protect the organization from this claim
  - Existence and scope of any exclusion in insurance contract or other contractual transfer that may bar recovery for organization if claimant is granted funds
  - Nature of "proof of loss" required by insurer or other transferee/indemnitor
  - Limitation on amounts payable to organization by insurer or other transferee

Although the preceding outline is specific to products liability claims against an organization that it, or its insurer, might have to pay, similar types of information should be determined for all accidental losses with which an organization may become involved (if these losses are sufficiently substantial, individually or in the aggregate, to merit the cost of gathering this information).

NEGOTIATION

As the parties involved in a claim investigate the issues from their different perspectives, they are very likely to differ on how they view two major issues in an investigation: first, who is entitled to the compensation from whom, and second, how much should be paid. These differences are almost certain to arise for any type of claim as exemplified in the following:

- When an organization retains its property, net income, or personnel loss, the managers of the involved departments within the organization may disagree as to who was at fault and/or whose budgets should bear how much of the cost of restoring the loss.
- When an organization's losses are covered by insurance, the representatives of the insurer and of the insured may disagree as to whether the loss is covered, the extent of the loss, and/or the amount of the insurer's obligation to pay the loss to, or on behalf of, the insured.

- When an organization looks to an indemnitor that is not an insurer to pay its losses or to hold the organization harmless from liability claims brought by third parties, the representatives of the transferor/indemnitee organization may disagree with those of the transferee/indemnitor on much the same issues, but with the added complications that the contract between them may not be as precisely worded as a typical insurance contract and that the transferee/indemnitor may be of lesser financial strength.
- When the claim calls upon the organization to be the indemnitor for others' losses either under a contractual transfer or through the civil law of torts or contracts, the organization may be resisting rather than attempting to collect a claim—thus, the organization is in a different position than it was in the three preceding examples.

In each of these situations the effectiveness of an organization's risk financing plans depends first on the skill of the negotiator representing the organization and second on the use of appropriate negotiating procedures.

Characteristics of a Good Negotiator

Effective negotiators use certain tactics and behave in ways that make them especially successful in persuading others to accept their position. Any person seeking to negotiate effectively should be familiar with these tactics and should strive to develop these behaviors. Many of these tactics are shown in Exhibit 12-1.

In addition to these tactics, certain behaviors make a good negotiator. An influential negotiator is generally friendly toward people. This makes them more confident that the negotiator truly cares about them and seeks to resolve their dispute in ways that will ultimately be beneficial despite the fact that they are, for the moment, "opponents."

A competent negotiator is informed about the situation underlying the conflict being negotiated to the extent that the overall situation can be viewed from each party's perspective. Such a global, yet detailed, grasp of the situation enables a good negotiator to recognize alternative resolutions to the conflict that do not jeopardize the key requirements of the party the negotiator represents.

A good negotiator is patient—willing to take time to explain matters opponents do not fully understand, to listen to the contentions of the opponents (especially for points of mutual agreement), and to allow the members of the negotiator's (or the opponent's) bargaining

Exhibit 12-1
Ten Tactics of a Good Negotiator*

1. Seek mutual agreement, not unilateral victory.
2. Let all parties win something; make no one a complete loser.
3. Find common ground, staying mindful of opponents' interests.
4. Seek a competent opponent with whom to negotiate.
5. Negotiate for the long run.
6. Strive to make explicit your and your opponents' perceptions and assumptions.
7. Prepare for all negotiations and for each session of continuing negotiations.
8. Listen to what opponents say and to what they mean.
9. Ask questions so that both you and your opponents learn from the answers they give.
10. Be flexible in seeking conflict resolutions.

*Adapted with permission from George L. Head and Laurie J. Bilik, "Ten Tips for Negotiating Effectively," *Risk and Employee Benefits Management*, March 1986.

team and the senior management whom the negotiators represent to absorb, evaluate, and appreciate the positions of the contending parties. Patience is required not primarily because the negotiator needs time to understand and accept a given resolution, but because those whom the negotiator represents need time to learn to "live with" the resolution of their dispute.

A good negotiator behaves professionally at all times and maintains an even temper, even when consciously employing dramatic techniques to emphasize a point. To think clearly, every person must control his or her emotions, particularly when his or her actions as a negotiator can have an impact on the well-being of those represented.

Self-confidence also is important to a negotiator's success. A negotiator must honestly believe in the position of the represented party in order to convince others of its merits. Anxiety, uncertainty, or ignorance undermine self-confidence and, therefore, almost always dissipate the negotiator's persuasive skills.

An effective negotiator also knows when the time is right to break off negotiations temporarily or to press forward immediately to finalize agreement. Such a negotiator can sense when an opponent has yielded as much as possible without suffering humiliation. A good negotiator also knows how to project the same. When each party perceives that the other has conceded as much as possible, then each is ready either to adjourn or to strike a bargain, consolidating their respective gains.

A good negotiator also is honest in presenting facts that favor the represented party and in wanting to reach a mutually beneficial solution. Honesty is essential because, if an opponent ever discovers an untruth or an insincere proposal, that opponent will always have doubts about the veracity of any other statements or the sincerity of any positions a negotiator may present.

Finally, a good negotiator wants only to resolve the dispute, not to destroy or humiliate the opponent. Such a negotiator recognizes that the only "enemy" is disagreement, not the opposing parties in the negotiations. Furthermore, many of these parties are likely to meet again in future negotiations, their roles or strengths perhaps radically altered. For this reason and for current cooperation, a good negotiator tries to leave each party with some positive feeling, not memories of defeat and a desire for retribution.

Steps in the Negotiating Process

In any negotiation, the four essential steps are as follows:

1. preparation,
2. exploration,
3. exchanges of offers/counteroffers, and
4. closure/settlement.

Preparation The information in this chapter about claims investigation has been targeted to prepare for negotiation to settle a claim. The essence of preparation is knowledge—of (1) the facts of the claim as each negotiating party perceives them, (2) the strong and weak points of both parties' cases, (3) the bargaining position each party is initially likely to take and from which that party may or may not be willing to retreat, and (4) the personality, style, and expectations of each negotiator and party represented as an individual. From this knowledge—or from suppositions where knowledge is lacking—each negotiator can develop alternative strategies for resolving the conflict without embarrassing, or making a future enemy of, any opponent.

Exploration The opening discussions among negotiators normally should be devoted to exploring each other's positions, perceptions, and concerns as well as the common ground from which they can move to handle contested matters. Allowing each party to clarify its position in opening statements clears the air of matters that individual parties feel need to be said and of irrelevant matters that could later block meaningful bargaining.

Such exploratory statements in the early stages of negotiation and the discussions they are likely to spark also may reveal otherwise unnoticed areas of agreement. For example, while negotiations on risk financing issues normally focus on two essential issues—who shall pay whom and how much—an opening exploratory discussion may suggest a solution that does not involve explicit payments to anyone. A unanimously acceptable alternative may be that one party makes the other whole by providing some service or thing of value other than money. Alternatively, opening discussions may reveal that one party is making an assumption that another has not even considered; recognizing the discrepancy in their assumptions, the parties might align their perceptions and almost automatically resolve their dispute. Even if clarifying assumptions does not end the dispute, it may bring the parties closer to settlement, both factually and psychologically. Exploratory discussions early in the negotiations should at least clarify the issues and channel the really important upcoming bargaining.

Exchange of Offers/Counteroffers At the close of the exploratory phase of negotiations, an effective negotiator often will summarize orally or in writing for all the parties (1) the facts on which all agree, (2) the questions of fact known to be in dispute, and (3) the issues that consequently remain. Such a summary can do much to establish a cooperative and honest relationship and an atmosphere of fairness that fosters future negotiations. Such a summary also provides a foundation from which an effective negotiator can make a reasonable offer (to pay funds or to accept funds) to which the other party can respond with an alternative that to them seems equitable. Such an initial offer and counteroffer is the ideal way to set the boundaries for future bargaining.

While such progress may be ideal, making an opening offer that is premature or unreasonable may be a mistake. It is unwise to make an offer unless there is some reasonable possibility of reaching an agreement for an amount or on terms approximating the offer. An offer an opponent considers unreasonable may merely harden the opponent's determination to maintain its original position or to at least break off, and therefore delay, further negotiations. Too extreme an initial offer also may make it very difficult for the offeror to later modify that position without losing credibility.

For the offer/counteroffer process to work effectively, each party must maintain some flexibility and initiative, some ability to keep the process moving without yielding all control to an opponent. For this reason, it is usually best to avoid all ultimatums—"take it or leave it" offers—which force an opponent into complete capitulation or refusal. Too often, ultimatums stop negotiations only until tempers have cooled and the parties are able to resume discussions without at least one of them feeling or appearing to be humiliated.

If opposing parties are to resolve a dispute through negotiations without court action or other dispute resolution mechanisms, their exchanges of offers and counteroffers must narrow their differences, bringing them closer to settlement. If the negotiating process works as designed, the time will come when a *final offer* is appropriate. This usually happens when differences between the parties are narrowed to the point at which, if each party is willing to make some reasonable concession to the other—if each is willing to "give something to get something"—then the dispute can be ended. By experience or intuition, a skilled negotiator recognizes this point and then approaches an opponent in a friendly but firm manner with an offer couched in such terms as the following:

> We disagree on X and Y. I will grant you X if you will grant me Y, or perhaps each of us can take half of X and half of Y. But, in any case, let's settle.

If amicable, out-of-court settlement is possible, such an approach should achieve it.

Closure/Settlement *Closure* refers to a point in the negotiating process where the parties have actually or virtually resolved their differences, but have not yet formally expressed agreement. It is time for one or both of them to say, in effect,

> It looks like we agree on everything. Specifically, we agree that. . . .

Settlement refers to the actual agreement or to a document embodying the agreement. A settlement usually is accompanied by or incorporates a *release*. A release is a legally binding contract between the parties to a dispute that embodies their agreement, that obligates each of them to fulfill the terms of that agreement, and that releases them from further obligations to one another that relate to their dispute. To be valid, a release must include all the elements of a proper contract: (1) bargained offer and acceptance (2) between or among legally competent parties (3) accompanied by an exchange of legal consideration (4) to fulfill legal purposes. Insurers quite routinely secure releases when settling claims with their own insureds or with third-party claimants against their insureds. It is good risk financing as well as sound legal practice for any other parties who act as indemnitors in risk financing cases to secure comparable releases from those whom they indemnify or who may later seek indemnity.

General Release. A release normally provides that, in consideration of the specific sum paid to the indemnitee, the indemnitee releases the indemnitor from all claims arising out of a particular accident or other incident for which that sum is paid. Thus, the two aspects of legal consideration here are (1) the indemnitee's promise to refrain from bringing suit or further claim against the indemnitor and (2) payment by the indemnitor to the indemnitee (or on behalf of the indemnitee to some third person) of the money specified in the release. In practice, an indemnitee often signs such a settlement release before receiving the settlement check with the understanding that the check soon will be issued. To resolve any ambiguities, the back of the settlement check itself often specifies that the payee's endorsement or negotiation of the check constitutes acceptance of the settlement and release of further claims against the party in whose favor the release is drawn.

A general release is a very common, largely standardized document much like the one presented in Exhibit 12-2. It releases the indemnitor from any further liability to the indemnitee, while making clear that this release does not waive any rights the indemnitee may have against other parties involved. While this particular sample form is widely used when an insurer is the indemnitor and an insured or third-party claimant is the indemnitee, this agreement is readily adaptable to situations in which other parties are in the roles of indemnitor and indemnitee.

When several organizations or individuals each have similar claims against an indemnitor, a proper release of that indemnitor must be signed by all such parties if the purpose is to completely absolve the indemnitor. For example, in a claim involving a married claimant, the release should be signed by both spouses. This occurs because many states grant a wife as well as a husband a cause of action for loss of consortium if either spouse is injured. A release that contains only the signature of the injured spouse usually leaves the other free to make a claim for loss of its services of the injured person. As another illustration, if an injured driver of an automobile, as an indemnitee, is someone other than the owner of the automobile, the names and signatures of both the driver and the owner should be included in the release; otherwise, the driver's signature does not free the indemnitor from liability to the vehicle owner.

Special Releases. Many different types of releases have been developed to fit particular circumstances including those in which several wrongdoers together (joint tortfeasors) are liable to an indemnitee, when legal minors are involved, or when the intent is to release the indemnitor from only some duties to the indemnitee.

Exhibit 12-2
Typical General Release*

Know all men by these Presents, That we, the Undersigned, for the sole consideration of ___$ X (the agreed indemnity payment)___ dollars, the receipt of which is acknowledged, have released and discharged, and by these presents do hereby forever release and discharge ___[the Indemnitor]___ heirs, executors, administrators, employers, employees, principals, agents, insurers, successors and assigns, for and from any and all liability, claims, demands, controversies, damages, actions and causes of action on account of personal injuries, death, loss of services or consortium, property damage and any and all other loss and damage of every kind and nature sustained by or hereafter resulting to the undersigned or any person or persons for whom the undersigned is acting as executor, administrator or guardian, from an accident which occurred on or about the ___ day of ___, 19___ at ___

and of and from all liability, claims, demands, controversies, damages, actions, and causes of action whatsoever, either in law or equity, which the undersigned, individually or in any other capacity, their heirs, executors, administrators, successors and assigns, can, shall or may have by reason of or in any wise incident or resulting from the accident hereinbefore mentioned.

As inducement to the payment of the sum aforesaid the undersigned declare that we fully understand the terms of this settlement, and that we voluntarily accept said sum for the purpose of making full and final compromise, adjustment and settlement of all loss, damages and injuries hereinbefore mentioned or referred to, and that the payment of said sum for this release is not an admission of liability by the payor, but that the payor expressly denies liability.

It is understood and agreed by the parties hereto that the undersigned, by the execution of this instrument, do not release or discharge ___[Other Potential Indemnitors of Indemnitee]___ who was also involved in the above accident, from any claim or claims for damages arising out of such accident, which the undersigned may have against said ___[Other Potential Indemnitors]___, but on the contrary all such claims, demands, and causes of action against said ___[Other Potential Indemnitors]___ are hereby specifically reserved.

It is agreed that distribution of the above sum shall be made as follows ___[Any and Various Wordings, specifying in substance "all to indemnitee" or "divided among A, B, C as follows...."]___

In Witness Whereof, We hereunto set our hands and seals this ___ day of ___, 19___

In presence of

_____   _____ (Seal)

_____   _____ (Seal)
Name

_____   _____ (Seal)
Address

_____   _____ (Seal)
Name

_____   _____
Address

Witnesses sign here   Claimants sign here

*Reprinted with permission from Robert J. Prahl and Stephen M. Utrata, *Liability Claim Concepts and Practices*, 1st ed. (Malvern, PA: Insurance Institute of America, 1985), pp. 387-388.

Joint Tortfeasor Release. A *joint tortfeasor* is one of several organizations or individuals who together, by design or coincidence, commit a tort against one victim under circumstances that make it difficult to distinguish one wrongdoer's fault from another's or to distinguish the harm caused by one wrongdoer from that caused by another. Examples of joint tortfeasors are a gang of thieves that may assault a passerby; a railroad as an organization and several of its individual employees may share joint fault for a particular runaway train; or several manufacturing firms releasing pollutants into the environment may be jointly liable to numerous neighbors whose properties become polluted by a mixture of the effluents.

Common law holds each joint tortfeasor individually liable to the victim for all the harm caused by any of the joint tortfeasors, and correspondingly, holds that a release of any one tortfeasor by the victim releases all tortfeasors even though they may not have been party to the release agreement. Often, however, it is not practical for a victim/claimant to collect from any one tortfeasor compensation for all the harm that has been suffered. Therefore, to prevent a claimant's settlement with and release of one tortfeasor from waiving the claimant's rights against other tortfeasors, special releases, such as the one in Exhibit 12-3, have been developed exclusively for joint tortfeasor situations. These preserve the claimant's rights against other wrong-doers not explicitly released.

Covenant Not To Sue. A covenant not to sue, permitted by state law, is an alternative settlement document for a claimant/indemnitee who may have claims against several wrongdoers involved in a particular accident, but usually in situations where it is possible to distinguish the harm caused by one wrongdoer from that caused by another. For example, if a healthy pedestrian breaks an ankle as a result of being struck by one negligently driven automobile, but is able to stagger on for some distance before being struck and killed by a second negligently driven vehicle, the operator and/or owner of the first vehicle is not liable for the pedestrian's death. This is one situation in which it may be advantageous for a claimant to agree not to sue one wrongdoer in order to obtain that wrongdoer's cooperation in proceeding against other, more culpable, potential indemnitors. For such situations, a covenant not to sue, shown in Exhibit 12-4, may be appropriate. The following is an excerpt of the most relevant portions of such an agreement. The claimant, in exchange for a specified sum of money from one indemnitor, acknowledges that:

> ... this settlement is a compromise of a doubtful and disputed claim [against the first indemnitor] against whom I/we will never at any time make any [further] demand or claim, or commence to prosecute, cause or permit to be prosecuted, any action at law or in equity....

Exhibit 12-3
Joint Tortfeasor Release*

Know all men by these Presents, That we, the Undersigned, for the sole consideration of [Specific Amount] dollars, the receipt of which is acknowledged, have released and discharged, and by these presents do hereby forever release and discharge [One Joint Tortfeasor] heirs, executors, administrators, employers, employees, principals, agents, insurers, successors and assigns, for and from any and all liability, claims, demands, controversies, damages, actions and causes of action on account of personal injuries, death, loss of services or consortium, property damage and any and all other loss and damage of every kind and nature sustained by or hereafter resulting to the undersigned or any person or persons for whom the undersigned is acting as executor, administrator or guardian, from an accident which occurred on or about the _____ day of _____, 19____ at [Precise Location of Accident]

and of and from all liability, claims, demands, controversies, damages, actions, and causes of action whatsoever, either in law or equity, which the undersigned, individually or in any other capacity, their heirs, executors, administrators, successors and assigns, can, shall or may have by reason of or in any wise incident or resulting from the accident hereinbefore mentioned.

As inducement to the payment of the sum aforesaid the undersigned declare that we fully understand the terms of this settlement, and that we voluntarily accept said sum for the purpose of making full and final compromise, adjustment and settlement of all loss, damages and injuries hereinbefore mentioned or referred to, and that the payment of said sum for this release is not an admission of liability by the payor, but that the payor expressly denies liability.

It is understood and agreed by the parties hereto that the undersigned, by the execution of this instrument, do not release or discharge [Other Named Joint Tortfeasors] , who was also involved in the above accident, from any claim or claims for damages arising out of such accident, which the undersigned may have against said [Same Specified Parties] , but on the contrary all such claims, demands, and causes of action against said [Same Specified Parties] are hereby specifically reserved.

It is agreed that distribution of the above sum shall be made as follows _____

In Witness Whereof, We hereunto set our hands and seals this _____ day of _____ , 19____

In presence of

Name _____ (Seal)

Address _____ (Seal)

Name _____ (Seal)

Address _____ (Seal)

Name _____ (Seal)

Address _____ (Seal)

Witnesses sign here   Claimants sign here

* Reprinted with permission from Robert J. Prahl and Stephen M. Utrata, *Liability Claim Concepts and Practices*, 1st ed. (Malvern, PA: Insurance Institute of America, 1985), pp. 391-392.

[But] I/we specifically reserve the right to make claim and/or prosecute actions against any and every such other person, firm, or corporation not a party to this agreement for damages arising from the said accident.

Where recognized by the courts and not prohibited by state statutes, such a covenant not to sue eliminates any ambiguity as to whether release of one party might also absolve another party. However, some state statutes do not permit an individual or organization to waive its constitutional right to sue another.

High/Low Agreement. A high/low agreement is a type of settlement agreement in which a claimant and a potential indemnitor, contemplating or already engaged in a lawsuit, agree to abide by the court verdict, subject to a separate guarantee between them that the indemnity payment will be between a specified minimum and maximum. The court's verdict establishes the actual payment only if it is between these upper and lower bounds.

This type of agreement has particular application where the defendant and the plaintiff both want the case to be finally adjudicated to establish their rights, but they want to minimize the risk of an extremely high or low payment. For example, the defendant's liability may be questionable, creating some likelihood that the plaintiff will collect nothing. At the same time, the actual harm to the plaintiff may be so substantial that the defendant, if found liable, is exposed to a large judgment. Through a high/low agreement, the plaintiff benefits by being guaranteed some recovery even if the case is lost, whereas the defendant has a ceiling on its liability should a massive verdict for the plaintiff be rendered. High/low agreements are sometimes controversial because, for example, they may foster otherwise avoidable litigation or constitute concealed tampering with the legal process. However, such agreements can expedite legal proceedings and allow all parties some measure of legal or financial "victory" and security.

Releases Involving Minors. The statutes of all states specify the minimum age at which people can bind themselves to various kinds of contracts such as releases. A release executed by a minor is not binding; the minor may later disavow the release and continue to press his or her claim. Therefore, to obtain release from a minor who is a potential claimant/indemnitee, the prospective indemnitor must secure the signature of a parent or guardian on a release specifically drafted to explicitly waive whatever rights the legally incompetent minor may have against this indemnitor. Moreover, because some states want to further protect minors, they require both a parent's or guardian's signature and court approval of such a release. As an additional complication, in states that recognize parents' rights derived from their children's rights, the signatures of both parents—waiving their own

Exhibit 12-4
Convenant Not to Sue*

FOR AND IN CONSIDERATION of the payment to me/us at this time of the sum of __X Dollars__ Dollars ($ __X__), the receipt of which is hereby acknowledged, I/we being of lawful age, do hereby convenant and agree jointly and severally, that I/we never at any time make any demand or claim, or commence, prosecute, cause or permit to be prosecuted, any action at law or in equity, or any proceeding of any description against [Potential Indemnitor No. 1]

because of any or all damages, costs, loss of services, expenses and/or compensation, on account of, or in any way growing out of, any and all known and unknown personal injuries and property damage resulting, or to result, from an accident that occurred on or about the _____ day of _____ 19_____ , at or near _____

I/we further promise and bind myself/ourselves jointly and severally, my/our heirs, administrators and executors to indemnify and hold forever harmless the said [Potential Indemnitor No. 1] heirs, successors and assigns and agree to repay any sum of money and expense, that he/she/they may hereafter be compelled to pay because of the said known and unknown personal injuries and property damage.

I/we hereby declare and represent that the injuries sustained are permanent and progressive and that recovery therefrom is uncertain and indefinite, and in making this convenant and agreement it is understood and agreed that I/we rely wholly upon my/our own judgement, belief and knowledge of the nature, extent and duration of said injuries, and that I/we have not been influenced to any extent whatever in making this convenant by any representations or statements regarding said injuries, or regarding any other matters, made by the persons, firms or corporations herein mentioned, or by any person or persons representing him or them, or by any physician or surgeon by him or them employed.

I/we specifically reserve the right to make claim and prosecute actions against any and every other person, firm or corporation not a party of this agreement for damages arising from the said accident.

It is further understood and agreed that this settlement is the compromise of a doubtful and disputed claim, and that the payment is not to be construed as an admission of liability on the part of ____[Potential Indemnitor No. 2]____ by whom liability is expressly denied.

This Covenant Not To Sue contains the ENTIRE AGREEMENT between the parties hereto, and the terms of this agreement are contractual and not a mere recital.

I/we further state that I/we have carefully read the foregoing instrument and know the contents thereof, and I/we sign the same as my/our own free act.

WITNESS _____ hand _____ and seal _____ this _____ day of _____ 19_____

CAUTION! READ BEFORE SIGNING

_____ _____ (Seal)

_____ _____ (Seal)

State of _____

County of _____ ss.

On this _____ day of _____ 19 _____, before me personally appeared _____ to me known to be the person, described herein, and who executed the foregoing instrument and _____ acknowledged that _____ voluntarily executed the same.

My term expires, _____ 19_____   _____ Notary Public

(If this agreement is acknowledged before a Notary Public, no witnesses' signatures are necessary)

*Reprinted with permission from Robert J. Prahl and Stephen M. Utrata, *Liability Claim Concepts and Practices*, 1st ed. (Malvern, PA: Insurance Institute of America, 1985), p. 395.

parental rights—also may be required to make a release totally effective.

Nominal, or Dollar, Releases.   Accidents or other harmful events often occur in the presence of bystanders or others who appear to have suffered no harm. However, there is the possibility that any one of these apparently unharmed persons may later experience actual or genuinely perceived psychological trauma or other harm stemming from the event. To forestall claims based on such late-manifesting or supposed harm, an organization or individual who may later be called upon to provide compensation often is well advised to secure nominal (or dollar) releases from such potential claimants.

To make such a release a binding contract supported by legal consideration, the party being released from future liability should pay a nominal amount (once considered to be as little as one dollar) to each party signing such a release. To prevent an overturn of such a release on grounds of misrepresentation or duress, it is important that the release be fully explained and voluntarily signed by those waiving their future rights.

Open-End Releases.   Although a potential indemnitor prefers a closed claim to a pending one, there often are situations in which a claimant/indemnitee is unwilling to sign a full release because the extent of the harm suffered or the amounts of the indemnity payments that may be appropriate in the future are unknown. An open-end release can address the claimant's/indemnitee's concerns while limiting the potential indemnitor's liability.

Such a release is best used when the extent of the harm suffered by the claimant is known, and the bulk of the medical, property, or other restoration needed by the claimant has already been rendered. Both the indemnitor and claimant recognize, however, that some additional, relatively small restorative payments, services, or treatments may well be required in the reasonably forseeable future. The indemnitor, willing to finance such limited restoration in the future while wanting to limit the dollar amount and time horizon of its liability, is likely to propose an open-end settlement. Under such an agreement (1) the indemnitor agrees to make future payments to, or on behalf of, the indemnitee up to a given maximum amount for specified types of treatment or other restorative sources the indemnitee may require because of a given accident for which the indemnitor is in some way liable; and (2) the claimant relinquishes any further claims against the indemnitor arising from this accident. A sample open-end release tailored to the type of medical expense claim with which these releases are most frequently used appears as Exhibit 12-5.

Exhibit 12-5
Open-end Release*

RELEASE OF ALL CLAIMS EXCEPT FUTURE MEDICAL EXPENSE

Know all men by these Presents. That we the Undersigned, for the sole consideration of [Specified Amount] dollars, the receipt of which is acknowledged, and in further consideration of the promise to pay such additional reasonable medical expenses as may be incurred within the next ___X___ months up to a maximum of ___Y___ dollars ($ _____) as a result of the accident described below do hereby release and discharge, and by these presents do hereby forever release and discharge [Indemnitor] heirs, executors, administrators, employers, employees, principals, agents, insurers, successors and assigns, for and from any and all liability, claims, demands, controversies, damages, actions and causes of action on account of personal injuries, death, loss of services or consortium, property damage and any and all other loss and damage of every kind and nature sustained by or hereafter resulting to the undersigned or any person or persons for whom the undersigned is acting as executor, administrator or guardian, from an accident which occurred on or about the ___ day of ___, 19___, at [Specified Location] and of and from all liability, claims, demands, controversies, damages, actions, and causes of action whatsoever, either in law or equity, which the undersigned, individually or in any other capacity, their heirs, executors, administrators, successors and assigns, can, shall or may have by reason of or in any wise incident or resulting from the accident hereinbefore mentioned.

As inducement to the payment of the sum aforesaid the undersigned declare that we fully understand the terms of this settlement and that we voluntarily accept said sum for the purpose of making full and final compromise, adjustment and settlement of all loss, damages and injuries hereinbefore mentioned or referred to, and that the payment of said sum for this release is not an admission of liability by the payor, but that the payor expressly denies liability.

It is understood and agreed by the parties hereto that the undersigned, by the execution of this instrument, do ___ not release or discharge [Other Specified Potential Indemnitors] who was also involved in the above accident, from any claim or claims for damages arising out of such accident, which the undersigned may have against said [Same Potential Indemnitors] but on the contrary all such claims, demands, and causes of action against said [Same Potential Indemnitors] are hereby specifically reserved.

It is agreed that distribution of the above sum shall be made as follows _____

_____

_____

In Witness Whereof, We hereunto set our hands and seals this ___ day ___, 19___

In presence of

Name _____   _____ (Seal)
Address _____   _____ (Seal)
Name _____   _____ (Seal)
Address _____   _____ (Seal)
Name _____   _____ (Seal)
Address _____   _____ (Seal)
Witnesses sign here   Claimants sign here

---

*Reprinted with permission from Robert J. Prahl and Stephen M. Utrata, *Liability Claim Concepts and Practices*, 1st ed. (Malvern, PA: Insurance Institute of America, 1985), pp. 411.

No-Release Settlements. When an organization handles complaints or minor claims brought by others, particularly its customers, or members of the public, it will often authorize middle and upper managers, as well as claims administration personnel, to offer immediate settlements, of no more than a relatively small dollar amount, without securing a release from the person lodging the complaint or claim. Such streamlined settlements are offered primarily to maintain the good will of customers and to foster a positive public image. There is also the unspoken hope that such treatment will forestall any future legal claims. In fact, one reason for not seeking a release is that any mention whatsoever of legal rights or lawsuits might remind potential claimants of possibilities the organization would rather they never consider. However, because even the most sympathetically treated customer who does not sign a release may someday sue, some organizations shun no-release settlements. Instead, they always require a release from those with whom they settle by this otherwise informal procedure.

Alternative Dispute Resolution (ADR) Techniques[4]

When the parties involved in a disputed risk financing case cannot resolve their differences by themselves or through their negotiating representatives, each party may mistakenly think its only alternative is to sue in court—to replace the largely unstructured negotiating process with the highly regimented formal procedures of court. In fact, however, there are at least two other alternatives that are both more structured than negotiations and less formal than court procedures. These alternatives are mediation and arbitration.

Mediation In the context of claims negotiation, mediate means to intercede, to seek agreement between parties through persuasion or good will. A *mediator* acts informally in the attempt to get disputing parties to discuss their conflicts first alone with the mediator and then as a group in the mediator's presence. Relying on expertise, or the friendship and trust of the contending parties, a mediator often recommends compromises for resolving a dispute and actively tries to persuade the parties to agree to this recommendation. The essence of mediation is to foster willing agreement between once differing parties, not to impose a settlement.

Mediation is used to resolve a wide variety of disputes involving business relationships. It may be used because a contract underlying a particular relationship calls for mediation, or because once a dispute has arisen, one or more of the parties suggests mediation as an alternative to litigation and the other parties agree. A contract that calls for mediation often specifies (1) the type of issues to be mediated (as risk financing examples, perhaps disputes on the valuation of losses or the adequacy of an indemnitee's cooperation with an indemnitor in defending the indemnitee against a lawsuit) and/or (2) the individual or organization that is acceptable to all parties as a mediator. The *Federal Mediation and Conciliation Service*, headquartered in Washington,

D.C., and the *American Arbitration Association,* whose headquarters is in New York City, both offer mediation services throughout the United States.

Arbitration   In general, arbitration is a process whereby two or more parties agree to submit an existing dispute, or some specified class of possible future disputes, to some impartial person or persons for final decision. The *arbitrator* (or board of arbitrators) is to decide each case on its merits, not to act as a mediator or as a compromiser. In this sense, arbitrators function as judges.

When disputing parties agree to arbitrate a dispute, they are said to be undertaking *voluntary arbitration. Compulsory arbitration* refers to the relatively rare statutory right of one party to require that another party submit a dispute to arbitration even though the second party may never have agreed to such arbitration and would prefer a court proceeding. Thus, statutes in some states require that certain classes of disputes—for example, real estate disputes involving less than a small specified sum such as $3,000—be settled by arbitration rather than in court, especially because of overburdened court dockets.

The type of voluntary arbitration most relevant to risk financing disputes is known as *commercial arbitration,* that is, arbitration of business controversies. Voluntary commercial arbitration can come about in one of three ways: (1) most frequently, the disputing parties agree to submit an existing dispute to arbitration; (2) the original contract between the parties provides for the arbitration of specified types of disputes; and (3) some trade and professional associations require members to submit to arbitration with other association members so that the association can resolve these differences internally without resorting to the sometimes less knowledgeable civil courts and risking often damaging publicity. To illustrate association-centered arbitration, primary insurers and reinsurers at odds about who is responsible for an insured's clearly covered loss have long arbitrated these disputes rather than use the court system. Such arbitration procedures are logically just as applicable in resolving differences between noninsurance indemnitors and indemnitees.

Early in the development of common law, arbitration was viewed with suspicion—a private attempt to evade or to oust the jurisdiction of the civil courts. Nevertheless, about half the states now have statutes that give voluntary arbitration judgments much the same force as a court verdict. In these states most agreements to arbitrate are binding, and an arbitrator's decision will, if necessary, be enforced by the civil courts and by the police power of the state, subject to only five general exceptions. A court will vacate, or declare void, an award granted through voluntary arbitration only if (1) the arbitrator has exceeded its jurisdiction, attempting to decide a matter that had not been properly submitted; (2) the arbitrator's award left something open for future decision; (3) the arbitrator's award was procured by fraud, corruption, or misbehavior; (4) the arbitration proceedings lacked due process; or (5) the award is contrary to law or public policy. Because arbitrators are almost always highly expert in the matters they handle and judge, or because the arbitrators are individuals chosen by the opposing parties, it is indeed rare that an arbitration award is seriously challenged in a civil court.

Beyond finally and promptly resolving the dispute, voluntary arbitration of business disputes has a number of distinct advantages. These are likely to include resolution of disputes within weeks rather than years, as in usual civil courts, much lower legal costs, the great expertise of most arbitrators in contrast to some lay juries, and the much less formal rules of evidence and procedure that make it more likely that an arbitrated dispute will be resolved on its merits rather than on a legal technicality. However, arbitration also has disadvantages compared to a court proceeding. For example, some arbitrators may feel less bound by precedent than are the civil law courts, and the less formal procedures of arbitration may involve some sacrifice of the protection that the rules of courtroom civil procedure were developed to provide.

REDUCING CLAIM COSTS

The idea that "a loss is a loss is a loss" and should have a definite value regardless of who is paying to finance recovery may suggest that any given claim should be "worth" a fixed, irreducible amount of money. While this suggestion has some merit, other discussions in the ARM Program—particularly in ARM 54 and ARM 55—have indicated that many kinds of risk control actions can be taken after an accident has occurred to reduce the eventual severity of the losses from that accident. Furthermore, from the standpoint of an organization that must pay its own or others' losses, the ability to call upon some other party to share or undertake all of the financing burden may reduce the first indemnitor's claim costs. Also, given the time value of money, an organization indemnifying others' losses can reduce the present value of its claims payments by making them on an installment basis rather than as a lump sum.

The material in this section describes how an organization can reduce the costs of restoring its own or others' losses through (1) advance payments to claimants to help them reduce their actual losses after an accident; (2) subrogation opportunities for requiring others to share part or all of the losses they have wrongfully caused; and (3) structured settlements for paying claims to others on an installment, rather than a lump-sum, basis.

Advance Payments

A person or organization suffering an accidental loss often needs funds for medical expenses, to repair damaged property or protect undamaged property, to facilitate or expedite setting up temporary business facilities, and to meet other costs needed for an appropriate emergency response. Having these funds available promptly enables an individual or organization to minimize its own losses and to return more quickly to normal activity.

When a person or organization faces an emergency because of an accident that is the legal responsibility of another, that person or organization probably can eventually require the responsible party (or that party's insurer) to be an indemnitor of its losses. If this indemnitor can promptly provide funds, the losses to the indemnitee will be minimized, and therefore, so will the aggregate amount the indemnitor will eventually pay. Therefore, under the proper circumstances, it may well be in the best interest of an indemnitor to make what are known as *advance payments* to potential claimants, thus reducing the ultimate value of the claims against it. These payments are advance in the sense that they come before any final determination of the indemnitor's liability and any final claim settlement.

Many liability insurers recognize the merits of advance payments in reducing insured liability claims payable to third parties whom their insureds have harmed and for which these insurers will almost certainly need to respond. Noninsurance indemnitors of others' losses can benefit from these insurers' experience, which has demonstrated that advance payments generally reduce claim costs when the harm to claimants is fairly serious, where some immediate cash will reduce the long-term consequences of this harm, where the indemnitor's eventual legal liability is quite clear, and where potential claimants already have demonstrated both financial need and a reasonably cooperative attitude. By offering to pay for partial or whole losses resulting from an accident, the indemnitor can create a positive claims administration environment by relieving the claimant's concerns about meeting emergency expenses. In such an environment, the potential claimant may come to see the indemnitor as an ally rather than as an adversary. Receiving such advance payment gives potential claimants reasons for believing that their cases are understood by the indemnitor who wishes to help them.

In appropriate circumstances an insurer or other indemnitor

Exhibit 12-6
Receipt for Advance Payment*

(This is not a release)

This is to acknowledge receipt of $ ____X____ paid on behalf of ____[Indemnities]____ to be credited to the total amount of any final settlement or judgment in my/our favor for alleged damages resulting from an accident on _____, 19 _____ at _____
I/We authorize that the above sum be distributed as follows: _____
[$ A to Physical, $ B to Building Contractor, $ C to Self]

Date _____   _____ (L.S.)

_____   _____ (L.S.)
          Witness

          _____ (L.S.)

_____   _____ (L.S.)
          Witness

---

*Reprinted with permission from Robert J. Prahl and Stephen M. Utrata, *Liability Claim Concepts and Practices*, 1st ed. (Malvern, PA: Insurance Institute of America, 1985), pp. 407.

normally offers advance payments without requesting any legal release in exchange. It is usual, however, to obtain an *advance payment receipt* like the one shown in Exhibit 12-6 whenever an advance payment is issued. The receipt states that it is not a release and indicates that the advance payment will be offset against the total amount of the final settlement or judgment. The advance payment may be made directly to the claimant or, at the claimant's direction, to a medical provider, building contractor, or other source of assistance in recovering from the loss. If the indemnitee is a married individual who has suffered bodily injury, it is best that the receipt be signed by both spouses to remove any doubt that the advance payment also may, if necessary, be deducted from any claim the uninjured spouse may collect for loss of consortium.

Advance payments are not a settlement or closure technique; they are a way of financing loss reduction for the claimant, thereby reducing the loss the indemnitor presumably will have to finance. It is only after the ultimate value of the claimant's loss has been determined and can be evaluated that negotiations for a final settlement can begin. Once a settlement value has been agreed upon, a full and final release—or an open-end release—should be requested from the claimant. The release should summarize the nature, timing, and amounts of any advance payments, and the total of these advance payments should be deducted from the amount paid at final settlement. The total amount of payments shown on the release should equal the sum of the advance payments plus payments upon the signing of the release, plus the maximum potential amount of any remaining liability of the indemnitor under any open-end settlement.

Subrogation

A basic principle of common law and morality is that a person or organization whose conduct harms another should be held financially responsible for that harm and should not be relieved of this responsibility merely because the victim happens to have other sources of compensation.

Thus, if a reckless driver collides with and damages a bakery's delivery truck, the reckless driver (or that driver's liability insurer) should be required to pay for the resulting damage to the truck, even though the bakery has alternative sources of funds to pay for the damage from, say, its risk retention capacity or its own vehicle physical damage insurance. If the bakery pays for the damage it clearly may sue the reckless driver for its cost of repairs. If the bakery's automobile insurer pays to repair the truck, then it, rather than the bakery, may sue the reckless driver for the indemnity it has paid. In the second case, the right of the insurer to sue the reckless driver is said to be gained through subrogation. It is a right that virtually all indemnitors receive upon having paid a loss to an indemnitee (the bakery) that is legally the fault of some third party (the reckless driver). Subrogation usually arises under such circumstances regardless of whether the contract of indemnity (here, the insurance policy) explicitly provides for it. Subrogation set forth in the indemnity contract is known as *contractual subrogation;* subrogation arising from common law is known as *equitable subrogation.*

Concept and Rationale of Subrogation The word subrogation is derived from the Latin *subrogare,* which means "to put in place of another or to substitute." Substitution partially describes the process of subrogation, but it does not reveal the precise legal meaning or the substance of the current doctrine. A more accurate definition is as follows: "Subrogation is a right, equitable in origin and enforceable in common law, whereby a nonvolunteer who has made payment to another party by reason of a debt for which the nonvolunteer is only secondarily responsible, takes over that party's rights and remedies against the third party who is primarily responsible for such debt."[5]

This definition contains the following essential elements of subrogation:

- the party claiming the right of subrogation shall have first paid the debt,
- the party claiming subrogation is not a mere volunteer, but has a legal obligation to pay the debt,
- the party claiming subrogation is only secondarily liable for the debt,
- a third party is primarily liable for the debt, and
- no injustice will be done by allowing the subrogation to be exercised by the party claiming the right.

If these elements are present, the subrogee (the insurer in the bakery truck example) is subrogated to whatever rights and remedies the subrogor (the bakery) may have against the third party (the reckless driver). The *subrogee* is the nonvolunteer who is claiming the right of subrogation. The *subrogor* is the party whose rights and remedies are succeeded to—that is, the party who receives payment from the subrogee and whose rights are taken over by the subrogee.

Subrogation is just for all parties in the sense that it allows compensation for indemnitors (like the insurer) and indemnitees (the bakery), while holding wrongdoers responsible for their misdeeds. In the absence of subrogation, the indemnitee would receive a windfall, collecting from the indemnitor and possibly from the wrongdoer through a successful lawsuit. If, however, the indemnitee collected only from the indemnitor without troubling to pursue the wrongdoer, then the wrongdoer would either benefit from or "get away with" its misdeed. Furthermore, the cost of the harm would be borne by insurers (or other transferee/indemnitors) who, in turn, would pass on this cost to the entire group of policyholders (or others from whom these indemnitors receive their revenues).

With subrogation, however, the financial consequences of a wrongful act or omission are the financial responsibility of the party that the law holds primarily liable. To the extent that the law achieves this purpose, some of the most important functions of subrogation are the following:

- preventing the unjust enrichment of the third-party wrongdoer,
- preventing the windfall of a double recovery by the indemnitee, thus preserving the principle of indemnity, and
- ensuring equitable price structures that properly allocate losses to those responsible.

Moreover, subrogation recoveries are not a windfall gain for insurers and other transferees/indemnitors. To illustrate, for each line of insurance to which subrogation applies, the amounts recovered by insurers (less the expenses of recovery) enter into their premium rate structures as reductions in the incurred losses upon which these rates are based. To deny insurers subrogation would cause a significant increase in the rates charged for many lines of insurance. For instance, it has been estimated that the abolition of insurer subrogation rights would require rate increases of at least 31 percent, 18 percent, and 12 percent in surety bonds, fidelity bonds, and auto collision insurance, respectively. Similarly, without subrogation, other transferees/indemnitors would find their costs of business rising, presumably forcing them to raise their prices to their customers.

Effects of Subrogation on Risk Financing Costs Subrogation saves insurers in loss costs, so other organizations can in principle save in funds they expend to pay for their retained losses or for others' losses. To illustrate, if the bakery were retaining physical damage losses to its owned trucks, then any money it could collect from the reckless driver (or that driver's insurer) would reduce its cost of losses. The resulting reduction would be the amount collected less the legal and administrative costs of collecting it. (Because the bakery would be collecting from the wrongdoer for its own loss, not for another's loss that it had already indemnified, the amount collected would not technically be a subrogation recovery; however, the essence of the transaction—collecting from wrongdoers for harm they have caused—would remain unchanged.)

Similarly, when an organization acts as an indemnitor of another's losses, any funds collected from a third party legally responsible for the indemnitee's loss reduces the indemnitor's overall risk financing costs. For example, if the bakery had subcontracted its delivery activities—using the subcontractor's employees and trucks in exchange for a promise to indemnify the subcontractor for any damage to its trucks while making bakery deliveries—then the bakery, having once paid to repair the damage to the subcontractor's truck, would become subrogated to the subcontractor's rights to collect from the reckless driver. Any such collection (less legal and administrative costs) would reduce the risk financing costs of the bakery in its role as an indemnitor of the subcontractor.

Structured Settlements

Structured settlements are a third means of reducing the costs of restoring a loss. Under a structured settlement, a claimant—typically someone who has suffered a severe or disabling bodily injury—receives a series of periodic payments rather than the more traditional, single lump-sum settlement. For this reason, such settlements sometimes are termed *periodic payment settlements*. These payments may be made for a fixed period or for the claimant's life. Some structured settlements also incorporate lump-sum payments, which are often scheduled at key times in the claimant's disability, to meet the needs of disabled claimants and their dependents.

Along with the structured settlement, the settlement agreement often includes an initial cash payment that may be used by the claimant to pay for such items as unpaid medical or hospital expenses, other financial needs, or attorney fees. A separate structured settlement agreement may be arranged to pay the attorney's fees as well if the attorney is interested in such an agreement.

Actually, considerable flexibility and creativity may be exercised depending upon the individual needs of the claimant and the imagination of the structured settlement broker or consultant. Structured or periodic payment consultants are available to assist claim people both in identifying cases appropriate for such settlements and in negotiating such cases.

The primary method of funding structured settlements is through an *annuity*, which is usually purchased through a life insurance company. (An annuity is a type of life insurance policy or contract that makes periodic payments to the recipient for a fixed period or for life in exchange for a specified premium). Other options, however, including trusts or the purchase of stock/bond portfolios are also available to fund such settlements.

Advantages of Structured Settlements Structured settlements, in helping to reduce claim costs, are beneficial for most of the individuals involved in a claim. A structured settlement costs an indemnitor less than a lump-sum settlement that provides the same benefits. This is so because the cost of an annuity, which takes into account the time value of money and life expectancy, is based on the present value of future benefits paid out over the claimant's lifetime. This present value is substantially less than the lump-sum settlement of the same amount.

For example, a case worth anywhere from $100,000 to $125,000 on a lump-sum basis might be structured at a cost of, say, $75,000 or less (the cost of the annuity), but the structured settlement will generate considerably more than $125,000 in benefits over the claimant's lifetime.

Probably the prime benefit to the claimant of a structured settlement is its *tax-free* nature. The proceeds of the settlement (which may be paid out regularly over the claimant's lifetime) are not taxable to the claimant recipient as income. The Internal Revenue Code excludes from gross income claim payments received for injury or sickness regardless of whether they are received as a lump-sum or as periodic payments.

While it is true that a lump-sum settlement received by the claimant is also tax-free, any income generated by investing that sum *is* taxable. On the contrary, the benefits received by the claimant over his or her lifetime from a structured settlement are *not* taxable as long as the custody and control of the annuity is not with the claimant. Thus, in order to maintain the tax-free status of a structured settlement, the claimant cannot alter the original settlement agreement in any way. It is therefore also important that the indemnitor exercise control over the periodic payment process to make the benefits tax-free to the claimant; this day-to-day responsibility normally can be delegated to the insurer issuing the annuity, although the overall control ultimately rests with the indemnitor.

Another related benefit is that a structured settlement provides sound money management for the claimant because a steady flow of funds is guaranteed over the claimant's life and, in many instances, for a longer period to beneficiaries. This builds financial security for the claimant and may tend to enhance the credit rating as well. It is also particularly important in cases involving minors, uneducated claimants, or individuals who have great difficulty in managing money. Indications are that many recipients of windfalls from lotteries or court awards spend the money within a few years. A structured settlement protects such individuals from their own shortcomings. Use of annuities provides especially strong protection against unwise or unauthorized use of the claimant's money because annuity payments can almost never be pledged, assigned, encumbered, or transferred by the annuitant.

Unlike money received by the claimant, money received by the claimant's attorney is treated as income and is, therefore, taxable to the attorney. However, the attorney may mitigate the tax impact by spreading payments over several years. In this way, the attorney is able to defer taxes that would otherwise be payable all at once had he or she settled on a lump-sum basis and received the full contingent fee at one time.

Finally, society benefits from structured settlements to the extent that they relieve court congestion and minimize situations in which lump-sum settlements are squandered by claimants causing them to be without proper care or to be placed on welfare.

Cases Appropriate for Structured Settlements Before a case should be considered for a structured settlement, it should be evident that the settlement will benefit both the indemnitor and the claimant. The structured settlement should enable the indemnitor to reduce the cost of the claim as well as provide the claimant with long-term financial benefits beyond those afforded by a lump-sum settlement. Once again, the particular needs of the claimant will substantially influence whether a structured settlement is utilized to dispose of the claim.

Although structured settlements originally were seen as being applicable only to large claims involving serious injuries and disability particularly to claims involving children, this is no longer the case. While at one time $100,000 might have been viewed as a starting point for a structured settlement, many companies are now proposing such settlements for claims valued at much lesser amounts. The kinds of claims for which structured settlements may be appropriate include those, as mentioned, where individuals have difficulty managing money. Children, whose settlements frequently require court approval, are good subjects for structured settlements. In addition, structured settlements seem most appropriate in cases where claimants are seriously injured or disabled. Brain damage, paralysis, spinal cord injuries, loss of a limb, or burn cases are examples of the kinds of injury claims which seem suitable for structured settlements. Death claims where dependents are involved represent ideal cases for structured settlements as well.

Presentation of a Structured Settlement Offer The presentation of a structured settlement offer by an indemnitor is most important, particularly when claimants or their attorneys are not experienced with structured settlements. Negotiations should open with the lowest reasonable offer. The offer should be presented to highlight the claimant's total financial picture. In addition to stating the total benefits, the offer should state how much pre-tax income the claimant would have had to earn to yield the tax-free benefits offered by the structured settlements. Consideration should be given to including collateral source income such as workers compensation, social security payments, or medicare benefits available to the claimant.

In more serious cases, a settlements expert who can be present for the negotiating session or pre-trial conference can be invaluable. Ideally, this expert would have had experience handling and negotiating claims and would feel comfortable in a negotiating environment. The expert would explain how a structured settlement works, would be able to provide costs as the negotiations change the components of the structured settlement package, and would guard against violations to the IRS rulings which make the future benefits tax-free to the claimant. The following example shows how the restoration of a loss can be organized as a structured settlement.

- *Facts.* The organization's automobile made a left turn into the path of the claimant, age twenty-nine, who was driving his motorcycle. The claimant's motorcycle was being operated without a functioning front brake, which probably reduced his ability to stop.
- *Liability.* Questionable to probable. The claimant can be charged with some negligence in this comparative negligence state in view of the nonoperating front brake.
- *Injuries.* Compression fracture of the claimant's second lumbar vertebra with impingement of the spinal cord. The claimant suffered initial paralysis but in time improved to the point where he is now ambulating fairly well with some loss of sensation. The claimant's annual income is $12,500. There are approximately $8,500 in medical bills plus loss of wages of about $10,000 and total medical and rehabilitation costs of about $18,500.
- *Evaluation.* The case was evaluated on a lump-sum basis at about $85,000, to be raised or lowered depending upon the actual extent of recovery. As this amount reflects what the claim person feels the case would be worth on a clear liability basis, it can be reduced somewhat due to the fact that the claimant can be charged with some contributory negligence.
- *Final settlement.* The case was closed on a structured settlement basis. Two annuities were purchased for a total of $26,549. One annuity cost $20,549 and funded the payout for the claimant; the other annuity cost $6,000 and represented the loss of consortium claim of the claimant's spouse, and funded periodic payments for her.

The periodic payments were to be received as follows:

1. Claimant
   a. $200 per month for life or for 30 years (360 months) guaranteed, whichever is longer.
   b. Deferred periodic payments to be received on:

Date	Amount
September 1, 1992	$3,750
September 1, 2002	7,500

2. Claimant's spouse
   a. $50 per month for life or for 30 years (360 months) guaranteed, whichever is longer.
   b. Deferred periodic payments to be received on:

Date	Amount
September 1, 1992	$1,250
September 1, 2002	2,500

3. Initial payment in the amount of $30,000 representing the claimant's attorney's fee. $8,500 had been previously paid to the claimant as an advance payment.

Total cost of settlement to the organization: $65,049.

Limitation of Structured Settlements There are some plaintiff attorneys who insist on lump-sum payments for their clients because they question the extent to which benefits really accrue to the claimant in typical structured settlement agreements. In the opinion of one notable plaintiff attorney, the wise investment of a lump-sum settlement is preferable to a nontaxable annuity, the present value of which has no relationship to the real value of the case. This attorney believes that court approval should be required in all structured settlements as it is in the case of infant claims and wrongful death actions. In addition, he believes that actuarial proof of present value should be disclosed to the claimant and attorney.

Another potential problem in structured settlements is the so-called *contingent liability* of the original indemnitor. Despite the fact that an annuity typically is purchased from a life insurance company, the indemnitor owns the annuity and remains responsible for the continued funding of the payments to the claimant. If the life insurance company becomes insolvent, the indemnitor is obligated to continue making the periodic payments. For this as well as for tax reasons, indemnitors who make structured settlements should maintain their claim files until all stipulated payments are made. The claim file may be closed but should not be destroyed in the normal destruction process. (Some indemnitors believe that a reserve should be carried even after a structured settlement is executed because of this contingent liability.)

However, if an indemnitor becomes insolvent, the claimant faces a dilemma because there are no rights to the life insurance company annuity. In effect, the claimant becomes a general creditor of the indemnitor and, as such, must share this status with all other general creditors. The chances of the claimant collecting on future payments may be reduced under such circumstances.

LOSS RESERVING

An organization ready to finance recovery from its own or others' losses operates as an "insurer" in the sense that the organization must have enough available funds to pay these losses. Thus, even though current income tax laws do not allow an organization (other than an actual insurer) to recognize additions to reserves for future losses (to itself or others) as currently deductible business expenses, sound risk financing requires an organization serving as an indemnitor to establish—*for managerial accounting purposes*—adequate loss reserves.

It is recognized that such reserves are a potential encumbrance on an organization's resources; to remain viable, the organization must be assured that this burden is not too great. The amount of such loss includes reserves—estimates of future outlays for losses plus loss adjusting expenses; the sum often is reduced to a present value if, in fact, loss reserves represent actual cash that can be invested to earn a positive rate of return. This amount represents the organization's best estimate, for managerial accounting rather than financial accounting purposes, of the likely burden imposed by risk financing commitments. The organization's senior management should view these reserves as potential liabilities that, if they become too large and because severe accidental losses must be paid, could seriously jeopardize the survival of the organization.

Therefore, senior management seeks estimates of loss reserves that are realistic, sufficient to cover losses as they occur, yet not so large that they jeopardize the organization's solvency and/or ability to raise funds for other productive, normal business purposes.

Importance of Accurate Loss Reserving

Tax and financial accounting considerations aside, an organization's senior executives need to have reliable estimates of the drain caused by financing accidental losses through retention. This information is needed regardless of whether the organization pays for losses through current expensing, funded or unfunded reserves, or borrowing. (Like premiums for commercial insurance, payments to captive insurers—usually another form of retention—are quite easily recognized and recorded by standard financial accounting procedures, and thus need not be highlighted here.) Without adequate loss reserving procedures, the senior management of an organization retaining its or others' accidental losses may fail to understand the extent of this burden.

Accurate loss reserving techniques are essential. The consistent over-reserving or under-reserving of funds for future losses almost surely will give senior management a mistaken view of the importance of these losses and/or of the organization's true financial condition (regardless of what may be reported for public accounting or tax purposes). *Under-reserving* is underestimating the present value of future losses (plus related loss adjustment or claim settlement expenses) for which the organization will act as an indemnitor—to itself or to others. This is a likely error. Under-reserving gives management an unrealistically low estimate of the true cost of losses, perhaps leading management to devote too little resources to preventing or paying for them. The ultimate effect is that management underestimates the significance of sound risk management, or its absence, for these exposures. Under-reserving also tends to inflate senior management's estimate of the operating efficiency of an organization by underestimating a potentially significant future cost. Having once under-reserved any serious actual losses, the organization may not have the funds to restore losses that it had promised to others—and to itself for retained losses.

Over-reserving occurs less often than under-reserving. By placing too high a value on future accidental losses and related loss adjustment expenses, over-reserving has most of the opposite effects from under-reserving. Over-reserving gives management an unrealistically high estimate of the cost of losses. Thus thinking itself overburdened with potential losses, management ends up with a deflated estimate of its organization's operating efficiency. One result is to curtail activities and/or to mistakenly think that it cannot retain higher levels of potential losses. Another result of over-reserving is that management will eventually lose faith in its organization's loss reserving procedures. These managers will also lose faith in reserve estimates for future losses—"Real losses always seem to be less than we think they will be."

Challenge of Loss Reserving

The difficulty of accurately reserving for a claim depends on (1) the type of claim, (2) the predictability of the related loss adjusting expenses, and (3) the time likely to pass between the initial reporting of a claim and its final settlement (an interval during which the effects of both interest earnings on invested reserves and price inflation of the claimant's losses must be considered). For some property losses, it is possible to determine the amount of the loss rather quickly, and the loss will be paid promptly, thus simplifying the reserving process. (This is why, for example, the loss reserves of property insurers tend to be much smaller relative to their premium volumes than do those of liability insurers.)

In contrast, many liability claims—especially where there are grievous initial bodily injuries and a long period of rehabilitation—may remain pending for several years after having been first reported. Moreover, as the concept of liability (particularly professional liability) has broadened, many years may elapse between an act for which an organization may be responsible and the first report of any claim arising from that act. This delay frequently stems from the fact that the person harmed has not realized the injury or has not been able to sue for a number of years. For example, a minor who has had medical treatment may not discover any alleged medical malpractice for some years, and even then, suit may not be instituted until the age of legal majority is reached. Throughout this period, an organization that stands to be the indemnitor of such a claim must maintain loss reserves for at least the reported cases (and if the organization is financially conservative, for claims presumed to have been incurred but not yet reported). The reserves for such cases must cover not only the present value of the amounts claimants are likely to receive in settlement but also the present value of future claim settlement costs—all of which is likely to be increased by inflation.

Methods for Establishing Reserves

There is relatively little uniformity in loss reserving techniques even among insurers. It is therefore understandable that noninsurance organizations' reserving techniques are even more diverse, especially since standard financial accounting and tax accounting rules do not permit deductions for additions to reserves for losses whose exact value (or even definite occurrence) has not yet been determined. Nonetheless, the claims reserving methods for property and liability losses that have become most widely recognized are (1) the individual case estimate method, (2) the average value method, (3) the fast-track reserving method, (4) the loss ratio or formula method, and (5) the tabular method. Beyond reserves for reported claims, others often are established for claims incurred but not reported (IBNR) and for allocated loss adjustment expenses. Because almost all organizations will at one time or another retain losses, they would do well to use any of these methods that insurers employ to estimate the cost of losses and, thus, the amount of reserves.

Individual Case Estimate Method The individual case estimate method, or case basis reserve, is used by virtually all claims administrators as part of the claims reporting procedure. Some estimate of loss severity on an individual claim must be made. The details of the claims investigation must be reported, and statements or estimates of the extent of a property loss accompany the investigation report. Likewise, with liability claims much evidence comes from supporting invoices or estimates of damage. Based on this evidence, the claims administrator frequently must give an evaluation of claims particularly on bodily injuries, including an estimate of the cost of settling the claim. This evaluation involves (1) assessing the extent of injuries and the physician's prognosis, (2) knowing the probable cost of medical treatment, (3) weighing the likelihood that the injured party will go to an attorney, (4) determining the legal merits of the claim, and (5) considering other factors involved. The claims representative plays an important role in the establishment of loss reserves when the individual case method of reserving is utilized.

The great majority of losses, especially in property cases, involve claims where there is no controversy over questions of coverage and little negotiation over the amount of the loss. In the case of fire insurance, for example, it is common to obtain a reasonable estimate of the value of the fire insurance claim immediately following the loss. Insureds are usually eager to receive compensation for their losses, or they wish to proceed immediately with repair of damages. Thus, this method of loss reserving is particularly useful when the amount of the claim is definite and there is no delay in reaching a settlement.

The individual case estimate method is also useful in situations where there may be an absence of loss data that can assist in the loss reserve calculation. For example, when a new type of coverage or extension of coverage is afforded the public, it usually takes several years of experience before insurance companies can rely upon average claims values to assist in the determination of reserves. After the insurance company has acquired several years of experience in writing the new line of coverage, it is able to establish loss reserves on a more scientific basis, utilizing one of the other methods of loss reserve determination, such as the *average value* method.

Average Value Method Reserves established by the average value method are generally used temporarily until enough details of the loss are known to establish an individual case estimate. It relies on the experience of the indemnitors, the industries, or others. The advantages of this type of reserving are that it is simple and economical. Claims of various types are categorized, and the average value of each type of claim is computed. The aggregate loss reserve is determined by multiplying the number of unsettled claims by the average case value of claims that have previously been settled. However, the indemnitor still needs to judge the extent to which other factors, especially inflation, will influence the value of a claim.

For example, the average claim has increased over the years as medical care providers, automobile parts and equipment suppliers, and repair persons of various categories have significantly increased their prices. Particularly in the area of medical care, inflation has been an unusually serious problem in the reserving of losses. In addition, the inflation of jury and court awards has added to average claim amounts.

Liability claims pose a unique problem since it may be years before they are settled. Installments may be paid under advance payments procedures, and cases may ultimately culminate in litigation that extends the time that a claim remains open and is subject to loss reserving.

There are other types of claims for which average values are quite reliable. For example, simple property losses usually settle rapidly, and the range of exposure is somewhat narrow. Thus, it is relatively simple to apply an average reserving system to a property claim.

Fast-Track Reserving Method The fast-track or "one-shot" method of reserving is generally used for small claims that are expected to be settled quickly. Claims therefore will qualify for fast-track reserving until they reach some specified age. If the claim exceeds that established age without being settled, it will then be handled under a different reserving method. In addition, fast-track treatment will be applied only on claims that are estimated to settle within a specified dollar limit. Fast-track claims are generally those for which a claims file is not created.

Loss Ratio or Formula Reserve Method Loss reserves, particularly for bodily injury liability and workers compensation claims, have frequently been determined by a formula prescribed by state statute. Reserves are based on an assumed percentage that represents the portion of the annual insurance premium that presumably would be paid out in claims. A ratio of losses and loss adjustment expenses to premiums is prescribed for a particular line of insurance. Thus, this assumed or expected loss and loss adjustment expense ratio of premiums earned under workers compensation insurance, for example, is established at 65 percent of the earned premium involved. A statutory reserve for liability insurance is based on a 60 percent loss ratio, less any amount already paid for losses and loss expenses. The statutory reserve of 60 percent of liability insurance premiums and 65 percent of earned premiums on workers compensation is based upon the three most recent years' losses paid arising from such premiums.

Tabular Value Method Disability of a tort victim or other indemnitee presents a problem of loss reserving under long-term permanent disability insurance and workers compensation coverage. In the case of workers compensation, reserving disability claims and death claims presents peculiar problems. If disability benefits are payable for life, it is necessary to arrive at some determination of the life expectancy of the claimant. Thus, the calculation of tabular reserves requires reference to mortality tables that reflect the life expectancy of an injured worker or of a surviving spouse unless he or she remarries.

Incurred But Not Reported (IBNR) Reserves   Establishing reserves for incurred but not reported losses is one of the most difficult problems in loss reserving. A supplemental reserve is sometimes recorded as a *pure* IBNR reserve; and in other cases, a reserve for all incurred cases not recorded on the books, plus a reserve for deficiencies, is established. Incurred but not reported claims may be projected according to the number of claims that have been reported, extended by an average severity. Projections may also be based on previous relationships of unreported to reported claims, an organization's revenues, or other level of activity. In addition to such projections, or a pure IBNR reserve, companies will sometimes adopt a residual reserve supplement to guard against inadequate reserving. Supplemental reserves, of course, are utilized by companies to guard against deficiencies in reserves for losses that have been reported and are pending.

Allocated Loss Adjustment Expenses   Pending and IBNR claims will incur a considerable expense for loss adjustment. Thus, a number of organizations maintain case reserves for allocated loss adjustment expenses. Using an appropriate method for the establishment of loss reserves, companies frequently use historical data to allocate anticipated expenses for the adjustment of losses covered under the loss reserves. They use such allocated loss adjustment expense reserves primarily for financial statement purposes or for internal analysis. It is also possible to anticipate legal expenses that may be forthcoming in the defense of open claims.

SUMMARY

Claims administration encompasses all the activities associated with making or receiving timely, adequate payments to restore accidental losses. Within any organization, claims administration entails the investigation, evaluation, negotiation, settlement/closure, and payment for losses that (1) the organization has suffered and that it restores with its or others' funds (through retention or transfer, respectively) and (2) others' losses for which the organization is responsible (and, again, for which the organization may pay with its funds or with funds from other organizations to which it has transferred this obligation). To monitor its claims administration activity, an organization should have a claims administration system and a claims auditing procedure. These gather data on the payments for all losses, regardless of whether they have been retained or transferred.

People with varied skills and who represent diverse interests are likely to become involved in claims administration. An organization's risk management personnel will almost certainly be included in addition to the managers of the departments or activities within the organization that have incurred losses and to whom, or on whose behalf, losses must be paid. The alternative to relying on internal personnel is to retain a contract claims administrator. This person performs any or all of the duties related to collecting or paying funds. Also likely to be involved are insurers' adjusters (staff, independent, and/or insurance agents or brokers, and attorneys representing any of the various financially interested parties.

All claims—all situations which call for an organization to pay for its own or others' losses—require an investigation of the loss-causing event to determine who should pay for a loss (the organization, its insurer or other contractual transferee, or some wrongdoer to whom the financial burden of loss is transferred by operation of law) and if funds are payable, how much should be paid. With these issues in focus, the investigative steps need to be tailored to (1) the type of loss (property, net income, liability, or personnel), (2) the prospective sources of funds to pay for the loss (internal to the organization, under an insurance or other indemnity contract protecting the organization, or through civil law), and (3) the particular peril and/or hazard giving rise to the loss.

Because many claims call for one organization to pay funds to or receive funds from another—and because organizations generally prefer to receive rather than to pay money—many claims spawn disputes. These can be resolved through negotiation, in the courts, or by alternative dispute resolution procedures. For negotiations, an organization should be represented by one or more very good negotiators skilled in the steps of preparation, exploration of others' positions and alternatives, exchanges of offers and counteroffers, and closure techniques for reaching settlement. When acting as an indemnitor, it is important that an organization obtain an appropriate general or special release upon reaching settlement. Should negotiations break down, many organizations prefer the speedier and less costly alternatives of mediation or arbitration to a court trial.

For an organization obligated to finance recovery from its own or others' losses that have already occurred, the financial burden on an organization of restoring losses can be reduced through (1) making advance payments to provide the claimant/indemnitee with funds to mitigate its own losses, (2) contract or equitable subrogation, that obligates a wrongdoer to reimburse an indemnitor for another's losses that have been caused by the wrongdoer, and (3) structured (or installment payment) settlements that enable the indemnitor to pay only the present value of funds due an indemnitee and, meanwhile, to enjoy investment earnings on the unpaid balance rather than allowing the indemnitee to reap this investment income.

For any losses it will be required to pay, an organization should establish—for managerial accounting (not financial or tax accounting) purposes—loss reserves. In doing so, the organization helps its management to properly weigh the financial burden of these losses on the organization. For actual reported losses, for allocated claims administration expenses (identifiable loss adjustment expenses), and for losses that presumably have been incurred but not reported, an organization should adopt any of the established reserving procedures that insurers use to estimate their obligations to policyholders.

Chapter Notes

1. Unless other sources are cited, much of the remainder of this chapter is adapted from Robert J. Prahl and Stephen M. Utrata, *Liability Claim Concepts and Practices*, 1st ed. (Malvern, PA: Insurance Institute of America, 1985), pp. 1–34, 341–425, and 457–476.
2. The material under this heading is adapted from Paul I. Thomas and Prentiss B. Reed, Sr., *Adjustment of Property Losses*, 4th ed. (New York: McGraw-Hill Book Company, 1977), p. 4.
3. The material under this heading draws upon James E. Carroll and Edward L. Gallagher, *Claims Management* (New York: Risk and Insurance Management Society, Inc., looseleaf notebook for seminar, no date), pp. XII-28 to XII-31.
4. The material under this heading is drawn primarily from two sources. The first is Bernard F. Cataldo, Frederick G. Kempin, Jr., John M. Stockton, and Charles M. Weber, *Introduction to Law and the Legal Process*, 2nd ed. (New York: John Wiley & Sons, Inc., 1973), pp. 20–23. The second is Ronald A. Anderson, *Social Forces and the Law* (Cincinnati, OH: South-Western Publishing Co., 1969), pp. 420–423.
5. Ronald C. Horn, *Subrogation in Insurance Theory and Practice* (Homewood, IL: Richard D. Irwin, Inc., 1964), pp. 13, 14.

CHAPTER 13

Risk Management Cost Allocation

INTRODUCTION

The effective management of any organization requires that its costs are identified and attributed to their source. Effective risk management programs require that their costs be similarly allocated to the departments that generate them. A properly designed risk management cost allocation system promotes effective risk management by encouraging risk control, early claims reporting, and good claims management. It simultaneously allows for cost-based product and service pricing. A poorly designed risk management cost allocation system not only fails to promote these functions, but it also may actually encourage the reverse.

This chapter describes and explains the uses of a risk management cost allocation system. It covers the objectives of an allocation system, the types of costs to be allocated, the approaches and bases through which these costs may be allocated, other practical considerations, and a summary of how to implement a cost allocation system. The principles discussed in this chapter are also applicable to allocating costs among participants in a group risk financing program, such as a pool or a risk retention group. The chapter concludes with an example of a risk management cost allocation system. Throughout the chapter, "cost allocation" refers, for convenience, to allocation of risk management costs among segments of an organization, such as departments, locations, or profit centers.

THE OBJECTIVES OF A COST ALLOCATION SYSTEM

A risk management cost allocation system is a means of distributing the cost of risk throughout an organization. In designing an effective cost allocation system, the risk management professional should ensure that it meets the following objectives:

- Promotes risk control by providing incentives for management and other personnel,
- Balances risk-bearing and risk-sharing,
- Provides managers with cost information,
- Facilitates implementation of a risk retention program,
- Is simple to understand, and
- Is not subject to manipulation.

Promotes Risk Control by Providing Incentives

Effective risk control reduces the long-term cost of risk for an organization. A primary objective of a risk management cost allocation system is, therefore, to promote risk control. One way a cost allocation system does this is by motivating personnel to reduce the frequency and/or severity of an organization's losses. This is achieved by allocating costs to the departments that generate them. A cost allocation system also rewards effective loss reduction in any department. The most direct means to reflect the results of sound risk control efforts, therefore, is to link risk management costs to each department's actual losses. Each department therefore knows that it will either be "charged" or rewarded for the results of its risk control efforts.

An organization's risk control program and its cost allocation system are thus interactive. For example, the system may provide credits in allocated property insurance premiums to a department that meets high standards for property protection. Conversely, changes in the risk control program may necessitate changes in the cost allocation system. For example, investing in risk control equipment that benefits a single department increases the risk control cost allocated to that department. However, the cost of risk control equipment used by and benefiting the entire organization should be apportioned throughout all departments.

Balances Risk Bearing and Risk Sharing

Most cost allocation systems seek to distribute costs so that all departments benefit from the system. Although it has been stated that one objective of the allocation system is to provide an incentive for risk control by distributing costs according to losses, this type of *risk-bearing system* does not recognize the fact that some loss-causing events are entirely matters of chance. Such losses are related more to the exposures of a particular department than to how effectively it is managed. So while an organization as a whole may wish to retain large exposures, charging any related "fortuitous" losses only to the department that generates them can destabilize the financial results of that department from one accounting period to the next. This is particularly true for catastrophic losses that may occur rarely, but may be extremely expensive. Especially for small departments, the fluctuations that result from bearing its own costs may be too much to withstand. For them, some sharing of costs among departments is necessary for their financial integrity and that of the entire organization. This is known as a *risk-sharing* system.

A cost allocation system that is completely *risk-sharing* allocates all costs in proportion to each department's exposure. This type of system does not subject departments to large fluctuations in payments from one period to the next. It also may facilitate department budgeting and long-range planning. However, such a system does not consider actual loss experience. As a result, it cannot sufficiently respond to changes in loss experience that result from changes in a department's risk control activities. The motivation of a risk-bearing system is therefore lost in a completely risk-sharing system.

For most organizations, neither extreme is a reasonable way of allocating costs. The objective of an effective cost allocation system is to find a balance between the two. This balance depends on the risk management goals and the other needs of an organization. In most cases, motivating departments to focus on risk control activities takes precedence over minimizing fluctuations in department costs. So the "balance" may be "tipped" to some degree toward a risk-bearing system.

Provides Managers with Information

Another objective of a risk management cost allocation system is to provide operating information to managers. Again, because a good system links risk control and risk financing costs to their sources, management can identify potential problem areas. Allocating these costs to departments may identify loss frequency and/or severity problems that would not otherwise come to light. For example, allocating costs to the departments of a hospital may show that there is a safety problem with a gate in a parking lot. This problem might not be noticed in the ordinary course of events because of the small dollars involved in settling claims for cars dented by this gate. If the building manager who is also responsible for the parking lot must address this problem in dealing with the risk management cost allocation system as it relates to financial planning, it will be easier to see what areas are producing the most losses and how to handle them.

Facilitates Risk Retention

A cost allocation system also should allow the organization to implement a program of risk retention. The overall willingness and ability of an organization to retain exposures generally exceeds that of an individual department. A cost allocation system, consequently, should allow the entire organization to take advantage of the economies of scale of risk retention, while not unduly exposing the individual departments to excessive fluctuations in their cost of risk.

Is Simple to Understand and Administer

A cost allocation system should be easily understood by all managers and other organization personnel. Systems that become too complex do not provide clear incentives for performance. Nor are they easily administered. The information entering the allocation system should be verifiable. Claim runs, exposure reports, and other documents providing data for allocating costs should follow a clear format. The system also should be explained in writing and discussed in presentations to the management of each department.

Is Not Subject to Manipulation

Risk management cost allocation systems are subject to two types of manipulation, internal and external. Internal manipulation is caused by actions of a department to which costs are being allocated. External manipulation is caused by upper management or other forces.

Common examples of internal manipulation are suppressing claims reporting or, if a claim has been reported, presenting the "facts" so that case reserves are lower than they should be. The first tactic is effective if the cost allocation system uses reported claims with no correction for subsequent reporting. The second tactic can be effective if the cost allocation system utilizes case reserves with no correction for subsequent case valuations as a basis for allocating costs. The cost allocation system can be designed to prevent or discourage internal manipulation. Monitoring can also be used to verify that the system is functioning as intended.

External manipulation usually occurs when a cost allocation system does not meet the non-risk management needs of the organization's owners or senior management. For example, if the organization prices its products to reflect production costs, and if risk management costs are allocated to departments without regard to the fact that one of the departments produces a "loss leader" for the rest of the organization, upper management may challenge the allocation of risk management costs to this department because they would unduly raise its operating costs and resulting price of the "loss leader" items. The best way to avoid external manipulation is to design the cost allocation system to reflect the organization's non-risk management objectives and to obtain prior approval of the system by senior management.

TYPES OF COSTS TO BE ALLOCATED

There are four categories of costs that potentially can be allocated. Together they comprise an organization's cost of risk:

- retained losses and related loss adjustment expenses,
- insurance premiums,
- risk control expenses, and
- administrative overhead.

Any combination of these costs may be allocated to any departments.

Having identified its costs according to these categories, the organization must determine or estimate the value of each category for the period for which it is to be allocated. The organization must also determine how to allocate the costs. In some cases, such as guaranteed-cost insurance premiums, allocation is relatively easy once these costs are evaluated. With other costs, such as retained losses, valuation and allocation are likely to be more complex.

An organization may use a different method to allocate each type of cost. For example, an organization may have distinct allocation systems for general liability, automobile liability, workers compensation, property, and other risk management department costs. Some of these costs may be fully allocated to the responsible department; others may be partially allocated to the department and partially absorbed by the entire organization; still others may simply be charged to overhead.

Retained Losses and Related Loss Adjustment Expenses

Most retained losses and related adjustment expenses are apportioned by the cost allocation system. Losses are measured by the dollars incurred by an accident or occurrence that are charged to each department. Dollars needed to cover retained losses may arise from an explicit retention program, retrospectively rated insurance coverages, a retrospectively rated pool, or from any other loss-sensitive risk financing technique.

Some loss adjustment expenses can be allocated to a particular loss or claim, and others cannot. *Allocated loss adjustment expenses* (ALAE) can be specifically related to and/or identified with a particular loss or claim. Such expenses include investigation, negotiating, and legal costs as well as salvage, debris removal, and similar costs associated with administering claims. If an organization retains ALAE, then regardless of the specifics of the cost allocation system, ALAE can be distributed by that system. Some retrospectively rated insurance programs and pools do not handle ALAE through the general risk management allocation system but treat ALAE as a part of the overhead cost of the program. These programs do not lend themselves to including ALAE in the risk management cost allocation system.

Unallocated loss adjustment expenses (ULAE) are not easily identified with a particular claim. However, if an organization retains ULAE, then regardless of the specifics of the cost allocation system, ULAE can still be distributed by that system; that is, although ULAE cannot be linked to particular claims, they can, for the most part, be charged to a particular department. For example, an organization that retains its workers compensation losses may pay a third-party administrator to handle claims. This administrator's fee can be charged to each department that generates claims handled by this administrator. However, some retrospectively rated insurance programs and pools do not allocate ULAE to the organizations associated with particular losses. These programs do not lend themselves to including ULAE in any participant's risk management cost allocation system.

An important part of determining how much of retained losses to allocate is the choice of an appropriate basis by which the values and other risk management costs of losses are calculated. (Losses not allocated are treated as overhead.) Losses may be calculated by one of three bases: incurred loss, claims made, or claims paid. The *incurred loss basis* estimates the total ultimate value of losses that will be incurred within the accounting period regardless of when they are reported or paid. This total value includes amounts paid, additions to reserves for pending claims, and estimates of the incurred but not reported losses. The *claims-made basis* calculates losses by using only the actual payments and changes in reserves for claims made during the accounting period. The *claims-paid basis* estimates the amount paid on losses during the accounting period regardless of when they were incurred.

Each basis for calculating losses may or may not include a *risk margin*. As explained in Chapter 2, a risk margin is an amount added to an organization's expected losses to cover potential adverse fluctuations in experience. Some organizations want to accumulate a risk margin for the organization as a whole, while others establish annual department risk margins for each accounting period. These reserves are recouped for the organization at the end of an accounting period for which a department does not need them.

According to generally accepted financial accounting standards, an organization should indicate on its financial statements its incurred but unpaid liabilities. If an organization funds for losses on other than an occurrence basis, it should show on its financial statements a liability for claims resulting from accidental losses that is greater than any accumulated fund held for this purpose. This liability reflects incurred but not reported losses that the organization anticipates financing through retention. In contrast, a risk margin is not a liability and should not be shown as such on financial statements. It may be shown as a segregated part of the organization's equity.

Estimating and allocating retained losses can be quite challenging and often requires sophisticated actuarial techniques such as those discussed in Chapter 2. Sometimes it is appropriate to hire an actuary to assist in calculating these amounts.

Premiums

In the terminology of risk management cost allocation, insurance premiums include premiums paid for guaranteed-cost insurance together with such "premiums" paid to "captives." These premiums often do not change between renewals and can be directly attributed to a department. For example, aircraft product liability premiums may be directly allocated to a department that manufactures aircraft or aircraft components. In contrast, certain coverages, such as directors and officers liability insurance, may provide more general benefit for an entire organization. Costs associated with these coverages do not have a specific source of exposure and are thus usually absorbed by the organization as a whole.

Risk Control Expenses

Risk control expenses include either long-term capital investments such as a fire detection/suppression system or occasional expenditures to purchase, for example, safety shoes or the services of a driver training instructor. Capital investments create or add to depreciable assets; occasional expenditures usually are charged against the accounting period in which they produce services or other benefits for the organization. In either case, most risk control expenditures are clearly allocable to a particular department. When a risk control expenditure is not closely linked to a particular department—for example, the annual salary for an industrial hygienist employed by a chemical manufacturer—this cost usually is treated as part of the administrative overhead for the risk management function or is absorbed by the organization as a whole.

Administrative Overhead

Administrative overhead includes the operating budget of the risk management department and time charges for executives from other departments or other resources from other departments devoted to risk management. Some risk management departments allocate their entire operating budgets to the other departments in an organization so that risk management's "bottom line" is zero. In this case the risk management department is not shown as a cost or a profit center. Other risk management departments allocate to other departments only those costs associated with certain types of exposures clearly arising from those departments. These costs may include the salary and benefits of those people working in workers compensation claims administration departments and the cost of their furniture, supplies, and other needs. These allocated costs also may include the percentage of the risk management professional's salary and employee benefits that represent the time this manager spends on the workers compensation program for each department. In this case the risk management department is reported as a cost center responsible for controlling the operating costs that are not clearly chargeable to other departments.

Other administrative expenses are not so easily attributable to particular departments and therefore often are not charged as such. Examples include a consultant's audit of the entire risk management program, an actuarial evaluation of a risk retention proposal or program, and management services for the organization's "captive."

APPROACHES TO COST ALLOCATION

There are two broad approaches to risk management cost allocation, *prospective* and *retrospective*. This distinction refers to differences in determining (1) the initial allocation and (2) the final payment of losses and other risk management costs. In a prospective system, costs are estimated and allocated at the beginning of the accounting period in which they are expected to be incurred. Once allocated, these costs are not changed for that period. In a retrospective system costs also are estimated and allocated at the beginning of the accounting period in which they are to be incurred. However, they may be reallocated one or more times during or after the close of the period, with payments or returns being made "retrospectively" according to changes in loss experience. A prospective cost allocation system is similar to experience rating in insurance; a retrospective cost allocation system is similar to retrospective rating in insurance. Both systems seek a balance between loss experience and loss exposure. In a prospective system, costs are allocated primarily on the basis of potential exposures to loss and secondarily on the basis of recent actual loss experience. In a retrospective system, the reverse is true: actual loss experience is the primary basis for allocation.

The primary advantage of a prospective cost allocation system is that costs are presumed to be known before the beginning of the accounting period and are not changed. This facilitates budgeting and related financial planning activities. The corresponding disadvantage of this approach is that the actual costs may be much different from those allocated. While these differences may be corrected in subsequent periods, the corrected costs will not be associated with the output of the period to which they are charged. Another disadvantage of prospective allocations is that an increase (or decrease) in risk control activity may be separated by several accounting periods from the corresponding reduction (or increase) in actual losses. As a result, it is difficult to correlate specific risk control efforts with changes in loss experience, making it difficult to determine the true effectiveness of a risk control program.

The primary advantage of a retrospective cost allocation system is that costs are more accurately attributed to the period (and the output) with which they are associated. This means that an increase (or decrease) in risk control activity and corresponding reduction (or increase) in loss costs are much more closely linked. As a result, it is easier to see how well a risk control program is working. The corresponding disadvantage is that final risk management costs are not closely determinable until well after the end of the period in which the costs were incurred. This can complicate risk management budgeting.

BASES OF ALLOCATION

After the types and amounts of an organization's risk management costs have been determined, the next significant matter is the basis on which they should be allocated to each department. Costs may be allocated on the basis of loss exposure or loss experience. A fully exposure-based system would allocate costs to departments only on the basis of its exposures regardless of its loss experience. In this case, the proportionate costs charged to any department would not change as long as its exposures did not change. A fully experience-based system would allocate costs to a department strictly on its pro rata portion of historical losses and would subject small departments to significant fluctuations in costs from one period to the next.

Actual practice frequently shows that costs are allocated according to a blend of exposure and experience. In general, systems for allocating costs associated with exposures that generate frequent claims (such as workers compensation as opposed to property losses) rely more on loss experience than on exposures. Furthermore, managers of large and more financially capable departments generally seek to have their costs allocated on the basis of loss experience more than exposures because this would tend to lower their allocated costs below what their department's size alone would suggest. An example of the blending of allocation bases would be an organization composed of two departments—one generating $100 million in revenues and the other $50 million in revenues. Risk management costs associated with property may be allocated to both departments based 90 percent on exposure and 10 percent on experience. In contrast, workers compensation costs may be allocated 75 percent on experience (25 percent on exposure) for the larger department and 50 percent on experience (50 percent on exposure) for the smaller department. These percentages should be chosen to reflect the relative degree of confidence that can be placed in the organization's own past experience as a predictor of its future experience—the "credibility" of the organization's own past losses. The more reliably past losses can be counted upon to predict future losses, the more nearly this loss experience approaches 100 percent credibility. In practice, credibility often is determined by a judgment or by actuarial calculations that are beyond the scope of this discussion.

The costs of loss-sensitive insurance may also be apportioned in layers. For example, in a system for allocating the costs for insuring general liability losses, each department may be responsible for paying all relatively small losses within its department deductible. Costs for losses above this deductible but within the organization's overall retention may be allocated to each department based 50 percent on experience and 50 percent on exposure. The costs for liability insurance above the organization's retention may be allocated wholly on the basis of each department's exposure.

Exposure Bases

There are different bases for determining and allocating risk management costs according to the type of exposure. For example, different bases are used to allocate general liability costs than are used to allocate workers compensation costs. Each base selected should, to the extent practical, reflect the underlying exposures. For each category of risk management costs mentioned earlier, exposure generally can be measured on the basis of size, nature of operations, and territory. In turn, each of these can be measured on the basis of some easily verified gauge. Size, for example may be measured on the basis of revenues, number of employees, or square footage. For example, a department with twice the revenues of another with identical operations may be considered to have twice the exposure, and thus, twice the allocated costs.

The nature of a department's operations also may determine exposure. A department making pharmaceutical products probably has a greater products liability exposure than one that manufactures soap. Therefore, the products liability risk management charges per dollar of revenue allocated to the pharmaceutical department probably should be greater than the risk management costs for each dollar of revenue charged to the soap-manufacturing department.

Territory also can be used to measure the cost of exposures because it reflects differences in benefit levels and socioeconomic/legal systems as they influence exposures. For example, a person injured in the United States probably will receive greater compensation than one similarly injured in Zimbabwe. Consequently, general liability risk management charges for each dollar of the organization's output in the United States should exceed charges for revenues generated in such other countries.

Insurance premiums for guaranteed-cost coverages for a particular department usually are calculated on a rate per unit of exposure. The rate for each department may differ substantially from the premium rate an insurer charges the organization as a whole because each department's degree of hazard may differ from the organization's composite rate. Consequently, the exposure base used by the insurer is usually a good starting point for determining an appropriate exposure base for the type of risk management cost being allocated. The following paragraphs describe some possible bases for allocating costs for general liability, automobile liability, workers compensation, property, and other exposures.

General Liability General liability exposures vary widely among different types of organizations. For some organizations, the general liability exposure primarily may arise from their premises and operations. For others, the general liability exposure may primarily come from products or the activities of independent contractors. To measure the dominant general liability exposure of an organization and to allocate general liability costs, commonly used bases include square footage of floor space, annual budget, payroll, full-time-equivalent workers, and sales. If an insurer charges an extra premium for an unusual exposure, such as a swimming pool, this premium usually is charged directly to the department responsible for it.

It is sometimes appropriate for an organization to modify an insurer's exposure base to better reflect in the organization's cost allocation system the degree of exposure associated with a particular department's activities. For example, budgets may provide a good indication of general liability exposure for each department in an organization except for the one with extremely high research and development activities (and costs) that generate no significant general liability exposure. This department's budget, if used as a basis for cost allocation, might well exclude the research and development costs because they do not add to the actual general liability exposure of that department.

Automobile Liability Automobile liability exposures differ for different types of departments and by types of vehicles operated by those departments. Some may use small trucks, some large trucks, some only passenger vehicles, and some essentially no vehicles whatever. The most commonly used exposure base for allocating automobile liability costs is the number of vehicles, with some adjustments for differences in types of vehicles. For example, a department operating both private passenger automobiles and taxi cabs might assign private passenger vehicles a relativity of 1.00 and taxi cabs a relativity of 5.00, reflecting the assumption that taxis typically generate five times the losses of an equal number of automobiles. Therefore, the number of vehicles counted as the allocation basis for this department would be computed as the number of private passenger vehicles plus five times the number of taxis. Such relativities used by insurers are often incorporated, with modifications, into an organization's cost allocation system.

Workers Compensation Workers compensation exposures differ for different types of departments and by job classifications within departments. The workers compensation exposure may involve highly hazardous mining operations or much safer office operation. The two most common exposure bases for allocating workers compensation costs are payroll and full-time-equivalent number of employees—often with rating adjustments for differences in exposure according to job classification. For example, office workers might have a payroll relativity of 1.00, and firefighting personnel might have a relativity of 12.00. Therefore, a department employing fifty office workers and two firefighters would be shown as having a total of seventy-four employees in the organization's workers compensation cost allocation system. The National Council on Compensation Insurance is often a good place to find rate relativities; these can be modified for particular departments.

Property Property exposures vary from one organization to the next and by type of building and occupancy within organizations. For some, the dominant property exposure may be manufacturing plants in rural locations; for others, it may be office buildings in urban areas. The two most common exposure bases for allocating risk management costs for property are square footage and property values (either replacement cost or actual cash value). When an insurer charges an extra premium for a particular exposure, such as a chemical mixing operation, this premium often will be charged directly to the department responsible for it.

The exposure base for property often needs to be modified to reflect accurately the associated exposure. For example, while property values may be good general indicators of exposure, one department may operate in a building that contains flammable chemicals. The property values for this department, when used in the cost allocation system, should be increased by a factor that more correctly reflects the increased degree of property hazard created by the presence of these chemicals. The effects of location, such as a building in a hurricane zone, also should be considered. Again, the relativities used by property insurers are often germane, but are usually appropriately modified for each organization.

Other Risk Management Costs and Exposure Bases Activities within the risk management program related to other exposures such as fidelity losses and products liability should—to the extent practical—have corresponding exposure bases for cost allocation. For example, risk management department overhead can be allocated in many different ways such as the following:

- in proportion to the total of other risk management department costs allocated for particular exposures,
- as a fixed percentage of some other base, such as sales, and
- as a combination of a flat fee per department (to cover fixed costs) and a percentage of some base, such as sales (to cover variable costs).

It may not be possible to use the "ideal" exposure base in all situations because one or more of the following problems may be present:

- The data that form an exposure base, such as the number of full-time-equivalent employees for allocating workers compensation costs, are not available on time or at a reasonable price.
- Department managers disagree about how an exposure base, such as total operating expenditures excluding capital investments for allocating general liability costs, should be calculated.
- The desired data, such as replacement cost property values, cannot be calculated each year in time to be used in a prospective cost allocation system.

However, in situations that effectively prohibit the use of the desired exposure base, it is usually possible to find an adequate, practical alternative. For the three preceding examples, acceptable alternative exposure bases are payroll for workers compensation, payroll for general liability, and replacement cost property values for the previous year with adjustments for more recent building acquisitions and disposals (again valued at the previous year's replacement cost).

Experience Bases

Claims experience is defined throughout this text as not only liability claims but also an organization's insured and retained losses. Claims experience often is used as a direct measure of the success of a risk management program. Claims experience is measured by the frequency or aggregate severity limited to some dollar amount.

Frequency does not reflect the size of claims, but it does help to assess whether more or fewer occurrences are causing loss. Claim frequency often is used when a management incentive system seeks to provide more immediate feedback on individual managers' performance related to risk management.

Aggregate severity also is commonly selected as the indicator of each department's claims experience. Each claim charged to a particular department is capped at a certain amount (for example, $25,000 per occurrence) and added to that department's experience. All claims reported for a given period are then cumulated to determine the department's experience.

Once a department's past claims experience has been measured by severity there are three primary bases for projecting its future experience and the related costs that will be allocated to it: changes in claims-paid, changes in payments plus case reserves, and changes in projected ultimate losses. When allocations are made according to changes in claims-paid, the costs to a department tend to fluctuate from one period to the next more than when the other two bases are used. Allocations based on changes in payments plus case reserves generate less fluctuation in cost; but there is the possibility that case reserves may be poorly estimated, thus artificially influencing any department's allocated costs. (However, if this artificial influence is uniform across all departments, it will not alter the distribution of costs among departments.) In addition, the use of payments plus case reserves overlooks difficulties that may arise because of different reporting and payment patterns for different types of claims that are characteristic of different departments. In these situations, projected ultimate losses (estimated ultimate payouts for certain claims) may be a better choice. If presumably incurred but unreported losses are allocated to departments in proportion to reported claims (as measured by payments plus case reserves), allocations based on payments plus case reserves and allocations based on projected ultimate losses produce the same results.

Regardless of which experience base is used, there are several important considerations in calculating the aggregate severity of a department's claims. Three of them are the per-occurrence limit, the aggregate limit, and the experience period used in each particular cost allocation system.

Per-Occurrence Limit Effective risk management programs work to reduce both the number of occurrences that result in claims and the amount of each claim that does arise. However, claim frequency usually is easier to control than claim severity. As a result, most risk management cost allocation systems are designed to be *frequency-sensitive*. This means that they react more to the number of claims than to the amounts of individual claims and their related ALAE. The most common method of making a cost allocation system frequency-sensitive is to limit the individual amounts of claims and ALAE charged against any given department to a specified amount per claim, such as $25,000. The amount of each claim and related ALAE in excess of the per-occurrence limit may be allocated among all departments based on their exposures rather than experience in order to reflect the more fortuitous nature of more catastrophic events and losses. Alternatively, and essentially equivalently, the excess amount of these claims may be absorbed by the organization as a whole rather than by its departments.

Aggregate Limit It also is possible to experience a series of many fortuitous, separate, relatively small claims that aggregate to a large total in a short period. Some cost allocation systems consequently limit the aggregate amount of claims and related ALAE that can be allocated to a department for any accounting period. If aggregate limits are so low that many departments exceed them, their managers are likely to be less motivated to emphasize risk control since reducing claims will have little or no impact on their department results. Furthermore, unduly low aggregate limits may require supplemental charges against various departments in order to reasonably allocate all claims and related ALAE to the appropriate departments. Such a second or third round of allocations in any given accounting period is costly and undermines the credibility of the allocation system.

Experience Period Any experience-based cost allocation system distributes current claims and related ALAE among departments in proportion to each department's claims and related ALAE over some period of past years. For prospective plans, experience periods usually range from two to five years; for retrospective plans, the experience period is usually one to three years.

The shorter the experience period, the more responsive the cost allocation formula will be to changes in recent past loss experience. As a result, a shorter period more quickly reflects the results of recent changes in risk management activity. For example, the shorter the experience period, the sooner will a manager who improves safety results enjoy lower risk management cost allocations to his or her department. However, a shorter experience period also tends to subject individual departments to more widely fluctuating charges resulting from unusually good or bad claims experience. This problem can be mitigated by placing maximums and minimums on the amounts of claims that can be included in any one department's experience base. Furthermore, multi-year experience periods may be weighted so that more recent experience is more heavily counted. Thus, experience accumulated over five years may be used to develop a weighted average in which each of the two most recent years are weighted by 30 percent, the third year receives a 20 percent weighting, and each of the two most distant years contribute 10 percent to the average.

PRACTICAL CONSIDERATIONS

Many practical factors affect the design of an allocation system and the actual or perceived equity of the system. First, an organization's accounting system may influence the design of its allocation system. Exposure bases often rely on data, such as sales and payroll, which are maintained as part of the organization's overall accounting system. In addition to the possibility that the desired data may not be readily available, the departments, locations, or activities to which risk management costs ideally should be allocated may be different from those for which the accounting system maintains information.

Second, for organizations with operations subject to different tax rates and systems—such as multi-national corporations or holding companies owning many domestic and/or foreign subsidiaries—allocating costs among departments may have significant tax consequences that prohibit or encourage otherwise appropriate risk management cost allocations.

Third, for some organizations, it is appropriate for each department to be charged at least a minimum amount for risk management services regardless of its exposures or claims experience; or, in an allocation of costs associated with a workers compensation retention program, each department might have as its minimum charge the costs of risk control, risk management department overhead, and excess insurance premiums; these would be allocated by payroll and adjusted for differences in job classifications. These services and the protection afforded by the excess insurance benefit all departments regardless of experience. Similarly, it may be appropriate to establish a maximum that a department can be charged despite even the worst possible experience. The usual purpose for a maximum is to reduce the fluctuations in allocated costs from one accounting period to the next. Such a maximum often is expressed as a percentage, such as 125 percent, of the prior year's allocated risk management costs.

Fourth, if an organization is highly decentralized, it may allow department managers to purchase their own insurance rather than participate in a risk management cost allocation system. These managers may then feel particularly motivated to practice sound risk control and risk financing. Although this result is generally positive, it can undercut the interdepartmental cooperation that develops when all departments participate in the same system. The managers may become unwilling to share the risk. This can disrupt the balance between risk sharing and risk bearing already described. Education and communication can, however, restore balance and the appropriate cooperation.

Fifth, for an organization with a small aggregate cost of risk relative to its total budget, the results of cost allocation may be insignificant. Risk management costs may be so small that they are lost in "budget noise." In this case, there is probably no need for a risk management cost allocation system in the first place. For instance, the manager of a department with a $10 million budget is not likely to care if he or she is charged $10,000 instead of $25,000 for workers compensation coverage.

Sixth, a cost allocation system should have the effect of penalizing or rewarding each department manager according to that department's costs. This can be accomplished by having managers' bonuses reflect their allocated risk management as well as other operating results. Moreover, the total budget of a department should not be adjusted to compensate for changes in risk management results, which would tend to cushion or cancel the manager's penalties or rewards. For example, if a department's workers compensation cost allocation increases from $1 million to $5 million because of its deteriorating experience, increasing its total budget by $4 million does not penalize its manager appropriately and may fail to motivate cooperation in improving the department's workers compensation results.

IMPLEMENTING AN ALLOCATION SYSTEM

The tasks required to implement a risk management cost allocation system are summarized as follows:

1. Review the attributes of a theoretically good risk management cost allocation system and decide what the organization's practical objectives for and constraints on such a system should be.
2. Determine the categories of costs to be allocated for each of the organization's major exposures.
3. For each category, decide whether a prospective or retrospective allocation better meets the organization's needs.
4. For each cost to be allocated, choose from the following to determine its value and how it will be allocated:
   - exposure base,
   - experience base,
   - per-occurrence limit,
   - aggregate limit, and
   - experience period.
5. Review the following practical considerations in light of the cost allocation system:
   - the accounting system,
   - the organization's tax situation,
   - any minimum and/or maximum on costs to be allocated for each account period,
   - the independence of departments,
   - the significance of risk management costs in each department's budget, and
   - how cost allocations may influence each manager's individual motivation and performance.
6. Perform trial calculations to determine whether the proposed system meets the organization's needs; if not, make adjustments, and repeat this step as necessary.

Throughout this process, it is important to work with department and senior management to develop an efficient system that is supported by all participants. Such support is necessary in both (1) collecting the data required to make the allocation and (2) fostering understanding and cooperation between department and senior management. An appropriately cooperative climate can be fostered by including all key managers in the development process.

Risk management costs usually are allocated once a year. To perform allocations in the second and succeeding years, the risk management department must continue to collect data required for the allocations and to communicate with department managers and top executives to be certain that the system is meeting the corporation's needs.

Risk management cost allocation systems should be changed as often as necessary, but should be as consistent as possible to remain reasonably stable. Situations that often trigger system changes include material shifts in the organization's operations (for example, the purchase of a large subsidiary or a decision to make one product a loss leader), inflation, which could cause almost every loss to exceed a per-occurrence limit, or a restructuring of the organization's departments or lines of authority. In any case the risk management cost allocation system should be reviewed in depth at least every three years to ensure that it is current. This review should follow the six preceding steps.

AN EXAMPLE

This section presents an example of how one organization developed and implemented a risk management cost allocation system for its primary general liability risk financing program. It illustrates the need for an "organization-specific" system, showing that there is no "right" or "wrong" approach, only an approach that makes sense for a given organization within the preceding guidelines.

The Lorac Management Corporation is a privately held organization that owns and manages five commercial properties located in three cities as shown in Exhibit 13-1. Each property is treated as a profit center, and separate accounting information is maintained to develop separate profit and loss statements. The manager of each property is on an incentive compensation system that also reflects the profitability of each property, including its risk management costs.

Last year Lorac purchased fixed-cost, occurrence-basis, primary general liability insurance for a total premium of $300,000. This premium had been allocated as shown in Exhibit 13-2. This approach provided a convenient, easily understood basis for allocating this

Exhibit 13-1
Listing of Lorac Properties

Location	Occupancy
Los Angeles, California	Hotel
Los Angeles, California	Apartment Building
Denver, Colorado	Hotel
Denver, Colorado	Office Building
Houston, Texas	Hotel

Exhibit 13-2
Allocation of Costs Based on Square Footage

(1) Location	(2) Occupancy	(3) Square Footage	(4) Percent of Total	(5) Allocated Cost
Los Angeles	Hotel	200,000	20%	$ 60,000
Los Angeles	Apartment Building	300,000	30	90,000
Denver	Hotel	200,000	20	60,000
Denver	Office Building	100,000	10	30,000
Houston	Hotel	200,000	20	$ 60,000
Totals		1,000,000	100%	$300,000

insurance cost. Furthermore, it was not likely to produce fluctuations in allocated costs beyond the annual changes in premiums as the square footage at each property remained fairly constant.

After last year's allocations some of the property managers complained about the general liability costs. The manager of the hotel in Houston, which had a significantly lower occupancy rate than the two others, felt that the Houston property was subsidizing the others. In contrast, the managers of the apartment and office buildings, which historically had fewer claims, felt that they were subsidizing the hotels.

For the forthcoming renewal Lorac's risk manager has realized that, because of market conditions and deteriorating claims experience, Lorac's guaranteed-cost general liability premium probably will increase from last year's $300,000 to $500,000 for the coming year. She also has realized that allocation according to square footage has not encouraged risk control activities at the properties. The risk manager also has worked with an outside consultant to develop a basic risk control program that addresses many of the causes of past accidents. She has also made certain that senior management supports having the risk management cost allocation process influence the property managers' bonuses so that each of them will have a personal incentive to cooperate in the new risk control program.

The program recommended by the consultant includes a $10,000 per-occurrence deductible for the general liability coverage. Lorac's acceptance of this deductible has induced the underwriter to lower the guaranteed-cost premium for the coming year to $250,000. The risk manager has determined that annual claims within the $10,000 per-occurrence deductible can be expected to aggregate to $150,000. She consequently estimates that the total primary general liability risk financing cost for the coming year will be $400,000, consisting of $250,000 in premiums and $150,000 in retained claims (including both adjustment expense for insured and uninsured claims). She also has concluded that it is important to maintain a prospective cost allocation system because the property managers desire budgetable costs. Changes in claims experience for each year will consequently influence only cost allocations for the next year.

The risk manager thus needs to evaluate how these costs will be allocated for the coming year. She has decided that the projected $150,000 in retained claims should be allocated on the basis of the last three years of claims up to $10,000 per occurrence. In contrast, the guaranteed-cost insurance premium should be allocated principally on relative exposure with some adjustment for large claims. This dual approach should reflect the risk manager's belief that the frequency of claims within the $10,000 deductible is controllable.

The next step is to perform the calculations. For the $150,000 projected annual claims within the $10,000 per-occurrence deductible, the risk manager has calculated by location the past three years of paid and reserved claims increased to reflect inflation and capped at $10,000 per occurrence. This calculation is shown in Columns (3), (4), and (5) of Exhibit 13-3; the sum of these three columns appears in Column (6). The amounts in Column (6) have been used to calculate the percentages that appear in Column (7). Each percentage in Column (7) has been computed by dividing the total claims at each location by the $400,000 of claims at all locations. The allocated costs in Column (8) apportion the $150,000 of projected retained claims by the percentages in Column (7).

The risk manager has also noticed that the Los Angeles hotel has generated a large portion of the claims that would have fallen within the $10,000 deductible. While this hotel represents 20 percent of the total square footage, it has sustained 47.5 percent of the amount of all the inflation-adjusted claims capped at $10,000. The risk manager believes that square footage is not sufficiently indicative of exposure. While square footage captures size relativities, it does not reflect differences in operational exposures; that is, the differences between

Exhibit 13-3
Allocation of Retained Claims by Three Years' Cumulative Claims Experience Capped at $10,000 Per Occurrence

(1)	(2)	(3)	(4)	(5)	(6)	(7)	(8)
		Least Recent		Most Recent	Total Claims		Cost Allocation
					(Col. 3 + Col 4	Percent	(Col. 7 x
Location	Occupancy	Year 1	Year 2	Year 3	+ Col. 5)	of Total	$150,000)
Los Angeles	Hotel	$ 75,000	$ 75,000	$ 40,000	$190,000	47.5%	$ 71,250
Los Angeles	Apartment Building	30,000	25,000	15,000	70,000	17.5	26,250
Denver	Hotel	40,000	40,000	20,000	100,000	25	37,500
Denver	Office Building	8,000	2,000	0	10,000	2.5	3,750
Houston	Hotel	2,000	10,000	18,000	30,000	7.5	11,250
	Totals	$155,000	$152,000	$ 93,000	$400,000	100%	$150,000

hotel, apartment, and office occupancies. Furthermore, square footage does not account for territorial relativities—the differences in, for example, the legal environments of Los Angeles, Denver, and Houston.

The risk manager has relied on insurance premium rates for different occupancies in these states to reflect the relativities shown in Column (4) of Exhibit 13-4. (Notice that these relativities are weighting factors that, unlike percentages, need not add up to 1.00.) Applying these relativities to the square footage in column (3) of Exhibit 13-4 has enabled the risk manager to adjust square footage so that it more closely reflects exposure as shown in Column (5). Column (6) shows the resulting changes in the percent of the total premium allocated to each location. The actual cost based on these percentages is shown in Column (7). These calculations conclude the exposure-based allocation of retained losses.

To build an experience-based allocation of the fixed-cost insurance premium, the risk manager decided to use larger claims (that is, inflation-adjusted claims between $10,000 and $50,000) as the allocation base and five years of experience because of the low frequency of larger claims. The results of this process are shown in Exhibit 13-5 in which Column (8) cumulates the relevant claims from Columns (3) through (7). Column (9) expresses the experience base for each location as a percentage of their $400,000 total. The allocated insurance premium in Column (10) is based on these percentages.

The risk manager has decided to allocate the $250,000 premium 80 percent on the basis of exposure and 20 percent on the basis of claims experience from Exhibit 13-5. The results shown in Exhibit 13-6 were obtained by taking the exposure percentages from Column (7) of Exhibit 13-4 and multiplying them by 80 percent. The risk manager then took the experience percentages from Column (9) of Exhibit 13-5 and multiplied them by 20 percent. The sum of these two percentages, the overall allocation percentage, is shown for each property in Column (7) of Exhibit 13-6. Applying these percentages to the $250,000 premium generates the insurance costs allocated to each location as shown in Column (8) of Exhibit 13-6.

The risk manager has decided to use the costs in Column (6) of Exhibit 13-7 as a first approximation of the final allocation for the coming year. She knows that there will be lively discussion concerning the significant shifts in cost—particularly toward the Los Angeles and Denver hotels. She considers this the ideal means to draw senior and operating management attention to the costs of claims as well as to the new risk control measures to reduce these claims. While the final cost allocations may not represent such a dramatic departure from the previous year, they should improve Lorac Management Corporation's risk control efforts and overall risk management program.

Exhibit 13-4
Allocation of Insurance Premium Based on Adjusted Square Footage

(1) Location	(2) Occupancy	(3) Square Footage	(4) Rate	(5) Adjusted Exposure (Col. 3 x Col. 4)	(6) Percent of Total	(7) Allocation of Insurance Premium
Los Angeles	Hotel	200,000	0.225	45,000	30%	$ 75,000
Los Angeles	Apartment Building	300,000	0.10	30,000	20	50,000
Denver	Hotel	200,000	0.20	40,000	27	67,500
Denver	Office Building	100,000	0.05	5,000	3	7,500
Houston	Hotel	200,000	0.15	30,000	20	50,000
Totals		1,000,000		150,000	100%	$250,000

Exhibit 13-5
Allocation of Insurance Premium Based on Five Years of Claims Experience Between $10,000 and $50,000 Per Occurrence

(1)	(2)	(3) Least Recent Year 1	(4) Year 2	(5) Year 3	(6) Year 4	(7) Most Recent Year 5	(8) Cummulative Total Claims	(9) Percent of Total	(10) Allocation of Insurance Premium
Location	Occupancy								
Los Angeles	Hotel	$ 0	$60,000	$60,000	$30,000	$30,000	$180,000	45%	$112,500
Los Angeles	Apartment Building	20,000	0	10,000	10,000	40,000	80,000	20%	50,000
Denver	Hotel	40,000	10,000	20,000	40,000	10,000	120,000	30%	75,000
Denver	Office Building	0	0	0	0	0	0	0%	0
Houston	Hotel	10,000	0	0	0	10,000	20,000	5%	12,500
	Totals	$70,000	$70,000	$90,000	$80,000	$90,000	$400,000	100%	$250,000

Exhibit 13-6
Allocation of Insurance Premium Based on Experience and Exposure

(1) Location	(2) Occupancy	(3) Exposure Percentage	(4) Exposure Percentage (80% of Col. 3)	(5) Experience Percentage	(6) Experience Percentage (20% of Col. 5)	(7) Total Percent Allocation (Col. 4 + Col. 6)	(8) Premium Allocation (Col. 7 x $250,000)
Los Angeles	Hotel	30%	24%	45%	9%	33%	$ 82,500
Los Angeles	Apartment Building	20	16	20	4	20	50,000
Denver	Hotel	27	21.6	30	6	27.6	69,000
Denver	Office Building	3	2.4	0	0	2.4	6,000
Houston	Hotel	20	16	5	1	17	42,500
	Totals	100%	80%	100%	20%	100%	$250,000

Exhibit 13-7
Comparison of Final to Initial Cost Allocation

(1) Location	(2) Occupancy	(3) Final Premium Allocation	(4) Final Retained Claim Allocation	(5) Final Total Cost Allocation (Col. 3 + Col. 4)	(6) Initial Cost Allocation (Ex. 13-2)	(7) Percentage of Change
Los Angeles	Hotel	82,500	$ 71,250	$153,750	$ 60,000	156%
Los Angeles	Apartment Building	50,000	26,250	76,250	90,000	(15%)
Denver	Hotel	69,000	37,500	106,500	60,000	78
Denver	Office Building	6,000	3,750	9,750	30,000	(67%)
Houston	Hotel	42,500	11,250	53,750	60,000	(10%)
Totals		$250,000	$150,000	$400,000	$300,000	33%

SUMMARY

Many managers need to know the costs of their organizations' operations to properly (1) monitor them, (2) price the goods or products flowing from them, and (3) motivate (and perhaps correct) the work of those who perform and manage these operations. Since each operation generates exposures to loss, each also imposes a cost of risk on the organization—a cost that, like all others, managers must consider. However, the cost of risk for a particular operation, department, or profit center is more difficult to measure than many other costs. It is also often particularly slow to manifest itself, becoming apparent only after several accounting periods after the managerial decisions that affected that cost have been made. Therefore, perhaps more than for other more evident types of costs, an allocation system for the cost of risk should be extremely definitive, reflecting the characteristics of an ideal allocation system. For risk management costs in particular, an allocation system should (1) motivate personnel to perform very well the activity of risk management, (2) strike an appropriate balance between costs that should be charged to individual departments and those that should be borne by the entire organization (that is, a balance between risk bearing and risk sharing), (3) be simple to understand and administer, (4) be sufficiently responsive without being subject to undue fluctuations, and (5) be highly resistant to manipulation.

Every sound risk management cost allocation system should account for the four cost categories that make up an organization's cost of risk: retained losses, insurance premiums, risk control expenditures, and the overhead administrative costs of the risk management department's general operations. For any given accounting period, each of these categories of cost may be allocated among the organization's departments (or charged to the organization as a whole) through a prospective or a retrospective approach to allocation. In a prospective approach the portion an organization's risk management costs charged to a particular department can be determined before that accounting period begins. This can be done because the percentages of costs that are allocated are based on each department's experience (that is, claims records), its beginning-of-period exposures to loss, or some combination of experience and exposure. In a retrospective approach the portion of risk management costs charged to a particular department for a given accounting period depend, at least in part, on its claims experience or other risk management performance during that period. Thus, prospective approaches to cost allocation are much like experience rating in property and liability insurance: past performance influences current costs. Retrospective cost allocation shares much with retrospective rating of property and liability insurance because the experience of the current period substantially affects the amounts and proportions of costs to be charged to each department for the current period.

Both prospective and retrospective approaches to allocation may apportion the risk management costs for any given accounting period on the basis of a department's exposures to possible loss, its actual experience, or some combination of both. Exposure bases for risk management cost allocation systems are generally quite similar to those used in rating the various lines of commercial property and liability insurance, although an organization may choose a different allocation base to meet its particular needs. When risk management costs are allocated on the basis of experience, a credible statistical foundation must be developed as a data base. This usually requires accumulating at least three (and often five) years' claims experience for each department. As an experience-based allocation system matures, more current data may be added to the base, perhaps some early data years may be dropped from the base, and more recent data can be more heavily weighted in determining an average of past claims for each department. To prevent the experience of any one year from unduly destabilizing the risk management costs charged to a particular department, the amount of any individual claim—or the total of any year's aggregate claims—added to the experience base for that department may be limited.

To keep a risk management cost allocation system relatively easy to understand and administer, and to ensure that it remains consistent with organization objectives, a number of practical considerations, possibly conflicting with theoretically proper cost allocations, must be considered. These practical considerations include interactions between the organization's risk management cost allocation and general accounting systems, the tax implications of its risk management allocations, the need for maximums and minimums in the risk management costs charged to any one department in any given period, the relative degree of decentralization throughout the organization, the significance of a department's risk management cost in its total budget, and how each manager's motivation and performance are likely to be affected by the risk management costs apportioned to that department.

Bibliography

Anderson, Ronald A. *Social Forces and the Law*. Cincinnati, OH: South-Western Publishing Co., 1969.

Cambridge Economic History of Europe (London: Cambridge University Press, 1977), Vol. 5: *The Economic Organization of Early Modern Europe*, ed. E. E. Richard and C. H. Wilson.

Carroll, James E. and Gallagher, Edward L. *Claims Management*. New York: Risk and Insurance Management Society, Inc., looseleaf notebook for seminar, no date.

Cataldo, Bernard F., Kempin, Frederick G. Jr., Stockton, John M., and Weber, Charles M. *Introduction to Law and the Legal Process*, 2nd ed. New York: John Wiley & Sons, Inc., 1973.

Committee on Definitions of the American Marketing Association, *Marketing Definitions*, Chicago: American Marketing Association, 1960, p. 15.

Crist, G. W., Jr. *Corporate Suretyship*, 3rd ed. New York: McGraw-Hill Book Company, 1950.

Georgia Chapter of the Society of Chartered Property Casualty Underwriters. *The Hold Harmless Agreement*, 3rd ed. Cincinnati, OH: The National Underwriter Company, 1977.

Hollingsworth, E. P. and Launie, J. J. *Commercial Property and Multiple-Lines Underwriting*, 2nd ed. Malvern, PA: Insurance Institute of America, 1984.

Horn, Ronald C. *Subrogation in Insurance Theory and Practice*. Homewood, IL: Richard D. Irwin, Inc., 1964.

"Marketing," Section 8 of *The Risk Management Manual*, Santa Monica, CA: The Merritt Company, loose-leaf, revised and supplemented periodically, May 1981.

Mehr, Robert I. and Hedges, Bob A. *Risk Management: Concepts and Applications*. Homewood, IL: Richard D. Irwin, Inc., 1974.

_____. *Risk Management in the Business Enterprise*. Homewood, IL: Richard D. Irwin, Inc., 1963.

Pearce, Alan M. "Legal Prohibitions Against Use of Hold Harmless Agreements," *Risk Management*, April 1977.

Prahl, Robert J. and Utrata, Stephen M. *Liability Claim Concepts and Practices*, 1st ed. Malvern, PA: Insurance Institute of America, 1985.

Rosenbloom, Jerry S. and Hallman, G. Victor. *Employee Benefit Planning*, 2nd ed. Englewwod Cliffs, NJ: Prentice-Hall, Inc., 1986.

Strauss, George and Sayles, L. R. *Personnel—The Human Problems of Management*, 4th ed. Englewood Cliffs, NJ: Prentice-Hall, Inc., 1980.

Thomas, Paul I. and Reed, Prentiss B., Sr. *Adjustment of Property Losses*, 4th ed. New York: McGraw-Hill Book Company, 1977.

Warren, David and McIntosh, Ros. "Consultants," Topic H4 in *Practical Risk Management*, Oakland, CA: Warren, McVeigh, & Griffin, loose-leaf, revised and supplemented periodically, January 1985.

———. "Marketing a Large Insurance Program," Topic A4 in *Practical Risk Management*, Oakland, CA: Warren, McVeigh, & Griffin, May 1986.

Yohalem, Martha Remy. "Employee-Benefit Plan" 1975, *Social Security Bulletin*, Vol. 40, No. 11, November 1977.

Index

A

Account, insurance, *215*
Accrued actuarial liability, *177*
Accrued benefits method, *182*
Accrued liability, *177*
Activity standards, *75*
Actuarial accrued liability, *177*
Actuarial assumptions, *179*
Actuarial cost method, selecting, *182*
Actuarial liability, *177*
  unfunded, *177*
Actuarial services, *237*
Actuarial surplus, *177*
Actuarial valuations, *179*
Additional, retro, *42*
Adjuster, *260*
Adjusters, independent, *261*
  insurers', *260*
  public, *262*
  telephone, *261*
Administrative controls, general, *131*
Administrative overhead, allocating, *216*
Administrator, contract with, *264*
  selecting, *263*
ADR (alternative dispute resolution), *287*
Advance funding, *178*
Advance payment receipt, *291*
Advance payments, *290*

Affiliated ("captive") insurer, *26*
Aggregate limit, *323*
Aggregate severity, *322*
Aggressive strategy, *131*
Agreement, exculpatory, *100*
  excusing, *100*
  guaranty, *96*
  high/low, *283*
  suretyship, *96*
Agreements, construction, *104*
  equipment lease, *109*
  hold harmless, *85*, *101*, *102*
  indemnity, *85*, *101*
  lease of premises, *108*
  purchase order, *106*
  service, *105*
  waiver, *85*
Agreements classified by extent of responsibility transferred, *115*
ALAE (allocated loss adjustment expenses), *305*, *314*, *323*
Allocated costs, types of, *313*
Allocated loss adjustment expenses (ALAE), *305*, *314*, *323*
Alphabet house brokerage, *207*
Alphabet house organizations, international, *227*
Alternative dispute resolution (ADR), *287*
American Arbitration Association, *288*
American Marketing Association, *215*

M

N